MASSEY COLLEGE
in the University of Toronto

MASTER

(handwritten, left margin — partially cut off)
...lings J. & R.
...f my first day at Annagh—
... for it has three walls
...fortable & big bedroom,
...with a terrible mattress
...& an ancient eider-
...ressing-room with
...om has the electricity.
...ic: would rather go
...w.c. A river old
...full of junk—
...th, two pianos
...ite safe. Big:
...m thing & the Park,
...selves,
...mam—
...rats of
...ruit which
...vre, mop-
...v.

(vertical handwritten note)
We welcome you to the W. of T. & still...
I am the maximum, & still I, the young ghost, always, with cat?...

Dear Douglas:

Delighted by the news... a novel, and look forward... reading it. What a satisfying form... And I well believe that yours is beaut-ful, and am keenly interested to hear that it is also brutal. I am myself working on a novel which will not be brutal, but is certainly far more serious in tone than anything I have attempted, and is at root an attempt to explore a region of my own life and thought which I have never put in a book before—my desire to experience regions of feeling which are not orthodox called religious. It is taking a long time, and as well as breaking new ground I am trying to correct faults which have plagued me, and irritated my critics, for years—my very personal and farouche tone, and a leaning toward the farcical and farouche which suggests shallowness of feeling, but is (I truly believe) the consequence of trying to conceal a nakedness and rawness of spirit which I have only now persuaded myself to display to readers... Do you think we shall be a nest of those birds at the U. of T.? It would be fun, wouldn't it? All the best to you and Sally from us both...

Rob. E Davies

---

361 Park St.
~~572 WELLER STREET~~
PETERBOROUGH, CANADA

Dear Grant:

Many thanks for your letter, your good wishes and the note to Miss Robson. I hope that this time we can make connections: last time she wrote charmingly. I cannot tell you how much I am obliged to you for this, or how truly I appreciate your readiness to intro-duce me to your friends, for I know that you do not do so lightly and unadvisedly, as they say in the Marriage Service. Already I am in yr debt for a wonderful hour with Athene Seyler.

We have moved, and are frankly de-lighted with the new house, which you must visit as soon as possible. The Front Parlour is our Macdonald Room by the way, no lesser artist allowed — and yr pic-tures look fine, as they are not crowded, and get a decent light, most of the day.

Our love to you, and we shall send you a comic post card from Llan fairpwll gwyngyllgogerychwrndrobwll-llantisiliogogogoch.

July 15.

Rob.

The Master's Lodging: Massey College
4 DEVONSHIRE PLACE, TORONTO 5

Dear Gordon:

We returned on Monday night, and I got your letter—the one of June 10—on Tuesday morning first thing, and it was a smack in the eye, I can tell you! My instinct was to write at once, but on second thoughts 'which are the best', I decided to defer writing until I knew what I was going to say, and to refrain from spray-ing you with emotion and sympathy which might be stupid and obtrusive. So I have been dithering for some days, during which I have had good news of you through Moira. But after all, we are old friends, and you are I think the most truly good and unselfish man I know, and if one doesn't speak frankly when you are seriously ill, when?

This is your second very serious encounter with that great Balancer and Revenger, the Belly. Only you know just what goes on in there, but to an outsider— a very concerned and truly affection-ate outsider none the less—me— it seems that this is the place where you harbour all the frus-trations and bitternesses which in another kind of man would find vent in complaint and railimg against the gods, and a few men. And of course it eats

(left margin, cut off)
...ould
...a
...use
...cs as

Discoveries

ROBERTSON DAVIES

Discoveries

Early Letters 1938-1975

Selected and Edited by JUDITH SKELTON GRANT

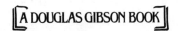

National Library of Canada Cataloguing in Publication

Davies, Robertson, 1913-1995
    Discoveries : early letters 1938-1975 / Robertson Davies; selected and edited by Judith Skelton Grant.

Includes bibliographical references and index.
ISBN 0-7710-3540-3

1. Davies, Robertson, 1913-1995 – Correspondence. 2. Authors, Canadian (English) – 20th century – Correspondence.   I. Grant, Judith Skelton, 1941- .
II. Title.

PS8507.A67Z54 2002   C813'.54   C2002-901547-2
PR9199.3.D3Z48 2002

We acknowledge the financial support of the Government of Canada through the Book Publishing Industry Development Program for our publishing activities. We further acknowledge the support of the Canada Council for the Arts and the Ontario Arts Council for our publishing program.

Typeset in Bembo by M&S, Toronto
Printed and bound in Canada

This book is printed on acid-free paper that is 100% ancient
forest friendly (100% post-consumer recycled).

A Douglas Gibson Book
McClelland & Stewart Ltd.
The Canadian Publishers
481 University Avenue
Toronto, Ontario
M5G 2E9
www.mcclelland.com

1 2 3 4 5   06 05 04 03 02

For John

Contents

PREFACE

n 1938, when these letters begin, the patriarchal, snowily bearded Robertson Davies of the Deptford and Cornish trilogies was still far in the future. But Davies, who was 25 that August, was already attracting attention. He liked to wear broad-brimmed hats; by 1941 he was affecting sweeping dark moustachios; and by 1943 he had added the familiar beard that he would wear for the rest of his life. Six solid feet in height, he made an imposing and eye-catching figure. And he set himself apart in other ways as well. By 1940 he had abandoned his Canadian pronunciation and substituted an actor's mid-Atlantic accent, honed in vocal training during two seasons with the Old Vic Theatre in London. His letters were penned in an elegant hand and on fine paper, often in several colours of ink. Recipients made a point of preserving those letters, not just for their appearance but because their sender was already an exceptional person.

For Your Eye Alone, the companion volume published in 1999, focused on the last twenty years of Davies' life. By that time he had become famous, a "great man" whose views were solicited on many subjects. But this selection, which covers the period from 1938 to 1975, from his 25th to his 62nd year, shows us the younger Davies in the long years of striving.

Some letters do survive from an even earlier period, starting with a group written to Donald Ryerson in 1930–35. Davies got to know Ryerson at Upper Canada College and collaborated with him on several operettas while they were at school and university. Eleanor Sweezey, with whom he fell in love as an undergraduate at Queen's University, Kingston, received many letters in 1934–36, especially when he was across the sea in his first year at Oxford. There is a bundle of notes (many of them brief) written to fellow student John Espey in 1937–38 at Oxford, for Espey had "decided from the start to save everything from Rob, certain that he would make his mark." Another group of charming love letters, written in 1939 to Birgitta Rydbeck, a Swedish drama student Davies thought he loved during his period at the Old Vic, survive, and so do a few others.

So why not begin at the beginning? Unfortunately, Davies himself put a ban on publication of the most important parts of this early correspondence, the letters to Eleanor Sweezey and Birgitta Rydbeck. In the latter case, Davies forbade me access while I was preparing to write his biography. In the case of the Sweezey correspondence, most of which was returned to him, he typed 38 single-spaced pages of excerpts for my use, then destroyed the originals. The extant passages no longer have the shape of letters, and, what is worse, it is impossible to tell how much has been omitted, or whether he "improved" them. In my view, neither the surviving Sweezey letters nor the ones to Ryerson, Espey, Rydbeck, and others, show Davies in a poor light: indeed, they reveal him to have been a young man of fancy and infatuations, occasionally despairing, often amusing, full of energy and accomplishment. But the older Davies didn't wish to expose the vulnerabilities of his younger self to public view. Shortly before his death, he did agree that his letters might be gathered for publication, but time precluded a discussion that might have permitted the early letters to be included.

What was Robertson Davies up to in the years from 1938 to 1975? His range of accomplishment was astonishing. Having graduated from Oxford with a thesis deemed worthy of publication, he quickly transformed it into a saleable general-interest book. He became a member of the Old Vic Company in London, England, on Tyrone Guthrie's invitation, but his chance to explore his capacities as an actor, and possibly as a director, was cut short by the war. Having returned to Canada in 1940, he accepted his father's invitation to edit the *Peterborough Examiner*, and made it one of the most frequently quoted papers in the country. After the war, he became such an important figure in the world of Canadian theatre, as a playwright, a director, and an energizer of others, that observers expected Peterborough, not Stratford, to become the locus of an influential annual Festival. In the late 1940s and 1950s, he became one of the best-known comic writers in Canada on the strength of the Samuel Marchbanks books and the Salterton novels. During the 1950s, he revealed himself to be a literary observer of extraordinary range and authority as the Books editor of *Saturday Night*. In 1961, he became the founding Master of Massey College, Canada's first graduate college, and in 1962, a full professor of English and drama at the University of Toronto. Finally, with the writing of the Deptford trilogy, he transcended the Canadian scene, emerging as a novelist whose works would in later years be read worldwide.

A few of the letters in this volume were written by the "public man," such as the one from "the editor of the *Peterborough Examiner*" to an arrogant job applicant (July 21, 1945) and the one from "the university professor" to a Ph.D. student about to sit his doctoral oral examination (fall 1975). But most of them reveal the private Davies. Writing itself is a frequent topic in his letters, and it is treated from every conceivable angle. In the 1940s Davies had to market his work himself (a necessity he hated), since there were at that time no Canadian literary agents to do it for him. So we see him sending his plays to theatre companies, producers, actors, and publishers, entering the plays into competitions and retrieving the typescripts. Many things moved him to discuss his writing and the experience of being a writer. When his publishers proposed cuts to *The Diary of Samuel Marchbanks* or to *Tempest-Tost*, for example, he felt compelled to explain the basic thrust of the Marchbanks columns, the reasons for the attempted suicide in *Tempest-Tost*, and the difference between a funny book and a comic book. When critics charged him with undue "talkiness" in his plays, he discussed the matter with theatre critic Herbert Whittaker. When his wife, Brenda, his usual confidante, was away in 1954, he unbuttoned himself to his old friends the McInneses about a sudden, unaccustomed loss of artistic confidence that had struck him midway through the writing of *Leaven of Malice*. And when he needed specialized information, whether it be an appropriate disease with which to dispatch Ma Gall in *A Mixture of Frailties* or information on village carnivals for *World of Wonders*, he beguiled old friends and chance acquaintances into becoming his research assistants.

Although Davies was intensely busy with his own writing and directing, he was asked from time to time to reflect on the state of "Canadian culture," and his perspective on these occasions still seems fresh today. There are also penetrating responses to books by a number of Canada's authors, among them Emily Carr's *The House of All Sorts*, Graham McInnes's *Lost Island*, Robert Finch's poems, Scott Symons' *Place d'Armes*, Margaret Laurence's *A Bird in the House*, and Margaret Atwood's *Survival*. When his own books appeared, and Canadian writers wrote appreciatively of his work in letters or reviews, his responses often display great critical insight about what he was doing.

Davies' passionate engagement with theatre – as playwright, director, professor of drama, and keen theatre-goer – emerges again and again in his correspondence. There are shrieks of anguish over the mutilations wrought by blundering amateurs on his plays, and practical ideas on topics such as the costuming of boys for *A Masque of Aesop*. In the letters to the director Tyrone Guthrie and professor Gordon Roper, among others, there are insights into many of the classics of the English stage repertoire. Davies was a frequent source of good counsel to young playwrights, and answered queries from the Stratford Festival about the world of Shakespeare's time.

A number of Davies' correspondents were friends of very long standing. Several of them had been comrades at Oxford in the 1930s. But every decade produced new ones. Among the most important letters here are those he wrote to Gordon Roper, a professor of English and a friend from the war years in Peterborough. Roper was an early, sympathetic, and astute reader of Davies' work. It was he who first recognized how profoundly Davies' thinking had been influenced by C. G. Jung, and his 1972 article on the subject made a strong impact on subsequent Davies criticism. It was in that year, when he was preparing to write the first serious book-length study of Davies and his work, that Roper fell seriously ill. To rally him, Davies opened his mind to him in a succession of letters over a period of several months in the summer and fall of 1972, the period when *The Manticore* was published and *World of Wonders* was taking shape. These letters expose Davies' moments of insecurity, his sudden rushes of inspiration, his surface preoccupations, and his profound concerns.

Much the most important correspondence to have come to light in the interval since the publication of *For Your Eye Alone* are letters that Davies wrote to his wife, Brenda, in his first days as editor of the *Peterborough*

Examiner in 1942, and in 1952 when she was visiting her mother and sister in Australia. Together with the letters he wrote to her from Ireland in 1959, when he was collaborating with Tyrone Guthrie on an adaptation of *Leaven of Malice*, they afford an intimate insight into the strong, loving partnership that steadied and warmed Davies throughout this period, and indeed until his death.

In making this collection, I had thousands of letters to choose from. A basic resource was the copies of letters made by Davies' secretaries at the *Peterborough Examiner* and at Massey College, most notably Moira Whalon, who began to work for him in 1956 and did his secretarial work for the balance of his life. His dictated business correspondence includes many letters on the subject of his writing – letters, for instance, to editors, to agents, and to readers – but it also includes an occasional letter to a friend, dictated when Davies was pressed for time. (Square brackets around Davies' signature indicate that a secretarial copy is the source.) For Davies, there was an important difference between dictated and written material, not just in the matter of privacy. He wrote almost all his "personal" letters himself – to friends, to readers who asked serious questions, and to editors who had become friends. Only occasionally was a copy made of such correspondence. The presence of many of the letters in this volume has therefore depended on correspondents' decisions to keep them and, of course, on their willingness to share them. Before Davies' death I made a list of the people I thought might have been correspondents, and he augmented it for me in our one discussion about this project. A search through major libraries and archives in Canada and selected libraries in the United States turned up a further range of letters, most notably to other Canadian writers.

A challenge – an amusing one – in making this collection was what to do about "fictional" letters. It was easy enough to exclude the letters written by characters in Davies' novels. (There are a fair number of them – recall, for example, the postcard from Liesl Vitzliputzli to Dunstan Ramsay at the end of *Fifth Business*, and the series of notes about his genealogical researches from Adrian Pledger-Brown to David Staunton in *The Manticore*.) Likewise, excluding Samuel Marchbanks' correspondence with Haubergon Hydra, Esq., Mervyn Noseigh, M.A., Rev. Simon Goaste, B.D., Richard Dandiprat, Esq., Chandos Fribble, and so on was straightforward, because, like the letters in the novels, they belong to imagined characters in a fictional context rather than to Davies himself, and, in any case, they are already in the public domain. But what about the letters to the editor of the *Peterborough Examiner* signed with such pseudonyms as "Mother of Three" or "Indignant Taxpayer," opposing Davies' own editorial positions in the hope of encouraging other readers to write? I excluded these as expressing views opposed to Davies' own. For the same reason, I have left out the letters attributed to "Dolly Gray," whose *Examiner* column parodied syndicated advice columns for a time in 1957 and 1958.

And what about the hoax letters – like the one tucked into a 19th century photograph album of Peterborough residents which Davies gave to the Peterborough Historical Society? Carefully "aged" and penned in a 19th century hand, it revealed a scandal about the revered wife of one of Peterborough's founders, but entertaining as it was, I excluded it on the ground that it was just as fictional as the letters in Davies' novels. (The Historical Society, initially persuaded of the letter's authenticity, worried about the embarrassment it might cause for the lady's descendants and considered suppressing it. But they caught on quickly, and then were delighted to have a story to tell.) I have, however, included several letters, signed with a pseudonym, that form part of a larger correspondence, and represent extreme and delightful instances of Davies' habitual heightening of experience. See, for example, the letter to Herbert Whittaker written on April 10, 1953, that begins "Dear Mr. Whittaker, alannah!" and is signed "Barney O'Lunacy," and the letter to Tanya Moiseiwitsch in June 1962, from the firm of Friar Bacon & Friar Bungay, Necromantic Suppliers and Supernatural Warehousemen.

We begin in 1938, with Davies' first approach to a publisher.

Dear Madam:

I think I understood you to say, in your Wednesday night radio address, _that the tempo of living in Australia is markedly slower than that of this continent_. Madam, beware! You have trodden on the rattlesnake of local patriotism! Here in Peterborough I venture to say that we can show you a tempo of living slower than any in the world! Let the kangaroo tremble in his bed! The Beaver of the Kawarthas can out-drowse him any day of the week! Adieu, rash Antipodean —

One of the Seventy Times Seven
Sleepers of Peterborough

SECTION

I

JUNE 1938–NOVEMBER 1947 – *SHAKESPEARE'S BOY ACTORS* REVISED AND PUB-
LISHED, *SHAKESPEARE FOR YOUNG PLAYERS* WRITTEN AND PUBLISHED, SEVERAL ONE-
ACT AND FULL-LENGTH PLAYS WRITTEN, *THE DIARY OF SAMUEL MARCHBANKS*
WRITTEN AND PUBLISHED

y 1938, the year he turned 25, Robertson Davies had made his mark at Oxford. His B. Litt. thesis on Shakespeare's boy actors had been recommended by his examiners for publication, and he had caught the eye of Tyrone Guthrie, the director of the Old Vic Theatre in London, with his Oxford University Dramatic Society performance as Malvolio in *Twelfth Night*.

Bent on an acting career, he was delighted to accept Guthrie's invitation to join the Old Vic Company. During his two seasons he contributed variously as a dramaturge, an understudy, an actor (in modest parts), and as a teacher in the drama school, but the experience made it clear that he would not reach the upper ranks as an actor. Early in 1940, after the company had disbanded on account of the war, he married its young Australian stage manager, Brenda Mathews, and brought her home to

Canada. Their relationship quickly became a love match and a partnership on many levels.

During the 1930s, Davies had come to know and love Wales, from which his father, Rupert, had emigrated to Canada at the age of 15 and where Rupert owned a succession of houses as summer retreats from 1932 onward. Every year from that time forward he would make special note of the day sacred to its patron saint, David – March 1. But Wales was not the country "bred in his bone," as it was for his father, and he knew it.

Arrived in Canada, Davies and Brenda spent several months living with Rupert and Florence Davies in Kingston, Ontario, while he filled in at his father's newspaper, the Kingston *Whig-Standard*, and cast about for work. His father then gave him more serious employment: beginning August 1, he was to write a thrice-a-week column under the pseudonym Samuel Marchbanks for Rupert's two newspapers, *The Peterborough Examiner* and the *Whig*. Called "Cap and Bells" at first, the column focused on the arts. After a couple of years, it appeared only twice a week and became largely a column of book reviews. Late in 1943, the Saturday column became a diary in which Marchbanks gradually expanded into a full-blown character. *The Diary of Samuel Marchbanks* (published by Clarke, Irwin in 1947) was drawn from these Saturday columns.

Assured of a modest income, the Davieses moved to Toronto in July 1940, and by November, B. K. Sandwell, the respected editor of *Saturday Night*, at that time a highly influential weekly, had hired him as the paper's literary editor. In addition to managing and writing reviews for "The Bookshelf" he contributed editorials, dance and music reviews, and seasonal pieces to the paper.

Coupled with the months he had spent at the *Whig*, this apprenticeship in journalism prepared him admirably for the editorship of *The Peterborough Examiner*, which he assumed at his father's invitation at the beginning of March 1942. For several years Davies carried the editorial columns alone, but the load was lightened when he was able to hire an assistant editor in 1946. His first truly satisfactory assistant, Thomas J. Allen, joined the paper in September of 1947.

The war was ever-present in these years. *Saturday Night* and the *Examiner* were preoccupied with it. Davies was called up twice, but was rejected both times because of poor eyesight. From Davies' point of view, one of the more discouraging aspects of those years was the virtual disappearance of the arts outside the main Canadian cities: amateur theatrical performances, musical groups, and the like were suspended for the duration. The move from Toronto to Peterborough was thus, more than it would otherwise have been, a move into cultural darkness.

Writing was Davies' lifeline. His *Shakespeare for Young Players: A Junior Course* was published by Clarke, Irwin in 1942 and sold well for many years. By 1943 his aspiration was to make his mark as a playwright. He wrote for the London stage and for amateur groups in Canada, but found that he had to place his work himself: at this time there were no literary agents in Canada. Undaunted, he reached out to such Canadian groups as there were, and sought help from English contacts. Twice he submitted plays to the Ottawa Drama League's one-act playwriting competition, and on both occasions won the prize (and public attention), in 1946 with *Overlaid* and in 1947 with *Eros at Breakfast*.

His first real chance at producing live theatre came after the war in 1946, when he and Brenda brought his adaptation of the Coventry Nativity Play to little St. George's Anglican Church in Peterborough. The second chance came in 1947 when a group of school teachers asked him to help them mount a play. He and Brenda took them on, turned them into the Peterborough Little Theatre, and as this section of the letters ends, were preparing for their first public performance early in 1948.

The Davieses moved house three times in this eight-year period, first to a furnished second-floor flat on Selby Street in Toronto in July 1940, next to a row house on Aylmer Avenue in 1941, and, in June 1942, to 572 Weller Street in Peterborough. Their three daughters, Miranda, Jennifer, and Rosamond, were born, in December 1940, October 1942, and April 1947.

To E. F. BOZMAN

Balliol Coll.
Oxford
24: vi: 38

E. F. Bozman was editorial director of the English publishing house J. M. Dent & Sons.

Dear Mr. Bozman

The Rev. Mr. Ridley* of Balliol has been kind enough to refer me to you, and has, I believe, sent you a letter which may act as an introduction.

I have just been given my B. Litt. Degree here for a thesis on "The Influence of the Boy-Actor on Shakespeare's Dramatic Technique" and my examiners, Sir Edmund Chambers and Dr. Percy Simpson,* were so complimentary as to urge me to publish it. The subject has not been given much attention and, as I cannot agree with most of what has been written about it, my own work on the point has some claim to originality.

I should not like to see it published as it stands, for as you know, academic theses make very dreary reading, but I should like to revise it and include certain information which was not suitable for a strictly academic work but which would, I think, make the book more entertaining to read.

Would Dent's, do you think, be at all interested in such a book? If so I shall be in London on Tuesday, Wednesday and Thursday next, and should be very grateful for an opportunity to discuss it with you. I am,

Yours sincerely,

W. Robertson Davies

To HUGH R. DENT

Fronfraith Hall*
Abermule, Montgomeryshire
North Wales
21: vii: 38

Hugh Railton Dent (1874–1938), English, was chairman of the English publishing house J. M. Dent & Sons 1926–38. He was a son of Joseph Malaby Dent (1849–1926), the firm's founder.

Dear Mr. Hugh Dent

Thank you for your letter of July 19, which reached me this morning.

The terms which you quote seem quite satisfactory to me.

With reference to revision, my own opinion was substantially that of Mr. Granville-Barker,* whose favourable criticism flattered me greatly. My plan was to rewrite the thing *entirely*, reducing the repetition of the middle part, placing greater stress on the chief characters in tragedy and comedy, and venturing one or two opinions which would not have been in place in an academic thesis.

I know as well as Mr. Granville-Barker that the whole thing is written in the vein of lickspittle caution and repetition necessary in a piece of writing meant rather to secure a degree than to make good reading. In the rewriting I should change all that. I had also meant to expand the work, at Mr. Bozman's suggestion, to 70,000 words, and the material which I meant to use for this purpose was:

a: A more detailed discussion of the chief women in tragedy and comedy, combining technical with aesthetic appreciation.

b: The introduction of contemporary criticism of the boy-actors culled from Puritan attacks on the stage, and particularly from Wm. Prynne's *Histrio-Mastix* (1632). This material is hard to come by and is "hot stuff," as much of it is vigorous denunciation of the morals of the boys. There is no doubt in my mind that a considerable part of the public which may not be keenly interested in Shakespeare will be curious about the lives of the boys, and Mr. Bozman and I agreed that this material, which was not strictly germane to my thesis, would make very lively reading in the book.

c: A closer comparison between the technique of the boy-actors and that of the modern actress with much implied criticism of the latter, and of modern methods of Shakespeare production, which give too slight a consideration to the obvious intent of the author. Mr. Bozman also approved this. You may depend upon me to use reasonable discretion in this part of the book, but I have had enough theatrical experience myself to write, I think, with justice. I should like to frame this part of the work so as to get the book some sale among theatrical folk, and to provoke interest and protest which would increase sales and perhaps gain me some recognition in the theatre.

My desire is so to revise the book that it will appeal to the academic public, the theatrical public and those who study theatrical technique, and to that part of the general public which likes non-fiction of a serious, but not ponderous nature, and, if possible, to excite controversy both in scholarly and theatrical circles.

Mr. Bozman asked me if it would be possible to find any pictures to make plates with which to dress the book. There are several which would be suitable.

I should be glad to have the typescript from you as soon as possible so that I may begin revision seriously. I should also like to know when you want the finished MS. I could let you have it the first week in September, or earlier in portions, or later, as you wish.

If you should want to see me personally for further discussion I shall be in London on the 27th and 28th of this month, and an appointment in the afternoon of the first or at any time during the second of those days would be perfectly convenient. I am, Sir,

Yours faithfully

W. Robertson Davies

To VINCENT MASSEY

Fronfraith Hall
Abermule, Montgomeryshire
North Wales
2: vii: 39

Vincent Massey (1897–1967) was Canada's High Commissioner to London 1935–46. He was a friend of Rupert Davies and his sons Lionel and Hart had been at Upper Canada College and then at Balliol at the same time as Davies. This letter was written before war was declared; it elicited a polite response and nothing more.

Dear Mr. Vincent Massey

For some months past I have been wondering what sort of National Service I should offer myself for in the event of war. A close study of the Government Handbook on the subject has not been very helpful, and in any case, as a Canadian I should prefer to do something which would be of help to Canada if the need should arise.

At present I am working as an actor at the Old Vic, and as a teacher in the Dramatic School there, and also in propaganda and lecturing work connected with that theatre. This keeps me busy every weekday from 10.30 a.m. to 11.30 p.m. and often on Sundays, so that I really cannot find a minute for any other sort of training or work; in the case of war, however, I should like to be quite clear about what I am to do, as seriously defective eyesight closes the usual sorts of military service to me. As you know, my training has been entirely academic and literary, and I thought that this sort of skill might allow me to make myself useful in some capacity.

I am sorry to trouble you in this matter, but as I am resident in England and yet not English there seems to be no place where I fit in. If you can give me any advice in this matter I should be deeply grateful as at the moment I do not know quite what I should do. If you should want to get in touch with me a letter to the Old Vic, Waterloo Road, S. E. 1 will always reach me. I am

Yours most sincerely

Robertson Davies

To GRANT MACDONALD

[Aylmer Avenue
Toronto, Ontario]
Sunday [June 15 or 22, 1941]

Grant Macdonald (1909–87), Kingston, Ontario, artist, is best known for his drawings of theatrical celebrities. He had been a friend since December 1935 when Davies and he met on the voyage home from the U.K., Davies from Oxford and Macdonald from London.

Dear Grant:

Of course I should have written to you sooner, but with my customary dilatoriness I have not done so. I had yᴵ cheque & have got seats for the Guild plays.* Unhappily all the front seats in the centre section of the balcony were gone, but I got three in the 2nd row *in the aisle* which is a great convenience, & we both look forward to six delightful evenings with you next season.

Last week I had a chat with W. H. Clarke,* the president of the Oxford Press, & mentioned to him that you were preparing drawings for the Shakespeare book [Davies' *Shakespeare for Young Players*] on spec.; he was very interested & encouraging to the point where I think we may assume that some of them at least will be used.

I had a call from Mrs. Ahrens* on Friday, & she is sending me some clippings abt. her husband; I will probably do *two* Cap & Bells articles on him if there is enough material, as it would fit in well with the conference in Kingston.

I am extremely busy these days, as there is a rush on at the office, & Clarke wants the Shakes. book by early September. I will write you again abt. that next week. Brenda & I will be in Kingston for the last two weeks in August, & we can clean up details then.

Guy Roberts* brought the screen on Friday, & it is *so handsome* that we have hung it in the hall, as a picture. I think you will like it when you see how well it looks there. *Many, many thanks for this wonderful gift.* We both send love to you & Mary [Keens].*

Rob. D.

To BRENDA DAVIES

Peterborough Examiner
Peterborough, Ontario
4.10 p.m. Monday [March 2,
1942]

*Brenda Davies (1917–   ), Australian-born
Canadian, had become Davies' wife in
February 1940. They had both been
members of the Old Vic Theatre Company
in London, England: she as stage manager
and actress, and he as actor, student,
dramaturge, and teacher. At the beginning
of March 1942, their first daughter was a
year and two months old and the second
was due in October. The house they
were to occupy in Peterborough was
not free until June, so Brenda remained
in Toronto and Davies commuted to
Peterborough for the work week, staying
at the Empress Hotel.*

My very dearest Wiggen:

I am writing you a letter now to be absolutely sure that it gets to you tomorrow morning, which is half because I know you will want to hear from me and half because writing makes me feel nearer to you. Ever since I left the house this morning I have felt that I would give anything to have you with me. As you see, I am lonely & home-sick, but don't worry, as otherwise *I am Doin' Fine!**

The journey was uneventful. I have decided that the train trip to Peterborough is just something that must be Risen Above. I had a bad moment when I thought I was on the wrong train, but that was only because the CPR goes a rather different route to the CNR and passes through a different collection of dumps. I had thought to be a Great Editor on the train, but I felt quite unlike it, & so, instead of reading the weighty pamphlets I had with me I read the new Mr. Pinkerton instead & it is a v. good *poisoning* mystery, located at Richmond.* Do you remember the day we motored out there & had tea?

Arrived at Pbh. at 11.35 & got a taxi, driven by a palsied ancient who looked like Toby Turtle in a Disney. Like many small town taximen (as in Kingston) he was greedy, & put 2 others in with me, a young man for General Electric & a girl for Westclox. I engraved his appearance on Memory's Tablets & will not patronize him again. It was snowing when I got here, but is quite fair & warm now.

At the hotel got a good room, with a bath & an ancient sofa. Not stylish, but comfortable, though the bed (as you foresaw) is *not* by Ridpath.* Garner* called soon after I arrived & we had lunch together. He confided to me that he dislikes being a Rotarian & I told him that a man of wide interests, like himself, would find their doings rather small potatoes. Yesterday, as you will recall, was St. David's day.*

After lunch we came here & I met Craw,* who is Honest Craw, obviously. He is bald, shortsighted & has a paunch; he ought to do those Indian exercises. My office is v. nabby & *so quiet*! Elson, the fill-in, is doing editorials until Saturday, as they thought I would need time to get the hang of things. That makes it much easier. Everybody is v. nice & seems to stand in awe of me to some extent, which is satisfactory. I Breathed a Jolly but Grand Mood* & all went well. I spent the afternoon clearing Kennedy's* odds & bits out of my desk & am now well settled in. They knock off here about 3.30, so all is quiet now. As for mornings, I get in when I like, and shall arrive about 8.45, I think, until we are moved in. Then we'll see. The [radio] station* is still very much in the making, & Kelly (whom we met at Kingston) is bossing the installation. Wig, it is going to be really handsome, & you must get a foot in as soon as poss! We'll discuss it all when I know more. I don't think there'll be any difficulty, even if you are not Traffic Mgr. There will be a Grand Opening, when all is ready, for which you must come down.

I am going now to have a squint at the Bannister house from the outside. I will then phone to see if I can get inside it & will write, if I can do so. This is just my first letter; I'll send you another before I turn in, so I won't say goodbye, yet.

Am now going to see the Much Discussed House!

All my love

Rob

To BRENDA DAVIES

[The Empress Hotel]
Peterborough, Ontario
Monday Night 10:35 p.m. [March 2, 1942]

My dearest Pink.....

Congratulations on your Extreme Cleverness in getting us such a really excellent house. After writing you today I hoofed up to Weller Street, not getting lost any more than was decent, and began a long search for it. Have you noticed how the first time you go anywhere all the distances seem endless? At last I came to the foot of the hill, and had almost concluded that I had lost it, or had passed it, when it hove in sight around the corner of a horrid little frame dump. So I had a good stare at the outside, and departed well pleased. Called the Bannisters from the hotel and got the daughter, who does not seem to be Right Bright, but anyway she told me that I could come along tonight, as "someone was sure to be in." So I went tonight at 8.30, and indeed they were *all* in. Ma Bannister, who wears a deaf machine, let me in and conducted me round the place, moaning and groaning all the time about how awful they felt at leaving. I was excessively and obviously insincerely sympathetic, in a sort of Jewish way, not yielding an inch. She wants to sell us the lino on the kitchen floor for $5, and I think it is worth it. The house was in a fierce mess, as Ma is clearly an old dotard & so is Pop and so is the girl.

Beginning at the beginning, I thought the hall had very definite possibilities. It does not need much in it, but our military chest might be just the thing, with the mahogany mirror over it. Your notion of papering the hall & drawing room in the same paper (our pink watered) is undoubtedly a good one. It would make the thing much more of a unity, which would be nice. I think we could dispense with curtains on the arch unless it proved too draughty. I like the little arch with its plaster doodads. It has a good deal of charm. The drawing room is fine. I think we can furnish it very nicely with little more than we have. It will take an entirely different character when we have our stuff in it. The Bannister furniture is very ordinary. I thought the fireplace good; not by the Brothers Adam,* but better than one usually finds in all but very costly houses. We can do a good job with it. The glass doors I did not find objectionable. The dining room is much like the drawing room – better with our stuff. As for rugs, as I said on the phone, I think the two orange ones in the front room would be an awful crush, and the floors are really very nice, though not exquisite. A little wax would do wonders for them. I think you remember the dining room as being bigger than it really is. The kitchen is just a mess. What a lot of meaningless little cupboards! Still, I think our stove would *just* go where theirs is; but it would be better where the refrigerator is, & vice versa. The cellar isn't much to boast about. I doubt if a playroom could be rigged up there, but I couldn't say without having a good look; I had to do all my looking while the Deaf Adder pestered me with questions. At present the whole house is *cluttered*. We will only know what is what when we see it bare.

The stairs were a pleasant surprise. I think they are nice enough to be left bare. Not Versailles, you know, but with a certain *something*. The bathroom was better than I expected; a new John would be a big help, but the tub is of decent size and it is light and has a good window. The room with the bow window would make a bedroom, I think. I am almost certain that our beds and little chests would go in the alcove, but the real problem is – where to put our chests? The mirror, as you suggest, might be unshipped and put on the back of the door, though then you would always see yourself as a figure *backed* by the light, which isn't much good. We will have to go into the matter thoroughly. The other room is a good room, and that is about all one can say of it. As for the other two rooms, I thought the back one really rather commodious and nice. Old Pop's study is bigger than you think and would make either a room for both babies* (though a bit of a squeeze) or a study for me. Indeed, the upstairs possibilities are many. The square room could be a nursery, the back room an upstairs sitter and study, and Pop's den a tiny guest room, if you liked it that way. Anyway we are not tied down to only one plan and we must talk it over thoroughly. The maid's place is really fine. She gets the only view of the back garden, save that from the John and Pop's sty. Lots of cupboards and hideaways. Fine.

Ma tells me, with tears in her voice, that the garden is lovely and that they have planted out A Wealth of Flowers, and may they lug some of them away? By law they may not, but it is usually done. Still, they can't do it until we are there, I should think, and we can be a Restraining Influence so that they do not strip the place. But I think that they are of the Mrs. Lind type, and once they are gone will not have enough gumption to come and get their damned stuff. I thought the back garden a tremendous Feature, and see many a lazy afternoon there in the summer. Sunbaths for Pink; sunbaths and romps in the hose for Nemo; long lays in a deckchair for Tweeze.* Wheeeee! It is really very large for a town place. In front of the verandah Ma tells me that there are hydrangeas. Now isn't it odd that about two months ago or so I had one of my Foreseeings, or Visitations, in which I was talking to an old Deefie on a verandah about hydrangeas? When it happened I felt it all terribly clearly. If only one could harness these things. There are many trees on that place..... an enormous advantage. And the verandah is splendid. As you see, I am enthusiastic about it and I give you full marks and a bonus as a house-picker. *Clever, discerning, tasteful* Pinkie!

After leaving the house this afternoon (having had an outside look) I dropped in at the Catholic cathedral and had a sit and a think. Dearest Pinkie, I am so anxious that this shall be a right move for us, and that we shall be happy here. The opportunity for me is a big one, and I must make the very most of it, but that is only half. It must be a good thing for you. It is a curious fate which brings you from Australia in order to be the wife of an editor in a Canadian small city, and I don't suppose that it is one which you ever contemplated. But I get a feeling from the atmosphere here that you will be able to do the kind of radio work you want to do, in time. Garner is keen and open minded, and somehow this place *smells* adventurous, though a bit crude. Not Toronto, where there is so much inertia and ignorance posing as experience; and not Kingston, where there are too many second-rate professors who are too clever to be gullible, and not clever enough to be really any good at anything artistic. I have been looking about in the streets, and the people look crass and rough-hewn, in a way, but somehow more *real* than one has been used to. You will be a lone wolf, but there will not, I feel, be the barriers of stupidity and vanity which you would meet in either of the other places. It is very exciting and I think you will feel it too. But this *must* be a success for you, in spite of initial setbacks.

I felt terribly lonesome this morning, and would gladly have hopped on a train and rushed back to you. What a business it is to be in love with someone! Did you wish I was back! I bet you did. I wanted you and I wanted Nemo a little bit too. I have always been rather a baby about going to new places. But I feel much happier now, and very excited, and seeing the house and talking to you on the phone have bucked me up enormously. I am so glad you are going to the concert with Kitty;* have a wonderful time and look marvellous. How nice of her to ask you. And as for the sale, do what you think best, and don't let anything you want go for the lack of a few dollars. We will manage somehow, and there is the $400 we are borrowing from the firm, you know. That house deserves a bit of pinching for.

I shall write again tomorrow, and I shall have a letter from you tomorrow, you darling. Monday has gone now, and there are only Tuesday, Wednesday and Thursday before I shall see you again!

You know how much love, and a kiss for that Awful One.

Rob

To BRENDA DAVIES

Peterborough Examiner
Peterborough, Ontario
3:iii:42

Dearest Pinkie

This has been my first full day at this job, & things have gone very well. I have written four editorials and messed about a lot, getting pots of paste, and other such tasks. I haven't really been working hard. But I find that the time at *Saturday Night* has made [a] vast difference in the speed and facility with which I write, & I have hopes that this job may prove to be less onerous than I had thought. When I was filling in for Geo. McCracken* it was quite hard, though never drastic. I should think that if one became very exhausted or ill it would be an awful burden, but I have no intention of letting that happen. My office is very trig, & the light simply *blinding*!

Had a narrow squeak today after lunch. Was coming back here from the hotel, suspecting nothing, when, not far away, I spied a lank form, and with it a shorter form with long lank dull gold locks. It wore a grey cow[?] coat, & though I could not make out the face, some instinct in me cried "Juicy _____." So, with great presence of mind I at once assumed the figure & gait of an old man, & hobbled up an alley until they had passed. From now on I shall be constantly on the alert.

Felt much better today, though I miss you frightfully. One thing marriage has done for me was to provide a perpetual kind audience, & after 36 hours without anyone to talk to I feel almost uncomfortable with repressed conversation. I am getting crudity from held-in chit-chat. Of course I could talk to people at the hotel if I wanted to, but I don't. I listen to their conversations instead. They all say, over & over "Well, y'know, when March comes in like a lamb it goes out like a lion." I am tired of this threadbare witticism.

Hotel life is dull enough, but the food is endurable. Only I *wish* they wouldn't serve half-lemons and call them grapefruit! I had a bath last night, as I was chilly. Peterborough water is quite soft, but brown, like weak coffee. Odd. Then to bed with the poisoning case, which is really first-rate. Tonight I think I shall drown my sorrow in a double-feature at one of the local flicks.

Really the weather here is foul! Thaw, snow, rain & sun! And my gumboots merely serve to collect the slush & hold it close to my feet. I must get a pair of storm-rubbers. Fortunately the hotel is hot − almost stifling.

They have now got a carpet for my room. I burn to know what the pattern is. I need some pictures for this office. Naked women, preferably. If you see any going cheap at Roy's sale,* snap them up. The picture of Churchill wd. be far too conventional & anyway, Craw has one. I have a huge mantel which cries aloud for something over it. Bend yr. brain to it, Pink. What shall I have?

What I *have* got is a lovely new *Encyclopaedia Britannica* & a fine Oxford Dictionary. I haven't had a moment to dip into them yet, but I shall in time.

By the bye (m' dear friend) I never sent Simpson's a cheque for their window men. Are they raging? Do they storm? If so, give them eightpence, & I will pay you when I get back. Thanks for the $5. *Of course* you shall have the change *the minute* I get home. When that will be I shall let you know in my next letter. I shall ask about trains.

This town is bigger than we thought – almost as big as Kingston. It was 25,000 last census & Garner says it is nearer 31,000 now. The shops look to be about Kingston standard – many small locals, a few big locals, & all the usual Woolworth's, Laura Secord & whatnot. There are more shopping streets than in K., I should say. There is a very large shop called Canadian Departmental Stores, which I think is a branch of Eaton's in disguise.

Sorry Nemo has a sad tooth. I hope she is happier now. How welcome yr. letter was! I'll write again tomorrow sweetheart, unless something turns up, in which case I'll write again tonight.

All my love for you, & a small bit for Nemo

Rob

To JOAN MCINNES

[572 Weller Street
Peterborough, Ontario
the latter part of 1942]

*Joan Cecile McInnes (1914–2002),
Australian-born Canadian, was married to
Graham McInnes, art editor of Saturday
Night 1935–41. Davies' period as the
paper's literary editor (1940–42)
overlapped with McInnes'. The McInneses
and Davieses quickly became friends.*

Dear Madam:

I think I understood you to say, in your Wednesday night radio address, *that the tempo of living in Australia is markedly slower than that of this continent.* Madam, beware! You have trodden on the rattlesnake of local patriotism! Here in Peterborough I venture to say that we can show you a tempo of living slower than any in the world! Let the kangaroo tremble in his bed! The Beaver of the Kawarthas* can out-drowse him any day of the week! Adieu, rash Antipodean –

One of the Seventy Times Seven
Sleepers of Peterborough

To JOAN and GRAHAM
MCINNES

[572 Weller Street
Peterborough, Ontario
Autumn, 1943]

*Graham McInnes (1912–70), English-born
Canadian (raised in Australia), was by this
time settled in Ottawa where he had
joined the National Film Board as script
writer, film editor, director, and senior
producer, 1940–48.*

Dear Joan & Graham,

Y^r letter and its splendid news came this morning. What are you hoping for – a girl or another boy? But I can't see why it should restrict your occasional visits to us; travelling with two children is only slightly more hellish than travelling with one, and we will make a place for the baby very easily. Anyway, we shall all cross that bridge when we come to it. Meanwhile, I hope that Graham will be awfully careful about stairs, lifting heavy weights and sudden frights; personally, during the period of expectant fatherhood, I tend to feel it in the feet. If he fancies anything special, Joan, be sure to get it for him, or the baby may be born with a ration-coupon on its thigh.

How envious we feel, reading about you going to parties. Peterborough is deadly, as usual. Not that I am ungrateful – there are a few little treats. For instance, during the next two months I shall address the Lions, the Home and School Club, and the Rotarians; the latter contains the *élite* of the industrial *bon ton* – a swell bunch of guys. But except for these peaks, the landscape is flat indeed. Oh yes, I forgot to say that I am on the local Fuel Control Board, mingling freely with the Aristotles and Caesars of the coal and wood industry.

About *Precious Bane:** I am glad you have revised your earlier opinion of it. Of course, it's not everybody's meat, but I have always found it most congenial. *Cold Comfort Farm** was certainly meant to parody Mary Webb, among others, and although it has some grand passages – as when Old Adam is clettering the dishes wi' a thorn twig – I have never felt that the book as a whole quite made the grade. There is an intensity of feeling in Mary Webb which Stella Gibbons never fully comprehended, and so she was unable to reproduce it, even in the distortion of parody. I know the country of the Mary Webb books quite well – it is near our home in Wales. Beguildy, Sarn, the Devil's chair and so on are all within the range of an after-tea drive. The atmosphere of her books is exactly the atmosphere of that countryside, and when once it has been truly felt it cannot be forgotten.

I am in this draft, and have had a notice. However, it was from Toronto, for I only told them about my change of address a bare eighteen months ago, and they have not taken it in yet. So I have had my papers transferred to Kingston, which is the centre for this Military District. And I took the precaution of having an examination by my Dr., to see what my category would be – he is one of the local medical board. I am a "C," and so it is unlikely that I shall be called. When I had my exam, I could only read the big letters on the eye-chart with my right eye, and couldn't even see the chart with my left. Also I have dizzy spells, hypertension and nervous indigestion, not to mention painter's colic and dowager's hump. So I expect that I shall go on slapping the Jap from behind my desk. "What did you do in the Great War, daddy? I was rejected, you little misery!"

Once more, hurrah about the big news –

Rob

P.S. *Don't forget that Saturday next is National Newsboy Day – honour your newsboy, the merchandizer of the future!*

To W. H. CLARKE

[*Peterborough Examiner*
Peterborough, Ontario]
17: ix: 44

William Henry Clarke (1902–55), Canadian, was president of the Canadian educational publishing company Clarke, Irwin & Company, which brought out Davies' Shakespeare for Young Players in 1942 and remained his Canadian publisher until 1958.

Dear Mr. Clarke:

Thank you for the cheque for royalties on *Shakespeare For Young Players* which reached me yesterday. I hope that the book is being useful, and may even gain a reasonable popularity in time.

I have just returned from my vacation, during which I did some thinking about your proposal that I should write another book. I had in mind a book on English Composition for High School students – something which would encourage style and adventurousness by advocating Stevenson's method – that of "the sedulous ape."* I am not at all sure that it would appeal to teachers, but it might.

However, it would take quite a while to prepare such a book, and at present I am up to my neck in work – editing a daily paper, as well as writing book-reviews and a weekly Diary for it. In such spare time as I have, I have been writing plays. The theatre is my prime interest in life, and my eventual aim and hope is to be a playwright. I have sent one play to a London producer [probably Tyrone Guthrie]* who asked to have a look at it, and I expect to hear from him some time this autumn. I am now working on another play, and also on a one-act piece on a Canadian theme* – a little comedy about Frontenac and Bishop Laval who, you may recall, had a tiff about a production of Molière's *Tartuffe** at Quebec. I cannot imagine that you are interested in publishing plays – not many people like to read them – and a volume of unacted plays by an unknown Canadian author would be a poor risk. But the plays on which I am working are all classifiable as Improbable Histories – that is to say, things which may have happened, but probably did not – and all are comedies. If it would amuse you to see the one which is completed, I should be glad to send you a typescript.

Writing these comedies is my diversion at present: writing another textbook would be hard work, of which I have enough already. I should be glad to hear whether you are even faintly interested in the plays, and I shall quite understand if you are not.

Yours sincerely

Robertson Davies

To W. H. CLARKE

[*Peterborough Examiner*
Peterborough, Ontario]
December 1, 1944

Dear Mr. Clarke:

I am writing to tell you how much I enjoyed reading Emily Carr's new book* "The House Of All Sorts." It arrived yesterday morning, and I took it home at lunch time, and did not return to work until I had finished it. I think that it is in many ways the best of her books that you have published up to the present time, and a most valuable contribution to Canadian writing. She has that quality which is so rare among Canadian writers, and indeed among writers of any country, of being able to convey genuine and deep feeling directly, and not strained through an elaborate mesh of words. I hope that if you are writing to Miss Carr sometime soon, that you will mention to her that I am even more enthusiastic about her books than I was when the first one arrived.

Did you receive a letter from me in September concerning a book which you had asked me to consider writing for school use? On the day that I wrote that letter I also wrote another, to which I received no reply, and it struck me that through some accident, they might both have gone astray.

With best wishes to yourself and Mrs. Clarke, I am

Yours sincerely,

[Robertson Davies]
Editor

P.S.: I am writing a review of "The House Of All Sorts," which I will send to you as soon as it appears.

To SENATOR RUPERT DAVIES

[*Peterborough Examiner*
Peterborough, Ontario]
March 1, 1945

William Rupert Davies (1879–1967), Davies' Welsh-born Canadian father, lived in Kingston, Ontario. He owned the Kingston *Whig-Standard and the* Peterborough Examiner. *He was a Liberal appointment to the Senate in 1942.*

Dear Father:

I see that you have been quoting with approval from the *Winnipeg Tribune*. It might interest you to know that what the *Tribune* has said was quoted without alteration from *The Examiner*.

This is just to point out to you what a wide circulation we are getting in this district.

Yours sincerely,

[Rob]
Editor

To JAMES AGATE*

James Agate (1877–1947) was a prominent English drama, literary, and film critic.

[*Peterborough Examiner*
Peterborough, Ontario
shortly before May 15, 1945]

[Dear Mr. Agate:]

. . . If most Canadians do not understand the speech of English actors it is not because that speech is incomprehensible, but because the Common Man in Canada is averse from understanding anybody but his immediate associates, and them only on the most superficial level. The *Diary* which I publish weekly is expressed with almost unbearable timidity, since vigorous or forthright criticism of the national intelligence is resented with almost hysterical ferocity. Canada suffers from artistic malnutrition: music is the only art which commands respect and general support. There is no theatre except in Toronto and Montreal, and very little there. Few Canadians have seen a play, and few have seen a movie which was not made in Hollywood. There is little film criticism, and what there is is addressed to an inexperienced audience. But there is an audience for good English films among the more discerning Canadians: they welcome a relief from the childishness of Hollywood, and the prurient-pure, daintily salacious Hays Office* attitude towards sex. *Fanny by Gaslight** is causing some fuss here because the heroine is illegitimate: Canada, you must understand, is a very *nice* country. No, Canada does not actively dislike English films: it is just too dumb, as a usual thing, to understand anything which is not thoroughly familiar. . . .

[Robertson Davies
Editor]

To MRS. DORA MAVOR MOORE

[*Peterborough Examiner*
Peterborough, Ontario]
June 29, 1945

Dora Mavor Moore (1888–1979) was a Scottish-born Canadian actress, teacher, and director. The writing of this letter had long-term consequences. The New Play Society, a professional theatre company founded in Toronto by Moore and her son Mavor, ignored Davies' work, although it produced many new plays by other Canadian playwrights during its ten-season life (1946–56).

Dear Mrs. Mavor Moore:

During the past few weeks I have written to you twice asking for the return of the manuscript of my one-act play "Hope Deferred." I have not received a line from you in reply, nor did I ever receive an acknowledgement that you had received the play from me, although you were very anxious to get it, and organized a performance of it in Toronto.

I do not suppose that there is any point in continuing this correspondence. However, there are two things that I should like you to know: the first is that your action in this matter leaves me without a copy of this play, which is now irrecoverable, as far as I am concerned; the second is that I am really very much surprised at such shabby conduct on the part of a woman of your reputation and background. I am

Yours sincerely,

[Robertson Davies]
Editor

To MR. _____

[*Peterborough Examiner*
Peterborough, Ontario]
July 21, 1945

Dear Mr. _____:

Thank you very much for your letter of the fifth of July, and for your reminder written on Friday last. I have been away several days since your first letter came, and carelessly neglected to answer it before I left.

There is no position on *The Peterborough Examiner* which I could offer you, and to be perfectly frank, I would not be inclined to offer you a job if I had one, and I will tell you why. In your first letter to me, you adopted a very patronizing tone toward this paper, and gave me to understand that you had offers from large papers in Montreal and Toronto. I have had a certain amount of experience in dealing with applicants for positions, and I knew immediately that these offers either did not exist at all, or were so trifling that you did not want to be bothered with them. But you took the attitude that you were doing *The Examiner* a great favour by offering it your services. That, Mr. _____, is not the way to get a job. Now in your second letter you explained at some length what you would pledge yourself to do if you came to work on this paper. We do not require pledges of our employees, and if you came to work here, you would be expected to follow the directions of the Managing Editor, who would tell you what was and what was not expected. Again in your second letter you stressed the fact that the limitations of a paper like *The Examiner* would be "very strong." They are not, perhaps, as strong as you would imagine.

In the example of your writing which you have sent to me, you reveal a style which is pretentious, but without foundation. Consider your brief report of the Montreal Little Symphony. It contains far too many clichés, and contains also at least two badly misspelled words. Reporters are not expected to be expert spellers, but if you really knew the meaning of the word "meritorious" you would never spell it "meritious."

If you are going to learn the newspaper business, you will have to begin at the beginning, and learn first to write the English language. Also you will have to reduce by ninety per cent your extremely inflated opinion of your own abilities. We have not, at the moment, an opening for a junior, and I do not know of anyone who has. However, it is not particularly difficult to get into newspaper work, and I am sure that you will be able to find a position if you want one badly enough. But again, let me repeat my earlier advice to you: Bluff and impudence are of no value in any business. I am

Yours sincerely,

[Robertson Davies]
Editor

To H. L. MENCKEN

Peterborough Examiner
Peterborough, Ontario
Tuesday, Jan: 8. [1946]

Henry Louis Mencken (1880–1956) was a preeminent American newspaperman, philologist, author, and critic. He did not take Davies up on his offer to supply him with "Canadian raw material."

Dear Mr. Mencken:

My father (Senator Rupert Davies) has just sent me your letter of January 5, in which you acknowledge the receipt of reviews of your Supplement to *The American Language* from the Kingston *Whig-Standard* and the Peterborough *Examiner*, written by Samuel Marchbanks.* I confess that I am this Marchbanks, and I did not send you copies of the review myself because I thought it a poorly written and rather offensively expressed article: I offer the usual excuse – it had to be written in a great hurry, with many interruptions. That is not the way to review a book of lasting importance, but it couldn't be helped. It was most kind of you to speak as well of the review as you did. The only thing I can say in its defence is that our two papers were the only ones in provincial Ontario – that is, outside Toronto and Ottawa – to carry a review of the book at all; the indifference of our contemporaries to anything which might conceivably be important to their own trade (as your book was) is truly marvellous. Of course, we bought the book for our library.

You ask some questions in your letter which my father has referred to me. The generally accepted designation for a citizen of Ontario is *an Ontarian*, though the word is not needed very often and has an odd sound. A citizen of Kingston is, of course, *a Kingstonian*. A denizen of Peterborough is properly called a *Peterboronian*, though I have heard some of the less literate nobility and gentry hereabout talking of *Peterborovians*: but these designations are less common and less esteemed than the expression *a Peterborough man*, which implies not merely citizenship, but long residence (at least two or three generations). For instance, I overheard this conversation on a 'bus, concerning the local Crown Attorney, V. J. McElderry, K.C.; the speakers were two she-ancients of the place:

"Mr. McElderry is a fine man, isn't he?"
"Oh yes indeed; a very fine man."
"Everyone knows him, and everyone speaks highly of him."
"Yes, but he's not really what I call *a Peterborough man*."

McElderry came here from a town about 25 miles away 19 years ago, but he hasn't made the grade yet with the locals who, from their indifference to arts, letters and the finer graces of society, I have heard referred to as *Peterboors* by outsiders; this rude name is not, of course, worthy of public notice in your scholarly volume.

It may interest you to know that this town received its name in tribute to its founder, Peter Robinson, and is officially Peterborough, but the railway stations have shortened it to Peterboro for their signs, and clownish folk have taken up this spelling; the local radio station (manned by fellows who mouth and mangle every word) pronounces it Peter-bow-row, and not "burra" as is the old style.

May I say how much I have been delighted by your *Prejudices*, your autobiographical volumes, your *Dictionary of Quotations*, and by *The American Language*,* as well as by the fugitive pieces which I see here and there. In return for that pleasure may I offer (if I may do so without seeming pushful) to provide you with Canadian raw material when and as you want it? I am a bit of a crank about language, have a good ear, and Canadian and Oxford degrees in English, and was an actor for a time, so I think I can hear what really is said, and reproduce it accurately.....

Yours very sincerely,

Robertson Davies

To HERBERT WHITTAKER

The Evening Examiner
Peterborough, Ontario
March 17: 1946

*Herbert Whittaker (1911–   ), Canadian,
was then drama critic for* The Gazette *in
Montreal, Quebec. He was also a director,
designer, and adjudicator.*

Dear Mr. Whittaker:

Although we have never met, we have a mutual friend in Grant Macdonald, who has often spoken to me of you. Therefore I am writing to ask you for a bit of information: A CP item dated March 1 said that the Canadian Art Theatre of Montreal invited Canadian writers to send them MSS of one-act plays before March 31, but no address in Montreal was given; could you tell me where such plays should be sent, and under what circumstances?

I have been writing plays for some time, and have some one-acters on Canadian themes at hand. I should like to send one of them to Montreal if I can find out a little more about the Canadian Art Theatre and its doings. I should be most grateful if you could tell me where the play should be sent. I am

Yours sincerely

Robertson Davies

To TYRONE and JUDITH
GUTHRIE

[Peterborough, Ontario]
May 27, 1946

*Tyrone Guthrie (1900–71), English stage
director, and his wife, Judith (1903–72),
likewise English, had become friends of
the Davieses at the Old Vic Theatre
Company in London. Guthrie was its
resident director when Brenda
apprenticed in the drama school in 1936
and served as its stage manager 1936–39
and also when Davies joined the
company as a junior member 1938–39.
The Guthries had come to visit over
Christmas 1945 from New York, where
Guthrie was preparing his wife's
adaptation of Leonid Andreyev's* He Who
Gets Slapped *for the Theater Guild at the
Booth Theatre.*

Dear Tony & Judy:

I read you an early version of this [the one-act play *Overlaid*] at
Christmas & you urged me to extend it. I did so, & put the result in
the Ottawa Drama League competition, & got First Prize ($100) out
of a field of 47.

The adjudicator's* "remarks" were depressing: "A hilarious folk-
comedy that could stand comparison with the best of E. P. Conkle,"
said he. Upon looking up the said Conkle in French's* Catalogue I
discover him to be a concocter of gummy fantasies. A friend insists
that I call my next piece "He Honks To Conkle." Still $100 is not to
be sneezed at, whatever insult may go with it.

Yours till Niagara Falls,
(*this is the Conkle touch*)

Rob.

To TYRONE and JUDITH GUTHRIE

[Peterborough, Ontario
October 1946]

Dear Tony & Judy:

Nobody knows better than I do that the greater part of a year has passed since I wrote to you: I grovel: I eat y^r feet. I can only say that y^r visit is still so fresh in my mind that I have been saying for months: "Oh, no need to write yet; they've only just gone." But it is ten months since you went. What have we done since which you might like to hear about?

Well, to begin with, we went to New York in June to see the Vic. Like real provincials, we call it *The New York Visit*,* and date things by it. Bettina Cerf arranged for our tickets and cleverly got us the seats in the exact middle of the front row of the Circle for all four productions. We left the children with friends in Ottawa (Australians) & *motored*, which was wonderfully pleasant, for we stopped wherever we pleased and observed the quaint customs of the American peasantry at first-hand. The first night we lost our way in the Adirondacks, & found an hotel which was not yet open: they took pity on us, however, & we had the place to ourselves – mountain air and quietness, rather like Wales. The following day we went quite slowly, buying examples of such native work as waffles, fried chicken and beer, & a handsome brass knocker which now enriches our front door. We gawked at the Vanderbilt mansion, & agreed that we could be very happy in it: we wanted to burn incense at the home of the late F. D. Roosevelt, but it was closed. We dined at Tarrytown, where a horrible mishap befell me. It was an ancient hotel – Victorian posing as Colonial – & the lavatories were not plainly marked. Brenda found one, which she judged was for general, or heterosexual, use. She directed me to it, & I rushed in carelessly & took up a restful pose in a booth. *Judge of my alarm & shame* when, a moment later, three women came in and began to make female conversation! They were the "committee" of a female club, or lodge, which was dining in the hotel that night. Loudly & unbuttonedly they talked of club affairs, primping at the mirrors! Should Gert be first to speak, or Mamie? I tucked up my feet – the doors were half affairs – & froze like a rabbit, while visions of exposure, police court, & Sing Sing whizzed (in Technicolor) through my brain! But worse was to come. Madam Chairwoman (as Gert was called, officially) *tried my door*, while my heart stopped! Then she went into the next booth &, while sitting cheek by jowl with me (if I may employ that expression) released her personal Niagara with thunderous enjoyment, while keeping up her conversation with her friends outside, & asking – apocalyptic moment! – that "the lady next door" would excuse her! At last they went, & I, on spaghetti legs, dashed for the door, & was not myself until I had downed three Daiquiris.

In New York we had excellent treatment at the New Weston. It was all marvellous – every minute. To enjoy New York thoroughly, one must have had rather a lot of some place like Peterborough, The Gateway to the Kawarthas. The shops were grand: the streets were grand: the restaurants were grand. The bookshops were not to be compared with London or Oxford, but provided very good coarse browsing. Central Park I thought a dusty common. But we spent a whole wonderful day in the Metropolitan Museum: we both love museums: how well they display things! We ordered a bronze Greek horse – a superb thing – but it has not been cast yet. We had a good look at the Mus. of Mod. Art, as well, & a fine lunch in its garden: this gave a chance to try a California wine – decent, but not up to South African, if we *must* talk of anything but the noblest French vintages. On our free night we went out with Bettina & Fetzke; though we are not much alike I took to him at once & we discovered a common enthusiasm for Chinese food: he guided us to 21 Mott St., a low place where policemen, firemen & connoisseurs eat, & there we ordered, & devoured, the Ceremonial Banquet for Sixteen, with a couple of hogsheads of fine tea. Then we went to Staten Island on the ferry, & digested. A notable evening. We had previously called upon Bettina at the Knocking Shop [The Theater Guild] – (to our immense delight the "receptioniste" took us for actors looking for jobs) – where she was all *impressement* & *chic* & *élan*; but on her evening off she was v. happily Mrs. F., & marvelled prettily at her husband's knowledge of marine architecture. I thought them both charming.

As for the Vic performances, they were water in a thirsty land to us, for we had seen nothing comparable for four years. Nevertheless, we were not thrown flat on our back as many New Yorkers were, for we thought them *good Vic performances*, but not genuine bowel-shakers* like the Victorian *Dream*, the modern-dress *Hamlet*, the Coronation *Henry V* or *The Country Wife*. These were all yours, but I do not mean to flatter. *Oedipus* without Laurence Olivier wd. have been nothing in particular; the Chorus reminded me painfully of a coven of Welsh Baptist preachers in their bardic robes at an eisteddfod. *The Critic* was a lark, but wanted *style* in the sense that *The Good Natur'd Man** had it. The *Henry IV* was good, but I could not do with Ralph Richardson* − scratching his groin, clawing his false paunch & giving a fine clinical study of g.p.i. Perhaps his performance did not cross the ocean well, like some fine wines. Again, L.O. was v. fine, but the core of the play was Beau Hannen.* We saw this at a mat. & eve. session, when the temperature was above 90°F. Rather wearing for the actors, but Richardson too obviously threw in the towel, which was not what we had travelled 500 miles & paid a lot of money to see him do. In our opinion, the prize of the group was *Uncle Vanya*: marvellous performances by L.O., R.R. & Hannen. We were deeply moved, & still are when we recall it: I was confirmed, too, in my conviction that Ibsen & Chekhov are more comprehensible to Canadians than to Englishmen, on the whole. Because there is so much of the same sort of frustration & bonelessness in Canada, I mean. Joyce Redman told us that *Vanya* put her in mind of Western Ireland: we met her when we went behind to see Diana Boddington.*

No doubt about it, the Vic. hit New York hard, as the talk, jealousy & frank copying since has amply proved. Two weeks ago we went to Toronto to see José Ferrer do *Cyrano*,* rather poorly: some of the best touches of production in it were pinched from the Vic. The influence of the Vic. on New York is comparable only to the influence on London of the visit of the Duke of Saxe-Meiningen's company* in 1881, or Diaghilev's *Ballet Russe** after the First Great War. The L.O. *Henry V* movie has confirmed what the plays began.

L.O. is the nearest thing to a *great* actor I have ever seen: if only he
had a bit more nobility & poetry I should not qualify my appreciation. How I long to see him in *Lear*! – We left New York much
refreshed, & grateful that such things still happened in the theatre.

What else have I to tell you? Oh, yes. My father is now half-retired,
& has bought a new home in Montgomeryshire, for his term as High
Sheriff,* which begins on St. David's Day, 1947. My brother Arthur is
now president of *The Examiner*, & I am vice,* & have a commodious
& elegant new office, an assistant to do part of the writing, & a lot
of tiresome responsibility, which I hate. Sometimes I feel that I am
chained to Peterborough by fetters of gold, & with the Income Tax
what it is, a fetter of gold is a damned swindle, no better than a fetter
of iron. Some day I shall have to hew my way out with a bloody axe.

I wrote Dame Sybil* about the Welsh play [*A Jig for the Gypsy*], &
got a kind reply: sent her the MSS in March: got it back two weeks ago,
much dog-eared & tumbled, & last week a note from Sir Lewis, deeply
regretting, etc. So much for that. At present I am getting together a
volume of my comic diary [*The Diary of Samuel Marchbanks*], which
the Oxford Press is bringing out: after that I shall complete a play
[*King Phoenix*] which I want to show to John Gielgud* when he is
in Canada next February. He won't want it, but I am going to show
it to him anyway. It is about Old King Cole, and the very peculiar
way in which he won his reputation as a Jolly Old Soul. It is as
though *Lear* had been written by Rabelais,* if I may so modestly
express myself.

And speaking of aspiring playwrights, I am haunted at the moment
by a Peterborough youth called _____ _____, whose desire, in his
own words, is "to crack the play-writing game." He appeals to me to
help him to "cut down the inevitable 5-year period of apprenticeship." He is "strictly interested in the money-angle" & his notion of
writing a play is to take Van Druten's* "There's Always Juliet" & *paraphrase* it, eliminating all grace & wit which it may have, & send it to
Broadway agents. When they return it he accuses them of lacking dis-
cernment. Sometimes he comes to my office, & I can only gape at
him, for he is such a cruel caricature of my own hopes & aspirations
that he appears to me as a horrible *Doppelgänger*, sent by Fate to mock

me. He does not know that I attempt to write plays: that only adds to the gruesomeness of his chattering inanity.

News: we expect another child in April, & Brenda's mother* is flying from Australia in February to be here for the event. Brenda hopes for a boy: I am of an open mind, & think three daughters a well-balanced family. The presence of Mrs. Newbold should make everything easy, as she is a magnificent coper.

News: We are doing *The Coventry Nativity Play* at the Rev. E. C. Moore's (you met him) church in December. I made a modernized version with some new bits in it, & some chunks from one of Bishop Bayle's moralities.* The actors are hard-handed men who work in Peterborough here, which never laboured in their minds till now, & have toiled their unbreathed memories with this same play.* The effect is fine, & quite moving, in places, and unbelievably bloody in others. But I think it will not disgrace us when completed. Moore is in the 7th Heaven & has declared that it is "the answer to prayer" so many times that Br. & I are beginning to feel rather incorporeal.

And now, enough, or you will cry out upon me for a tedious conceited fellow who is costive of his news for a twelvemonth & then spews out all in a merciless flux of words. In this household your visit is a thing of yesterday – an epiphany of the Great World which has left us open-mouthed. The children want to know when you will come again. Every blessing light upon you –

Brenda & Rob

PS: Have you read Sir Osbert Sitwell's *The Scarlet Tree?** *Frightfully* good – you'd *adore* it.

It won't be so long before I write again.

To GRANT MACDONALD

[572 Weller Street
Peterborough, Canada]
Wed: Nov 6. 1946

Dear Grant:

    I am writing this uncomfortably in bed: I have a cold in my throat & have retired with the steam-kettle: can you smell Friar's Balsam on this? Brenda & I both thank you for yᴵ note & yᴵ visit: glad you enjoyed it, for we loved having you. When you had gone, though, we both had a fit of the blues, for you live so much in the *Great World* (which for us means the Theatre) and we are so remote from it, & have such meagre hopes of ever returning to it.

    Yes: we want you to do Brenda *very* much, & we are thrilled by your notion of doing pictures of Miranda & Jenny. It would be a wonderful way of capturing their endearing young charms, before they become all legs & arms & adolescence. We shall hang all four in the dining-room & they will be our family portraits.

    I quite forgot to tell you that the Ottawa people had done my play *Overlaid** for I thought it of little account. Miss Hall was discouraging beforehand, though she wrote quite enthusiastically afterward: apparently the audience laughed more than she expected. Sometimes I think I have a more genuine idea of what is funny than many people credit me with. I don't think you've read *Overlaid* & when you come to see us again I'll dig up a copy: it is not like anything else I have done. A group in Kamloops B.C. is doing it quite soon.

    For the moment, farewell & thanks for your very kind offer to draw the children.

All the best from both of us

<u>Rob</u>.

To JOHN J. ESPEY

Peterborough Examiner
Peterborough, Ontario
Friday, March 7 [1947]

John J. Espey (1913–2000), American, was a writer and was to become a professor of English at UCLA. The son of a Presbyterian missionary, he was born and raised in Shanghai, and devoted his first books – including Minor Heresies *(1945) and* Tales Out of School *(1947) – to his childhood in China. He and Davies became friends at Oxford 1935–38 and were to remain sporadic correspondents.*

Dear John:

Thanks for your letter of Feb. 15. I meant to reply at once, but a great weight of troublesome business descended upon me and I have just got 'round to it. Glad to hear that you are getting back to health. What fine things you are doing in your writing! I was greatly tickled by *Minor Heresies*, as you know, and I have been following the school stories in the *New Yorker** with even more pleasure. The last one I saw – about the Jew who fell foul of the young Christians – was brilliant; it made me so much more angry than the full-page ads in the N. Y. *Times* which show aged rabbis being kicked in the rump, while lush Rebeccas and kids with 100-watt eyes look on with grimaces of pain. Incidentally I think the U.S. Jews are behaving awfully badly about Palestine, but you probably do, too. When *Pine Tree Patrol* comes out I entreat a signed copy; I may even be able to do a little bit about it, for my book reviews are beginning to attract some notice, and I now have a sworn circulation for them of 80,000 – many of them literate. I see *Minor Heresies* now and again in the bigger book shops here, and I never fail to brandish it about and say "Here's a remarkably fine thing" to my wife; this, I am convinced, eggs on other buyers, for I now have a beard, weigh 230 pounds, and look as though I knew what I was talking about, even when I don't.

My family continues to grow. Two daughters, as you know, and right after Easter another which we hope will be a boy called Nicholas. My wife is very keen about boys, though I don't care much for them myself. Also, next week, my wife's mother [Muriel Newbold] arrives from Australia, for six months or so. She is a most charming person, and I am looking forward to seeing her again – an uncommon attitude toward Mas-in-law, I believe. My elder daughter, Miranda, shows signs of unusual musical ability, and we are fussing about getting the right teaching for her; I teach her now, but I am a born genius-ruiner, being explosive and impatient when I should be tactful and torpid. But she is a dear child, and we get on splendidly most of the time; already she shows signs of an entertaining wit. The other girl, Jennifer, is deeply set on her mother, and fears me, though for no good reason as I spend hours trying to win her. Ours is a lively household, for my wife is the only member of the family who has any evenness of temper.

I continue to write plays, though just today I shipped off a book of nonsense in diary form [*The Diary of Samuel Marchbanks*] to a publisher who will be bringing it out soon, and I shall send you a copy. But I am set on plays, and they are the very devil to get rid of. I have done quite well with amateur productions and whatnot, but that is not the Real Thing. However, John Gielgud was in Toronto in February, and I renewed acquaintance with him then and he read my stuff and was very kind and encouraging about it. He was particularly keen on a play about Ethelred the Unready ["The King Who Could Not Dream"], but did not like the last act. I am going to re-do it and see how he likes it then. There is some hint, also, of the formation of a professional theatre in Canada, and I have had a note from the impresario which sounded quite encouraging. Altogether, things are looking up a bit, and in twenty years or so I may have had a play done somewhere, and got some money for it.

But oh! the dreariness of provincial life in Canada! Ibsen, living in that Pompeian atmosphere of 19th century Norway, didn't know how lucky he was! I waste my days among people who hate the Arts because they are Immoral, and wear themselves to skin and bone worrying about the Decline of Church-Going, the evils of breaking the Sabbath, and the horrendous increases in the divorce rate. It is enough to make a man erect a statue of Priapus on his front lawn – a fountain statue, with Canadian whisky pouring from its erected penis night and day.

Brenda and I exist only by luring friends to come and visit us – pagans, suckled in creeds outworn, for preference. You don't happen to want a Northern holiday, do you?

May the Lord God, who sees every secret, save you, and make you perfect and strong.....

Yours in the bowels of Christ,

<u>Rob</u>

P.S. I have lost track of LePan,* who went to war as a gunner. I have no doubt he is doing something *worthy* somewhere.

To ETHEL WAGNER

Peterborough Examiner
Peterborough, Ontario
March 12, 1947

Ethel Wagner was a sixth grade teacher at Seventeenth Street School in Niagara Falls, New York.

Dear Miss Wagner:

I was very much surprised and pleased to receive the letters from the boys and girls of your class, about the letter which I wrote some time ago to the *New York Times.** It is possible that some of your children received a wrong impression from my letter as it appeared in that paper, because to my great annoyance about a third of what I had written was cut out of it, and the remainder had been re-written in such a way as to give a much more severe impression than I had intended. The reason for my letter was this: I saw an article in the *New York Times* written by a woman who had visited England for about three weeks, and who was extremely critical of social distinctions there; she gave it as her opinion that democracy could not exist in a country where there are distinctions of class. This seems to me to be a most dangerous and foolish sort of cant, because although I have travelled in a number of countries, I have never been in one yet where there were no distinctions of class, and I think that it is more honest and healthy to acknowledge that fact than to ignore it. Certainly I do not think that it could be maintained successfully that there are no distinctions of class in the United States. With this in mind I wrote a letter to the *Times*, drawing attention to the advertisement for the Nash car, which seemed to me to be a particularly vulgar example of class distinction, based upon nothing but money.

I was impressed by the letters which the children wrote. The majority of them show an extremely pleasant and healthy attitude towards social distinctions. I have written a little note to each child on the letter which it wrote, and in some of them I have tried to draw attention to a tendency to pretend that something is so, which quite obviously is not so. As you yourself are aware, democracy, as it exists in England and to a considerable extent in Canada, is Political Democracy – that is equality of all men before the law; Social Democracy – that is the assumption that all men are of equal value to the state, is not so highly valued, because we cannot convince ourselves that it is either a true or a valuable belief. Social Democracy, as it concerns good manners between all sections of the population, however, we value very highly indeed.

I am sending some new Canadian stamps with this letter, and I hope that there will be one for each child in your class. This stamp commemorates the invention of the telephone in Brantford, Ontario, by Alexander Graham Bell. It may surprise some of your pupils to learn that the telephone was not invented in their own country. Some of them may be stamp collectors, and even if they are not, they may like to have this stamp as a little recognition of my gratitude for their letters, and the friendship which I feel toward them.

With every good wish to yourself and your class, I am

Sincerely yours,

[Robertson Davies]
Editor

To MARY KEENS

Peterborough Examiner
Peterborough, Ontario
April 8, 1947

Mary Keens was a helpful, kind, single woman, considerably older than the Davieses, a lover of art and the theatre and a friend of Grant Macdonald's. A Torontonian, she visited them in Peterborough from time to time. The Davieses' third daughter, Rosamond, was born on April 6.

Dear Mary:

This is just to let you know that the baby was born on Sunday at 12:50 o'clock, and that Brenda and the child are both very well.

It is a girl, and weighs eight pounds; it is quite a nice looking child, though it is impossible to tell much about it at present. It has a very big nose, and some black hair, and has a rather communist expression. The other children are very excited about it, and seem to expect it to come home almost any minute. We haven't a name for it, as we had rather expected that it would be a boy, but the question of names is getting the most serious consideration at present. Brenda's Mother makes the whole thing very simple, as she is able to keep an eye on the house, and keep the children in good control, and see that everything works smoothly. Brenda sends you her love, and will write after a few days, and I will send you a picture of the baby when I can get some taken.

With best wishes, I am

Yours sincerely,

[Rob]

To THE EDITOR OF *SATURDAY NIGHT**

Peterborough, Ontario
[on or soon after April 19, 1947]

[Dear Sir:]

May I add a few words to the discussion of Mr. Donald Wolfit's performances (S.N. April 19)?* First, may I ask whom Mr. Nat Benson is quoting when he says that "those who saw him claim the immortal Sir H. was a ranter and roarer of cataclysmic proportions"?

Irvingana has been a hobby of mine for some time, and I have made notes of about fifty conversations which I have had with people who saw the late Sir Henry Irving act; some of my informants were critics, and a number of them were old actors who had appeared in Irving's company; not one of them said anything which would support Mr. Benson's statement. Irving's principal accomplishments as an actor appear to have been an ability to communicate emotion of a feverish intensity to his audience, and the power to refine that emotion, giving it a daemonic or poetic quality, as he wished. Irving's pupil, the late Martin Harvey,* possessed this quality in a lesser degree, but still strongly. No critic, so far as I know, has attributed either refinement or poetry to Mr. Wolfit though many have granted him a quality of intensity. Mr. Benson should read the opinion of Irving* held by his sternest critic, Bernard Shaw.

I was able to see only "Lear" and "Volpone"* when Mr. Wolfit visited Toronto. The audience received the first of these kindly, but I think that many who saw it will agree with me that Mr. Wolfit's best acting was done during his curtain calls. His air of exhaustion – of being barely able to sustain the adulation of the ravished audience – was carried off with far more real histrionic skill than he gave to his performance of the old King, which impressed me as petulant, vulgarly conceived, and altogether hammy except in the cursing passages, where he showed something of the fire and vigour which undoubtedly led Charles Cochran* and James Agate to link his name with Irving's. But after the play and during the intervals I talked to several judicious playgoers, all of whom were saying that New York would never put up with so much ham, so many bad actors, such tatty scenery and the general air of haste, slap-dash and "Come on, boys, let's finish it before the pubs close!"

Many Canadians who saw him in this country were not at all surprised by the cool reception Mr. Wolfit received in New York; he played in the theatre which housed the Old Vic company last spring and invited comparison with that famous repertory group; that is precisely what New York gave him. The verdict was the same as England's where, as a revue artist puts it, "Olivier's 'Lear'* is a *tour de force*, while Wolfit's is forced to tour." Respect for Shakespeare seemed to blind many Canadian newspaper critics to the faults of a company which it is kindness to call mediocre.

Robertson Davies

To THE CHILDREN OF THE SIXTH GRADE, SEVENTEENTH STREET SCHOOL, NIAGARA FALLS, N.Y.

Peterborough Examiner
Peterborough, Ontario
June 9, 1947

Dear Boys and Girls:

It is not often that I get thirty-seven friendly letters in one delivery of the mail, and I cannot tell you how pleased I was to hear from you again, and to know that you thought about the little notes which I put on the last group of letters. I enjoyed reading what every one of you had written, and I was glad to see that some of you, with whom I had disagreed, had thought again on the subject of democracy. I do not, for a moment, want you to agree with what I say unless you really think that it is true, but I am very anxious that you should not form opinions about an important thing like democracy without really thinking the matter over very carefully for yourself. I was especially glad that one or two of you, whose letters I remembered particularly, like Shirley DiOranco and Joseph Baccelli, had reversed their opinions, and I thought that their letters were extremely interesting. I liked the letter from Sam Selafani too, but because I mention the letters of two or three of you, I hope that you will not think that I paid no attention to the others. I must repeat that I read them all with great pleasure. I would like to explain to Phyllis White, however, that I am not in the least bored with children, and am in fact very fond of them, and have three daughters of my own. I should like to tell Rose Martinez that I did not win the Pulitzer prize, but only a rather small prize for writing a play, which is not nearly so important.

Several of you were kind enough to ask for a photograph of me in your letter, but I really think that it would be better for me not to send one to you. [If you were to] see my picture you might not like me as well as you do now. There are people who look well, and there are people who write well, and it is very rarely that any one person is able to do both. Let me say again how glad I am to have had this correspondence with you, and I hope that it has given you a somewhat more friendly feeling toward Canada; certainly it has given me a friendly feeling toward the children of the Seventeenth Street School in Niagara Falls.

With best wishes, I am

Yours sincerely,

[Robertson Davies]
Editor

To R. W. W. ROBERTSON

572 Weller Street
Peterborough, Canada
Sunday, Sept. 21. [1947]

R. W. W. Robertson was Davies' editor at Clarke, Irwin. In a letter written September 19, he had given several reasons for eliminating Davies' dedication and four mock verse quotations from The Diary of Samuel Marchbanks: *"They are not in the spirit of the book" and "We hope that it is going to have a great success and we feel that it is going to give our fellow Canadians a much needed lesson in the art of not taking ourselves too seriously but we don't want to do anything to destroy that lesson by going one inch too far." Robertson prevailed: the excisions stood.*

Dear Mr. Robertson:

I am returning the page proofs to you under separate cover. I have made Hengist Marchbanks an *uncle* throughout: I have cleared up the confusion about Christmas and New Year's: I have put heading "IV" in its proper place, and I have made a few other corrections – the small caps on page 172, for instance, agree with the usage elsewhere in the book.

I disagree completely with yᵉ letter of 19 September. I have been writing & publishing this DIARY for 4 years, & in that time I have put everything under the sun into it, including a great deal of verse of the type of these mock quotations. The public thinks them funny, and that is what counts. The *Diary* is a grab-bag: some like one thing in it, & some another. It has no homogeneity & no plan. When you talk about "the spirit of the book" you talk of something which, so far as I am concerned, does not exist. In writing the *Diary* I have been guided by one principle & one only – "*Anything for a laugh.*" If the dedication & half-title quotes make a few readers laugh, that is all to the good.

Perhaps you mistake my motive in writing the *Diary*. It is not, as you suggest "to give our fellow Canadians a much-needed lesson in the art of not taking ourselves too seriously": it is, simply, to say my say as I please: there is nothing educative or highbrow about it. If I may say so, I think that you take the *Diary* too seriously when you say that it is not meant to be funny; it was never meant to be anything else. – In short, I should like the half titles used, though you may can the dedication if you don't like it. And I think that the Autumn quote –

   Crows doze, choughs cough, shrews snooze etc
should be attributed to Hardy, rather than Crabbe.*

With good wishes

<u>Robertson Davies</u>

To GRANT MACDONALD

[Peterborough, Ontario]
Sunday, Nov. 23, 1947

Dear Grant:

   We were very sorry to put you off at the last minute, but it is quite impossible to entertain anyone this weekend. All three children have chickenpox, and Brenda and Jennie have mumps as well. I am head nurse, aided by a D.P. girl* whom we have at last got – don't know what I'd do without her. The place is a lazar-house. The Victorian Order nurses and public health nurses will not go near infectious disease; their specialty, it appears, is badgering and harrying the poor and getting great kudos for it. Trained nurses are as scarce here as anywhere. It is at times like these that married men think that bachelors have the best of it.

   However, things should clear up soon, and if possible we should like to see you the weekend of December 5 or 6; our Nativity Play* opens the night of Sunday the 7th, and we should like you to see it if that is not inconvenient. I am a bit muddled; did you say you wanted to do a picture of me for *Mayfair*?* And if so, for what particular reason? I should love to sit for you again; I am just curious as to what interest *Mayfair* has in my doings.

My book [*The Diary of Samuel Marchbanks*] is out, after prolonged pains on the part of R. W. W. Robertson and his midwife Holy Henry Clarke. I have had an annoying time with them; they are so insufferably pretentious in theory and such botchers in practice..... But more of that when we see you – and I want to give you a copy of the book, as well, so don't spend your money foolishly buying it..... Can you let us know about the weekend?.... In haste.....

ROB

361 Park St.
~~572 WELLER STREET~~
PETERBOROUGH, CANADA

Dear Grant:

Many thanks for your letter, your good wishes and the note to Miss Robson. I hope that this time we can make connections: last time she wrote charmingly. I cannot tell you how much I am obliged to you for this, or how truly I appreciate your readiness to introduce me to your friends, for I know that you do not do so lightly and unadvisedly, as they say in the Marriage Service. Already I am in yr debt for a wonderful hour with Athene Seyler.

We have moved, and are frankly de-lighted with the new house, which you must visit as soon as possible. The Front Parlour, by the way, is our Macdonald Room — no lesser artist allowed — and yr pictures look fine, as they are not crowded, and get a decent light, most of the day.

Our love to you, and we shall send you a comic post card from Llanfairpwll-gwyngyllgogerychwyrndrobwllllantisiliogogogoch.

July 15.   Rob.

Queen's University Archives

SECTION

II

JANUARY 1948–MARCH 1952 – *THE TABLE TALK OF SAMUEL MARCHBANKS* PUBLISHED; *OVERLAID, FORTUNE, MY FOE, EROS AT BREAKFAST AND OTHER PLAYS,* AND *AT MY HEART'S CORE* PUBLISHED, *TEMPEST-TOST* WRITTEN AND PUBLISHED, *A MASQUE OF AESOP* WRITTEN

n January of 1948, now 34, Davies entered a period of extraordinary activity, made possible in part by Tom Allen's capable editorial assistance at the *Examiner*. Allen had joined the paper the previous September, and the two had begun a book review column (with others' contributions as well) that replaced Davies' mid-week Marchbanks column. However, Davies continued with his Saturday diary column until 1953, drawing a second compilation from it in 1949 – *The Table Talk of Samuel Marchbanks* – that won him warm reviews.

By now, with the Second World War well past, theatre was not just reviving but flourishing in Canada, and Davies was in the thick of it. He served on the executive of Canada's recently revived great coast-to-coast amateur drama competition, the Dominion Drama Festival, and directed many amateur and summer stock productions, always with Brenda as one of his key actors. Throughout this period he directed the Peterborough

Little Theatre each year in adventuresome productions and entered them in the regional competitions of the DDF. He directed his own play *Fortune, My Foe* (set in Kingston) for Arthur Sullivan's International Players in Kingston in 1948. And when, in 1949, a summer stock group set up shop in Peterborough as the Peterborough Summer Theatre, Davies directed four of the ten plays presented. The following summer he directed two more plays, including his own *At My Heart's Core*, written to commemorate Peterborough's centennial. In 1951, with the Summer Theatre successfully launched, he directed *At My Heart's Core* for the Brae Manor Theatre at Knowlton, Quebec.

Fortune, My Foe and *At My Heart's Core* were not the only plays he wrote or published in this period. In 1948, Samuel French brought out an acting edition of *Overlaid*, and in 1949 five of his one-act plays were collected as *Eros at Breakfast and Other Plays*. In 1951–52 he wrote *A Masque of Aesop* for his old school, Upper Canada College. All these plays quickly entered the repertory of amateur groups all across the country.

Given the extraordinary productivity of these years, it is startling to realize that Davies was diagnosed (possibly erroneously) with Hodgkin's disease (cancer of the lymph nodes and spleen, then usually fatal), and in April/May of 1948 underwent a long course of debilitating deep X-ray treatments in Toronto.

In spite of Davies' signal success in getting his plays published and widely performed in Canada, the amateurism of many of the performances rankled deeply. In 1950, he decided to turn an idea that he had originally roughed out as a play into a novel. The result was *Tempest-Tost*, which became the first of the Salterton trilogy. It was published in 1951 in Canada and the following year in the United Kingdom and the United States.

Davies and Brenda returned to Britain twice in these years. The first trip, in 1949, was occasioned by the DDF's decision to send the Ottawa Drama League to the Edinburgh Festival with *Eros at Breakfast*; the second, in 1951, by Rupert Davies' appointment to the ceremonial role of High Sheriff of Montgomeryshire. They revelled in a great deal of theatre-going and the renewal of theatrical contacts they had made before the war. This was also the period when they moved from 572 Weller Street into a gracious 1850 house at 361 Park Street that would give them tremendous pleasure.

To MR. _____ :

Peterborough Examiner
Peterborough, Ontario
January 21, 1948

Dear Mr. _____ :

I am not surprised that you would rather not have your name appear in *The Examiner* at the end of the letter which you have signed "Fair Play." The letter contains several libellous statements and an incitement to a violent illegal act. If we were to print this letter, this newspaper would be responsible upon both counts. I am returning the letter to you, and I suggest that you send it directly to the Humane Society, though I would strongly advise you to re-phrase it before doing so.

Yours sincerely,

[Robertson Davies]
Editor

To AMELIA HALL

Peterborough Examiner
Peterborough, Ontario
June 22, 1948

Amelia Hall (1916–84), English-born Canadian director and actress, was director of the Ottawa Drama League whose playwriting competition Davies won in 1946 with Overlaid *and in 1947 with* Eros at Breakfast. *The ODL entered* Overlaid *in the Eastern Ontario Drama Festival in 1947, and in 1948 their production of* Eros at Breakfast *took several prizes.*

Dear Miss H. –

. . . About the turtle & cruelty: I think you are wrong in trying to wipe out all vestiges of cruelty in yourself. I feel that the best we can hope to do is to recognize & control such things – giving them an occasional outlet when the moment seems appropriate. I abhor cruelty to animals & children, but if I did not give some adults an occasional twist I should burst. But to say that we have no proof that cruelty & destruction are evil is the most utter bunk: we have the example & precept of virtually every great teacher in history. Have you read *The Abolition of Man* by C. S. Lewis? The answer is most forcibly given there, & in Huxley's *The Perennial Philosophy*.* Most decidedly we do know what is right & what is wrong in broad issues, but for some inexplicable reason most people prefer to sit in judgement upon the minute transgressions of their neighbours, rather than apply themselves to larger decisions in this field. They try to work from the particular to the general – which is impossible – rather than the other way about.

As for Canadians, there are just as many crooked-minded scoundrels among us as elsewhere – but they look so clean & commonplace! You are quite right: we must beware of them. . . .

With good wishes & renewed thanks for *your* good wishes,

<u>Robertson Davies</u>

To EARLE BIRNEY

Peterborough Examiner
Peterborough, Ontario
July 14, 1948

Earle Birney (1904–95), Canadian poet, novelist, playwright, editor, professor, and Chaucer scholar, was one of the fathers of Canadian literature.

Dear Mr. Birney:

I am not a regular reader of *The Canadian Home Journal*, but when I visited my doctor yesterday, I picked up a copy which was in his waiting room, and was greatly pleased to find your article about Canadian reading in it. Although I have not had the pleasure of meeting you, I know you of course by reputation, and I was delighted by the forceful manner in which you dealt with this subject. It has been one of my complaints for some years that Canadians as a nation are indifferent to reading of all kinds, and that our boasted standard of education loses fully half its effectiveness when we realize that our schools do not impart a real love of learning to our people. I do not know precisely how to express what I mean about this matter; I do not think that it can truly be said that Canadians lack zest for life; but I believe that it is true that as a people we are ignorant of the enrichment of life which can come through literature and the arts which are allied to it. Music is the one art which has fared well in Canada, and even in the case of music I know a great many people who consider themselves to be musical enthusiasts who think that four concerts a year is quite an adequate musical ration. As for the theatre, which is my own particular enthusiasm, I am sometimes depressed to find what a very small portion of the population is interested in the Little Theatre movement, and how small a portion of the interested group cares for nothing more than amateur imitations of New York and London successes.

I deeply hope that your article will reach a great number of readers, for it says most eloquently what many of us have been saying in one way or another about our country.

With every good wish, I am

Yours sincerely,

<u>Robertson Davies</u>
Editor

It is painful, also, to find that of the Canadians who *do* read, many are incapable of holding their culture like gentlemen. Dreadful, too, are the women's organizations which look upon culture in all its forms as "refining" – something which eunuchizes men & renders women barren. To hell with the whole bloody lot!

Appreciated y^r remarks abt. the Canadian Authors Association. So far I have declined to join as it appears to me to have the fault of the worst trade unions: i.e., it protects incompetent craftsmen. Anybody who can make his X, apparently, is free to join.

Yours
RD.

To PHILIP JOHN STEAD

Peterborough Examiner
Peterborough, Ontario
August 12, 1948

Philip John Stead (1916–), a friend from Oxford, was, in the period after the war, dramatic critic for The Times *of London, reviewer for the* Times Literary Supplement, *and lecturer at the University of London. He was to become director and later dean of academic studies at the Police College, Bramshill, 1953–74.*

Dear John:

Your letter of August 7 arrived just as my own feelings of guilt were driving me to the typewriter to address you. I have a reasonable excuse for my silence: just after I last wrote to you my Dr. discovered that I was in the grip of a nasty malady called Hodgkin's Disease; briefly, it enlarges the glands of your neck and chokes you to death. It was fatal until a few years ago, but now clever chaps thwart it with X-ray, and I had to have 24 very nasty bouts with a big electrical machine, which left me very low. But it seems to have done for H.D., and I am deeply grateful to have been Spared – as my grandmother* used to phrase it.

So glad you liked [*The Diary of Samuel*] *Marchbanks*. I feared it might be rather low and simple for your distinguished palate. I run a gob of the same every Saturday in three papers here,* and it is much appreciated by the simple, fun-loving Canadian public. Another book of it will appear next autumn (1949). Next spring a book of my one-act plays comes out, called "Eros at Breakfast, and Other Plays." I shall send you a copy. Furthermore, to my great delight, a three-act piece of mine called "Fortune, My Foe" is to be done by a quite good rep. company in Kingston, Ont; at the end of this month. As the play is on a Canadian theme, and is set in the city of Kingston, I hope it will attract some attention. I yearn, burn and churn to be a playwright, even on a small scale, and I have been very lucky in the past two years in getting quite a lot of productions – some of them good.

Was fascinated by your news of _____ and the Merry Widow; She is an Indian, you say? Is she black? A sari, perhaps? Does she chew betel and giggle and say "Sahib, him belly stlong mans; him jig-a-jig belly fine?" I thirst for detail. You may recall that during our term at _____, the Master confided to us that he had [a] B–g P — k; is there any marked alteration in his character now that he has a garage for same? This is not, as you might think, mere lascivious curiosity. Nothing human is alien to me* – not even the sexual life of theatrical adventurers.

Haven't seen *The Last Romantic** yet, but await it with eagerness, for M-H [Sir John Martin-Harvey] was the first actor of any consequence I saw, & I saw him subsequently in a repertory which reached into the dark backward and abysm of time,* and which he did with a grace and distinction which I have never seen equalled. Gielgud comes nearest, but he is moonlight; M-H was the sunlight of an autumn afternoon. I shall never forget him, & I use him as a measure against which other actors are tried. M-H had nobility and pathos in a measure I have never seen anyone else equal.

Do you really think Marchbanks would be read in England? My publishers anticipate a sale of about 5,000 here, which is big for a book of non-fiction in Canada. That brings me a little over a thousand dollars, which is taxed as *unearned* income! Writing in Canada is purely a labour of love. If you think an agent* might like to see a copy I shall gladly send one to yours, & it is most kind of you to suggest it.

It will be a long time, I fear, before I have the money or time to visit England. But let us try to keep up a correspondence, however desultory, for I am sure that we shall meet again at some future time, and when I write to you I feel as though I had parted from you but yesterday. Do you know anything of Harry the Horse,* by the way?

Was he a victim of enemy action? Did a spiv get him? Our linked fate was short, but I loved him dearly. I always hoped to bash somebody with him, for he was certainly the heaviest stick I ever met with.

All the best to you & your wife. I sometimes go to Montreal and shall hunt up Vincent Rother* next trip.

[No signature in original]

To GRANT MACDONALD

572 Weller Street
Peterborough, Canada
Aug 18, 1948

Davies was shortly to direct and Brenda to act in Fortune, My Foe *with Arthur Sutherland's International Players in Kingston. The play includes a play-within-a-play performed by marionettes which are managed by Szabo, an European master. Mr. Punch, of* Punch and Judy, *also has a part.*

Dear Grant:

What a wonderful fellow you are! Brenda & I were plunged in the depths of dark despair about the puppets, & you calmly produce a life-long puppeteer from nowhere! Indeed we had sunk so low as to begin the puppet job ourselves – with heavy hearts, for a poor show would hit the play hard after all Szabo's brave talk. Now we breathe again! But we are bringing Mr. Punch (Act I) with us. He is copied from Piccini's Italian Punch.* I have made his head from a doll's head – all wrong, with fat cheeks – & painted it with oils – my first experience of them, & v. crude. However, I think he will do if you will revise my grossest errors with a few touches. At present he looks like a demon with mumps.

Brenda has written Mary [Keens] about the play, & she may descend – though not on you & N.N., I trust, for sheer maidenliness. She would never have spoken to us again if we had kept it from her. Lots of people are coming, I hope, including Amy & Clair [Stewart].*

I only hope Kingston produces a few paying customers. I am waiving any royalty, but I don't want Sutherland* to lose his shirt.

Again, our heartfelt thanks!

RD . . .

To RICHARD BURBAGE

Peterborough Examiner
Peterborough, Ontario
January 11, 1949

Richard Burbage, an Englishman in Canada only since June 1948, was adjudicating and also directing plays for the Woodstock, Ontario, Little Theatre.

Dear Mr. Burbage:

Thank you for the letter which you were kind enough to write to me on the 10th of December about the Kitchener production of *Fortune, My Foe.* I am sorry that I have been so long in replying to it, but circumstances have made it difficult for me recently to do a great many things which I had intended to do before Christmas.

I agree with you that the Kitchener production was very bad. I was particularly depressed by the fact that so far as I could tell not a single line of the play was spoken as I had written it, and what the audience heard was a clumsy paraphrase in which all the points had been blunted. The play has a great deal of talk in it, but when it is properly produced it does not seem slow for this reason. I do not understand why the Kitchener director kept his people sitting in their chairs as if they were glued to them through all of the first act. Nor do I understand why he allowed the important character of Weir to be played in that clownish fashion. The Professor, of course, gave no hint of being a man of strong passions or brilliant imagination, and this, combined with the fact that the part of Nicholas was very dully played, managed to ruin the whole piece. What the producer did not realize was that the play is not intended to be a realistic piece, and that it required a much broader style of acting and a much wider emotional range than he had attempted to give to it.

Writing plays in Canada is a rather difficult business, because I find that most Canadians are convinced that a play written by a Canadian must be inferior to one written by an American or an Englishman, and is not worth giving a careful production. However, the Ottawa production of *Fortune, My Foe* was an extremely successful one, and gave evidence that the play can be very good when it is properly treated. I am quite happy to have plays of mine done by Little Theatre in Canada, but I wish it were possible for me to obtain some guarantee beforehand that they would be given at least the same care in production as a play which had already appeared somewhere else. I hope that we shall meet soon, and if I can ever do anything for you, please let me know.

Yours sincerely,

[Robertson Davies]
Editor

To DORIS FRENCH

Peterborough Examiner
Peterborough, Ontario
March 28, 1949

Doris French (1918–   ), Canadian freelance journalist, later became a CBC broadcaster and an author, and was twice a federal New Democratic Party candidate. In an otherwise warm letter about The Diary of Samuel Marchbanks, *she asked, "Don't you know any nice socialists? Perhaps Peterborough is particularly barren of these – otherwise I find your recent reference to socialism hard to explain."*

Dear Mrs. French:

Thank you for your nice letter of March 23rd. I believe that I say somewhere in the Marchbanks' *Diary* that my political opinions are sharply influenced by the people that I happen to be with. When I am being lectured by Tories, I become a much more advanced socialist than any parliamentary representative of the C.C.F. [Co-operative Commonwealth Federation]; when I am being hounded by socialists, I am likely to change quickly into an eighteenth century Tory. As a matter of fact, I think that we are moving very rapidly toward a socialist state in Canada, and that most of the things which are done in this direction are genuine advances. But I am sick to death of doctrinaire socialists who think that the advance of socialism will bring about some striking change in the human heart, and will make people pleasanter than they are now by a series of acts of parliament. I am no particular enemy of socialism, but I am a violent enemy of mediocrity, and it often seems to me that some people of socialist belief are eager to make over the whole of mankind on the pattern of their own tiresome selves. I gather from your letter that you are a socialist in politics, but I think that you will admit that all politics – conservative, liberal, and socialist – contain their share of fatheads who make the party theories repulsive to any right-thinking person.

I am glad that you liked the *Diary*. A new collection of Marchbanks' pieces will be coming out in the autumn, and I hope that the public will treat it as kindly as they did the earlier book.

With every good wish, I am

Yours sincerely,

[Robertson Davies]
Editor

To EARLE BIRNEY

Peterborough Examiner
Peterborough, Ontario
November 17, 1949

Dear Earle Birney:

Thank you for your note of November 14th. The review of *Turvey*
in *The Examiner* was written by Mrs. Hilda Kirkwood,* and not by
myself as you appear to think. I am glad that you liked it. On the
strength of Mrs. Kirkwood's review, I bought a copy of the book, and
read it with great enjoyment.

As you have yourself brought up the subject of our book reviews,
I would like to tell you a little bit about them, because I think that
they are rather uncommon in a Canadian daily newspaper this size.
We have three reviewers; Mrs. Kirkwood does most of our reviewing of fiction and of poetry; she writes very good verse herself, and
has had a fair amount of it published, and I think that she is a good
judge of books. My assistant editor, who is a Canadian with a degree
from Oxford in English Literature, does most of our reviews of historical books, essays, and non-fiction works generally. I myself like
to write about books that concern the theatre or literary criticism,
and take the opportunity whenever one occurs of commenting on
a reprint of a classic or a book of proven worth. These reviews
appear in this paper and also in the Kingston *Whig-Standard*, which
gives them a total circulation of about 32,000. So far as I can see,
most papers of our size do not review books, and if they do so, they
take very little trouble about it. However, we have a feeling that a
newspaper ought to have something to say about books, and
although we have very little evidence that our readers are interested
in the book reviews, we feel that they ought to be so, and continue
to print them.

Book reviewing in Canada seems to be in a very bad way. Even
Saturday Night has now come down to treating books as news, rather

than as works of art, and a book whose author has recently committed suicide appears to be of more importance than one which is merely well-written. Certainly one of the things that Canada needs most badly is a group of critics with higher standards and broader qualifications for their work.

Do not be too cast down because the Saskatoon *Star-Phoenix* has jumped on *Turvey*. The critic of the *Star-Phoenix* has very strong opinions of her own, and I remember that when *The Diary of Samuel Marchbanks* appeared, she threatened and bullied me* for nearly a column because the book was not respectful enough toward somebody that she called the common man. As I have never met a common man, or anybody who is prepared to describe himself in that way, I regard him as a myth, and want to have nothing to do with him. The fantods of the *Star-Phoenix* are not to be taken too seriously.

With congratulations on your book, and warmest good wishes, I am

Yours sincerely,

Robertson Davies
Editor

To PHYLLIS A. MOORE

[572 Weller Street
Peterborough, Ontario]
Dec 13, 1949

Phyllis Moore was Jennifer Davies' teacher in Grade 1 and for five months in Grade 2 at Queen Mary School in Peterborough. Miss Moore recalled that "when Jennifer gave me the note, she said that her father had written it for her mother, so he signed it 'Brenda Davies.'"

Dear Miss Moore:

Jennifer has had intestinal 'flu, and is now recovered. However, I would not have allowed her to return to school today if she had not wanted to do so very much: Dr. Fitzpatrick* does not advise going out too early. Would it be troublesome if she remained indoors at recess today – not to avoid fresh air, but too strenuous play.

Yours sincerely,

Brenda Davies

To HERBERT WHITTAKER

Peterborough Examiner
Peterborough, Ontario
February 21, 1950

Herbert Whittaker, now drama critic for The Globe and Mail, *was preparing the North Toronto Theatre Guild to enter Davies' play* King Phoenix *in a regional competition of the Dominion Drama Festival.*

Dear Herbert:

Thank you for your letter of February 21st. Your report on the progress of *King Phoenix* is most encouraging, and I am greatly looking forward to seeing it. Grant Macdonald was visiting us at the week-end, and I think he is going to try to get up to Toronto for the Festival, in order to have a look at it. . . .

The Peterborough Little Theatre plays* are now over, and I am afraid that most of our audience found *The Play of the Weather* confusing but not amusing. We had nice costumes for it, and that carried it through with reasonable success. The surprise of the group was *The Tinker's Wedding*, which seems to have given violent offence to certain Catholics in town, because as you will remember a priest gets pushed around rather badly in it. I think that this is probably my fault, because I am extremely fond of the play, not for its plot, but for the richness and poetic nature of its writing. It has been my experience, however, that Catholics take offence very readily, and that such questions as literary worth are of very small importance to them. The result is that we are having a hullabaloo about it in the newspaper, and some of the Little Theatre people are very upset. They are all school teachers, and their capacity for alarm is somewhat greater than that of ordinary people. However, I think that it will be a lesson to me that audiences in even quite large towns like this are inclined to forget that a play is a piece of make-believe, and to read into it all kinds of meanings which the author and the actors never put there. I am sure that if J. M. Synge is looking down on Peterborough from heaven, he is astounded and sad to see how grouchy and humourless his beloved Irishmen become when they are transported to a new country.

  With every good wish, I am

Yours sincerely,

[Rob]
Editor

To PHILIP JOHN STEAD

Peterborough Examiner
Peterborough, Ontario
April 6, 1950

Dear John:

  This is just a note to tell you that Chatto & Windus are going to publish *The Table Talk* in England in the autumn. My Canadian publishers arranged this, and are very pleased about it as, of course, I am. I do not know whether this will make it any easier to interest people in the plays, but when the book appears it might make a little difference.

  King Phoenix was done here recently in the Toronto section of the Dominion Drama Festival, and was jumped up and down on and kicked all over the place by an English adjudicator named Maxwell Wray.* I do not know whether you know anything of this Wray, but I do not think that he is a particularly prominent figure in the English theatre, and when he proclaimed an absolute and violent dislike of *The Lady's Not for Burning*,* I mentally classified him as a boob and dismissed him from serious consideration. He is a great man for realism in the theatre, and insists that doors in stage settings should not have real locks on them, as this interferes with an actor's exit. He said that *King Phoenix* was "artistic hooey" and had bored him and made him miserable. If you should ever have an opportunity to do this man a bad turn,★ will you be good enough to seize it, and render any necessary bill to me.

　　With every good wish to you and your wife, I am

Yours sincerely,

Rob
Editor

★Assassination, for instance.

To HERBERT WHITTAKER

572 Weller Street
Peterborough, Canada
Easter Sunday, 1950

The play that Davies anticipates writing in this letter became Tempest-Tost, *the first of the Salterton novels.*

Dear Herbert:

　　You will think that I am continually plaguing you with letters; however, yours of April 5ᵗʰ demands an answer.

　　FIRST: You are quite right that *King Phoenix* wants cutting. All of Gogmagog's stuff about his soul should be replaced by a short speech. I am sorry to see it go, for I liked that stuff about the journey to the North, but it does not hold the audience. Some tightening in Scene Two is wanted as well..... You are quite wrong in thinking that I resent criticism from you of this or any of my plays. I deeply dislike the people who want to chop & change my work only to show how clever they are, & to put me in my place, but you are not of that number. I have a powerful respect for your judgement because I believe that you love & understand the theatre, & are not a critic primarily to show off your own cleverness. As I have told you before, I think you are the best critic in Canada, & better than that might be taken to imply. Though you might not guess it, I am really quite humble about my plays: I know that mine is still a 'prentice hand. But I am serious about writing plays, & I cannot endure criticism from people who niggle at my stuff merely to make some personal advantage – to seem clever or to whittle down what they imagine to be my conceit. Anything you have to say about my work, I assure you, falls upon a receptive ear.

SECOND: I offer you the new piece because I think you are a fine director; I don't care what group you work with. The University Alumnae have been sounding me out about a play: would they be interested? I should like it to have a [Dominion Drama] Festival showing. The New Play Soc. wd. not do a play of mine. I once offended Ma Moore & Mavor* seems to carry on the war.

About the play itself: I do not contemplate a piece too narrowly hitched to DDF; indeed it might not mention that brawl, but would touch it indirectly. Roughly, I intend a play about a production (an out-of-doors, summer job) of a Shakespeare play, by a group of amateurs who have induced a professional – a woman – to help them. Amateurism on its many levels will be probed. But the plot is about a man nearing middle-age – a schoolteacher – who has a late blossoming & falls for the leading-lady, who is 20, or so, & gets his heart broken in the process. He looks funny to others – is truly pathetic also. I have it in scenario and it will make a comedy. I want it to be a laugh-piece, but I seem unable to write a play which is without some sadness in it. If you want this piece it can be in your hands by autumn.

On Friday I completed my latest job, called *At My Heart's Core*. It will be done at the Summer Theatre here, & also at Ottawa, I think, and by Robᵗ Gill* next Spring in Toronto. Brenda likes it greatly. It is about Peterborough in 1837 & the chief characters are all historical. It is a 5 f., 3 m., piece & I think it says a few things about pioneering which have not been said before. I have eschewed all logging-bees, square dances and other appurtenances of pioneer drama, though I have fallen for a Comic Irishman and an Indian (female). I would greatly like to have your opinion of it.

NOW: Could you, later in the Spring, spend a weekend with us here? We have a bed. We also have 3 children, but you are used to streetcars and other background noises. On such a jaunt you might have a look at a script of *A.M.H.C.* & discuss a point or so in the new play, as well as cracking a crock & meeting a few people.

We are going to Calgary.* The program leaves me cold but I suppose it will be better than I foresee, and Saint-Denis should be well worth the journey. We hope to see you there.

With good wishes from us both

Rob

To W. H. CLARKE | *The play/novel under discussion in this letter is* Tempest-Tost.

Peterborough Examiner,
Peterborough, Ontario
June 20th, 1950

Dear Mr. Clarke:

. . . This is not the time, perhaps, to bother you with such a question but I have been thinking recently about writing a novel. I have a play worked out in considerable detail and the more I think about it the more it seems to me that it would do just as well as a novel. I have never tried to write a novel and do not know how it will work out. However, I am becoming a little discouraged with the difficulties of working with Canadian Little Theatre groups. I am actually appealing to you for advice in this matter: do you think that the success of the Marchbanks books has laid the sort of foundation upon which a novel could be rested? It would, I may say, be a light and amusing story with a Canadian setting and my experience as a book reviewer tells me that light and amusing stories are rather uncommon at present.

Yours sincerely,

Robertson Davies

To HERBERT WHITTAKER

[*Peterborough Examiner*
Peterborough, Ontario]
July 6th, 1950

Dear Herbert:

. . . Somebody sent me a copy of *The Forum** yesterday which had some remarks by W. S. Milne about the Toronto Festival. He was quite nice about *King Phoenix* but suggested that it was rather full of talk. This is a criticism which is very frequently directed against my plays and I am not altogether sure what it means because every play is full of talk and if there were no talk the curtain would never go up. Do they mean the speeches are too long, or that they take too long to make their point, or that the dialogue is boring, or what precisely do they mean? My observation has been that when people are in critical situations they behave in two clearly defined ways: fools are inarticulate, say nothing and get themselves into terrible trouble even to the point of death, and wise people talk a very great deal and eventually settle the problem. I take care in every play of mine to include at least one fool and the part is usually marked by the sparseness of dialogue. The power of speech is that which more than any other separates man from brute and people who like brutish drama have my full permission to go to circuses where they will get it at its best. In other words I shall continue to write plays which are full of talk.

Your letters are a great refreshment and I should be delighted to hear from you again any time you can bring yourself to write. I find that by accusing you of being a bad correspondent I can almost always goad you into writing a letter.

Yours hopefully,

[Rob]

To HERBERT WHITTAKER

Peterborough Examiner
Peterborough, Ontario
July 10th, 1950

Dear Herbert:

. . . Thank you for your excellent advice about talkiness in plays. You have, of course, put your finger on a very weak spot in my equipment of which I am conscious but which I do not seem to be able to correct. The plots in my plays tend to be very slight and I cannot work up much interest in them. I have a feeling, which may only be self-justification, that a play which depends on its plot is in a very weak position because once people know the plot the play has no further interest for them. I feel this to be so with *Harvey** which I predict will become laughably out of date in quite a short time. I myself have known for two years that *Harvey* is about a drunk who thinks he sees a big rabbit; when I went to the play I expected to find rather more in it than that. But for two and a half hours I was exposed to a drunk who thought he saw a big rabbit and I went away with a feeling of dissatisfaction. Indeed if I had paid for my ticket I would have been down-right angry. But a play which provides a large evening of elaborate and amusing talk never fails to delight me. However, I see your point and I am most grateful to you for the tactful and pleasing way in which you have expressed it. I shall be interested to know what you think of *At My Heart's Core* because I feel it has rather more plot than you may be accustomed to finding in plays of mine, and I don't think that there are many speeches in it which shoot off on tangents from the main theme except in act three where a character sings a song. He does this for a particular purpose but it is true that the song has no direct bearing on the plot. A playwright, you see, can always maintain the talk he puts in the mouth of a character illuminates that character and thereby contributes to the plot. Furthermore, I took a solemn oath some years ago that if it were humanly possible I would never write a play which did not contain a song or a dance and both if possible. When the theatre gets away from songs and dances it is getting into very dangerous mud. I particularly specified in *Fortune, My Foe* that the tramp should dance, but I have yet to see a performance in which he does so. The average Canadian amateur actor is a clod untroubled by a spark and any suggestion that he should sing or dance fills him with comic dismay. I am getting to hate and despise actors more every day. . . .

Yours sincerely,

[Rob]

To MIRANDA DAVIES

Miranda Davies, aged nine, was at Glen Bernard Camp, Sundridge, Ontario.

Peterborough Examiner
Peterborough, Ontario
August 14th, 1950

Dear Miranda:

When Mummy and I came home from Niagara Falls, we found a splendid letter from you. I must compliment you on your good writing and the interesting things that you put in your letters. It is important to be a good letter writer because everybody likes to receive letters and good letters are quite uncommon.

Mummy is writing to you about the bathing shoes. I am sending you a small parcel which I hope will help to pass the time if you have a dull day.

I am sorry that you do not get along well with _____. She is a tease just as her father used to be and if you let her make you angry, she will go on doing it. But I would not worry too much about it.

Much love,

[Daddy]

To MICHAEL SADLIER

Peterborough Examiner
Peterborough, Ontario
August 9th, 1950

Michael Sadlier, Irish-born Canadian actor, was managing director of the Peterborough Summer Theatre. The 10th and last play of its season was to be Davies' At My Heart's Core *which concerns three of the Peterborough area's exceptional pioneers: the botanist Catharine Parr Traill (1802–99); her sister, author Susanna Moodie (1803–85); and the letter-writer Frances Stewart (1794–1872), whose husband Thomas was one of the founders of Peterborough.*

Dear Michael:

Shortly after I had seen you this morning, I ventured out into the street and was immediately pounced upon by an elderly lady who said "Mr. Davies, I hope you are not going to make my grandmother scrub floors in your play." She then launched into a long tale about herself and proved to be a granddaughter of Mrs. Frances Stewart. She told me that a lot of the older people, and particularly those of pioneer descent, in the city are keenly interested in the play but have heard rumours that it is going to make cruel fun of their forebears. I assured her that this was not so and urged her to spread the word among her friends. I am sure that I will be an old man before this play is on and over.

This lady's name was Miss Mabel Collins and she lives at 406 Water Street. She wrung from me the information that the Miss Attwoods had been asked to the play as descendants of the Moodies and Traills and the least I could do was extend a similar invitation to her. Would you be good enough, therefore, to drop her a note of invitation? I think that we must draw the line here as it is absolutely out of the question that everybody who has pioneer ancestors should also have a free seat for the play. However, Miss Collins seemed to be in a great state of excitement and I bought her good will for a couple of tickets.

This is precisely what I was afraid of – rumour and bad feeling among the ancients of the city. However, I think that I have dealt with Miss Collins and assured her that her grandmother would be dealt with most kindly. In the course of the conversation she told me some things about Mrs. Moodie and Mrs. Traill which I would not dare to put in any play. I expect that there will be some great old knife throwing among the old families if the play stirs up any interest.

Yours sincerely,

[Rob]

To R. W. W. ROBERTSON

Peterborough Examiner
Peterborough, Ontario
November 16th, 1950

Dear Mr. Robertson:

I received my copies of *At My Heart's Core* today and like the look of it very much. I feel that it was wise to stick to the same style as *Fortune, My Foe*. I hardly expect that much notice* will be taken of it, particularly at a time when so many new books are coming on the market. However, it may be hoped that over a period of two or three years it will sell satisfactorily.

As you probably know, I had a talk with Mr. Clarke in September, in the course of which I spoke to him about my resolve to try my hand at a novel [*Tempest-Tost*]. I hope to send you the typescript of it by the beginning of June next year so that if you should wish to publish it, it will be possible to get it out for autumn. I would very much appreciate some advice from you on the matter of length. I had decided that a hundred and twenty thousand words would be about the right length for a novel of this kind, but I see that a great many novels are appearing now which are decidedly shorter than that. It is my own feeling that most novels are much too long. A great many of them run to a hundred and fifty thousand words and upward, and I frequently think as I read them that they would be improved by pruning. If you feel that a hundred and twenty thousand words is too long, I could, of course, reduce the number.

It may seem curious to you that I should make an enquiry of you at this time when the novel is still in the process of being written. It is very often said that a story must find its own length and that the number of words contained in it should be sufficient to tell its story adequately and no more. However, I seem to function rather like Anthony Trollope than like the artistic gentlemen who talk in the terms which I have mentioned above, and if I am told that a piece of work should be a certain length, I adjust my inner machine accordingly and it appears at that length. I suppose this is because I am basically a low journalist and not an artist. If you can find time to let me have your opinion on this matter, I should value it greatly.

With many thanks for the care which you have taken of *At My Heart's Core*, I am,

Yours sincerely,

Robertson Davies

PS: It is to be a comic novel, & one cannot go on being funny indefinitely: even Dickens couldn't.

To EDWIN C. GUILLET

Peterborough Examiner
Peterborough, Ontario
January 8th, 1951

Edwin C. Guillet (1898–1975) was a Canadian author, teacher, and historian. The play under discussion is Davies' At My Heart's Core. *Nothing appears to have come of the suggestion at the end of this letter that an essay be written about the impact of Irish on Ontario speech.*

Dear Mr. Guillet:

I was very glad to get your letter which touches on a point which is of particular interest to me. The pronunciation of "my" as "me" is still good English usage according to the Oxford dictionary. As you say, it was general during the eighteenth century on both sides of the Atlantic and persisted, and indeed still persists, in Ireland. It was the Irish characters in the play – the Stewarts and Mr. Cantwell – who used it, as I particularly instructed them to do. Mrs. Traill and Mrs. Moodie used the more modern pronunciation. In modern Ireland, I am told, the stylish thing among the middle classes is to say "my," but in the country districts and among people with long tradition of education, the older form is still used. I like it, personally, because in spoken English it gives a dash and raciness which is impeded by the long sound of "my." To continue on this point, I must stress that in my play it was the two uneducated Irish settlers who actually said "me"; the form used by the three people of education and breeding was much more like "mih." I think that the change in the pronunciation of this word came about through the spread of general education which caused a lot of people who were learning to read for the first time to pronounce words as they were spelled rather than as they would be pronounced according to historical and traditional usage.

I must say that I am delighted that you picked out this special point in the play because I am greatly interested in speech and have for a long time been curious about the forms of speech which our ancestors brought to this country. My mother's family was of long duration in Canada and I can recall pronunciations among her relatives which certainly had their beginnings in the eighteenth century – the pronunciation of balconey with the accent on the second syllable for instance. It is possible by listening carefully to hear traces of many kinds of speech in modern Canadian usage. I am often amused by the insistence of the Scots in Canada that they have had a powerful influence upon this country and have given it much of its characteristic cultural flavour, but the fact is that in Ontario at least, the Irish have triumphed in matters of speech and although our intonation is different, the speech of most people in Ontario smacks strongly of Ireland – some from the north, some from the south. A really good essay on this subject would be uncommonly interesting. I do not feel qualified to undertake such a job myself but it may be that you with your wide connection among people with strong historical interests and training may know of someone who could do it.

I hope that it is not too late to wish you the greatest happiness in 1951.

Yours sincerely,

[Robertson Davies]

To H. S. SOUTHAM

Peterborough Examiner
Peterborough, Ontario
January 15th, 1951.

Harry Stevenson Southam (c. 1880–1954), Canadian, had been the publisher of the Ottawa Citizen *since 1920.*

Dear Mr. Southam:

Thank you for the very kind and encouraging telegram which you sent to the theatre for me on Saturday night. I must thank you and *The Citizen*, also, for the most generous support you gave the play during its week in Ottawa* and for the kindness which you showed toward my wife, which we both appreciate very deeply.

I am delighted that you liked *At My Heart's Core*. I was particularly happy that it should be given a production in Ottawa for a reason which I think you will readily understand: The Ottawa Drama League has performed a number of my plays and I feel greatly indebted to them. When I wrote *At My Heart's Core*, therefore, I sent it to them for production without a royalty, as I had made up my mind that I should send them anything new of mine without royalty as long as they continued to want them. I was a little put out, therefore, not by their refusal to do the play – which, of course, was their right and a matter of taste – but the rather disagreeable assertion by some members of their committee that the play was badly written and unactable, and that they would most certainly lose a large sum of money if they attempted to perform it. Though I hope that I am not vain about my capacity as a playwright, I have not found anyone in the O.D.L. whose opinion I seek on difficult matters in this particular work – in short I thought I knew a good deal more about it than they did. I was most happy, therefore, to be vindicated by the Canadian Repertory Theatre and particularly happy that they had a week of very good business. The satisfaction of the audiences and their readiness to part with money to see the play seems to me to finish the argument between me and the Ottawa Drama League.

I do not know whether you are interested in such matters or not, but I presume that as a financial supporter of the C.R.T., you may be concerned with the development of playwriting in Canada. For the past two or three years plays of mine have been performed by professional groups in Canada and I have found in every case that although they prepare the plays much faster than the Little Theatres, they perform them very much better. They adopt a thoroughly businesslike attitude toward the play, their artistic standards are high and what particularly pleases me as a playwright is that they allow me to know my own business and do not itch to re-write and tinker with my plays. I have made up my mind, therefore, that in future I shall do business whenever I can with the professional Canadian theatre for whose managers I have the highest regard and let the Little Theatres alone. The remarkable advance which professional theatre companies have made in Canada since 1945 leads me to think that it will not be too many years before we have a professional theatre of very high standard in Canada and as I regard myself as a professional writer and not an amateur, it is with them that I shall cast my lot.

With renewed thanks for your many kindnesses and with warmest good wishes from my wife and myself, I am

Yours sincerely,

[Robertson Davies]

To GRANT MACDONALD

361 Park Street
Peterborough, Canada
July 15 [1951]

Davies, Brenda, and the children were about to leave for Britain to visit Rupert Davies and his new wife in Leighton Hall (his recently acquired huge home in Wales), and to see some plays in London. The Davieses had just moved from their first home in Peterborough at 572 Weller Street to the charming 1850 house at 361 Park Street, not far away.

Dear Grant:

Many thanks for your letter, your good wishes and the note to Miss Robson.* I hope that this time we can make connections: last time she wrote charmingly. I cannot tell you how much I am obliged to you for this, or how truly I appreciate your readiness to introduce me to your friends, for I know that you do not do so lightly and unadvisedly, as they say in the Marriage Service. Already I am in y^r debt for a wonderful hour with Athene Seyler.*

We have moved, and are frankly *delighted* with the new house, which you must visit as soon as possible. The Front Parlour, by the way, is our Macdonald Room – no lesser artist allowed – and y^r pictures look fine, as they are not crowded, and get a decent light, most of the day.

Our love to you, and we shall send you a comic post card from Llanfairpwllgwyngyllgogerychwyrndrobwllllantysiliogogogoch.

Rob.

PS: The idiot photographer put my film in the wrong kind of developer & ruined my four shots of you, and all the pictures of *Heart's Core* at Knowlton!* But *The Listener** calls me "a man of letters" – to me a prouder name than Duke or Archbishop: it was Wm. Plomer who wrote that, at a column's length, and I wouldn't call the king my uncle, I'm that proud!

To HAROLD RAYMOND

Leighton Hall
Welshpool, Mont.
North Wales
July 28 [1951]

Harold Raymond (1887–1975), English, was a partner in the British publishing house Chatto and Windus. Cecil Day-Lewis (1904–72), the Irish-born English poet, translator, and writer of detective fiction, was a reader for Chatto and Windus.

Dear Mr. Raymond:

When I reached Wales yesterday I found a letter from Mr. W. H. Clarke of Clarke, Irwin, in which he tells me that you have decided to bring out my novel TEMPEST-TOST; of course this is most gratifying news and I am delighted to hear it. He also sent me a copy of Cecil Day Lewis' comments on the book, and gave me the gist of your own feelings about it. With his letter was a note from Mr. R. W. W. Robertson, the editor of Clarke, Irwin, discussing the matter and listing your objections in a conveniently tabulated form. May I discuss these with you as well as may be done in a letter, for although I may not be able to change your opinion I think I shall be able to explain why I have written the book as I have done. Changes at this date are not easy, for I am correcting the page proofs at this time, and the Canadian printer wants to get to work: further, my inner manufactory has stopped work on T-T, and so far as I am concerned it is finished. But let us see what can be done.

First Objection: the description of Hector [Mackilwraith]'s childhood is too long. Very well, I shall cut some of it, but I can't say just how much, for I must do the best I can without letting Clarke, Irwin in for a lot of costly re-setting.

Second Objection: the suicide is out of key with the book as a whole. I cannot agree and cannot change. May I explain? Suicides happen when people meet a situation they cannot face, and that is what happened to Hector. Suicides are often done to get pity, and that is what Hector wanted, as Cobbler says. He didn't even choose a strong enough rope. What is more, suicide may be funny, and I think Hector's was so, just as Mrs. Bridgetower's heart disease is funny. Or perhaps I should say comic. And at this point I must say that I think the book is more *comic* than funny, and by that I mean that it is a story rooted in truth and observing life from a special point of view, rather than a tale full of contrived incidents, like those serials in *Chums**about the boy-conjuror who upsets the school by putting eels in the headmaster's top hat. Mr. Cochrane of your firm suggests that more rumbling of the stomach might serve to bring Hector's story to an end. No, that is feeble, and recalls Richmal Crompton* to my mind. Suicide it must be. But – and I do not know why neither you nor Clarke, Irwin have noticed this – it is a suicide which was foredoomed to failure; it wasn't really in Hector's nature to kill himself, and in the end he is as safe as he can be.

Though his bark *may not be lost*
Yet it shall be tempest-tost.*

Why do you suppose I chose that title? Originally I wanted a sub-title: "The Strange Love, Tragical Death and Glorious Resurrection of Hector Mackilwraith, B.A." Hector goes through an experience comparable to the mystical re-birth achieved by all great heroes; he has a tough time, he descends into hell, and he rises purified and renewed. Tummy-rumblings at the Ball! Never, while I have my strength! The action of the comedy is not complete without the mock-death, and if some of the public do not like it now they will see the necessity and the goodness of it in twenty years or so.

Third Objection: nobody likes the horse's penis. All right, out it comes. But I once saw a horse electrocuted,* and what I have made Old Bill do wasn't a circumstance to what the horse really did. Once again I think you have mistaken my book for a *funny* book, to be read by old ladies at Torquay on winter afternoons. It is a *comic* book, and one of the comic things about life is the way in which the lovable and venerable may, in a moment, in the twinkling of an eye, become hideous, grotesque and even hateful. Does it not amuse you that, although Old Bill was a shameful sight at one end, Mr. Leakey was so much a slave of convention that he decently veiled him at the other? And neither you nor anyone at Clarke, Irwin seems to have tumbled to the fact that what happened to Old Bill was, in miniature, what happened to Hector when he left his proper sphere and was whisked into the theatre: honoured and successful where he belonged, he certainly trod on a live wire when he left his proper job, and with comparable effect.

Fourth Objection: the party at Mrs. Leakey's interrupts the book and should be cut. Sorry – no cut here. As Mr. Robertson says in his letter to me "that party is pure and authentic Canadiana"; I am a Canadian author writing about Canada, and Mrs. Leakey's party will recall many such revels to my Canadian readers. If English readers, including Mr. Day Lewis, don't like it, they can skip it. They'll learn to like it in twenty years.

Fifth Objection: the drinking scene is too long and should be cut. Very well, I'll cut what I can, with expense in mind.

Sixth Objection: the auction scene is too long. I'll see what I can do, but the bids jump ten dollars at a time as things stand.

Authors are, as you undoubtedly know, very touchy fellows. We bring forth our children in pain and struggle, and we do not like it when passers-by – even midwives – point out that the child's nose is flat, or that it is hump-backed. And, as with flesh-and-blood children, the hump-backed ones sometimes do better in the world than those with more regular bodies. But I shall try what surgery can do for my tuberculous whelp.

The B.B.C. talks people have asked me to do [a] fifteen minute talk, in the character of Samuel Marchbanks, for them when I am in London. Had you heard about this? Is it a good omen? Should I do it? They want me to give Marchbanks' impressions of Britain. They seem to have some notion that I am a newcomer to these shores, chewing tobacco and swinging my lariat as I gape at the sights. I shall strive to oblige.

May I have the pleasure of making your acquaintance when I am in London, which will be from the 20th to the 25th of August? My wife will accompany me, and we would be most happy if you would lunch with us on one of our days in the Wen, if you will suggest the place. And if my letter seems snarling and contumelious in tone, set it down to the wolfish acerbity of an author defending his own; if you wish to discuss the novel further we might gore and toss one another delightfully when we meet. With good wishes.....

Robertson Davies

P. S. You understand, of course, that my protests against changes in the book are not simply pig-headed; I genuinely feel that too much tinkering would be fatal. I am too conscious of the kindness and forbearance which you, personally, have shown toward me and my work, and the efforts which you have exerted to bring it before the public, to attempt to thwart you merely as a show of personal pride. But not only for this book, but for future books, I feel that I must get off on the right foot as a serious writer – which is not of course, the same thing as a *solemn* writer. The story of Hector Mackilwraith is not funny; it has its very sad side. But I prefer to allow the reader to feel sad on his own responsibility. But I do not want to make it impossible for him to do so by robbing Hector of his suicide, which friends of mine who have read the book and whose opinion I respect, tell me comes very near to making them cry, even as they laugh. That is the way I like readers to feel.

R.D.

To W. H. CLARKE

[Peterborough, Ontario]
November 8, 1951

Dear W. H. Clarke:

I was sorry indeed to hear that you are unwell – sorrier still to hear that you temerariously refuse to believe that you *are* unwell, and insist upon going to your office. To me, as a malingerer of lifelong habit, this is an incomprehensible desire on your part. What do you want to go to work for? You have an excellent staff: why do you not seize upon this opportunity to lie in bed, coddled by your family, and an object of affectionate concern to your employees? I urge you to give up your ill-considered excursion into Christian Science at once, and accept the fact that you are ill and must rest until you are well. You are, at this moment, that happiest of creatures, a Licensed Loafer: why don't you loaf?

I am almost minded to send you a bottle of what I take myself when convalescing – Madeira wine. But it promotes a sense of well-being, and I understand that it is an excess of well-being which prompts you to go to work before you are fit for such exertion: therefore I shall keep the Madeira, and send you, instead, this good advice: stay at home, and preferably in bed, until you are *quite* well. Then stay in bed another day or two, for good measure. I am a hypochondriac of long experience, and I know how dangerous too sudden a resumption of work can be.

With every good wish for your recovery under the treatment prescribed above.

Robertson Davies

PS: If you get up, you may have to shovel snow! Think of *that*!

To GORDON ROPER

Peterborough Examiner
Peterborough, Ontario
November 20, 1951

*Gordon Roper (1911–   ), Canadian, and
his wife, Helen, had become good friends
in Peterborough during the war. In 1946,
Roper joined the English Department at
Trinity College, University of Toronto,
where he remained until 1969. He had
written his doctoral thesis on* Moby Dick,
*the great novel by American writer
Herman Melville (1819–91). Titled
"Melville's 100 Year Old White Whale,"
the requested article appeared on page 4
of the* Examiner, December 18, 1951.

Dear Gordon:

Would you be able to write an article of about twelve hundred words for the *Examiner* on the fact that this is the centenary of *Moby Dick*? I think that we ought to pay some attention to it and you are the obvious man to do so. What you would write would appear in our Saturday Book Column which also appears in the *Kingston Whig-Standard*. The combined circulation of the newspapers is about thirty-five thousand, and we reckon on an audience of close to a hundred thousand. The payment for the article would be twenty-five dollars, and if you can do it, I would like to have it not later than the 12th of December so that we could use it as our Christmas Book Column. Christmas is a time when people tend to think in terms of old books and great books and I think it would make a first-rate column for that occasion.

You may think it a very cool proposal that you should offer something of your specialized knowledge on this subject for newspaper publication at what I recognize is a small fee. I am quite aware that this is so. However, there are certain points which I would like to make in connection with what I have said. You are, yourself, a Peterborough boy, and I think that it is a good thing that Peterborough should be reminded that not all its sons become business men and that there is a relation between the world of scholarship and this city. Another point is that you never can tell who is going to see what you have written or what its influence may be. It always sticks in my mind that some years ago, Hugh Kenner* told me that he had never heard of James Joyce until he read a book review which I had written in the *Examiner* about Joyce; as you know, Kenner is now one of the rising young men in the field of Joyce scholarship. I do not feel the *Examiner* can claim an immense amount of credit for this, but I am greatly pleased that we had something to do with it. We have, more than ever before, and more than most Canadian newspapers, a great number of readers of high school age, and I would very much like them to hear about Melville and who better should introduce them to Melville than yourself?

I recognize, of course, I have left it rather late to make this proposal to you and that you may be too busy to take it on. However, I would like you to think about it.

With every good wish to yourself and Helen, I am,

Yours sincerely,

Robertson Davies

To VERNON MOULD

Peterborough Examiner
Peterborough, Ontario
December 6, 1951

*Vernon Mould (1927–   ), Canadian, art
master at Upper Canada College
Preparatory School in Toronto, was in
charge of costumes for the one-act play
Davies was writing to mark the Prep's
Jubilee Year. Titled* A Masque of Aesop, *it
concerned the Greek fabulist Aesop and
was to be performed on May 2–3, 1952.
Alan G. A. Stephen (1902–73), English-
born Canadian, was the Prep's
headmaster 1934–66.*

Dear Mr. Mould:

I am sorry to have taken so long in answering your letter, but I have been very busy with the play itself and until now, have not been able to get around to it.

I presume that Mr. Stephen has shown you the list of characters for the play. I do not think that it would be wise or needful to attempt any sort of "historic" costumes for the supposed Greek people. I think it would be much better to achieve a handsome and interesting appearance for the play than to try anything like that, and for this reason, I would suggest that you use lots of colour. For the crowd, for instance, I do not see why it would not be perfectly satisfactory to dress them in their own white shirts and flannel shorts, knee socks and soft shoes, provided that each one can also wear some sort of brilliant cloak. It might be wise, also, to provide them with coloured caps, perhaps in the Phrygian design as their heads will be the part of them which will be seen most. For the god Apollo, something magnificent is required, and perhaps it would be possible to manage a purple cloak with gold on it for him, and if it were possible, he would look well in a wig with gold curls on it. I do not, of course, mean a sort of Shirley Temple wig, but the sort of stiff and formal wig which is often seen in ballet. In fact, I think that you might take your cue from ballet design all through. I have specified in the stage directions that Aesop is to be humpbacked. Please do not underdo this effect. I cannot urge you strongly enough to exaggerate the visual effects for the play. I think it is particularly important that the boys should wear interesting things on their heads for boys never have enough hair or big enough faces to look interesting at a distance.

About the fables contained in the play: you ought to be able to work up something amusing for the Cock and the Hen and the Chicks. I suggest that they should all wear masks, and perhaps cloaks with cloth sewn to them in such a way as to represent feathers. As you undoubtedly know, you can get wonderful effects by painting on costumes which would cost hours of time and much money to get by actual sewing. I think that the Town Mouse and the Country Mouse ought to have mouse masks. It is necessary, of course, that none of these masks should come more than half way down the face because these characters have to sing. I want the Town Mouse and Country Mouse to look like an old-fashioned vaudeville team – the Town Mouse being very smart and stylish and the Country Mouse dressed in exceedingly unfashionable and ill-fitting clothes.

The most difficult fable to costume will be the Belly and the Members. My own suggestion is that all the characters in this should wear black cloaks. The Arms and Legs might wear head-dresses from which an arm or a leg stuck up into the air. The Belly itself should have an enormous pink belly to wear on its front with a nice big pants button sewn in the middle of it. The Head might wear a hat which was built up to look like an enormous brain. I think that the Bottom should simply have a very large cushion tied on behind with his cloak hanging over it. Nobody will be likely to misunderstand what he is.

Once again, I urge you not to worry too much about details but to aim for big and striking effects. An audience can be bored to death after looking for an hour at pretty costumes which do not provide much variety, but if they are continually refreshed by bright colours in changing positions, they are perfectly happy. I hope this gives you the information you want. I am going to try to let Mr. Stephen have the full text of the play by the 2nd of January.

With good wishes, I am,

Yours sincerely,

<u>Robertson Davies</u>

To BRENDA DAVIES

[Peterborough, Ontario]
Tuesday, March 4 [1952]

Brenda was making her first visit to Australia since leaving for England in 1936 to apprentice at the Old Vic. She had not seen her sister Maisie in all those years, though she had had a good visit with her mother in 1947 when Mrs. Newbold came to Peterborough for a long visit around the time of Rosamond's birth. Malton (now Lester B. Pearson International) was Toronto's airport.

My dearest Pinkie:

After you went out onto the field at Malton, Clair and Amy [Stewart] and I invested thirty cents in going up to the lookout on the roof where we watched your plane go to the runway and at last soar up into the sky. We stayed there until you were just a speck. We could not see you at a window, and hoped that you had got a good seat. Then we went back to town, put the Pontiac in dock at Hawthorne Gdns [Rupert Davies' home in Rosedale, Toronto], and turned in for a three-hour nap. We came to for dinner, and chatted yawningly till ten, then to bed again, and I did not stir till nine on Monday.

You got away at a good time for the weather has been foul – half rain, half snow, and a bitter wind. The only ray of sunshine on Monday was Herbert's nice piece,* which I have sent to you. This is what it is to give lifts to critics! Monday morning I visited Clarke, Irwin, and hounded Clayton Ridpath* to such purpose that he revealed that he had had our new lamp for some weeks, and really meant to get around to sending it! I wrung from him a promise to have it here by the weekend, but I regard that merely as the first foray in a low campaign of devilling.

Attended an early rehearsal of *Aesop* at Upper Canada College and was annoyed to find that Galt,* the master in charge, had tinkered my play quite a bit. For one thing, he completely missed the point of one of the songs, which was written with assonance instead of rhyme; he apparently thought I wanted to rhyme and couldn't. I desired the Headmaster to enlighten him on this matter. How vile all teachers are! They mix with kids so long that they treat everybody as a pupil.

However, I gave his cast a talk on acting and particularly the speaking of English which gave him a red face. Also heard some of the music, which is not bad – sort of Purcell strained through a dirty sock. There is a misery about *Aesop*, by the way; they are doing it the week we shall be in St. John,* and it can't be changed. However, I fear the U.C.C. performance might annoy me; Dr. Sowby* has already made them change a line because it echoed the Bible and was thus blasphemous! Having once escaped from schoolmasters, why do I put myself in their gripe again? Some deep urge toward self-torture, I conclude.

Laid about me to such purpose at U.C.C. that I missed the 5.35, so dined with the Stewarts and caught the 7.15 and got home to find the family in bed, but wide awake, demanding news.

And so today we began the great adventure: Discipline by Daddy, Décor by Anna Pedak, Shoes by Gamba, Wigs by Clarkson.* Already Mrs. P. has given the house the indefinable air of a Prussian pension in which she excels. The table is constantly set, dominated by my napkin in its ring. I arrived home after work to find Mrs. Shields and Mrs. P. wrestling with what looked like twenty small fry, but proved to be only Boo, Catherine and Cawoll.* The crime sheet was a short one; a whole bag of liquorice all-sorts had disappeared since noon, and after an exhaustive examination it was decided that these had been taken by some person or persons unknown. Breaths were smelt, but to no avail. Scotland Yard is on the alert.

The flavour of the Festival* lingers, and many are the compliments being passed. Even Elva [Mrs. H. L. Garner] has put herself on record as asserting that "everything of a cultural nature Peterborough has, pretty nearly, springs from the Davies." Approbation from Sir Hubert Stanley is praise indeed.* When people tell me how superb you looked* on Saturday night, I modestly admit that this was the case – but how I long to seize them by the shoulders and cry "She is the Goddess Venus with the nature of the Blessed Saint Mellangel,* and when I think of her my body freezes with ecstasy!".... But this might be judged eccentric.

I judge that by now you must be near to Sydney, and will be in Melbourne quite soon. Do, do enjoy yourself, my love, and get the most complete rest and change you can. Give my love to your Mother..... There is no more news, except the old news that I love you so much that I am in hourly danger of spontaneous combustion, and so good night and God bless you.

Rob

PS: I resolved that while you were away I would not write too much, as it might seem a way of horning in on your holiday – but I feel a terrible writing spell coming on.

To BRENDA DAVIES

[*Peterborough Examiner* and
572 Weller Street
Peterborough, Ontario]
Tuesday, March 18 [1952]

Dearest Pink:

I am snatching a few minutes at the office to write to you, before going home, for things are pretty lively there, and I shall be involved in a round of story-reading and whatnot as soon as I get in. Please do not be alarmed, but all three children are now back in bed, with colds and coughs which Ross Matthews* takes a dim view of. The reason for the dim view is, of course, the skating carnival, for they are all Cain-raised to be in it, and he has promised them to do his best to have them up and ready for rehearsal by Saturday. This has meant monstrous doses of sulfa, which I administer three times a day, as well as a wet medicine, nose drops, and sedative pills. There is $9 worth of medicine sitting on the nursery chest at this moment. The sulfa makes them a bit feverish and low, and last night was rather a night, for Rosamond and Jennie were pretty upset. But by tomorrow noon they will have had the full dose, and R.M. hopes to have them on the mend. Now I have debated *keeping this from you*, for I don't want you to fuss. They are not dying, or even seriously ill, but they are being given The Works in order that they may skate in the carnival. But after consideration I thought I had better tell you, but you are not to fuss; they are being nursed and coddled and tended like nobody's business, and are getting to be Spoiled Beasts. By the time this reaches you they will be perfectly well and skating like mad dogs.

I will confide to you secretly that I begin to weary, ever so slightly, of this skating carnival. Yesterday at lunch time I settled down for a much needed snooze and within twenty-five minutes I had five phone calls, all about the carnival rehearsals, or carnival costumes, or enquiries about the children. During the day I had nine phone calls, of which seven were carnival, and two Little Theatre, fretting about the one-act play festival. The carnival people are agog about their show, and remembering how agog we were about the festival, I keep my temper with them. "Every man's dung smells sweet i' his own nose," as the dramatist Marston* so trenchantly puts it.

The costume problem* was a vexing one, for Mrs. Susi has let Mrs. P. down and Mrs. P. cannot cope. I phoned Gwenny to get the old woman with the bald head, but she is out of commission, and three other dress-makers were full up. But miraculously Mrs. Mitchell, who sings in the Coventry Singers, heard of our plight from Gwenny, and turned up last night and took away all the stuff and swears she will make them all! This piece of unsought and unexpected kindness quite floors me, and I shall send her a great big plant, with a nice note. All would be well if the kids wouldn't fuss and devil me so, but they are in agony lest something should keep them from the carnival; it is a feverish obsession with them. Today at noon I lay down for another snooze and had three calls – two carnival and one for the C.N.R. This ground me, as I was up a lot in the night with J and R.

I am still in doubt as to whether I should be telling you this or not, for I am anxious that nothing should shadow your holiday. But you must treat it as a comic hooroosh several thousand miles away, and laugh heartily, as though at the funny papers. I laugh most of the time, but last night, when Jenny sat up in bed, with her hair streaming down and a look of invalid malignance on her face, she looked so much like my Mother* that I nearly gave her a good clout. Jenny can get more drama out of a small pill than anybody except her late Grandmamma. But basically we are all very bobbish. I put the boots to Cawol today at noon, for she was hanging around, and none of the kids was up to doing anything with her. Her mother, who seems to be a Great Sawney,* had sent her down, without warning, to spend the morning. If the little muckworm gets a cold, it will be no more than bare justice.

Very bobbish: yes. But when you asked me in your last letter if I was getting over the Festival I laughed so loud that the children jumped in their beds. I have, as it were, merged beautifully from the Festival into the Skating Carnival, and there are moments when Reason totters on her throne. But I must claim for myself that I have never yet spoken of the carnival to the children in other terms than those of high regard.

It really seems as though at your exit from Peterborough, all hell broke loose. . . .

Your letters are a great delight. It was a fine thing for you to go back to Melbourne, and especially to see your childhood home before it breaks up. One ought always to keep one's line of recollection in good repair, like a strong rope which runs through the whole of one's life. You will get many things in perspective which were not so before. At eighteen one puts one's stresses in some odd places. It is particularly a good idea for you to see where you had trouble with your stepfather,* for you left Australia with that bulking big in your mind. But now – he is, one trusts, in Hell and it is a question whether a completely conventional childhood would have done anything for you that your own somewhat frampold* experience did not do. And

Australia ought to give you a line on Maisie.* As you know, it was very bitter to me that after twelve years of uncommonly happy marriage Maisie was able to put a wedge between us in a couple of hours. She is your elder sister, but when one is grown up that ought to be balanced by a more objective view.

Really, of course, I ought to be there, so that you could see me in the surroundings which will probably always be the backdrop to your most intimate thoughts. Then you could decide whether you are really going to keep me or not. Actually, I am glad I am not there, for nothing looks such a fool as a man in a houseful of women when he has no logical reason to be there. I would love to see the scenes of your early life, but not just now; when the children are older, shall we make a visit to Australia? I have been thinking a good deal on this subject, as a matter of fact, and if war doesn't intervene I don't see why, when Boodie [Rosamond] is a few years older, we shouldn't travel a good deal. I weary of Pbro and Canada and long to see the great world. But to get back to my subject; have a really good look – a searching look – at everything. It gave me a great thrill when you wrote that you had climbed that tree. And do bring back a wad of family photographs; I warm greatly to Richard Larking, with his camera and black velvet cloth.* You know that I have a strong feeling for the *continuity* of life; one is a bead in a string, and it is good to know what the other beads are like. Perhaps that is how we seem to God – all generations milling about, without regard for accidents of Time. At any rate, to think like that gives one a decent respect for one's ancestors. To regard oneself as the Consummation of all Evolution is a wicked and vain fancy. So have a jolly good wallow in your past, and when you come back I want to hear all about it.

I reckon that this will reach you about Wednesday March 26. Therefore I shall not be able to write you many more letters that will reach you. So let me say now how very happy – deeply happy – I am that you have made this journey, for I feel it will be a turning point in our life together. It will, I hope, hitch you up again to a whole train of thoughts and feelings which our marriage seemed to cut you off from. Coming to live in Canada was a wrench and a nervous adventure, and I never forget or undervalue the great courage and the trust in me which you brought to it. But from now on you will have, so to speak, all your luggage with you, and Australia, whatever it may mean to you, will never seem so far away again. . . .

I have not been able to complete a single one of these letters without a protest of my love for you. Dearest Brenda, it is the compass of my life. Until I met you I was a wanderer in life; since, I have always been able to get my bearings. And if you were not a great person, I could not love you as greatly as I do. It is the best and truest and noblest thing about me. I do not think I ever wrote you a love-letter before we were married. Now that you are away my thoughts are all one long love-letter to you, my dearest dear.

Now to the drug store to post this and get some ginger ale for the tiny lazars above to take after their sulfa; I can hear them shrieking merrily.

<u>Rob</u>. . . .

To BRENDA DAVIES

[*Peterborough Examiner*,
Peterborough, Ontario]
Saturday, March 22 [1952]

My dearest Pinkie:

You are always terribly modest about your letters, though actually you are the best letter-writer I know, because your stuff is always so immediate and fresh and vivid, but you would have been flattered if you could have seen how your letters were received here today. The American crowds standing on the dock at New York, shouting to the approaching ship for the latest installment of Dickens' novels, was nothing to it. We each got a letter and it has raised us from gloom to a kind of drunken good cheer.

Reason for Gloom: Dr. Matthews found that his sulfa treatment was not working, and issued an edict that the kids must *not* under any circs be in the skating carnival. They were very good about it, I must say, and just took it without comment, but it was plain to be seen that they were stricken to the heart. At night, after lights out, there were tears. But I have done my best: we are buying the costumes, anyhow, as they want them for dress-ups; we are planning a state visit to *Quo Vadis* next week; we are visiting *Lady Precious Stream** as guests of the director; we are going to the matinee of the carnival. . . .

I reckon that this is the last letter I can write to you with certainty that it will reach you before you return. I don't know what I shall do next week, for I have looked forward so much to writing to you. Doubtless I have moaned a bit, but the writing was sheer pleasure. Next week I shall have to send at least one cable, just for the fun of sending something to you. Have you enough money? And have you your visa for the U.S.? I had an awful dream last night that you had not been able to get it and the U.S. people in Australia had to send it all to the States and get it back by slow boat, and that you weren't sure you would be back even by summer or perhaps ever. Woke up in a sweat, I can tell you.

Return, Persephone, from the Underworld, and bring Spring with you. I must now go and get some promised ice-cream, to celebrate the fact of everybody getting letters from you.

By the time this reaches you we shall have stopped counting the days and will be counting the hours. Floods of love from us all.....

<u>Rob</u>

PS: Your things which you are bringing back sound wonderful, and the information about your family fascinating. I'll check with Customs about it and cable you what they say. Thank your Mother for her kind and heart-warming letter. She knows just the things I want to hear.

Love ——

R

September 11, 1954

Dear Alan:

Thanks for your letter of September 10th. It will give me the greatest pleasure to go to the performance of <u>A Masque of Aesop</u> in December and I would be very greatly obliged if you could extend your invitation to include my daughters who are extremely anxious to see the play.

I really haven't any idea what could be done with the $250; I am absolutely and unshakeably against having it spent on a picture of me as I have no desire to see my mug perpetuated in oil paints and I would regard such a use of the money as a robbery of the school. Nor do I think it would be a good idea to use the money as a prize in dramatics as the people who get such prizes are often merely the showiest and most shameless boys or girls in any school, whereas children of greater potential talent may be unable to express it at that age. I do offer one suggestion, however, which springs, I think, from a real understanding of what dramatic

SECTION

III

n many ways, 1953 was a watershed year for Davies. For a start,
it was the opening year of the Stratford Shakespearean Festival,
whose founding artistic director was his mentor Tyrone Guthrie.
Davies did everything in his power to ensure the Festival's success. He
provided an informed voice on its board of governors for eighteen years,
collaborated with Guthrie, artist Grant Macdonald, and designer Tanya
Moiseiwitsch on three commemorative volumes about its first three years,
wrote influential annual assessments for *Saturday Night*, and contributed
many articles to souvenir programs. He also agreed to adapt Ben Jonson's
sprawling play *Bartholomew Fair* for Stratford, but the Festival rejected it.

In 1953, too, Davies became literary editor of *Saturday Night* once
again. He held the post until 1959, turning out a succession of lead
book review articles that reveal him at the top of his bent, writing with

93

assurance, generosity, and authority on a remarkable range of subjects.

In 1953, Davies began to find himself increasingly at odds with Clarke, Irwin. The publisher rejected a projected third Marchbanks compilation, citing several reasons, most particularly its use of "low" humour. The following year Davies began to use an American agent, Willis Kingsley Wing; and he moved to Macmillan of Canada in 1958. 1953 was also marked by a disconcerting, and highly uncharacteristic, loss of artistic confidence. Davies had completed the first two sections of *Leaven of Malice*, the second novel of the Salterton trilogy, in November 1952. He then plunged into additional work for Stratford and *Saturday Night*, while still editing the *Examiner* and directing for the Peterborough Little Theatre and at Brae Manor, and exhausted himself in the effort. He underwent a kind of soul scrape, and recognized the need for a period of regeneration. It was at this point that he began to explore the works of the psychologist C. G. Jung. Jung's influence on Davies was profound, but it is not visible in *Leaven of Malice*, which he completed in 1953 and the early months of 1954. A Jungian world view is clearly in evidence in *A Mixture of Frailties* (written in the fall of 1956 and much of 1957), in which Davies' heroine, Monica Gall, undergoes a self-searching period of training and expansion of outlook, helping her to realize her full potential. Jung's influence is evident too in *General Confession*, the play Davies wrote in 1958 about the final years of Casanova.

The Davieses travelled to the U.K. twice in this period, indulging themselves again in a great deal of theatre-going. The first visit, in 1954, was occasioned by a production of Davies' Welsh play *A Jig for the Gypsy* by a try-out company in London, and the second, in 1958, was a two-month family excursion. Davies' two elder daughters became boarders at Bishop Strachan School in Toronto, Miranda in 1953 and Jennifer in 1955.

To PERCY GHENT

[Peterborough, Ontario
shortly before October 23,
1952]

*Percy P. Ghent (d. 1952), Canadian
radiographer who entered the X-ray field
in 1910, wrote special articles for the
Toronto press, including "In the
Spotlight," for the editorial page of the
Toronto Telegram. In this column, he
mentioned owning a holograph letter
written by Sir Henry Irving. Davies wrote
and offered to purchase it, and was
instead made a present of it.*

Dear Mr. Ghent:

I cannot tell you how grateful I am to you for the Irving letter. I have been keenly interested in Irving ever since I was a boy because both my parents, who were keen theatregoers, had seen him and regarded him as far above the level even of the remarkable group of actors who appeared in Britain and the U.S.A. at the turn of the century. The thing which interested me, I believe, was that everyone who spoke of Irving seemed to regard him, not so much as an actor, as a very great man with whom they had the good fortune to establish some contact. Even as a boy of twelve I was curious as to why this should be so, and since that time I have questioned everyone whom I have met who ever saw Irving; now, alas, they are becoming rather uncommon.

Although Irving's personality appears to have been of extraordinary strength, it is remarkable what very different impressions he produced upon different people. Portraits and sketches of him by very capable artists differ so greatly that it would be hard to recognize them as the same man. The voice which was the subject of endless criticism during his lifetime has been imitated for me by at least a dozen people, some of them very capable actors, but none of these imitations appear to be of the same voice. It is interesting also that the death-mask of Irving, which is preserved at the Stratford Memorial Theatre, looks only superficially like the portraits of him which exist.

These, and many other things which have come my way in my quest for the real Henry Irving, suggest to me that this very great actor had a quality which no other actor to my knowledge has possessed. So personal was the impression that he made upon everyone who saw him that he appears to have struck deeper into the hearts and minds of those who met him than actors usually do. Disagreement about the quality of an actor is common enough, but it does not go to the point where two observant spectators appear to have seen two entirely different men. It was often said that Irving excelled in the portrayal of saintly and devilish characters; saints and devils, from what we hear about them, seem to make their appearances in a very personal way to everyone who encounters them.

Robertson Davies

To W. H. CLARKE

Peterborough Examiner
Peterborough, Ontario
December 15th, 1952

W. O. A. Langs, the subject of this letter and a cousin of Davies' mother, was born in 1863 in Canada.

Dear W. H. Clarke:

I was amused by your letter of December 10th, but I am pleased that my aged kinsman, whose full name is William Orpheus Alfred Langs, has bought a copy of [*The Masque of*] *Aesop*. He is an odd old party, now 89 years old who qualified as a doctor during the reign of William IV,* I believe, but was disappointed in love and retired from practice before he had actually begun. He has devoted his life to breeding pigeons, attempting to discover perpetual motion and studying the history of South America. Every time I write a book I get a letter from him which always runs like this: "Dear Cousin, I have read your book and call your attention to the following typographical errors....." He is an eccentric of a type which seems to be disappearing.

With every good wish to yourself and Mrs. Clarke for a Merry Christmas, I am

Yours sincerely,

Robertson Davies
Editor

To W. H. CLARKE

[Peterborough, Ontario
shortly before March 28, 1953]

A third collection of Marchbanks columns was under discussion between Davies and his publisher. Initially the volume was to have been centred on the correspondence that became a feature of the column between September 1949 and December 1950. But when that didn't suit, there was some thought of an Almanack.

Dear W. H. Clarke:

No secretary, so am typing this myself; please excuse typographical enormities.

I like MARCHBANKS ALMANACK very much as a title, and could work out a scheme to include the material I have in hand under such a heading. However, I have also been thinking about THE SECRETARY OF SAMUEL MARCHBANKS, or if you liked it better MARCHBANKS SECRETARY, and had thought to arrange it thus:

Preface, explaining that while "secretary" means a young person of obstreperous efficiency and curiosity to most people, to me it means the *secretaire*, or bureau, which I have inherited from my French fore-bear Gaston L'Immerdu Marchbanks (he who mapped the sewers of Paris for Napoleon) and that I intend to make public its contents.

The contents would be divided into Drawers and Pigeon Holes, Secret Hiding Places, and Spillings (these last being fished up from behind the Drawers). It would contain letters to and from Marchbanks,

Fragments from Works in Progress (*A Day With Marchbanks*, pending volume in "Days With Poets" series, and *A Little Journey to the Home of a Great Reformer* – all about Marchbanks) and also Fugitive Pieces composed at the request of friends.

I thought that here and there we might use a cut of a pointing hand to refer readers back to the Preface, in which a general plan of the work would be outlined, to create and maintain confusion.

I would write more and more politely, but I hate typing, and do not do a good job. Will be interested to hear from you. I enclose the title page we spoke of, but I don't like it.

[No signature in original]

To HERBERT WHITTAKER

Royal York Hotel
Toronto
[April 10, 1953]

Dear Mr. Whittaker, alannah!

   Sure, and 'twas myself was readin' in this mornin's *Globe* about the Art Theayter conducted by Mrs. Goulding,* God bless and protect her! You were givin' her many a kind word for performin' behind a scrim. Begob, it's himself is the crafty one, sez I. He'll be afther takin a leaf outa the old trout's book, sez I. And when he puts on *The Family Reunion* in Victoria,* sure he'll do it without so much as raisin' the curtain, sez I. And that'll be subtle, b'jeez.

   May the blessed saints Peter & Patrick & Mary Magdalene lick ye from head to foot with their honeyed tongues. –

Barney O'Lunacy
director –
Abbey Theatre
Oakville.

To GRAHAM and JOAN
MCINNES

[Peterborough, Ontario]
April 21 (birthday of You
Know Who) 1954*

*Graham McInnes had joined Canada's
Department of External Affairs in 1948
and in 1954–55 was serving at
Wellington, New Zealand.*

Dear G & J:

Graham's letter of April 9 reached me on the 15th. Yes, there is to be a Stratford Festival this year: *The Shrew, Measure For Measure*, and *Oedipus Rex* (Yeats'* translation). Star, James Mason.* I have seen the designs and plans, and I think it will top last year. [Tyrone] Guthrie, [Grant] Macdonald & I are going to do another book,* and we have plans to make it much better than *Renown [at Stratford]*, which was rather a rush job. The pictures were done first, before there was any talk of a book; then I had to fit text to them, which was not always satisfactory. But this year Tyrone Guthrie will do a day-to-day producer's log. Grant Macdonald will do only important actors, and a lot of sketches of workshop, rehearsal, etc. and this will set me free to write a more coherent comment on the whole biz, I hope.

But your kind words about *Renown* cheered me greatly. Regarding Macdonald's work, I *do* feel that you have rather undervalued him, and I put it down to a lack of personal sympathy; he is rather putting-off, and some of his work makes me squirm, as it does you. But he is a close friend of mine, and I value him highly, because he is a *real* artist; his work is the communication of a very personal vision of life, and while it is not everybody's cuppa I think that at its finest it is very fine indeed. His is a moonlit, remote world, and all his own. During the past three years he has been going through a very bad patch – debt, the prolonged illness and death of his Father, and a feeling of being neglected and undervalued which he fights, but cannot wholly defeat. He has grown more withdrawn and crotchety and nesh, poor devil, and his work is more moonstruck than ever. But he is a steely spirit, and I know he will recover, and embark on quite a different style. B and I worry about him a good deal, but he is not the kind of man one can help. His battles and his triumphs are all his own.

The news about your book is *very* good and I shall be watching out for it. What a lively agent you have! Do you think you will get some money out of *Lost Island*? B and I have great guessing games as to what the book will be about. Very romantic, we are sure, for you are very romantic – a real story-teller and shonnachie, like your father. *Saturday Night** will do its best for you.

I am sadly conscious that it is nearly a year since I wrote to you. I won't say I couldn't have written. But I will say I couldn't have written cheerfully. I have been in rather a bad way, and if you don't mind, I shall tell you about it, as you are tried friends. I have had a kind of prolonged crisis – as it were an artistic menopause – caused partly by overwork and partly by painfully getting better acquainted with myself. The outward symptoms were exhaustion and a nasty skin disease called *lichen planus* – what the Bible calls a tetter.* Horrid scaly outbreaks on hands, feet, tum and (final misery and degradation) my privy parts. Dermatologist says this will take several months to heal and sure enough it is only just gone, leaving a few blotches. Nervous exhaustion, says he. Mentally it expressed itself in self-doubt, failure of my inventive faculty and endless fits of The Drears. But I am out of it now, I think, and know myself better. I have set aside much of the destroying ambition which has possessed me for so long, and have rec- ognized that I have a very limited talent, and that any really marked success as a writer is not for me.

What! you say; what about all those books and plays? Well, first of all they are none of them really much good, and they have never made any money. Now you know me well enough to know that I do not make money the final test of worth, but I would feel better if my returns from my writing were more than peanuts – I would feel more like a real author, and not like an amateur. But I am driven to write by a compulsion which I cannot control, and I am reconciled to being, in the literary world, what the Sunday painter is in the world of art.

However, *Renown* was my 10th published book. And during all this soul-strife I have written another novel, to appear in the middle of August. It is called *Leaven of Malice*, and the publishers say it is a lot better than *Tempest-Tost*. It is about newspaper life in a small Canadian city, and it uses the setting and many of the people from *T-T*. Now *T-T* was criticised for having a thin plot; *LM* has enough plot for a Trollope novel.* *T-T* introduced comic wheezes for laughs; *LM* is amusing too, I believe, but the wheezes are more organic (if an organic wheeze is ever desirable). I hope it is a better book, but really I do not give a bugger whether it is or not. I had to write it because I am a man with the writing disease – Scribblo, ergo sum, as the fella says. It is done now, and shortly I must deliver a comedy [*A Jig for the Gypsy*]* to the Crest Theatre in Toronto (very good new group) and I must do Renown Number Two before the end of Aug. Then I hope to pause and take stock of my position. I am now forty, and I ought to know what the hell I am doing, and why.

Recently B and I were asked to Govt. House for a weekend. For our fine characters? Because H.E. [His Excellency, Vincent Massey, Canada's Governor General]* desires us to demonstrate Hindu love-postures in the Drawing Room after dinner? No. He hankers after an Ottawa Festival of the Arts, and he wanted ideas. I gave him a basin-ful of these, including a Masque of Government, acted in the Commons Chamber, using Canadian actors, ballet, music, Film Board (a complex wheeze on which I am v. keen). A Mock Battle and assault on Parliament Hill from the River, with the audience mounted on a log-boom supplied by Eddys.* A festival of liturgical music in the Cathedral. And such-like goings-on. He was enchanted. So something may happen. But for some reason which I cannot fathom this is all excruciatingly Hush Hush, so do not whisper it to a soul. If I am allowed to play Ben Jonson-Inigo Jones to the James I* of H.E. I shall enjoy myself very much. But a Gorgon lurks in the path. It is Charlotte Whitton.* My notion is to do a festival with the buildings which now exist, including both Senate and Commons chambers (Senate dreamy for small concerts and Yankees will pay $10 a seat to sit in real traditional-type chairs) but Lottie wants a Big Ottawa Auditorium. Well, we shall see. Meanwhile I dream happily of using real soldiers for the Mock Battle.

I hope this letter hasn't been dreary. B is in New York at present, giving good advice to a pal who is about to marry for the second time. So I am alone and introspective..... The Kingston *Whig* has hired a Queen's professor of English, Arnold Edinborough,* as its new editor. A delightful fellow. This is part of my Papa's campaign for Canadian editors who can spell and count up to 10.

Hoping this finds you in the pink as it leaves me at present.

Rob.

To GRAHAM and JOAN MCINNES

[Peterborough, Ontario]
September 1 [1954]

Dear G & J:

Let us dispense with the usual "I am sorry to have been so long in writing etc." and get on with the letter. My metaphorical organs have been in the mangle for some months, and I have only just been able to detach them for long enough to send you a note. . . .

I enjoyed the book, and hope you are going to do some more. I think that vein of adventure and fantasy mingled with a lot of factual detail is very much your dish, and it is also the dish of hundreds of thousands of readers who want a book which gives them a sense of adventure and a wider life. I hope you won't be put out if I say it reminded me of my old favourite R. M. Ballantyne,* but with a nice bit of sex where old Ballantyne had to worry along without it. I am very happy that you are in covers at last – I mean fiction, and not the books of criticism. I think you are a *book* man, and not a magazine man; you need space to develop your people and your plots, and the short piece simply does not permit it. Have you ever given any thought to really *good* mystery tales – not whodunits so much as why-dunits? I think *Lost Island* shows a first-class sense of suspense and *good* mystery, and you have also a talent for detail which should enable you to construct beautiful plots – much like your kinsman Rudyard, but without his Manlydom, as Max Beerbohm* calls it.

My new novel, called *Leaven of Malice*, appears on the 18th of this month and shall speed to you on a dolphin's back. I am very worried about it, for I don't think the newspaper reviewers will like it. Chatto are doing it in London, but Rinehart, Knopf and Harcourt Brace have turned it down in the States as being "too English." Funny, when the English rather patronize me for being "provincial" in a Canadian way. Aren't big nations snotty? However, it is now with a good American agent,* who is going to see what he can do.

I got an agent because of your example and also because another writer friend of mine urged me to get one. Clarke, Irwin have now brought out ten of my books, and I haven't had much money out of them, because CI always cry a poor mouth, and say they can't make any money on Canadian books. So I asked Clarke, straight out, if he *lost* money on me, and if so, why he went on publishing me. He gurgled a bit, then said he *did* lose money on me, if he counted all his expenses of warehousing, promotion, etc. but he loved literature and thought it lent prestige to his firm to publish me, and he had a duty to Canadian writers, etc. But I think there is a blackamoor in the wood-heap somewhere, and it is the agent's job to find it. Anyhow *Leaven* will be my 11th book, and in November there will be *Twice Have The Trumpets Sounded* – another book about the Stratford Festival – which will make twelve. If Clarke is losing money he is a bear for punishment. I hate to be treated as if I were a charity, or the wan figure of Canadian letters, or something diminishing of the sort.

On Monday last my new play *A Jig for the Gypsy* went into rehearsal at the Crest Theatre in Toronto. Good cast, good designer, nice management & good director – a very fine setup, for which I am grateful. It opens on the 14th, for a fortnight and I am very excited. Monday I read the whole job to the actors – one way of guaranteeing that these dear but featherheaded souls will all know what it is all about, for they tend to read only their own parts. Herbert Whittaker is producing, and he is good, imaginative, and has a great regard for the script, which is not true of all directors. Odd – he can't act, and doesn't say much, but he seems to boost the actors to create, and then he criticises and moulds their creation; a good method – indeed the best, I think.

As Brenda has told you, the Questors Theatre* in London does the play for a fortnight, from September 25; they are a good tryout company and have sold some West End shows. I do not dare even to hope that they can do so with mine, but miracles sometimes happen. We fly to England on the 22nd, to see the opening, then go on a jaunt for four weeks – a real holiday. I am tired from work, and also from my soul-struggle of recent months about my relations with my publisher. As I think I told you, his wife favoured me with a lot of advice about my work, based on *Leaven* – I am harsh toward mankind, and this springs from the fact that my life has always been easy and I do not understand the troubles of less favoured people. It may be true; on the other hand, it may not. But she is a professional Christian, and ought to know that we are all as God made us, and when God made Ella Wheeler Wilcox and Godfrey Winn* he did not choose to pour me into the same mould. This opinion of my private character has not made me any more happy with Clarke, Irwin, who appear to me to be Christian in word but Shylocky in deed.

Enough of this egocentricity. Your descriptions of life on the Socialist Paradise are deeply interesting, and I have struck New Zealand from my list of Places I Really Must Visit. But of course we do not blat abroad what you say; it would be as though my real opinion of Peterborough were to become widely known. Indeed, N. Z. sounds much like a vast Peterborough.

The Stratford Festival this year was better than in 1953 – not startlingly better but truly and surely and solidly better, and I think that venture is now set to do fine things for some time to come. James Mason, whatever you may hear, was *not* a failure, but a damned good actor; the thing was that several of the Canadians were very nearly as good and sometimes better, and the people who expected J. M. to bring fire from heaven were disappointed. He was also, it appears, a very fine person and much liked by all. On the last night of his appearance the cast applauded him and the audience gave him a big farewell, and he was understandably much touched. But Mrs. M.* seems to be a tiresome lady, and she nagged him and snooted the others in a very teasing fashion. Her values are those of Hollywood, and theatre does not appeal to her – particularly in what she considers to be a backward part of the world. Alas!

I have been dieting and have dropped from 225 lbs to 197; my doctor only says "try to get off another 10 lbs." He is a wee bone of a man, and obviously thinks a glass of milk and a biscuit a feast for a king. Sometimes I wake up in the night sweating, having dreamed that I am eating a whole mountain of cottage cheese, thickly overgrown with lettuce. Visions of fruit-cake and whipped cream haunt my waking hours. I fear that our month in the Land o' Stodge will undo much of this painstaking work, but I am determined that I shall not grow fat again.

Must close, as I still have an editorial to write. Love to you both and my good wishes to Michael, Susan and Simon,* who seem to grow visibly in your snaps.....

Rob

To ALAN G. A. STEPHEN

Peterborough Examiner
Peterborough, Ontario
September 11, 1954

When A Masque of Aesop *was published in 1952, Davies gave the performance fees and the royalties to the Upper Canada College Preparatory School. As schools across Canada performed the play, the fees the Prep collected mounted up. Stephen asked Davies how the resultant sum should be spent.*

Dear Alan:

Thanks for your letter of September 10th. It will give me the greatest pleasure to go to the performance of *A Masque of Aesop* in December and I would be very greatly obliged if you could extend your invitation to include my daughters who are extremely anxious to see the play.

I really haven't any idea what could be done with $250; I am absolutely and unshakeably against having it spent on a picture of me as I have no desire to see my mug perpetuated in oil paints and I would regard such a use of the money as a robbery of the school. Nor do I think it would be a good idea to use the money as a prize in dramatics as the people who get such prizes are often merely the showiest and most shameless boys or girls in any school, whereas children of greater potential talent may be unable to express it at that age. I do offer one suggestion, however, which springs, I think, from a real understanding of what dramatic presentations do to the people who are engaged in them: what about spending a reasonable sum of the money for as long as it lasts on a really large and splendid cake to be eaten by the Dramatic Society after they have given a performance? There is nothing that makes people so hungry as acting and I would rather think of the boys having something to eat than looking at a picture of me or watching one of their companions, who happens to have a particularly brassy nature, getting a copy of Macaulay's *Essays**
on prize day.

With every good wish, I am,

Yours sincerely,

Rob

To GORDON ROPER

Peterborough Examiner
Peterborough, Ontario
February 8 [1955]

Dear Gordon:

Your letter cheered me immensely, for I never think of my *Saturday Night* articles as penetrating to the Common Room at Trinity. My piece about the Tillotsons was splenetic, I admit, but they give me acute rectal distress, and so does Dr. Leavis.* They try to deal with Thackeray, and the Brontës as if they were really human beings enjoying full citizenship, but there is always a strong hint that these artists are not really the mental equals of their academic critics. Now I suppose this may be true, though Thackeray was a mighty shrewd critic himself. But my point is that a creative writer is neither the equal or the superior of a professor; he is just a different kind of creature, and he does his level best with whatever talent he has; to rap him on the knuckles, or pity his ineptitude, is not playing fair. Poor Emily, when she sweated out *Wuthering Heights*, was not trying an examination for the Greatest Novelist degree; she was suffering like hell, and suffering demands some compassion and understanding in the beholder. People who are not prepared to go a little way with an author in feeling ought not, I think, to write critical books about him. Both Tillotsons write in the pinched, refined, *dull* way which is the worst product of English criticism. It is educated, perhaps, but only in brain; the hearts are middle-class and mean. They are *emotionally* illiterate.

Of course I agree that a great critic is a great fellow, and a book like *The Road to Xanadu** is superbly stimulating, rich and seminal. In a coming *SN* article* I whoop it up for a book on Ruskin and one on Byron which are criticism of a high standard. But I tremble for students who get the notion that creators are really straining for academic approval, and not to purge the soul of the reader with pity and terror. Don't think I hate profs. But I have known so many good ones – C. S. Lewis and Dr. Chapman, to name but two, and Edmund Chambers* – that I must explode at the snottier brethren.

Paul Bacon* seems a good chap, and I was able to give him a lead for a job, though it may not work. I razzed him a bit for his notion that the smaller papers are basically "training-grounds" for the *Globe*. To be 45, and a reporter on any big paper, is not an enviable fate. The fun of chasing fire engines dulls as the joints stiffen and the gonads cool. He has lots of brains and with luck he should go a long way. For 20 he is remarkably mature in his ideas.

So glad your friend in the French Dept. thought well of the seduction in *Leaven*. I have had some very nice compliments about it, and some slaps in the puss, too..... "There are so many sordid things in life that we don't really want to meet them in our reading..... etc." But I firmly believe that is how most seductions are – not on the silk chaise-longue, with sips of champagne, but hasty encounters when opportunity serves, in circumstances which are comic or tragic, but not romantic. Which of us could endure a movie of our own most exalted moments of sexual passion? Stendhal's *Diaries** bear me out in my opinion.

You are one of the professors whom I admire for sufficient reasons – real appreciation, humanity and genuine liberalism of opinion, and many more which I will not embarrass you by detailing. Therefore I turn to you for an opinion: do you think my work satiric? So many people say so, yet that is not my intention. I think of myself as a serious writer – serious in my attitude toward life – who writes in a comic vein. I do not seek to hurt people, or ridicule the unfortunate, or poke fun at the illiterate. I try, rather, to write about people as nearly as possible as I see them. I do not go very deep because, as yet, I dare not; but I shall do so. In my next novel, now a-brewing, I want to get into my bathysphere and go as deep as I can; it is about a girl who is trying to rise above a sordid home background. But I hesitate somewhat to do so if I really give the impression that I am sneering at my characters. Of course not everybody says I do; but some people get that impression, and I want to correct it if I can. So I ask you: do you think these charges true, and if they are, what can I do to change that condition. I will not inject sugar into my stuff; I think that would be dishonest and truly cynical. But I try to be compassionate, which does not mean that I weep into my typewriter. I assure you that this is a genuine problem which occupies a great part of my thinking, and when you have a minute, I would greatly appreciate your judgement on it.

With every good wish to you & Helen and Susan & Mark

Rob

To MIRANDA DAVIES

[361 Park Street
Peterborough, Ontario]
Wednesday [April 27, 1955]

*Miranda Davies, then 14, was a boarder
at Bishop Strachan School in Toronto. She
believes that Davies dictated or typed this
letter from the second line of the second
paragraph on. Brenda Davies was
directing the Peterborough Little Theatre
in A. P. Herbert's* Two Gentlemen of Soho
for performance on November 19, 1955.

Dear Miranda:

I hope the parcel contained all the things you asked for. Some stub nibs recommended by Daddy are enclosed for the Italic writing, but who is going to teach it to you? I could only find two pairs of black pants, and if you need any more you had better order them from the school supply depot. Don't worry too much about having left so many things, but next time you unpack I think we had better make a list. The theory books were in the bookcase – not the one by the bed, but the other; Jennie discovered them. I am delighted you are doing so well at tennis and enjoying it. What do you want the ballet shoes for? I thought you had given up your ballet lessons.

I got some nice brown stuff and Mrs. Roy* is making Jennie a sailor dress. Daddy has been piteously ill, poor soul, and we have all felt deeply for him. He has borne it with his usual uncomplaining fortitude, which should be an example to us all, and now shows signs of improvement. His temperature is down, and he is spitting up heavy brown goo, like the suckings of Hooper's bulls-eyes, and has no voice at all. He also has weakening night sweats, and is quite poorly. But on Tuesday night he had a very poor time and dreamed he was being beaten by wicked dwarves; this was because the Dr. had filled him full of codeine. Nobody knows what Daddy goes through. Rosamond is back at school this afternoon, having had a lingering spell during which I could not get her temperature to keep at normal. She is full of bounce in the mornings, but tires very quickly, and is saucer-eyed by night. Nobody knows what Rosamond goes through. Puss-cat has not caught onto the fact that the screens have been put on the windows, and she nips up the vine and sits on the roof outside my bedroom window yowling piteously because she cannot get in. This means that Jennie and I have to climb a ladder and lure the fat headed thing down, which she does not want to do. Then, the minute she is free – yes, you guessed it. Nobody knows what Puss-cat goes through.

Saw *Hamlet** on the blower on Sunday night. Good in bits, but such a tiny image. Kate Reid stank; Ophelia must be played by a singer (see *Shakespeare's Boy Actors*). Much of the production had been hooked from the film. Still, a worthy try. Daddy could not see it, being in bed. Nobody knows etc. Rob Christie was an excellent Polonius, I thought, though Herbie Whittaker was unkind about him in the *G&M*. But secretly I think I have seen more *Hamlet*s and worked on *Hamlet* more than Herbie. This is just between ourselves.

Mrs. Pedak has her bottom teeth, and is finding a lot of fault with them. She can't pry them loose at night, they nip her, they slide about, etc. One cannot begin too early in life to develop a cheerful disposition. She is with Dr. Honey* now, having her valves ground, or something. The study has been painted and papered and looks very fine.

As you journey through the world, dear child, you will observe on every hand inequalities brought about by the disparities of economic circumstance – in other words, you will find that some people have more wampum than others. E_____ has seven new dresses; H_____ has none; you have two. This is tough for poor old H_____, who would probably like to cut a smart figure as well as the next one, but it is not fatal. She may marry a rich man, or she may get a wonderful job and make a lot of money herself. And you can judge whether E_____ is any nicer with seven dresses than she would be with a mere five. It is to observe this uneven spread of wampum – among other things – that we have sent you away to school. You must learn not to despise money, or fear it, or worship it, but to understand what it is or what it can do. Your family has neither a lot of money, nor is it pinched for money. This gives you an excellent start, and should keep you from falling victim to either of the two commonest and most romantic delusions about money which are (a) that it doesn't matter, and (b) that it matters more than anything else in the world.

In a few years you will meet a lot of poor young men who will talk very scornfully about money, and people who have it. But remember that it is just as silly to despise people for having money as for not having it. Not everybody who has money got it where E_____'s uncle got his.

Lots of love from

<u>Mummy</u>

P.S. "Two Gentlemen of Soho" is now cast, and I'm very glad to have the best available talent. Lloyd Hale, Glen Jagerman, Doug Sadler, Sylvia Cherney, Marcella Buck.* They all seem keen and I hope it will go with a bang.

Lots of love.

To HORACE W. and VIRGINIA DAVENPORT

[Peterborough, Ontario]
June 1 [1955]

Horace W. Davenport (1912–), an American physiologist, and Davies had become close friends at Balliol College, Oxford, 1935–38. At this point Davenport was chairman of the University of Utah's Division of Biological Sciences. His wife was Virginia Chapin Dickerson (1912–68), an American physiological chemist. The Davenports had asked Davies to be godfather to their second son, Robertson Davies Davenport. The porringer Davies sent was inscribed with a "Great Thought" from Heraclitus, "guaranteed," as he said in a note on July 31, to be applicable to every crisis in life: panta rhe, ouden mene (everything flows, nothing remains).

Dear Horace & Virginia:

I have never been so honoured or so flattered in my life! Only a day or so ago I was mumbling self-pityingly to myself "Nobody ever asks me to be a godfather" – and then –! I only hope that I can sustain this dignity in a fitting manner & do not get into a mess that will force your son to change to Benedict Arnold Davenport or something like that. – I have been walking about in a glow for several hours.

On Friday we go to Toronto and I shall dispatch from there the usual mug, or porringer, or coral teething-pole (with bells) or something more adventurous if I can find it. And please accept the love & congratulations of us all, including the children, and our most profound obeisance to R.D.D. – long may he prosper!

Rob

To HORACE W. DAVENPORT

[Peterborough, Ontario
September–October 1955]

Dear Horace:

I should have replied to your letter long ago; I was in Muskoka on a holiday, and wrote no letters. This was because the "holiday" meant directing a play* at a theatre there, and finishing a new one of my own which will be produced this autumn in Toronto,* and, I hope, elsewhere.

First: yes, I should be honoured to be named as guardian of your son, though I hope I shall not be called on to act in that capacity; I want you & Virginia to live long and happy lives, and if you do not, I shall be extremely angry with you. Still, this consideration does crop up, and you are right to meet it; if anything happens to you I shall do my level best for the boy, and in this promise Brenda joins me.

I am sorry that you are having a disturbing time.* But this is the proper period of life for it. Recently I met a friend of mine, an actor, at a party; we were both getting ready to celebrate our 42nd birthdays; we sat in a corner and had a perfect orgy of self-doubt, shattered hopes, unfulfilled ambitions and general misery, and emerged much brighter. In one's early forties one knows oneself; one knows that one is not really Leonardo, and one is faced with the job of doing the best one can with the few morsels of talent one can muster. The man in his forties is old enough to have lost some of his appetite for praise, but he is as sensitive as ever to blame. His glories seem mean, and his youthful dreams as, in the words of the Old Testament, but menstruous rags.* He knows himself half-lunatic, three-parts fool, knave, charlatan and gull. He is conscious of his aging body. He is a pitiable mess. Yet in this abyss he is upborne by the knowledge that he really can earn his living, that he has persuaded a woman to live with him and that she seems to endure him pretty well, that he has children who are far better equipped for life than he. He is also conscious – if he is you H.W.D., or me – that there are people who envy him and wish that they could do what he does, and who would love to topple him off his perch and seize his job and its emoluments. This knowledge sustains him somewhat, as does also a feeling that if he can wade through the Slough of Despond* he will get his second wind, and do some very neat work before he dies. So cheer up. You have always had a fine talent for gloom, but you know damn well that you are an enviable man.

I am very happy about the fine reception *Leaven of Malice* has received in the U.S.A. Apparently it is what publishers call "a sleeper," and is gaining ground all the time. Has been reprinted within a month of publication. Dramatic rights have been sold to a Broadway producer.* Very nice. But it has led my old friends, the Canadian critics, to assure me that I am no better than I should be, and have much to learn, presumably from them. Jealousy, my dear Davenport, is the canker of the literary world, and if there is one class of insect I especially dislike, it is the literary insect. When they assure me that I am no Dickens, I writhe not because they have said it, but because I am conscious of this fact to a degree far beyond anything they can imagine. I know myself to be a worm: but I do not like to be told so, in print, by some drunken phoney who could not write the jokes for comic toilet rolls.

But enough of this spleen. I hope the horizon clears for you soon. You deserve well of life. All that is wrong with you is that you are in the Horrible Forties..... I salute you & Virginia and *both* your sons. Why do you have sons and I have daughters? You're a biologist, and I suppose you know.

Rob

PS: Did you know that Eliot Emmanuel* was a psychiatrist in Montreal? Wrote me recently wanting to review books on psychology, showing where Freud was wrong. I was unable to accept this generous offer. If Freud was wrong, I'll learn it from someone other than E. E.

To BOB HATTON

[*Peterborough Examiner*
Peterborough, Ontario]
May 9th, 1956

*Robert J. Hatton (d. 1986), Canadian,
was then City Editor of the* Peterborough
Examiner. *He later became an English
teacher and head of the English
department at Adam Scott High School
in Peterborough. On the day Davies
wrote to Hatton, there was an article in
the* Examiner *headed "Choir Throws
Coffee Party."*

Will you please take care that no headings or reports appear in the *Examiner* in future in which a party is "thrown," or a deed, a crime, an imposture or a joke is "pulled." We are becoming much too careless about these colloquialisms which tend to appear particularly in headings, and unless we check them now they are likely to become regular *Examiner* style – which would be most regrettable.

RD

To R. W. W. ROBERTSON

Peterborough Examiner
Peterborough, Ontario
June 16, 1956

*The "Stratford book" under discussion in
this letter would have been a successor to
the three books which commemorate the
Festival's first three years – Renown at
Stratford (1953), Twice Have the Trumpets
Sounded (1954), and Thrice the Brinded
Cat Hath Mew'd (1955). Davies had done
most of the writing for them and they
were published by R. W. W. Robertson's
firm, Clarke, Irwin.*

Dear RWWR:

Since talking to you on the telephone on Friday morning I have given very serious thought to your proposal that I should write another Stratford book as a Samuel Marchbanks Scrapbook, and as I have decided that I really cannot do so, I feel that it is fairer to write to you at once than to wait until next Thursday as we had agreed.

My reasons are, first, that I cannot convince myself that the book would be a good one. It would have to be written in not more than ten weeks in what spare time I could get from my daily work, and it would involve a considerable amount of extra journeying to Stratford. I have always been convinced that the Marchbanks books gained some of their quality from the fact that they were chosen from a very large amount of material which was written in comparative leisure; I am not at all sure that the same kind of thing can be produced by forcing. Nor have I any desire to appear before the public as a hack who is determined to write about the Stratford Festival under any circumstances. . . .

There is no question of not being able to do the book if I sacrificed everything else to it and knocked myself out during the next two and a half months. But I have just completed a little more than two years in which I have been doing literary odd jobs of all sorts, writing under great pressure, adapting a play [Ben Jonson's *Bartholomew Fair*] for Stratford and doing a lot of things which, though interesting in themselves, were not in the direct line of creative work. I have been trying to get the decks cleared in order to give myself time and leisure to write first a play* and then another novel [*A Mixture of Frailties*]; having finally reached the point where I can do this I am not anxious to sacrifice them to a piece of hasty work, the only possible satisfaction of which would be that it might make some money. Experience has taught me that it is extremely unlikely that I shall ever make much money by writing and, therefore, there seems to be little reason why I should not write what I please rather than what immediately comes to hand. I hope, and think that you will agree, that it is far better for me and for Clarke, Irwin to take adequate time to write another novel with the genuine intention of making it better than the last one, instead of cramming in every possible piece of work that I can manage with the result that most of it will be scamped and will be done under conditions of fatigue.

I do not want to bore you with a long letter, but because I have a very great respect for your personal judgment I am anxious to explain my situation as fully as possible. There is another thing which is absolutely necessary to me at present and that is the achievement of a certain amount of time in which I can read and think. I very badly need some new ideas and a thorough overhaul of many of my old ones. I could name dozens of cases – and so could you – of authors who have rushed through life outfitted only with the ideas that they picked up between the ages of eighteen and twenty-four, which has not been enough provision for a lifetime. The result is that much of what they write after forty is old stuff which is only redeemed from mediocrity by the fact that their skill in writing has increased. I am extremely anxious to avoid this pitfall if I can and, therefore, I want to take some time to read and even more time in which to do absolutely nothing. The book which you mentioned would be a temporary success for us all in all likelihood, but I think that in the long run it would prove extremely costly.

With good wishes I am

Yours sincerely,

Robertson Davies

To HERBERT WHITTAKER

[*Peterborough Examiner*
Peterborough, Ontario]
July 10, 1956

[Dear Herbert:]

Here is a copy of the additional material which was introduced into *The Merry Wives of Windsor* at Stratford. Langham* introduced some lines from the Quarto text into his script for the production and asked me to provide the scenes – obviously lost somewhere through the ages – which fill out the story of the Host of the Garter and the German visitors. There is nothing I like better than trying on

Shakespeare's laurel wreath and I was so carried away that I even provided notes for the new text, for as you know Shakespeare without
notes is simply not respectable.

It amused me that some of the critics – you were an honourable
exception – did not hesitate to say that *The Merry Wives* is an
extremely bad play. If they do not know what is Shakespeare and what
is modern addition how can they possibly tell?

I am sending this to you for your private amusement, but if you
should want to make any public reference to it may I ask you to let
me know about it first as I am not quite sure what Langham's attitude would be and it might be necessary to ask him. I was not commissioned to do this work for the Festival, or paid for it, and so I
suppose I am free to show it to anybody I choose without regard for
consequences, but I would not like to do anything which might put
Langham in a funny position – particularly as he still has to decide
whether he is going to do my version of *Bartholomew Fair*.

With good wishes I am

Yours sincerely,

[Rob]

To WALLACE HAVELOCK ROBB

Peterborough Examiner
Peterborough, Ontario
September 12, 1956

*Wallace Havelock Robb (1888–1976) was
a Canadian poet, salesman, and
ornithologist who lived near Kingston,
Ontario.*

[Dear Mr. Robb:]

Your visitors from Peterborough have misinformed you about the
bells here. There is a carillon of twelve good bells which was either
given or purchased at some time during the last century, and which
were hung in the tower of St. John's Anglican Church, as it was the
only place that could accommodate them. They belong to the city and

are called The People's Chimes. There has been an understandable tendency for St. John's to consider that the bells are their own property, but from time to time their pride in this matter has to be reduced. Anybody may have the bells rung by tipping the Sexton $1.00, and a good many people do have them rung on their birthdays, when children are born, at times of death and on National days. A friend of mine usually presents me with a dollar's worth of Welsh airs on St. David's Day every year, and as the tower is directly opposite my office windows I get the full benefit of it. The one fly in the ointment in connection with this picturesque arrangement is that the Sexton has a deficient musical sense and his playing is distressing; all the hesitancy of a little girl hunting for the next note in her piano piece is brought by this man to his search for the next half-ton bell that he will ring.

With good wishes I am

Yours sincerely,

[Robertson Davies]

To YOUSUF KARSH

Peterborough Examiner
Peterborough, Ontario
October 11, 1956.

Yousuf Karsh (1908–2002) was a Canadian photographer (born in Armenian Turkey) who was known internationally for his portraits of famous personalities.

Dear Mʳ· Karsh:

The book that we were talking about on October 10th is called *In a Great Tradition, A Tribute to Dame Laurentia McLachlan by the Benedictines of Stanbrook;** I understand that it contains several of Shaw's letters to his friend who was a cloistered nun.

Referring to Shaw's remark that people should be photographed and painted naked, I have been able to trace the occasion of it, but not his exact words. It was in 1929 when he was on a holiday at Antibes and his photograph was taken sitting on a raft in a pair of bathing shorts, sunbathing. This picture was published rather widely and provoked unpleasant comments from some people who said that a man of Shaw's age – he was 73 at that time – should not exhibit himself naked. This was a silly remark because Shaw looks very healthy and well in the picture and has the physique of a much younger man. His reply to this criticism was that pictures of great men were of greater interest and value if the sitters were naked, as we were then able to see what they really looked like and were not confronted with a suit of more or less fashionable clothes with a head sticking out of the top of it. It is interesting that there should have been such a fuss about a pair of shorts in 1929; nowadays they would cause no comment whatever, even if the wearer were 100.

Last night I gave a good deal of thought to the questions you asked me about the important writers of the day* who might provide subjects for your book of portraits. I would like to repeat my plea for Sylvia Townsend Warner, who is at last being recognized as one of the really great masters of the short story in English. Among the men, I forgot to mention Christopher Fry, who is certainly the most considerable dramatist of the day, and of course Aldous Huxley, whose reputation has faded a little, but whose work continues on a level which nobody else living at the moment quite reaches. Among the poets I particularly draw your attention to Robert Graves. I am strongly convinced that in a hundred years he will be recognized as the greatest poet of our day, and the successor to W. B. Yeats. He has a magnificent head and you could do wonders with him. His home is in the island of Majorca but he is often in England.

With good wishes to yourself and Madame Karsh, and many thanks for an extremely pleasant morning, I am

Yours sincerely,

Robertson Davies

To BROOKS ATKINSON*

[*Peterborough Examiner*
Peterborough, Ontario]
October 17, 1956

Brooks Atkinson (1894–1984), American, was the influential drama editor and critic for The New York Times *1925–60.*

[Dear Mr. Atkinson:]

The Old Vic company, which is shortly to visit New York, has completed three weeks in Toronto where it played, among other things, *Richard II.* Although this play has long been familiar to me, it was only this time that I noticed a vital *crux* in it, which I would not have seen had I not been following Miss Nancy Mitford's revelations about U and Non-U speech.* It occurs in Act IV, scene 1 – the deposition scene in Westminster Hall – and it marks the *exact* moment when Richard loses all hope of his crown, not only in his own heart, but in the hearts of all right-thinking Englishmen. He cries (unstrung by anguish and thus revealing that he did not have a U-speaking Nanny) –

"An if my word be sterling yet in England
Let it command a *mirror* hither straight."

And Bolingbroke, with a U-sneer, corrects him –

"Go some of you and fetch a *looking-glass.*"

In the light of our new knowledge, this moment strikes upon the audience with well-nigh unbearable tragic force. Non-U! The pity of it! And him wanting to be a King!

I hope that this impertinence finds you in good health.

Yours sincerely,

Robertson Davies

To PETER H. BENNETT

Peterborough Examiner
Peterborough, Ontario
October 31, 1956

Peter H. Bennett, English-born Canadian, was managing director of the Stratford Shakespearean Festival.

[Dear Mr. Bennett:]

Thank you for your letter of October 29th in which you ask me for my frank comments on the matter of the adaptation of *Bartholomew Fair*.

The correspondence which we both have tells the story of this venture and there is no need to go over it all again. As you say, my letter of November 9th, 1955, gave the Festival a chance to get rid of this project, which was one of Tony's [Tyrone Guthrie's] ideas, because Michael Langham had succeeded Tony as Artistic Director and I did not want him to be embarrassed by a commitment which involved me. As I said in that letter, the revisions which Tony asked for when we went over the first drafts of the play on April 10th, 1955, were very extensive and involved a complete reworking of all the material and a considerable amount of new writing. I did not want to under-take this heavy job without a real assurance that Michael was interested in the project and, therefore, I arranged a meeting with him on January 4th, 1956, at which he expressed himself as greatly interested and told me to go ahead with the revisions as Tony had asked for them. On June 28th he wrote to me and this is the relative paragraph from his letter: –

"If you have finished a preliminary draft of 'Bartholomew Fair' I should dearly like to read it. I am keen that we should present three pieces next summer and would like one of them to be non-Shakespearean. Please send a script if you have one."

I had by that time completed the revised version which was sent to the Festival from Mr. Wing's office on June 28th. On August 8th I had a further talk with Michael in which he expressed satisfaction with *Bartholomew Fair* and repeated that he hoped to include it in the programme for 1957, but made it clear that if this were not possible the play would be done within two or three years.

The Minutes of the Executive Meeting of October 25th and your letter of October 29th tell me that Michael has now changed his mind and does not want the play. This leaves me high and dry with a piece of work which has occupied a considerable amount of my time and which is quite outside the budget of any other Canadian theatre. I do not think that it is putting the matter too strongly to describe this conduct as capricious – even considering the many strange aspects which business assumes in the theatre. I cannot, at the moment, tell you what my attitude to the matter* will be as I find that I am divided between two sides of myself: one side is a Governor and fervent well-wisher of the Stratford Festival, who is prepared to do almost anything to further its ends, and the other is a Canadian writer, not wholly without reputation, who feels that he has been led up the garden path. I am going to New York later this month and I shall certainly discuss this matter with my agent, Mr. Willis Kingsley Wing, and will seek his advice.

Yours sincerely,

[Robertson Davies]

To ANTHONY QUAYLE

Peterborough Examiner
Peterborough, Ontario
January 8, 1957

Anthony Quayle (1913–89) was a distin-guished English actor and producer for the stage. He also acted in films. He appears not to have responded to Davies' letter.

[Dear Mr. Quayle:]

. . . Contrary to your belief, I have known for some time that you were a director of the Reinhardt Company and that is another reason for having a very high opinion of you. And as you are one of the very few men who is divided between the publishing and the theatre worlds I should like to ask you a question which has troubled me for several years. My experience has been that when a writer sends a manuscript to a publisher he gets a courteous and direct answer quite quickly from somebody who obviously knows his business, and if the answer contains any critical opinion this too may be of real value. But when a writer sends a play to a producer's office, very frequently he gets no answer at all, very often the answer is long-delayed and when it comes he may find that his play has not been read by anybody whose opinion or criticism of it he can take seriously. I do not expect that you will want to answer this question or that you have any very satisfactory answer to give, but it has puzzled me for some time.

For the past twelve years I have been a writer of plays and novels and my relationships with book publishers have been thoroughly satisfactory; dealings with theatre companies, however, always seem to be entangled in a vast number of avoidable difficulties, and important decisions involving the fate, both of the producers and the author, often seem to be left in the hands of people who are unfitted for them. It is all very queer and I do not understand it in the least. I feel that I may ask this question because I do not think that I am a thwarted writer with an axe to grind; I am, on the contrary, an author who has had quite a bit of success and a reasonable amount of luck. But this strange split between the world of the theatre and the world of publishing has long surprised me, and as I have no quarrel with either I feel that I can ask the question without bias.

With every good wish for the new year, I am

Yours sincerely

[Robertson Davies]

To RALPH HANCOX

Peterborough Examiner
Peterborough, Ontario
January 9, 1957

Ralph Hancox (1929–   ), English-born Canadian, had applied for the job of editorial assistant at the Examiner. *For the previous two years he had been working his way up at the Kingston* Whig-Standard, *eventually writing a daily column. He came highly recommended by key figures at the* Whig *– Davies' brother Arthur (publisher and CEO), Robert D. Owen (executive editor), and Arnold Edinborough (editor).*

Dear Mr. Hancox:

Thank you for your letter of January 7th and for the newspaper clippings, which I have read and which I am returning to you under separate cover.

Your letter appealed to me and I think that we might be able to work well together. The experience that you have had, quite apart from your newspaper work, should give you a broad range of sympathies. There are one or two elements which I miss in your account of your training but I think that these are balanced by the breadth of your travel.

It must be said at once that your style, though well suited to news writing, is not quite what would be wanted for editorials. The editorials that you have shown me are good of their kind, but, as you yourself have pointed out, they are crusading editorials and have a somewhat shouting, buttonholing tone, which is suitable to crusades but is not a very good style for conveying information or for persuading people to leave one course of action and adopt another. The Crusades, as you will remember, were attempts to convert the heathen by hitting them over the head. This simply leaves you exhausted, and with a lot of dead heathen, which is not the object of editorial writing. I see no reason, however, why a man who can write as well as you do in one style should not be able to change his style and I do not regard this as a very serious objection. If you want to learn, I think that I am not a bad teacher.

Because of what you have shown me and told me in your letter, and because of the high recommendations given you by my brother and Mr. Owen and Mr. Edinborough, I am almost persuaded to appoint you to the position without further discussion. However, that might not be really wise for either of us and, therefore, I propose that we should not make a final arrangement until the weekend of January 19th. I shall be in Kingston on the 19th and I would like to see you during the morning, if that is possible. Perhaps it would be better – though there is no secrecy about this arrangement – that we should meet in the LaSalle Hotel rather than at the *Whig-Standard*. I should think that half an hour would suffice to say what we have to say to one another and if this arrangement is suitable to you we can fix a time for the meeting.

To refresh your mind about the proposal that I outlined to you on the telephone, it is that you should come here for the first year to learn the job and the particular characteristics of the city of Peterborough, at a salary upon which we will agree, and that at the end of the year if we are both satisfied we should reconsider the matter of the salary and appoint you to the position of Associate Editor. Meanwhile I suggest that you keep your eye on the *Examiner* and acquaint yourself in a general way with our Editorial Page and with the paper as a whole. If we settle it on the 19th, what chances are there that you could begin here on February 4th?

Yours sincerely,

Robertson Davies

To TOM PATTERSON

Peterborough Examiner
Peterborough, Ontario
May 16, 1957

*Tom Patterson (1920–) is a journalist
and native of Stratford, Ontario. It was
his idea to found the Stratford
Shakespearean Festival, which came
into being in a tent in 1953 and in a
permanent building in 1957.*

[Dear Tom:]

I enclose a cheque for $300. from my wife and myself in order to provide three of the named seats in the new theatre. The names which we should like to have attached to the seats are

Lilian Baylis*
Sir Edmund Chambers
Sir Henry Irving

My wife wanted some reference to Miss Baylis in the new theatre as she worked for her for some time and admired her greatly; I did some work on Shakespeare at Oxford with Sir Edmund Chambers, for whom I had the greatest admiration, and I think it fitting that at least one great Shakespearean scholar should be commemorated on one of these seats; the reason for the Irving name is obvious enough, particularly as he was the Shakespearean idol of an earlier generation of Canadians.

If any of these names has already been chosen* to be attached to a seat, could I ask you to let me know.

With every good wish I am

Yours sincerely,

[Rob]

To TANYA MOISEIWITSCH

[Peterborough, Ontario
July 4, 1957]

*Tanya Moiseiwitsch (1914–   ) is the
English designer of the Stratford
Festival's thrust stage and of many
Festival productions, including the 1957
Twelfth Night.*

Dear Tanya:

Cd. not get near you on Tues. night to say how lovely your costumes for *Twelfth Night* were: surely there must be some way of bringing back those hats for men? Adieu

Rob. Davies

To HORACE W. DAVENPORT

361 Park Street
Peterborough, Ontario
July 19, 1957

Dear Horace:

I have been very remiss about writing to thank you for the pictures of R.D.D. – not only the last group but several which have pre-
ceded it. What a handsome boy he is growing to be. I had a letter
from Virginia some months ago adjuring me not to send him things,
so I skipped his birthday. However, I do not think I shall do so again,
because I really like buying toys & things, and am very fond of children, in a selective sort of way. Children in the mass – no; specific
children – yes.

During the past three weeks I have been most disagreeably busy.
Our local police force is the subject of a Royal Commission investi-
gation, on allegations of corruption & incompetence in several nasty
degrees. Yesterday I was 1 hour & 5 minutes in the witness box giving
evidence about a conversation I had with the local Judge,* who

wanted my paper to say black was white. Nasty, in a small place & the Judge (a Cambridge man) shrieks as if I had cut his throat – which I may perhaps have done. But I have small appetite for playing the Hero – a role which I feel ill becomes a newspaper man. But compared with lawyers & cops, we're saints!

May I turn to you & Virginia for some help & advice? I need a disease. Specifically, I am at work on a novel [*A Mixture of Frailties*] in which the heroine's mother must die. She is a woman of vulgar nature, about 50–55, who has been a lifelong heavy eater, & in particular an eater of sweet things – jams, pastries, conserves & all the sugary stuff. What could she die of that is legitimate, yet has a touch of style to it? Science is so meddlesome nowadays that there are not too many good diseases left to fiction. I see by the *Encyclopaedia* that gormandizers may become *lardaceous*, but this is not fatal. Diabetes is no longer a killer. Is fatty degeneration still a possibility? And can it be combined with a nice, monstrous dropsy? I should be *so* much obliged for a good, authentic medical horror which a greedy woman could die of.

The novel eats up all my spare time. It is harder to write than anything I have yet attempted, & on a larger scale. It gives me the jim-jams, for in it I am not relying on my talents as a funny-man to get me by. I am – so help me – trying to be a serious novelist. Of course there are some larky bits in it, & some of the grotesquerie which is inseparable from my view of life, but basically it is serious. I wish you were nearer & I would plague you for an opinion on it. It is ¾ done but some of the hardest work is yet to be done. – By the way, my play *Hunting Stuart* may be done on Broadway this next winter: the producer is trying to find a star. The whole Broadway set-up makes me tremble – but they are very free with their money.

All good wishes to you & Virginia & the children from us all.

Rob

P.S. Poor Douglas LePan has had a heart attack – a very heavy smoker – 60 to 80 cigs a day: poor chap, it will cramp his excellent career in the diplomatic service.*

To TYRONE and JUDITH GUTHRIE

[Peterborough, Ontario]
Saturday October 19 [1957]

Dear Tony and Judy:

Very sorry you have been seedy; but how good of you to write when feeling languid! Glad you liked the wire for *Maria Stuart;** wires which one hopes will be comic in effect have a way of blunting, or going sour, in transmission. Yet one can't go on forever saying "Masses of love and great slobbering kisses darling" in first-night wires – it is trite. . . .

We want very much to see *Maria Stuart* but don't see how it can be done. The one weekend we could get down and see both *MS* and *Macropoulos** is a long-weekend for the girls from school, and as they have been very miserable with 'flu this term we must be with them and see that they have a cheery time. But we shall come down later to see *Mac.* But one so rarely has a chance to see a big piece of German roman-ticism that we are deeply disappointed not to be able to make it. Did we ever tell you about seeing *Faust* in Edinburgh,* in German? Wow!

Another complication is that my new novel [*A Mixture of Frailties*] is promised to the agent for December 1, and I am still writing the last section! And I have run into a very bad patch with my writing, and stuff keeps coming out which is pure *Peg's Paper* or even *The Happy Mag.** To my horror sentences frame themselves like this – "Judge of our heroine's amazement when she opened the door, only to discover that Truman Thoroughgood, deemed by her to be in Rome, stood on the threshold, his finely moulded lips parted in a shy, sweet smile." I seem to be in the grip of some evil sprite, and I am really getting into a tizzy. Indeed, my *lichen planis* (you may recall my fretting scall,* or tetter) has broken out again. The Dr. says it is nerves, but I know it is literary frustration. Writing will be the death of me, one of these days – probably in about forty or fifty years.

You ask about *Hunting Stuart.* Nothing seems to be happening, and I don't much care. More and more I feel that I am not really a play-wright, just a stage-struck fellow. I am committed to writing another play [*General Confession*] for the Crest, to be done next Spring, and I think that is about my speed. My N.Y. producer-man says plays must be SOCKO, and I am not a bit SOCKO – I am more what you might call SPLOSH. – But the novel, if I can only get out of the treacly abyss in which I wallow, will be the best thing I have ever written. I have felt it more deeply than anything else, and if it is a failure, do you know what I shall do – I shall just sit right down and write another and better one, that's what I'll do. It is my fate to write, whether I do very well at it or not, and more and more I do not care what people think of my stuff. I suppose this is the megalomania of the writer.

Speaking of megalomania, Brenda and I went on Thursday night to see a Passion Play which was done here in our Memorial Centre – that big barrack where you saw the Canadian Ballet. I attended as the Brooks Atkinson of the Kawarthas. It was a frightening mess, presented as the Oberammergau Passion Play,* but actually a gang of American tent-show hams, headed by a tricky wee thing called Val Balfour, who played the role of He whom Judy always speaks of – with a delicacy which leaves me breathless – as A Certain Person. He was a megalomaniac, if you like! *All* the light, arm's length space on every side, every possible effect – and a voice of brass, with personality to match.* Effective, in a ghastly fashion, for he scored off everybody, just like Ethel Barrymore in *The Corn Is Green*,* but irreverent, vulgar and hateful. And the music! I swear upon the bones of my grandmother – though I know you will think this a tale – that when Jesus died on the cross, the recorded sound-track broke into that poignant American ballad *Goin' Home*!* But it was like catnip to some of the God-intoxicated locals – though justice demands that I say that many others were as disgusted as we were. I gave it the skelping of a lifetime in the *Ex*,* so if you hear that Maddened Christus Axe-Slays Bearded Critic, you will know what has happened.

Adieu, and hope you will both soon be well.

Rob.

*Brenda described him as the Wolfit of the Bible-Belt.

To SAM AJZENSTAT

Peterborough Examiner
Peterborough, Ontario
January 24, 1958

Samuel Ajzenstat (1937–   ), Canadian,
was Associate Editor (Features) of The
Varsity, *the University of Toronto's student*
newspaper. He later became a professor
of philosophy at McMaster University in
Hamilton, Ontario. He had written to say
that The Varsity *was planning to publish*
an extensive survey of Canadian culture
and was seeking information from a
number of prominent figures, Davies
among them. The survey appeared on
February 21, 1958.

[Dear Mr. Ajzenstat:]

I shall try to reply to your letter of January 15th as briefly as possible. Regarding the state of Canadian writing at present, I think
that we have about as many good writers per thousand of population as the U.S.A. What we lack is that large body of writers who
may be called second-rate (by which I mean that they are able craftsmen and men of ideas, but not especially original in their outlook)
which contributes so heavily and so valuably to writing in Great
Britain. I think that this is a fault of our Canadian system of education which does not encourage really good writing, does not teach
grammar or rhetoric, and tends to encourage the pioneer idea that
there is something suspiciously glib about a man who expresses himself
clearly and easily.

It is not at all difficult for any decent writer to find a publisher in
Canada; publishers are crying aloud for writers and Canadian publishers are very considerate of the claims of their fellow countrymen.
Finding an audience, however, is a very different matter, for Canadians
are still rather shy of reading about themselves. The foolish sensitivity about reading a novel which is set in a recognizable Canadian town
is as great today as it was in 1934 when Morley Callaghan* published
Such Is My Beloved. A Canadian publisher thinks that he has done
well with a Canadian book if it sells 5,000 copies. This shows us in

a very unfavourable light in comparison with, for instance, Australia.

I don't really know what a Canadian subject is. A Canadian writer should be free to write about anything. However, there is beginning to be something which might be called a Canadian outlook in writing and at its best it is less sentimental than American writing, and not plagued with the fads which influence so much writing in England. I saw recently that someone was complaining that Canada had no Angry Young Men;* I think that Canadians are a little too shrewd and a little too close to the earth to fall for the Angry Young Man nonsense, just as they never got stewed up about the proletarian nonsense which was popular in the U.S.A. until recently. These are both forms of sentimentality and the Canadian writer at his best is not a sentimentalist. He has the fault which corresponds to this virtue however; his writing is apt to be chilly and unemotional.

Culture is simply the way in which people live. The culture of the cave man meant sitting on a rock gnawing a bone. The culture of Germany between 1935 and 1945 involved making soap out of Jews. One of our difficulties in Canada is that too many of us insist on thinking of culture as a kind of lacy frill which is attached to the edge of life, whereas to be worth anything it must be the whole fabric of life. We have a culture now which is in some respects remarkable, but which has not given rise to any art of a stature which commands the attention of the world. We may perhaps do so, but there is no reason why we should not absorb and make the fullest use of the art from other parts of the world. As Dr. W. A. MacKintosh of Queen's University said to the Royal Society* last June – "A national culture is not a direct object of endeavour. It is not created as a gown by a designer. It is a by-product. Further, a country can have a truly national culture, incredibly bad. Canadians should aim at what is excellent intellectually, aesthetically, socially. If it is real, it will ultimately prove to be Canadian but its justification will be that it is excellent."

There are excellent historical reasons why Canadians as a people tend to be somewhat chilly in temperament and emotionally thin-blooded. There is no good reason, however, why we should be considered as a nation as ignorant as we are, unless it is that we are intellectually lazy, but I think that coldness of temperament and narrowness of emotional

range beget intellectual laziness, and some of our national troubles
may have their roots in this barren soil.

Yours sincerely,

[Robertson Davies]

To LULIE WESTFELDT

361 Park Street
Peterborough, Ontario
October 27, 1958

*Lulie Westfeldt (1896–1965), American,
was a gifted Alexander teacher based in
New York City. She had been trained by
F. M. Alexander himself. Davies wrote this
testimonial for her book* F. Matthias
Alexander: The Man and His Work.

[Dear Miss Westfeldt:]

   ... by 1955 I needed Alexander treatment badly, for I was worried
by frequent and prolonged numbness in my left leg which had
become so troublesome that at times it would make me stumble. A
physician had examined it carefully, and could find nothing wrong,
though he established to his own satisfaction that it was numb (which
I had told him before) by sticking pins in it; his only proposal was
that I might have an exploratory operation to see if I had a slipped
disc, if the leg grew worse. Fortunately in November of this year I
met a pupil of yours, and made arrangements to see you for lessons
the following January.
   Circumstances made it impossible for me to take lessons for more
than a week, as I live at a considerable distance from New York, but
as my wife was also keenly interested we came to you together, and
you undertook to teach us in successive half-hours, so that while one
was being instructed, the other watched. I do not think that you were
confident that so short a period of lessons could do us much good,
but it did. By the end of the week my left leg was much more comfortable, and we went away determined to continue working at home
on the lines established by you.

Since that time we have visited you every six months, and have had, all told, about thirty lessons each. Between visits to you we have worked by ourselves, usually twice a day and missing, I think, no more than ten days in thirty months.

The results are of a kind difficult to describe, but fully bearing out [Aldous] Huxley's . . . statement,* that "such physical self-awareness and self-control leads to, and to some extent is actually a form of, mental and moral self-awareness and self control."

This sounds like tall talk, but in actual experience it is not so.

To be specific, the trouble in my left leg disappeared and has only returned on two or three occasions when I was particularly tired, and then yielded at once to some Alexander work. Apart from this I have had a marked increase in physical well-being, and have been free from the periods of exhaustion and nervous weariness which used to follow intense work.

My work (which is that of a writer and editor) forces me to spend long hours – ten hours a day is by no means uncommon – sitting at a desk, writing or reading. Only those who have done it for twenty years know how physically wearisome and demanding such immobility can be; in fact, it is not immobility, but a routine of twists, fidgets and jumps caused by thwarted muscles and nerves. Nature quite often gives the physiques of farm-labourers to those who do sedentary work. I am such a person, and the inactivity which my work requires is bought at a dear price, which is exacted in the currency of numb legs, dyspepsia, back-ache, head-ache, ill-temper, misanthropy and a weariness of body which demands violent physical exercise – which weariness of mind makes unendurably distasteful.

Lessons with you, and daily private exercise along the lines you point out, has made a most welcome change in this physical misery. I still sit at a desk all day and part of the night, but I sit in quite a different way; walking, which is my favourite exercise, has taken on a new quality of pleasure; because I am not nervously exacerbated, I plan my work better, and actually get more work done with less trouble; my misanthropy has dropped to quite a low level for one engaged in a notoriously misanthropic profession.

I know that you discourage your pupils from talking about psychological changes which follow work on Alexander's lines, and I appreciate the fact that cranks and featherweight messiahs must be discouraged. Nevertheless, I must add that during thirty months of Alexander work I have found new powers of endurance which are not solely physical. Everybody in their forties is trying to get their second wind for the second and hardest lap in the race of life; some people find it one way and some another, and a sad number do not find it at all, and seem to shrivel as the years pass. Whether I have found it in the Alexander lessons and their application I cannot, with complete confidence, say, but certainly they pointed the way to a development for which I had hoped, but could not have reached unaided. As you yourself have said, the work emphasizes and discloses what the pupil essentially *is*, and in my own case I regard it as a means of self-exploration, as well as a technique of physical re-training.

With every good wish, I am

Yours sincerely,

[Robertson Davies]

To HUGH MACLENNAN

Peterborough Examiner
Peterborough, Ontario
January 14, 1959

Hugh MacLennan (1907–90), Canadian novelist and essayist, was a defining voice in Canadian literature.

Dear Hugh:

I cannot thank you enough for your letter about *A Mixture of Frailties* for I value your opinion more than that of just about anybody in Canada. You *know* what writing a novel is, and they – including most of our fellow-novelists – don't. The more I write, the tougher the problems seem to be: you have grappled with them, and given them a fall, & your praise is very sweet.

I particularly thank you for what you say about my "innate tough-ness." The manner of writing which is native to me is mistaken by a great many readers & critics for an easy-going, mildly humorous one. I have been called an imitator of Angela Thirkell!* But what they mistake for frolic is often despair. I am strongly conscious of the pathos, irony & often tragedy of daily life, & I try to write of it with understanding, & some courage, but without whimpering, or resort-ing to wooden thunder. It is painful to be thought a lightweight, in consequence.

However, all this is familiar to you, for you have been through it all. It was good of you to know that I would welcome kind words from a real author, and not to withhold them. Be assured that I shall keep your letter, for I am very proud of it.

With every good wish

Rob.

Dearest Pink & Darlings J. & R.:

Here I am at the end of my first day at Annagh-ma-Kerrig, in a very comfortable & big bedroom, rather like a library, really, for it has three walls all of books, a big, old bed, with a terrible mattress & seven wool blankets & an ancient eider-down: also a hot bottle. A dressing-room with a candle in it, but the bedroom has the electricity—an Anglepoise lamp, v. good. A large white chummy which I am bidden to use, but won't: would rather go down a long dark passage to the w.c. A queer old house, this, somewhat ruinous & full of junk—part of the antlers of an Irish elk, two pianos in bad tune, endless chairs not quite safe. Big: not so big as Leighton, but big & rambling & inconvenient. A large lake in the park, icy cold, where T. & J. make themselves swim. A bouncy, happy wee dog, & a marma-lade cat. Plenty to eat, so far, but threats of having to eat fish from the lake. The fruit which isn't good enough to sell is kept for the house, & so wooden peaches turn up, & greenish rasp-berries. This sounds awful but is really v. pleasant.

This morning T. & I began work on the play. Read it all & he likes it very well but keeps saying 'Wouldn't it make a good film'. Has several good suggestions. That took all morning. Right after dinner I was put to work to pick raspberries, wild ones for the bottom of the baskets & tame ones on top. They fetch 1/3 a pound, apparently. Then tea & right to work proof-reading T's book. They seem to slave, & then stop & play patience. Judy's cough is, if anything, worse: I tremble for her. T. looks a good deal older & has an arthritic elbow which gives him a good deal of pain. Not surprised, for

SECTION

IV

FEBRUARY 1959–JULY 1963 – *A VOICE FROM THE ATTIC* COMPLETED AND PUBLISHED; *LEAVEN OF MALICE* ADAPTED AS THE PLAY *LOVE AND LIBEL*; *A MASQUE OF MR PUNCH* WRITTEN; MASSEY COLLEGE PLANNED

avies, 45 as this section begins, continued to edit the *Examiner* throughout this period. In 1960, however, he accepted responsibilities that took him out of Peterborough for part of every week, and began to shift responsibility onto the shoulders of associate editor Ralph Hancox, who had succeeded Tom Allen in 1957. In 1963, Hancox took over the editorship completely. Davies brought his second stint as literary editor of *Saturday Night* to a close early in 1959 when he committed himself to writing a weekly column called "A Writer's Diary" for the *Toronto Star* syndicate. His review articles on books for *Saturday Night* had meanwhile caught the attention of Alfred Knopf. In 1958 Knopf approached Davies for a book and by the end of 1959 Davies was revising the manuscript of *A Voice from the Attic* for him.

When he turned *Tempest-Tost* into a novel, Davies had ceased to think of the theatre as the place where he would make his mark; but he was now suddenly presented with an astonishing theatrical opportunity. The

Theater Guild of New York wanted to produce an adaptation of his novel *Leaven of Malice*, with Tyrone Guthrie as director. So, in the summer of 1959, draft script in hand, he made a pilgrimage to Guthrie's huge uncomfortable house "Annagh-ma-kerrig" in County Monaghan, where the two of them reworked the material. In the fall of 1960, the play, now called *Love and Libel*, went into rehearsal and opened in Toronto. It went on the road to Detroit and Boston before opening – and abruptly closing – in New York. Davies, acting as dramaturge, found himself required to make innumerable adjustments each day, and hated it.

At this juncture, fortunately, a new adventure presented itself: Vincent Massey invited him to become the founding Master of a new residential College for graduate students at the University of Toronto. Davies, no academic but by now hugely knowledgeable in certain areas, had earlier been asked to lecture on drama at the University's Trinity College, which had brought him to Toronto two days a week in the fall of 1960. But the Mastership of Massey College was an opportunity of a very different sort, and it carried with it an appointment in the Graduate School. For the next two years, he spent part of every week in Toronto, participating in planning sessions for the College and teaching undergraduate drama courses as background for the teaching he was to do for the Graduate School beginning in 1962–63.

Davies continued to travel to Stratford to attend meetings of the board of governors, and, with Brenda, to see each season's plays. He and Brenda took two trips abroad in this period, the first to Portugal and the second to the Netherlands, spending some of their time in the U.K. as had become their custom. The family moved from Peterborough into the Master's Lodgings of Massey College in Toronto in June of 1963.

To RALEIGH PARKIN

Peterborough Examiner
Peterborough, Ontario
February 26, 1959

*Raleigh Parkin (1896–1977) Canadian,
was Associate Treasurer of Sun Life
Assurance Company in Montreal. In
January 1959 Davies had begun to write a
Saturday column for the Toronto Star
syndicate, called "A Writer's Diary." For
the first three months he appended a bit of
"Canadiana" to each column – a
quotation and a little explanation of its
context – in order, he claimed, to remedy
Canada's lack of "a mythic history from
which we can draw refreshment, marvels
and grotesquerie."*

Dear Mʳ· Parkin:

Yes, I can give you the source of the quotation which was attributed to your father, the late Sir George Parkin;* it came entirely out
of my own imagination. However, when I was a schoolboy at Upper
Canada College I heard your father quoted so often, particularly by
the late William Mowbray,* that he has always figured in my mind as
a source of wise sayings. Unfortunately Mowbray's favourite gem
from your father's collection was "A gentleman never appears at
breakfast in his slippers," and this was always followed by a detention.

In the first of these columns which I published in the *Star*, I made
some general remarks to the effect that Canada has just as good a store
of legend and comment to draw upon as the U.S.A., and that it is a
pity that we overlook it. I said that under the general heading
Canadiana I would publish something of the sort every week, and
since then I have published remarks attributed to Pauline Johnson, Sir
William Osler, Sir John A. Macdonald, Goldwin Smith, Bliss Carman
and Sir William Peterson.* All of these I made up, not wantonly, but
with some consideration for what might have been said and where it
might have been said by the man in question. What I wanted to do
was to see how long it would be before somebody questioned these
quotations, because I have an unflattering theory about Canadians that

they will accept almost anything that is told to them with a sufficient degree of solemnity. My quotation from Sir William Peterson – "To discover the truth about a man consider the precise opposite of popular opinion on him; this will not give you the whole truth, but it will point the way," – seems to me to be quite in Sir William's vein; he was a great-uncle of my wife's and a good deal of what he said, and the way he said it, has come down through her family. When preparing the piece which I attributed to your father I did some reading about him and decided that one of his Johannesburg visits would be a good setting for such a remark.

When I mentioned in the *Star* that I was going to present these quotations I did not represent them as being other than fiction, but as I say, I wanted to see how long it would be before somebody found me out. You have done so, and it now lies in your power either to denounce me as a vicious trifler with the feelings of a large number of patriotic Canadians, or to keep your own counsel and see how long it will be before other people do what you have done.

Enclosed is clip of the column in which the quotation appeared.

With good wishes I am

Yours sincerely,

Robertson Davies

PS: If this use of Sir George's name hurts your feelings, I apologize, but I assure you that nothing in the way of serious imposture was meant.

To GRAHAM MCINNES

[Peterborough, Ontario]
June 26. [1959]

*Graham McInnes, still with Canada's
Department of External Affairs, was
Counsellor (and later Minister) at Canada
House in London 1959–62.*

Dear Graham:

Brenda has written to Joan, but I wanted to drop you a line myself, to say how sorry I am that we shall not be able to meet in London. . . .

The Queen is here now, and what a hubbub! The Toronto papers are determined to prove that the nation as a whole are indifferent or hostile to the visit, and are being bloody rude – trying to catch H.M. off balance, or snarling at Philip, or he at her, discovering that Philip scratched the paint on the yacht when docking it, warning him that he is not to be "arrogant" to Canadian reporters – it is nasty, but it is also provincial and petty to a sickening degree. Truly, we are a nation of clowns. The other side of the picture is the crowding and shoving to get at the Royal Person, the pitched battles about whose brat shall give her flowers, the offers to lend her a doggy, the parading of the blind, the halt and the Officially Piteous of all kinds. Last night on the telly we watched the Great Ball in Montreal; Mayor Fournier* belongs to that school of Noblesse which emphasizes all points by jabbing his forefinger at the royal bosom; Rabbi Whosis (in what seemed to be a spangled skullcap) showed her photographs of his grandchildren; Fournier, height four feet two, danced very decently, for you could have passed a top hat between his tum and the Queen's. It was a riot – almost literally, for Mounties had to chase the nobility and gentry off the dance floor. The telly announcer returned, again and again, with loving emphasis, to a royal coat-of-arms on the wall, which he assured us droolingly, was "entirely made of plastic"..... I wonder if the Queen and the Duke have hilarious post mortems in their bedroom, like the rest of us?

Will phone when I get to London just on the chance

Love to you both

Rob

To BRENDA, JENNIFER and
ROSAMOND DAVIES

Annagh-ma-kerrig
[Doohat: Co. Monaghan
Eire]
Friday: July 10. [1959]

Davies was in Ireland at Annagh-ma-kerrig, Tyrone and Judith Guthrie's home in County Monaghan, where he was to collaborate with Guthrie on turning his novel Leaven of Malice *into a play for the Theater Guild in New York. He brought with him a fresh outline and a two-act script.*

Dearest Pink & Darlings J. & R:

Here I am at the end of my first day at Annagh-ma-kerrig, in a very comfortable & big bedroom, rather like a library, really, for it has three walls all of books: a big, old bed, with a terrible mattress & *seven* wool blankets & an ancient eiderdown: also a hot bottle. A dressing-room with a candle in it, but the bedroom has the electricity – an Anglepoise lamp, v. good. A large white chummy which I am bidden to use, but won't: would rather go down a long dark passage to the w.c. A queer old house, this, somewhat ruinous & full of junk – part of the antlers of an Irish elk, two pianos in bad tune, endless chairs not quite safe. Big: not so big as Leighton, but big & rambling & inconvenient. A large lake in the park, icy cold, where T. & J. make themselves swim. A bouncy, yappy wee dog, & a marmalade cat. Plenty to eat, so far, but threats of having to eat fish from the lake. The fruit which isn't good enough to sell is kept for the house, & so wooden peaches turn up, & greenish raspberries. This sounds awful but is really v. pleasant.

This morning T. & I began work on the play. Read it all & he likes it very well but keeps saying "Wouldn't it make a good film." Has several good suggestions. That took all morning. Right after dinner I was put to work to pick raspberries, wild ones for the bottom of the baskets & tame ones on top. They fetch ⅓ a pound, apparently. Then tea & right to work proof-reading T's book.* They seem to slave, & then stop & play patience. Judy's cough is, if anything, worse: I tremble for her. T. looks a good deal older & has an arthritic elbow which gives him a good deal of pain. Not surprised, for it is terribly damp here. The countryside is pretty but rolling: no mountains. They are expecting a horde of guests* & one came today – T's sister's adopted son, Joe Hone,* who is v. handsome in the Irish way – big eyes, high colour & curly hair.

I am just beginning to feel human, for the flight was rather tiresome. I sat next to an old man who was very deaf & stupid, & kept hounding me about what I was reading. "I used to be a great reader" roared he: "read everything – love stories, Westerns & all. Deepest book I ever read was called *She* by a fella named Haggard:* ever hear of it?" I had enough of him before Prestwick. Then a long ride by bus to Glasgow, & another to Renfrew, to another airport. I got the Gs 200 State Express [cigarettes] on the plane & a bottle of whisky at Glasgow. Waited 2 hours at Renfrew, then by small plane to Belfast: Tony met me with his wee Morris,* & we drove 60 miles here. Rather exhausting & I had trouble sleeping as I felt the plane all night. The old deafie really was a bore: grabbed the stewardess by the arm as soon as he got on & yelled: "Got a men's room on this contraption? Not so young as I was and have to go a lot." She was flustered. On the bus I was treed by a Jewish lawyer from Chicago who explained to me how wasteful it was for the Scotch to build so many stone houses. I seem to attract the confidences of such people.

No doubt I shall settle down more as time goes on but at present I am restless. When we really get to work on the play I expect I shall feel better but just at present I find the atmosphere queer & disturbing. Hard to say why, for T. & J. are most hospitable, but the climate is odd – lovely sun today & roasting hot during the berry-picking – but damp & clammy at night, & though it is now dark it was light outside till 10.30. Tony says the climate is "very sluggish." But I am an awful old fusser & it isn't *clean*: disloyal to write this under my host's roof but it fidges [fidgets] me. Because I was in the w. c. today Tony peed in the face-basin! This sort of thing gives me the creeps, & I rather dread to wash. Call me North American if you will, but I don't like it.

Shall write again in a day or so when less discomposed. Do hope you are having a good time at Sandgate.* My regards to Lulie Westfeldt. Tell her my left leg has eased up a lot, revealing a stiffness in my right ankle, which seems slowly to be working itself free as my back gets stronger.

Must climb under the 7 blankets now. My love to you all & I wish you were here or I was there.

(Very special love to you, Pinkie dearest.)

Rob

To BRENDA DAVIES

Annagh-ma-kerrig
Doohat: Co. Monaghan
Eire
Wednesday, July 15 [1959]

Dearest Pink:

It is ten o'clock & I have come upstairs because I wanted electric light: in the drawing-room (which boasts *one* globe) they have not yet put it on, & though I can neither read nor write, Tony & Meg Davis are playing patience. Meg is about 75 & an old friend from Belfast & she & T. bully one another unmercifully: she "knew the garden" in T's mother's time, & insists it has gone to ruin & goads T. to great feats of weeding & transplanting. I was sucked in after tea for some heavy weeding: they have the scutch-grass very badly. It is locally called "twitch" & is in the box-hedges, so when Meg says to Judy "Ye've terrible twitch in your box" I know that no indecency is meant. Old Meg is the only person I have ever seen put Tony down. Tonight we had peaches & he & Judy carefully peeled theirs. "Nobody who is anybody at all eats a peach with the skin on" says T. "Trash!" says Meg; "nobody who is anybody cares tuppence whether anybody thinks they're anybody!" She wears a hearing-aid, & Tony bullies her about not hearing. Apparently last Christmas they had a dreadful Scene & wouldn't speak.

– The Reas & Peter Zeisler* left this morning: they were very nice & bid us look them up in New York. Tony & I did some good work on the play this morning: it is beginning to take shape: he wants more short scenes & Mrs. Bridgetower brought in. Also the plan of production begins to emerge – many small trucks with wee bits of setting on them. This means a good deal of patching & tinkering, but not as much work as I was prepared for: but tinkering takes time. Fortunately I have a nice room to work in, & Tony's beast of a typewriter. So most of the day I peg away, & turn up for meals. Last night he read us all the last chapter of his book, which is very good. Then we talked about *J. B.**

– Yesterday afternoon we all drove over to visit – who do you think? – Lord Rossmore* & his mother: he is about 28, & I told him of Mrs. Stewart* who, as Miss Frances Browne of Dublin, nearly married an ancestor of his, but went to Douro [near Peterborough, Ontario] instead. They have an extraordinary library, containing first editions of a great many eighteenth century plays, & a lot of treasures. But Lady R. is very casual: she has mislaid a Shakespeare Fourth Folio, & can't think what she has done with a first edition of *Pride & Prejudice*. She took it to bed one night "to pretend I was living a hundred years ago" & it got lost. Fell in the po. & was thrown out, I expect. They are very short of money & live in the dower house. The castle, built in 1870, is in ruins from dry-rot. It is hideous, but Mrs. Rea, like a real American, was in raptures over it & thought it was medieval. Lady R. does all the work herself, & has a rough woman twice a week. But she is having a fête for 100 tomorrow. They have a huge raspberry patch & took TWO TONS off it this season: this makes Judy's mouth water, as a rival in the berry trade. I don't understand Judy. This morning a farm girl came to order flowers for her wedding: two bunches, & three buttonholes for men: total payment 5/-, which Judy pouches with glee. I am either a snob, or common, or something, but I would not wish to do floral work for farm-girls if I were the lady of the manor. And they are! "The Docthor" is a very great local figure. Incidentally I find that Judy's father was a very strict & devout Baptist. Surely this explains her deep concern with what is & what is not common? But Old Meg takes no nonsense. "Trash!" she cries, at any sign of hoity-toitiness.

– Tony is a strange one. After the weeding I wanted a bath, to avoid stiffness. "Hurry up," he cried, "& I'll get into your water, so we won't run down the tank." And he did, & pushed in while I was having my bath & nakedly oerhung me while I was in the tub. Then hopped in & swilled around in my suds, with a right good will.

– My letters to you seem to be a long whimper about the dirtiness of the Gs, which I do not mean, but it is worrisome. The dishwashing! But Old Meg will have none of it. "Put that back, Tony it's DORTY!" she screams. I warm to her, I must say, & she to me, I think, for she offers me toffees from her personal store.

– Well, I am achieving what I came for, because the play goes ahead, & T's ideas are, on the whole, good. I remember Hugh McCraig's advice,* & handle him with kid gloves. But I don't think it will be done in January because he is committed to do *Hamlet* in London with Chris Plum,* then. The more I see of theatre things the more I marvel at their strange slipperiness. But he intends to do it all right, & is truly interested in the collaboration. He has bushels of ideas, & thank Heaven he leaves it to me to carry them out.

– Eleven o'clock now & quite dark outside. Goodnight, dearest Brenda: I miss you very much, & wish you were here to halve the discomfort & double the fun. Because there *is* a lot of fun, but the kind that would be twice as delightful if you were here to share it. It was very stupid of me to come away without a picture of you.

Much love to the girls & unreckoned heaps of it to you –

Rob

To BRENDA DAVIES

Annagh-ma-kerrig
Doohat: C<u>o</u> Monaghan
Eire
July 28 [1959]

Dearest Pinkie:

. . . Today, Tuesday I went to Dublin where I hadn't expected to get, with Tony, Joe Hone & Christopher Scaife.* Lovely drive & Dublin is a charming city, but smaller than I had foreseen. The Liffey is a dirty creek. Tony went off on biz. & Joe took Christopher & me to Trinity Coll. Library, a superb building, where we saw the Book of Kells, one of the greatest of all illuminated manuscripts – a thrill. Then we went to the National Gallery, which was not v. gd. – too many pictures of not very famous Irishmen by nobodies. Then to a v. gd. bookshop. Then to a famous bar, immortalized in *Ulysses* – Davy Byrnes' – a dump. Then I took the lot to a v. gd. restaurant for lunch & crammed them, & tanked them up with Canadian whisky, & washed them all over in wine, while they exclaimed at my princely extravagance. Total bill £4:15:0 [£4 15s. 0d.], which I do not call a lot for a first-rate lunch & wizard booze-up for four!

– Then we dropped Joe, & rushed Christopher to the airport, then Tony & I drove home & he talked casting for my play. His pick:* Prof. Vambrace – Micheál MacLiammóir: Mrs. Bridgetower – Esmé Church: Solly B'twr – Bill Shatner: Pearl, a N.Y. girl called Nancy Malone, v. pretty: Gloster Ridley – Bill Hutt: Swithin Shillito – Nick [Eric] House: Humphrey Cobbler – Douglas Campbell, the rest, Davy Gam, Esq. but perhaps Milly Hall for Edith Little. He thinks a Canadian cast, with a few of name, would have class, & MacLiammóir would bring great flamboyance. He will be in N. Y. in late Sept. & thinks we ought to see the Theater Guild together. Could we drive down then? Or go by 'plane? You *must* come; can't do any more on this play without you. It is practically done now, & much changed for the better: as you['ll] see, Mrs. B'twr is in as a principal character &

a good one. Tony has made me see it as a *play* & formerly I could not get rid of the idea of the novel. But what hard work it has been: I have really toiled, & I look forward eagerly to London for a rest & change. Today was my first real day off since coming here. I have plugged away Sundays & all, for T. wants everything done in a hurry.

Wish you were going to be in London with me: but we must have an autumn toit in N. Y. – Tell Jennie I was startled to see a collection box in a post office which said "Please put in something for the black babies"* – but it was for African missions & not what I thought.

Good Night my dearest: in two weeks exactly I shall be home. Huge hugs & kisses

Rob

To BRENDA DAVIES

Norfolk Hotel
Surrey St., London
July 31 [1959]

Dearest Pinkie:

Hope my cable abt. the phone call got to you in good time & was reassuring. I know I sounded idiotic on the phone, but I could hardly hear you, & a horde of people were milling about, excited by a call from Canada, & I could not say anything but grumpy nonsense. But I was thrilled to bits to hear your voice, & do thank you for calling.

– Yesterday (Thursday) was a brute. It is a long story. Tony sent back the first 60 corrected galleys of his book (about 150 pages) in the envelope his publishers sent them in. On this envelope was a sticker which said the name of the publisher and "Return postage guaranteed." Now everybody knows that only works if it is in the country of origin & then only if the parcel goes astray. But Tony gave the package to Joe Hone to post & Joe, like a real Irish genius, put no stamps on it, because of what the sticker said. He & Tony rejoiced at this piece of cleverness & *money-saving*. But as I foresaw the package did not reach the U.S.A. & is probably in the Dead Letter Office in Dublin. So the publishers cabled Tony in a sweat, asking him to do the second or duplicate set of galleys which they always send in case of emergency. That was bad enough, but Tony had written in quite a lot of new stuff, & like a dizzard had destroyed his MSS! So in his agony he turned to me & with just an hour for lunch we sat in his study & corrected proofs yesterday from 9.30 a.m. to 7.30 p.m. So if I talked like a loony on the phone it was because my wits were addled. But we got it all done at last, & Tony wrote some of the new stuff & I wrote some. It was a tough day & meant I did not get my play finally completed as I had hoped.

– Last night I went to bed early, but could not sleep, & woke at 3, & lay awake till 4.30, when it was time to get up & dress, have a sketchy bkfst. & set out to drive to Belfast. Dr. Steele* drove us in his big Citroen, a comfortable car, but the Gs mocked it because he loves it so. Made it in good time to get the plane at 8.30: bkfst. again on plane.

– I gave Judy £10 to buy napkins & told her formal designs – no kittens playing with balls of wool. So they will arrive some time & there will be duty to pay on them but we can do nothing about that.

– I am at the Norfolk, which is a mistake because I thought it was the Howard. It is smaller & dumpier, but what the hell, Archie;* it is v. *clean*. Will write again soon, so great big hugs . . . I count the hours till we are together again –

Rob.

To BRENDA DAVIES

[Norfolk Hotel
Surrey St., London]
Tuesday, August 4. [1959]

Dearest Pink:

No use writing any more after this, as I shall be home on Saturday
& the letter would follow me. Certainly I shall be glad to be back:
London is wonderful, but not alone. Curious the feeling you mention
in yᴵ letter that I might be so taken with the joys of solitude that I
would not come home: nothing could be less likely. I am a domestic
creature, quite apart from love for you, & the children. I quite like
travel, but don't really know how to do it. I can't *joy* in travel when
my heart is elsewhere. And my heart is where you are. In future we
must avoid these partings whenever we can – it may not always be
possible but we must try. – But as you say, your childhood did not
dispose you to think of husbands as home-loving creatures. Maybe
home wasn't as happy for them as mine is for me.

Now to affairs: . . . No, I don't think Miranda wants to "come out"
at the Mississauga Horse Ball: she's been presented; she's OUT. The
Ball is a lot of balls. But if you think she ought to go to seek Prince
Ch–rm–ng, we can decide when I get home. But Prince Ch–rm–ng
at the Horse Ball will be a Toronto Tory in his man–killer suit.

No sense giving you details about theatres & things. But I can tell
you this: the *Mermaid** was a disappointment – the show not the
theatre. Will tell *all* with gestures, when we meet.

Got a handsome present for WRD:* a pair of William IV wine
coolers, designed like our salts, beautiful melon bottoms, & a nice
simplicity. Wish they were for us? Should we bag them & give him
something else? They would look marvellous on our sideboard & just
the thing for flowers. What do you say? Got them in the silver vaults:
what awful trash most of the stuff down there is! Victorian junk. But
these have the real look. – I'll ponder the matter, but we've liked those
salts so much that I know we would like these too. And they would

be a nice reminder of my journey – I MUST stop selling myself those coolers! When I began to write to you there was no such notion in my head – honest!

How would it be if when I get home I get the play all corrected & ready for Miss W.* & then read it to you & Jenny? It will take a few days, but not too long. I like it very much in its present form.

Great hugs & kisses & I shall be watching out at Malton: if I'm long in Customs don't worry – no exemption & I'll have to declare one or two things.

Rob.

To THE VEN. ARCHDEACON C. SWANSON

Peterborough Examiner
Peterborough, Ontario
August 29, 1959

Cecil Swanson (1889–1984), English-born Canadian, was the rector of St. Paul's Church, 227 Bloor Street East, Toronto. The Anglican Church of Canada's draft report on the revision of The Book of Common Prayer *is under discussion in this letter.*

[Dear Archdeacon Swanson:]

Thank you for your letter of August 28th about Archbishop Trench's Glossary. I have been delighted with the interest which that article* appears to have caused, for I have heard from a number of people about it.

I was greatly interested in your comments on the revision of the Prayer Book. Although I can understand the reasons for revision, all my emotion is against them, for I grudge every change in the wording. When I am told that people do not understand some of the phrases in the Prayer Book I sometimes give offence by saying that I cannot see any reason why they should not take the very slight amount of trouble involved in acquainting themselves with that language. It appears that people are ready to take pains about almost anything except matters involving religion. It would not surely be a difficult matter to include a lecture on the language of the Prayer Book in the preparation for Confirmation.

In matters of language I am by no means persuaded that what is modern is necessarily good. If we study the history of any great language – Latin for instance – we find that it has a Golden Age which is likely to decline into a Silver Age, and may decline still further into what is sometimes called a Bronze Age. I occasionally receive the impression that English is right in the middle of the Plastic Age, and I do not see why the Prayer Book which was written in the Golden Age of English speech should be diminished in order to accord with latter-day taste.

Again thank you very much for your letter. I am

Yours sincerely,

[Robertson Davies]

To ALFRED A. KNOPF

Peterborough Examiner
Peterborough, Ontario
December 28, 1959

Alfred A. Knopf (1892–1984), the American publisher, was publishing Davies' A Voice from the Attic in 1960. The manuscript had been read, commented upon, and edited. Knopf had then written a warm letter to Davies drawing attention to the areas of concern, and the marked-up carbon copy had been sent to him for revision.

[Dear Alfred:]

I am covered with shame because Mr. Strauss has pointed out to me not only that I have been misusing the word comprise* all my life, but that I have shown a donkey-like spirit in not understanding his first explanation. After I had written to you I looked up the word again in Fowler's *The King's English* and discovered my way of using it listed under malapropisms, so instead of celebrating Christmas in the usual way, I went off into the woods for three days of ritual purification. The probable result will be that I shall never use the word again in my life, and of course I hope that Mr. Strauss will alter it suitably in the typescript. Will you please present him with my humble apologies and promises to try to do better in future. . . .

Yours sincerely,

[Rob]

To JOAN GRIFFITHS

Peterborough Examiner
Peterborough, Ontario
April 12, 1960

Joan Griffiths (1919–2001), Canadian, was headmistress of Bishop Strachan School for Girls 1958–62. Davies probably agreed to judge BSS's poetry competition because Miranda had been a student there 1953–59 and Jennifer, who came to the school in 1955, was still there. Marjorie Pickthall (1883–1922), the English-born Canadian poet after whom the competition was named, had been a student at BSS.

[Dear Miss Griffiths:]

I am returning the manuscripts of the entries in the Marjorie Pickthall competition. I have marked the winners and Honorable Mentions on the lists supplied by Miss Seaman* and will not repeat them here.

I hope that you will not be distressed by the fact that I have recommended that no prize be given in the senior poetry competition. I feel that the effect of any such prize would be to reduce the value of better work that has been done in the past. If I may offer a suggestion, I think that the girls would be much better off to concern themselves with the technique of verse and to moderate their desire to express thoughts and emotions which cannot bear the most friendly examination. It is not to be expected that they will be poets, but there is no reason in the world why they should not be competent verse technicians and some practice in this art would be invaluable to have in their study of English composition. I was struck by the poverty of vocabulary which handicapped them, and by a lack of a sense of the music of language and of congruity in the choice of words.

On many of the entries I have written extensive notes which I hope may be helpful to the contestants. As I have had no training as a teacher these notes may express opinions which will seem curious to the girls who read them, but I feel that they are questions which an interested and friendly person outside the educational world might suitably ask. I have been particularly careful to point out vagueness and pretension which are common faults of writers in their 'teens, and which, unless checked, can be ruinous in the university years. It was a most interesting experience to see the entries and I thoroughly enjoyed going through them.

With good wishes I am

Yours sincerely,

[Robertson Davies]

To ALFRED A. KNOPF

Peterborough Examiner
Peterborough, Ontario
June 13, 1960

[Dear Alfred:]

Thank you for your letter of June 7th. Everybody seems to like the Karsh picture, but me. I think it looks like a Y.M.C.A. secretary at a fancy dress ball, and greatly prefer the picture by Greenhill,* which you have. The *Post* commissioned that picture for its exclusive use, but Karsh has other portraits of me and would, I am sure, be glad to make one available if you wanted to use it.

I do not know whether you have ever had your portrait taken by Yousuf Karsh; if not I would be delighted to describe the experience to you when next we meet. Personally I find the unceasing flow of reminiscence about popes, emperors and celebrated adulterers who have been photographed somewhat depressing; I begin to feel that I am unworthy of so experienced a lens. I begin to wonder if a snapshot of a very small potato would not do just as well. This is not Mr. Karsh's intention. He wants me to feel that being photographed by him means that I have made the grade, but some twist in my nature produces exactly the opposite effect. I like Greenhill's picture, which I think makes me look like a man who can read a book without moving his lips and occasionally licking his thumb. However, if you like Karsh's pictures – and their publicity value is undeniable – he has one of me taken in the same posture as his famous photograph of Bernard Shaw,* in which I look like a sort of road company Shaw. There are also others in which I am doing fancy things with my hands which I would never dream of doing except under the spell of this extraordinary magician. Would you like me to send you a few samples?

With good wishes I am

Yours sincerely,

[Rob]

To HORACE W. DAVENPORT

[Peterborough, Ontario]
September 22, 1960

Dear Horace:

Delighted to hear from you, and very sorry the weekend won't work. . . .

However, Brenda and I hope to be in your part of the country in November. A play of mine, adapted from *Leaven of Malice* and now called *Love and Libel*, begins rehearsal in Toronto in two weeks, and will open there in November, and go on to Detroit for, I believe, a couple of weeks. If I am not much mistaken, Detroit is a reasonable distance from Ann Arbor, and if convenient we should like to run over for a day; we expect to have the car with us. After Detroit, Boston, and then into New York some time in mid-December.

It is being done by the Theater Guild, and is quite an elaborate affair, with an army of actors – about sixteen and understudies who also appear as crowd – and more scenery than the Oberammergau Passion Play. The director is Tyrone Guthrie, an old friend of mine, and absolutely first-rate at the job; designer David Hays* who does work that suits me perfectly – very modern in feeling but with a fine romantic dash. The actors mean nothing in New York, except for Dennis King* (whom you probably remember in *The Desert Song* a long time ago, but who is now a leading man, and not *quite* a big draw), but are mainly Canadians, trained in our Stratford Shakespearean Festival, and very capable; it is an ensemble play, rather than a star piece, and the Guild expects Guthrie to take the place of a star – which he may well do for some people, as *The Tenth Man*★ has been such a success. However, it is all on the knees of the gods.

Theatre people have been assuring me that the experience of having a play done in New York is a destructive and shredding one. Everybody sings this doleful lay, even Jacques Barzun,* who ought to have more philosophy. Perhaps it is so, but I must say that at 47 I am damned grateful to have the chance; if I am ever going to make a mark other than a rather local and tiny one, I had better get busy and do it. However, I am now too old, and have had too many plays done by quite good companies, to be simple-minded about it; neither am I capable of being destroyed by failure, or driven mad by success. The play is quite a decent piece of work, and I am sure the production will be first-rate. If it fails, well it fails, and not the first good piece of work to do so. However, Guthrie's plays do not fail ignominiously, so *un flop d'estime* is probably the worst I have to face. I hope you will be able to have a look at it in Detroit – though as I don't know about your distance this may be presumptuous – but if you can, I hope you will give me the pleasure of getting seats for you.

The reason for my being in Toronto on the 6th, to which I refer with far too much mystery above, is that this autumn and winter I am a visiting professor at Trinity College, University of Toronto, in English, and teach two days a week. I look forward to this with pleasure, as Trinity is an excellent place, and they are treating me with ill-deserved respect. It gets me out of Peterborough and into the company of quite a different kind of people, and Brenda appreciates this, too.

I am grateful for your occasional photographs of R.D.D., whom I have been neglecting shamefully in the matter of books, etc., but tell him that this is inadvertence and will be put right. What a handsome lad! I am anxious to meet him, though my touch with children is no surer than it ever was; they scare me, and I scare them, but eventually an uneasy sort of goodwill asserts itself, and when they get older we are much happier. This has happened with several children I have known.

Perhaps I should bring you up to date on our own. Miranda is now 19 and in second year university (English); she heads for the stage and next summer goes to Stratford as a festival apprentice, one of the seven chosen from over a hundred applicants. Jennifer will be 17 in two weeks, and is in her last year at school; was in Europe for two months this summer on one of those student tours. Rosamond is thirteen, and has just begun at boarding-school, which she likes greatly as she gets on well with people. We miss her at home, and that is one reason why Brenda is glad to get to Toronto for a couple of days a week, as she has friends there and lots to do.....

We both send our best wishes to you and Virginia . . .

<u>Rob</u>.

To THE CAST OF *LOVE AND LIBEL*

December 9. 1960

Davies posted this note at the Martin Beck Theatre in New York on the day Love and Libel *closed after only five performances. Amelia Hall, who played Edith Little, preserved it in one of her theatrical scrapbooks.*

My dear friends –

It is too bad that our venture should be so soon over, but – never explain, never apologise. It has been a great pleasure to work with you all, & I hope that I may do so again – soon, and under more favourable stars. Brenda & I wish you all the happiness & success you so plainly deserve.

Robertson Davies

To JOHN COOK

Peterborough Examiner
Peterborough, Ontario
May 26, 1961

John Cook (1918–), English composer, organist, and conductor, was writing the music for the Stratford Festival's production of Love's Labour's Lost, *one of many Stratford productions between 1955 and 1966 for which he created music. Michael Langham was directing the play. Davies had been on the Festival's Board of Governors since 1953 and was persuaded to remain until 1971.*

[Dear John:]

Following our talk by telephone on Thursday night, I did some digging in my Shakespeare books of reference and the situation about *Love's Labour's Lost*, Act 3, Scene 1, appears to be this: In the First Folio the first stage direction is simply "song"; the Quarto makes no mention of this song. The first words of the scene are –

Armado: Warble child..... and then the little boy sings Concolinel.

As I am sure you know, in Shakespeare's day "a warble" meant what we would now call a roulade – a charming vocal exercise without words. Therefore I would assume that Armado calls for a wordless warble by the boy, and that no song is necessary, unless you follow the Folio stage direction and have one before the scene begins.

If you mention this to Michael I wish you would tell him that I am resigning from the Board of Governors at the end of this season for very shame, as I feel that it would be indecent for me to stay on it any longer; however, he might appoint me Resident Pedant to the Theatre, which was what Tony Guthrie used to call me when I worked at the Old Vic, and used to be sent off to the British Museum to settle such questions as this.

With every good wish, I am

Yours sincerely

[Rob.]

To TANYA MOISEIWITSCH

[Peterborough, Ontario]
June 30 [1961]

In his review of Love's Labour's Lost *for the* Peterborough Examiner, *Davies had declared* (erroneously it would appear): "Tanya Moiseiwitsch, the designer, has dressed it in a style deriving from Watteau which suits it to perfection."*

Dear Tanya:

No, you may *not* call me Master! Pinhead, lackwit, slubberde-gullion druggel, sloppy journalist – you may call me all of these and any others that occur to you. I deserve them all. It was not simple ignorance: was I not hounded through the Louvre at the age of eleven by my Loving Parents, simply in order that I might have a rough notion of what Watteau looks like? Did I not make mental notes, thus:

WATTEAU, Antoine 1684–1721; pron. "What Ho!" French painter. General style; mushy. Subjects; chaps carrying on ineffectively with fattish girls. Characteristics; Arcadian romance with the goats left out; Special notes: watch out for satin drawers on gents.

But never in my life have I written a piece of criticism without making at least one Stupid Mistake. Furthermore, I observe that most critics do the same. This is a special chastening visited by the Spirit of Folly on those who presume to Know Best. (Example: Nathan Cohen attributing the music in *L.L.L.* to Lou Applebaum.)*

Or am I mixing up Watteau with Fragonard?* My confidence is at a low ebb. Years ago I saw a Watteau *As You Like It*,* at the Vic, designed, I believe by Molly McArthur. Edith Evans in satin bloomers bullying Michael Redgrave in same. Macabre if one let one's mind stray toward the Purely Physical. There was a swing on which Celia swang; very pretty. But Dame E.E. (whom I admire immensely, but on this side idolatry) gave the whole affair an Oedipal air which was unnerving to me, at that time about twenty-one and intolerant of Gifted Eld giving a marvellous impression of Ingenuous Youth. (The music was also 18th century, and I'm not sure that Arne's* "The Lass With The Indelicate Air" was not played during the witty love-duels.)

I shall not go on burdening you with my protestations of guilt. Let it suffice that I am punishing myself severely – I won't say how, as it is ugly and involves a chain – and promise never to do it again. Just accept this as an ABJECT CRAWL from.....

Rob.

To ARNOLD EDINBOROUGH

Peterborough Examiner
Peterborough, Ontario
August 21. [1961]

Arnold Edinborough (1922–   ), English-born Canadian academic, journalist, and editor, had just purchased Saturday Night *magazine. In February of 1961, Davies had been appointed Master of Massey College in the University of Toronto. The College was still in the planning stages and would not open until 1963.*

Dear Arnold:

Brenda told me your news at lunch today, & I take my Underwood in hand to congratulate you most heartily. This is the reward of boldness; you must have been under great strain while it was being cooked up, & you must feel gratified and limp now that all is in the bag. You have always been a darer. You dared to quit the cellars of Academe, as represented by Queen's, to take a plunge into journalism; you dared to leave a certain job for an uncertain one; now you have dared to stand up and holler when Jack Cooke* had put on the black cap. Hooray for you! Long may you dare and may your daring bring you everything you want. It is the daring ones who make the wheels go round.

I feel this strongly, because I am doing a spot of daring myself, in a direction that seems superficially to be the contrary of your own. I am leaving the comparative ease of being publisher of a paper for the certain unease of running a particular sort of college; I am leaving a world where few people cheek me for one where aged profs sneer at me because I am not and never will be their notion of a scholar; I am also making certain sacrifices of money in the hope that new work will keep me alive, as I am sure that another 20 years of provincial journalism would wrap me in the sleep of intellectual death.

I am also canning my *Star* column,* at Christmas, I expect. It pays handsomely, but it is whoredom. You are one of the few people I know who would understand this. To write about Corvo and Logan Pearsall Smith for housewives in Sioux Lookout is all right for a while, but in the end it makes one a Tinpot Pontiff – the peer of

T. Cholmondeley Frink in *Babbitt*,* if you happen to recall him. The *Star* can take their money and ingest it anally, if I make myself clear.

But I did not point my forefingers to tap about myself, but about you. I glory in your courage; may Fortune, who favours the bold, lick you all over with her honeyed tongue. I speak not only of money – though it has its naive charm – but of the prestige which your particular kind of iconoclasm entitles you to in this queer country. May you be to this unawakened earth the trumpet of a prophecy* (if I may quote an Oxford man slightly wrong).

I embrace you in the spirit,

<u>Rob</u>.

To ANTHONY B. ROTA

[*Peterborough Examiner*
Peterborough, Ontario]
December 29, 1961

*Bertram Rota Limited, Antiquarian
Booksellers, was a resource Davies had
been tapping since he was a student at
Oxford in the 1930s, and not just through
its catalogues. He visited Rota's whenever
he was in London, England.*

[Dear Mr. Rota:]

Thank you for your letter of December 27th. I am glad to have been in time to get the items that I did from your catalogue #125, and sorry to have lost the others, particularly #578 – the original costume designs by G. B. Shaw for *Arms and the Man*. My special reason is that I am changing my occupation and am now lecturing to graduate students at the University of Toronto on English drama from 1660 to the present day. I have a pleasant and growing collection of books, letters and other objects which directly relate to the drama of the 18th century, but am not nearly so well supplied with things relating to the drama of the late 19th and early 20th centuries. I feel very strongly, and have indeed demonstrated, that an opportunity to see and handle letters, manuscripts or books which have some association with celebrated dramatists or actors gives a life to such lectures as mine which cannot be secured in any other way. Especially for students in a country like Canada, it is important to make the writers and actors and critics of the past real in some special way. The Shaw designs would have been admirable for this purpose.

I know that you have to give careful consideration to the wants of all your customers and cannot play favourites among them, but as I am at a disadvantage in being at a considerable distance from you, so that your catalogues reach me some time after they have been circulated in the United Kingdom, may I ask you to keep me in mind if you should receive anything which sounds as though it might be along the lines that I have mentioned above? When I visited you in the spring of 1961, I was very fortunate in securing two fine Max Beerbohm manuscript poems and two of his books which he had embellished with his own drawings. I should greatly like to secure something rather special connected with Bernard Shaw or Sir James Barrie,* or indeed with any celebrated dramatist of the period which falls within your own concern. If at any time you wish to inform me of something of this character that had come to you by cable, I would be very glad to pay the cable charge.

The books and manuscripts of which I speak are used now for teaching, but my collection* will, in the end, go to the library of a College designed for graduate students and thus will not be dissipated or re-sold at higher prices or in other ways used for financial gain. I mention this because when I visited you in the spring of this year you mentioned in conversation that you had been active in forming several distinguished collections in colleges in the U.S.A. and I hope that the project of lending your expert knowledge to the formation of one in Canada might appeal to you.

With every good wish for 1962, I am

Yours sincerely,

[Robertson Davies]

To HORACE W. DAVENPORT

[Peterborough, Ontario]
Jan. 6. [1962]

Dear Horace:

For about ten months I have been dithering about writing to you, because I know your unfavourable opinion of the academic world in general, and thought you would probably think ill of what I have done. But now the Balliol *Record* has blabbed all, and the truth must be told.

Briefly, the Massey Foundation (you recall the Massey association with Balliol*) has undertaken to build and endow a residential college for graduates at the Univ. of Toronto. They have asked me to be first Master, and to plan and set the coll. on its feet. This is what I am doing. The job also carries a professorial appointment. I am in English, of course, doing post-graduate work in the Drama from 1660 to 1950 (death of GBS), not all in one bite, naturally, but 1660–1800, and 1800–1950.

Why? Because the thought of another twenty years as a newspaper editor appalls me, and at my age chances to change your job do not come often. Because this damned hick town is beginning to kill me. Because I want more time to write, which is promised as part of the new job, which has an element of Ornamental Hermit in it.

Because (and principally) I am much steamed up about the college idea. Out of a Grad. Schl. of nearly 3,000 we take roughly 100 of the best – half scientists and half humanists, and no mutts studying for degrees in pedagogy, library science or insurance selling admitted – and they live together when not working. The plan is part Oxford, part Princeton. We attempt a civilizing mission, but do not force this unduly. Our Senior Fellows are men of considerable distinction, and the young men get to know them, and also people who do important work in science, scholarship, industry and the professions, whom we lure in with good food and drink for that express purpose. Further, we house and entertain the visiting professors, the special lecturers, and kindred interesting people who visit the Univ., and they meet our Junior Fellows. It is, indeed, an attempt to treat young men of promise as men of learning, and to shoehorn them into the world which they hope to join.

We are now building a fine place for ourselves; first-class modern design; quadrangle form, with two fine libraries, Common Room, dining room, special examination room for post-grad vivas (very posh, it is, with a dome of many-coloured glass for a roof), and suites which are good but not of Persian luxury for the Junior Fellows, and somewhat more Persian accommodation for the Seniors.

A lot of tutorial work will be done there, and also symposiums, conferences and lectures of arcane significance from visiting grandees.

The coll. includes a handsome dwelling for the Master (and the Mistress); the coll. is for men, but we intend to provide buns and cocoa pretty frequently for the wives of the non-resident Junior Fellows (who will be twenty in number).

I am to run the place, assisted by a Bursar. I am planning it on lines dictated by my experience in business, so I hope it will not be so wasteful as some colleges which have 100 years of inconvenience behind them.

The Univ. of Toronto, as you may not know, is a federation of colleges – six, and some faculties which come under the University itself, such as law and a number of the sciences. Massey Coll. will be independent financially and in administration, but part of the whole. One of my reasons for taking the job is that I have a great regard for the President of the Univ. – Dr. Claude Bissell* – and share his ambition to make the graduate school a very good one. It is the best in Canada now, & attracts quite a few people from the U.S.A., as well as Africans, Indians, and West Indians, and some from the U.K. We are very Scotch about education up here, and I am happy to have a chance to do my dash. I am really serious about this, and am not merely pushing for a classy biography – *A Jowett* of the Snow Fields* or something of that sort.

You do not remember the Masseys with any affection,* I believe. But Vincent Massey, formerly Governor-General of this Dominion, is a strongly imaginative man, and I have a powerful respect for his

idea of a coll. Also for Lionel, who has become a first-class administrator (he is administrator of the Royal Ont. Museum, now) and is
working himself thin for this idea. The others* – Hart, Raymond (the
actor) and Raymond's son, don't have much to say; their financial
advisor is a first rate man, and is doing a fancy job on college invest-
ment. We shall not be rich to begin with, but a genteel sufficiency
should not be long in coming. It was Vincent Massey and Bissell who
persuaded me. (It was like persuading a delicately balanced rock to
roll down a mountain.)

Am organizing steadily now, teaching three days a week, and relax-
ing my hold on this paper. But we do not open until autumn of
1963..... So there you have it.

Every good wish to you & Virginia & the boys

<u>Rob</u>. . . .

To MOIRA WHALON

[*Peterborough Examiner*
Peterborough, Ontario
Between January and May
1962]

*Moira Aileen Whalon (1924–98),
English-born Canadian, had been
Davies' secretary at the* Peterborough
Examiner *since 1956 and continued to
work for him until his death in 1995.
Davies wrote this note as he left
Peterborough to go to Toronto.*

Miss Whalon:

If wanted – *really* wanted & not just longed for – I can be reached
at the Waldorf-Astoria, Charles St, or Trinity Coll. Back Friday a.m.

R. D.

To TANYA MOISEIWITSCH

Friar Bacon & Friar Bungay
Necromantic Suppliers and Supernatural Warehousemen
(Founded 1594)
[June 1962]

Dear Miss Moiseiwitsch:

It has been brought to our attention that in the current production
of *Macbeth* at Stratford, the first sixty-eight lines of Act Four, Scene
one [the witches' cauldron scene] have been omitted, doubtless
because of the difficulty of securing the properties necessary to its apt
performance. As a very old-established firm, who had the honour of
victualling this extremely effective scene for Mr. Shakespeare himself
in 1606, may we quote you the following attractive bundle, which
we can supply on receipt of a cable, our telegraphic address being
Paddockanon.

"Toad, that under cold stone
Days and nights has thirty-one
Sweltered venom sleeping got....."
    IMMEDIATELY AVAILABLE in unlimited quantity from our own
    gardens. True *Bufo vulgaris* as supplied to Mr. Shakespeare. $3.
    per doz.

"Fillet of a fenny snake"
    Blindworm, from the Norfolk Broads, $3 per doz. filleted and
    shipped in ice. We recommend, however, fillet of adder, as each
    order includes the "fork," thereby effecting a pleasing economy.
    Fillet of adder, $8 per doz. shipped in ice.

"Eye of newt and toe of frog"
    Pleasing minor items, shipped dry; soak for two hours before
    curtain time. Our MERLIN'S MIXTURE $2.50 per lb.

"Wool of bat"
Per generous hank, unwashed, $6. Washed, $12.

"Tongue of dog"
Recent difficulties with the R.S.P.C.A. make this formerly rea-
sonable item somewhat expensive. Mongrel: $1 per tongue.
Pedigreed: $5. Shown at Crufft's: $8.

"Adder's fork"
See above. Separately $6 per doz. dried. Exercise care in handling.

"Blindworm's sting"
A very attractive dried bunch, comprising approximately fifty
stings, $5.

"Lizard's leg"
Our South American special. Large: $1. Small: 25¢.

"Howlet's wing"
Genuine English howlet, warranted from churchyard or belfry,
"not a wing is sold till it's five years old." $12 per wing.

"Scale of dragon"
From Continental China, *guaranteed*, $18.50 per scale. From
Formosa, no guarantee, $5 per scale.

"Tooth of wolf"
Best Canadian timberwolf, $9 per tooth.

"Witch's mummy"
Increasingly difficult to obtain, and we must limit orders to
one pound per customer per month. Best quality, from the
Carpathians, $250 per pound. SPECIAL — While She Lasts! —
Dracula's Aunt Sybilla! A steal at $750 per pound, packed in her
own skin! Many personal hairs in each package! A MUST for the
large operator!

"..... maw and gulf
Of the ravined salt-sea shark"
  Fresh daily from Newfoundland. $35 per set.

"Root of hemlock digged i' the dark"
  Per root, $4. In powdered form, $3.50.

"Liver of blaspheming Jew"
  Since the founding of the State of Israel, an increasingly difficult
  item, and recent embargoes on exports from several mortuaries
  and cremation chapels in the Bronx, Forest Hill and similar
  centres have greatly limited supplies. Furthermore, the increase
  of interfaith fellowship has made it impossible to guarantee that
  any given Jew is a true blasphemer. He may be of the Reform
  persuasion. However, our laboratories have been at work, and
  we have had excellent results from our own –

PATÉ OF BLASPHEMER

  IN WHICH A SMALL QUANTITY OF THE ABOVE ITEM, as well as
  "nose of Turk and Tartar's lips" have been mingled in a paste
  composed of blasphemers against virtually everything. Very reasonable: per pound pot, $45.

"Gall of goat,"
  from Wales, packed in "slips of yew." Open with care as the fumes
  have been known to overcome experienced Stage Managers. Per
  gall, $28.

"Finger of birth-strangled babe
Ditch-delivered by a drab."
  From a Salvation Army home for Repentant Magdalens. Guar-
  anteed ditch-delivered, as the Chief Obstetrician is Dr. Duncan
  Ditch, FRCP, M.D.; per dozen, $4.

"Add thereto a tiger's chaudron....."
  An item rarer than it was in the great days of the Empire, but

still available. Royal Bengal Chaudrons, $80 each. A cheaper class of chaudron, from zoos and circuses, at $50 each. Delivered in ice, C.O.D.

"Cool it with a baboon's blood"
  True baboon, per carafe (approx. 1 litre) of superior bouquet and body, $15. Canadian native baboon, bottled by Bright's Winery (screw-top returnable bottle), $3.

We undertake contract work, supplying your stage Management nightly for the duration of your run, at an inclusive price of $38.50 each night. We have many letters on file attesting to the effectiveness of this service, and extraordinary manifestations are by no means uncommon in theatres where it is used.
  Awaiting the favour of your esteemed order, madam,

Leonard Greymalkin
for: Bacon and Bungay

To ALAN B. BEDDOE

400 Water Street
Peterborough, Ontario
December 3, 1962

Alan B. Beddoe styled himself "Designer and Consultant in Heraldry." The foremost Canadian authority on the subject, he became the founding president of the Heraldry Society of Canada 1966–67. Beddoe applied to the College of Heralds on Davies' behalf, and the modified Coat of Arms was approved in 1964. Davies used the arms on his bookplate and on his and Brenda's silverware, and Brenda worked it into a large piece of needlepoint for their living-room wall. See Man of Myth *491–92.*

[Dear Mr. Beddoe:]

I should like your professional advice on a matter relating to a Coat of Arms, not for Massey College this time, but for myself. In 1942* my father, Senator Rupert Davies, was given a Grant of Arms which he has used since, particularly during 1951 when he was High Sheriff of the County of Montgomeryshire. Naturally this is what I should like to use myself, but there are two points concerning it which I should like to be absolutely correct about.

The first is that, according to my understanding, my father's Coat of Arms ought to carry some mark which indicates that I am his third son.

The second is that I would prefer not to use my father's motto and would like your opinion on the possibility of having an altered motto for my own use. I believe that the motto is not an integral part of a Coat of Arms and that there is no particular objection to changing it.

I enclose a photograph of my father's Arms. The ground colour of the shield is red, the transverse band is white, the lion is black and the ink-balls, which indicate our connection with the printing and publishing trade, are gold. The demi-dragon on the crest is red with gold tongue and claws and the scaling ladder seems to be either dark brown or black. The colours of the mantling are white and red.

My father's motto, as you will see, is A Ymdrecho A Drecha [He Who Strives Hardest Shall Conquer]. This is a Welsh motto and I would prefer to change it to – Ymurandawed dyn a'i galon [Let a Man Listen to the Prompting of His Inner Voice] – which is much more suitable to my character and feeling about life.

I should be glad to hear from you on this subject, and if it is not necessary to consult the College of Heralds about these alterations, may I ask what your fee would be to prepare a drawing of the Coat of Arms as altered for my use.

Yours sincerely,

[Robertson Davies]

To RALPH HANCOX

[July 17, 1963]

> In June 1963, Davies moved to Toronto to take up his post as Master of Massey College. In July, he took a trip to Europe and sent this postcard (of Van Gogh's workhouse-inmate with battered top-hat and cane and viewed from the rear) to Ralph Hancox, who had succeeded him as editor of the Examiner.

This is not one of the well-known Van Goghs, but it shows that he cd. have been a good newspaper cartoonist if he had possessed a steady character. Holland is delightful: *such* nice people! And what a sense of town planning – shd. Pbro. send a deputation?

R.D.

MASSEY COLLEGE
in the University of Toronto

[1963]

MASTER

Me welcome you to the U. of T.! It is your home — I am the newcomer, & still a stranger, though kindly treated.

Dear Douglas,

Delighted by the news that you have written
a novel,and look forward with avidity to
reading it.What a satisfying form it is!
And I well believe that yours is beautiful,and am keenly interested to hear that
it is also brutal.I am myself working on
a novel which will not be brutal,but is
certainly far more serious in tone than
anything I have attempted,and is at root
an attempt to explore a region of my own
life and thought which I have never put
in a book before--my desire to experience
regions of feeling which are commonly
called religious,but are not orthodox
or churchy.It is taking a long time,and
as well as breaking new ground I am trying
to correct faults which have plagued me,
and irritated my critics,for years--my
very personal tone,and a leaning toward
the farcical and farouche which suggests
shallowness of feeling,but is (I truly
believe) the consequence of trying to
conceal a nakedness and rawness of spirit
which I have only now persuaded myself to
display to readers...Do you think we shall
be a nest of rare birds at the U.of T.?
It would be fun,wouldn't it? All the
best to you and Sally from us both...

Rob. [Davies]

SECTION

V

uring 1962–63 Davies had been able to settle into part of his new position, as a professor of English and drama in the Graduate School at the University of Toronto. But when Massey College opened its doors in the fall of 1963, his conception of the Mastership prescribed new, intensely interesting, activities. He spent the College's first year establishing a firm rhythm for its communal life – biweekly high tables, annual Gaudy Night and Christmas Dance, professional choral music at chapel services, concerts spaced through the year. He also marked out the role he would play as Master. He would comport himself with formality, presiding on special occasions and making himself available by appointment, but he would not be casually accessible at mealtimes or in the common room.

The College's first years were genuinely exhilarating for Davies, as he brought the founders' dream into being in the building they and he had so carefully planned. But the death in 1965 of Lionel Massey, Vincent's son, was a serious loss, since it was he who of all the family had been most in sympathy with Vincent's and Davies' view of what the College should be. An even greater blow was the death in 1967 of Vincent Massey himself. These events had serious consequences for the College and added significantly to Davies' burdens.

There was resentment in some university circles over his sudden assumption of a full professorship, and Davies thought it politic as a result to undertake two pieces of "academic" writing. One was a little book on Stephen Leacock for the New Canadian Library's series on Canadian writers, the other a substantial contribution to *The Revels History of Drama in English*. But the paperback publication of the novels of the Salterton trilogy and the appearance in 1967 of a third Marchbanks volume added more to his reputation as a writer.

Davies' involvement with live theatre continued to be intense. *A Masque of Mr Punch*, a one-act play he had written for performance by the Preparatory School at Upper Canada College in 1962, was published in the fall of 1963. In 1965–66, he helped create two theatricals for Canada's Centennial – a Centennial Spectacle (cancelled at the last moment) and a contribution to a *Centennial Play* (completed, performed, and published). He remained on the Stratford Festival's board of governors in these years, and he and Brenda continued their customary avid theatregoing, typically attending more than seventy performances a year.

The death of his father, Rupert, early in 1967 was a profound personal loss for Davies. It also precipitated the sale of the *Peterborough Examiner* in 1968, severing his involvement with the newspaper world; but it had a liberating effect on his writing. He could now make use of early experience in *Fifth Business* without the sense of constraint that had earlier held him back. The novel, simmering in him since the late 1950s, profited too from his long immersion in the works of C. G. Jung and from his expanded range of experience, including the travelling he and Brenda did in these years in Europe, Australia, and Mexico.

The Davieses' move from Peterborough to Toronto briefly reintegrated the family, since two of their daughters were finishing their schooling there and the third was working in Toronto, but they soon moved into their own quarters or went off to university elsewhere. Both Jennifer and Rosamond married in this period, Jennifer in 1966 and Rosamond in 1969.

To DOUGLAS LEPAN

Massey College
University of Toronto
[latter half of 1963]

*Douglas LePan (1914–98), Canadian poet
and diplomat, left the Department of
External Affairs in 1959. He taught at
Queen's University, Kingston, 1959–64,
and was shortly to move to the University
of Toronto to become principal of
University College 1964–70. The novel he
had written was* The Deserter.

Dear Douglas:

Delighted by the news that you have written a novel, and look forward with avidity to reading it. *What* a satisfying form it is! And I well believe that yours is beautiful, and am keenly interested to hear that it is also brutal. I am myself working on a novel [*Fifth Business*] which will not be brutal, but is certainly far more serious in tone than anything I have attempted, and is at root an attempt to explore a region of my own life and thought which I have never put in a book before – my desire to explore regions of feeling which are commonly called religious, but are not orthodox or churchy. It is taking a long time, and as well as breaking new ground I am trying to correct faults which have plagued me, and irritated my critics, for years – my very personal tone, and a leaning toward the farcical and farouche which suggests shallowness of feeling, but is (I truly believe) the consequence of trying to conceal a nakedness and rawness of spirit which I have only now persuaded myself to display to readers..... Do you think we shall be a nest of prose birds at the U. of T.? It would be fun, wouldn't it? All the best to you and Sally from us both.....

Rob.

Me welcome *you* to the U. of T.! It is your home – I am the newcomer, & still a stranger, though kindly treated.

To J. BURGON BICKERSTETH

Massey College
University of Toronto
June 12, 1964

*John Burgon Bickersteth (1888–1979),
Canadian (who was born and died in
England), was the first warden of Hart
House, centre for men students at the
University of Toronto, 1921–47. Like
Massey College, Hart House was a
benefaction of the Massey Foundation.
Davies sought Bickersteth's counsel when
Massey College was being planned, and
continued to keep in touch with him.*

Dear Burgon:

Our first formal year of college is over, and we have escaped without a major crisis, and with several positive gains, the best by far being
the strong feeling some of the men have developed for the place.
Several hated to go away; of those who will be here next year a large
group have already begun to make some plans to set things off on the
right foot when we reconvene in September. The Bursar [Colin
Friesen]* is happy because it looks as though he will have a full college
all summer, which is important for money; he has done a splendid
job – a much lower deficit than had been anticipated, and all achieved
without running down quality.

There have been some great surprises for Brenda and me. We know
something about girls, but not much about young men. We are stag-
gered at how childish very clever young men can be – so brilliant at
their work, and so petty, or monkey-like, in the ordinary affairs of
life. We are also rather astonished by their remarkable egotism, sometimes good and admirable, but sometimes grabby and selfish; it is sad
to see a brilliant man sacrifice dignity and decency merely to gyp
somebody out of a dollar or two. But on the whole they are first-rate,
and we have made some good friends among them. Yesterday eight
of them took their degrees – two doctorates and six masters – and
we had them to lunch beforehand. Odd how small attentions of this
sort mean a great deal to them; perhaps their egotism springs from
the fact that so few people seem ready to give them their due. But

they liked the luncheon very much, and all wore their college gowns to Convocation, and one of our men arranged that the two Esquire Bedels attending the Chancellor were also College men, so it was quite a Massey occasion.

I was greatly touched by your letter of June 2, in which you speak of leaving some books to the coll.; you may be assured that we shall cherish them, and because they are yours as much as for themselves. Our librarian [Douglas Lochhead]* is first-rate, and has been appointed Special Lecturer in bibliography to the university; so any rarities we have will be used directly in teaching, and will not go to sleep in the vault. Indeed, it is our ambition now to make the coll. the biblio-graphical centre for the university, and it will be the only thing of its kind in Canada. By next spring I hope we can show you the begin-nings of this project, for which we hope to get some money from the big foundations.

Brenda and I are off for a holiday on June 20 – to Spain and Italy to look at pictures and theatres. We will get to England before we come home, and when our plans are clearer will write to you again. Perhaps it will be possible to meet for a time, and tell you personally so many things that cannot quite be put into a letter – feelings rather than facts.

Love from us all,

Rob.

To MR. _____

Massey College
University of Toronto
January 14, 1965

[Dear Mr. _____:]

I cannot grant your request that your name should appear on the directory in your staircase in a manner which is different from that used for the other men. The College provides very great freedom in important matters, but in trivialities we cannot make concessions to personal whim.

Your request in this matter suggests to me that, in spite of our conversation on the subject on November 25th, you do not approve of the way that we do things here. I am sorry that this should be so because it is one of the purposes of the College to offer facilities to men of your proven ability, but this does not include making you an exception to our rules. I recommend that you give very careful thought to the question of whether you wish to apply to have your fellowship renewed for the 1965–66 academic year. I cannot believe that you enjoy spending valuable time in fighting a system with which you disagree, and escape from which is so easily achieved.

Yours faithfully,

[Robertson Davies]

To DONNA WALTON

Miss Donna Walton wrote from Westminster College, London, Ontario.

Massey College
University of Toronto
March 22, 1965

[Dear Miss Walton:]

Thank you for your letter of March 16th and your enquiry about Mr. Graham C. McInnes.

I have known Mr. McInnes since 1940; I met him then as he was writing criticism of pictures and sculpture for *Saturday Night*, and I was their book critic; the editor at that time was the late Dr. B. K. Sandwell.* I was drawn to G. C. McI. because he was an admirable conversationalist – eloquent, ready and witty – and his sense of humour agreed with my own. His literary bent comes to him naturally; the Mackail connection, the Burne-Jones connection,* the relationship to Kipling, his mother's great popularity as a novelist, his brother* Colin's reputation as a novelist – all of these things fortified his own interest in writing something more vigorous and important than criticism. There is a strongly romantic strain in his nature, which combines with an experience of life broader than the ordinary to give his writing a special flavour; if it is permissible to trace such things to heredity, I should think that the romance came from his father [James Campbell McInnes], who was a splendid interpretive artist, and the quality of strong observation and insight into the humours of human motive, from his mother [Angela Thirkell]. His choice of theme in his novels, *Lost Island*, *Sushila* etc., is romantic almost in the vein of Rider Haggard, but the description, character drawing, especially in some of his short stories, has a very sharp edge. He has a great relish for satire, and one of our amusements when we met at intervals, was to read aloud to one another from *Babbitt*. Perhaps it should be said also that his experience as a film director has sharpened and exercised his vision in a very special way. I think his best work is still to come, for romance and satirical observation are an unusual combination, and do not fully declare themselves in youth.

Yours sincerely,

[Robertson Davies]

To J. BURGON BICKERSTETH

Massey College
University of Toronto
Sat. March 27. [1965]

Dear Burgon:

I have delayed longer than I should in replying to your letter of March 7, but there were one or two developments here which I wanted to see in a more advanced state before writing of them to you, and which I knew would interest you.

First of all, my warmest and most grateful thanks for the Johnson and Jenkinson on *English Court Hand*.* We did *not* have this basic work, which is now quite hard to find, and costly when found. The Central Library has it, and Lochhead had been working with that, but of course it means much, much more to him to have a copy in our College library, from which he can have photographs made for use by his students, and which he can consult whenever he pleases. I know he is writing to you, but I must add my thanks to his, with a special word: I can imagine what these books mean to you; they have an air both of being used and cherished, and one does not part with such books without feelings of sadness; but your true kindness and goodwill in making such a gift add immeasurably to its sweetness. This college must be built, above all else, on *feeling*; that is my conclusion as its second year draws toward a close. The university and the world abound in places built on money, and ambition, and all sorts of things which are admirable in their way, but if we can invest Massey Coll. with a genuine tenderness (not soppiness) of feeling, from its beginning, we shall have made an unusual and perhaps a great place. Your gift, then, carries special blessing, because of the feeling that surrounds it.

During the past months I have been worrying a good deal about the chapel, but have been greatly aided by one of our Junior Fellows, a Rev. John N. Buchanan, a Presbyterian minister who has given up parish work to become a history don. Young – under thirty – very intelligent, and of a firm character; Scots background – from the Maritimes but has lived everywhere in Canada, and got some of his training in Cambridge and Edinburgh. For the past few weeks – since Christmas – he has been taking services for us, and does it uncommonly well, because as a very intelligent man he refrains from talking simple-mindedly to people who are quick to accuse the Church of childishness.

He has made the grade academically; next autumn he begins his teaching career as an Assistant Professor, which is as high as one *can* begin. I have been persuading him, and at last he has consented to act as permanent chaplain to the College; will have a room here, will see the men frequently at meals and in the Common Room, will be a part of the college, but not identified solely as a chaplain, because he is manifestly a history don who is also a parson.

I think this good, and so does he, for he is somewhat dubious about chaplaincy in the universities; he has filled a chaplain's post in B.C., and also in Saskatchewan, and found that the barrier to his work was that he was a clergyman, and nothing else, in universities where clergy seemed to have no place. So he thinks chaplains in universities ought to be like the "worker-priests" in France; doing what everybody else is doing, doing it well, but doing it from a religious point of view and with a religious motive. I hope the experiment works well; we get a good turnout now to our monthly afternoon services; maybe they come to hear the choir, but they come.

No news about a Warden; I don't think the President [Claude Bissell] was inclined to look seriously at John Barker,* as he was rather young and hadn't done enough. Also, the students are agitating to have a voice in the choice of a warden. Perhaps you have followed the news of the students' strike at Berkeley U. in Calif.; it has caused student unrest all over the country. The Berkeley people had a real grievance, but you know what sheep Canadian students are; they want anything that promises a lark and a disruption of work, including grievances and strikes. Of course they don't know what they need in a Warden; many of them think Joe McCulley* is wonderful. But there seem to be so many student politicians – mostly Jews, I regret to say – How *odd* of God, to choose the Jews!* – who will do anything to make the President's life a burden.

Another crisis at Hart House: Bob Gill has been drinking very heavily, and work there has been suffering. The last crisis came during work in February on a production of *The Cenci*,* when he had to be lugged off to the hospital, and has just been released, badly scared but I fear not scared enough. This creates a problem for the President, who does not want to dismiss Bob, who has been here so long and who did some fine work, but he is running the Theatre into the ground. The developments which are on the horizon will not please Bob; the university considers forming a special department to deal with Drama in all languages, and with links with Fine Art, the Museum, and other univ. departments which are relevant. This department will also control the Theatre, and dictate the policy and plays to be performed – making the Theatre a real academic theatre and not a partly commercial one as at present. This is all very fine, and a move in the right direction, but it leaves Bob somewhat high and – one hopes – dry, as he will probably be asked to lecture in the drama department, but will not control the Theatre, nor direct plays there except when asked. He won't like it a bit, but the President is very annoyed, and Bob is lucky his skin is safe. Not that the President is Puritanical, and simply down on Bob for his heavy drinking; it is because an important university facility is being outrageously abused.

The tricky part for me is that I am likely to be very much toward the top in the new drama set-up. The President sees it as being run by three men* – Clifford Leech, the head of the English Dept. at University College, Jack Sword as financial man, and myself. As I am an old Friend of Bob's, it will not be easy to get on well under such changed circumstances, but if we don't get on well we shall simply have to get on ill. The problem is that Bob has become deeply resentful during the past four or five years, toward his fate – thinks he is hardly-done-by, plotted against, etc. Nobody is plotting against him; indeed, his friends stuck by him most loyally during the recent bust-up, and the President hates disciplining him. In his excuse, it must be said that he has been in a great deal of pain during the last few years – something to do with his back – and drank a lot to bear it. But truth compels me to say that over ten years ago, before this trouble appeared, he was getting through a bottle of gin a day, because he stayed with us one summer and we were astonished.

No more news at present from the old diploma-mill, but I shall write again as soon as something turns up.

Love from us all,

Rob

To A. M. KIRKPATRICK

Massey College
University of Toronto
September 20, 1965

A. M. Kirkpatrick was Executive Director of the John Howard Society, which helps men in prison and in community correctional programs. The subject of this letter wrote Davies at least three letters (now in the National Archives) from the Don Jail in Toronto or from the Ontario Reformatory, Mimico (part of Toronto).

[Dear Mr. Kirkpatrick:]

I am writing to enquire if you can give me any information about a man called _____, who is at present in the Toronto jail. I met _____ many years ago when he was an actor, and tried to encourage him in some work that he was doing; since that time he has got into repeated trouble because of homosexuality combined with drunkenness, and is in and out of jail very often. Every time he gets out he comes to me for money, and so far I have tried to help him because of his fervent assurances that he is going to get back into decent work and keep out of trouble. However, this has now gone on for some years and I am beginning to have serious doubts as to whether he can ever get himself out of the mess in which he is involved. The last letter from the Toronto jail, dated August 31st, pleads with me to give him a job at this college as a cleaner or kitchen worker; this is out of the question because it would disrupt the rest of the staff, who are first-rate people, if I introduced this man, who is, I fear, somewhat deranged mentally, among them. I hate to desert _____ utterly, for very few people have much sympathy with actors who are down on their luck, but I do not feel that I can continue as I have done in the past. I would greatly appreciate any advice or information you can give me, especially if it led to anything that might keep _____ out of trouble. I fear, however, that only permanent restraint would do that.

Yours sincerely,

[Robertson Davies]

To JOHN N. BUCHANAN

Massey College
University of Toronto
December 3, 1965

John Nyren Buchanan (1931–   ) is a
Canadian of Scots background. A
Presbyterian minister, he served as
chaplain of Massey College 1965–68
while completing his doctoral thesis
Charles I and the Scots, 1637–1649 *and*
commencing his first academic
appointment as assistant professor.

[Dear Chaplain:]

What I have to say is a matter of such delicacy that I hesitate to talk to you about it face to face and have resorted to a note. The last time Holy Communion was celebrated in the Chapel the wine was sour, and I think that this is because it is kept in the small cruet which is not air-tight. This raises a theological point far beyond my understanding: should one notice the quality of the wine at Communion, or, on the contrary, does it give a bad impression of Almighty God if He serves terrible wine at His table? I leave this knotty problem up to you. I suggest, however, that it might be a good plan when wine has been used at Communion that the remainder of the bottle be returned to the Bursar, or conceivably that it become the perquisite of the Chaplain. I do feel that it is unsatisfactory to keep it for a month in a warm cupboard.

With good wishes,

Yours sincerely,

[Robertson Davies]

To FRANCES TOMPKINS

Massey College
University of Toronto
December 7, 1965

Frances Tompkins (1916–95), Canadian,
was employed at the Stratford
Shakespearean Festival 1953–83. She was
administration secretary until 1970 and
then secretary to the Foundation.

[Dear Mrs. Tompkins:]

I have just received the list of Festival Governors for 1966 and I
see that, as in the list for 1965, I am listed as having no known occupation. I feel that this is likely to lead other Board members to think
that I am an idle man and can do an enormous amount of extra
work. If anyone should enquire, I am a Professor in the University of
Toronto and the Master of Massey College. Strange though this may
look in a list where everybody else is at least President of something,
it is the shameful fact.

Yours sincerely,

[Robertson Davies]

To HORACE W. DAVENPORT

Massey College
University of Toronto
December 30. [1965]

Dear Horace:

Thanks for your letter and apologies for my delay in replying. I
shall not bore you with a long account of what has been keeping my
nose to the grindstone since last July; briefly, it has been the job of
getting an endowment for this college. I had not thought the necessity to do so would arise so soon, but in the summer – July 28 – Lionel
Massey had a stroke and died within twelve hours; as this college lives

by the favour of the Massey family, and as they are divided among themselves, it became necessary to press for some settlement of college finance as soon as possible, for Lionel was our warmest supporter apart from his father, who is now oldish and rather frail. Have you ever tried to persuade rich people to unbelt? Of course you have. Then you know what I have been up to. At last I think the job is done, and we are fairly secure, but it has demanded an awful lot of persuasion, cajolery, flattery and browbeating, not to speak of God knows how much letter-writing, budget preparing, and tiresome belabouring of one obvious fact – that if you found a college and give it your family name and then starve it to death half the world will think you mad and the other half will think you stupid. During the course of this blood-bath our Bursar [Colin Friesen] got an ulcer, the college solicitor [Wilmot H. Broughall] got so he could not keep any food on his stomach, and I got an intensification of my skin rash, combined with ennui and *taedium cordis*. But nothing is achieved without these horrors, and colleges are built on the bones of their servants.

Apart from this, we have had the excitement of our two older daughters becoming engaged, and the older one becoming subsequently disengaged, as the chap seemed to think that all the concessions should be on Miranda's side. (He is a Catholic – an intellectual Catholic, which seems often to mean more rigid than a simple dolly-worshiping Catholic.) Jenny's young man [Thomas Surridge]* is a scientist – studies the learning habits of animals, or some such thing, and seems very bright indeed. He has published a lot of papers, etc. I know nothing about it, but judge him on his personal character. These excitements gnaw at the parental nerve-endings. I go about humming, from *The Beggar's Opera** – "I wonder any man alive/Would ever rear a daughter!"

Glad to have news of Robbie; he sounds lively, and I am glad things are clearing up for him. I am always in a puzzle as to what to send him; books are obvious and dull, but if I launch into other things, I may make stupid mistakes, as I am not in the least well grounded in what such young men like and need. So if you ever feel like dropping a hint, I should be greatly obliged.

For the present, adieu. I think of you often. I hope that 1966 will bring you all great happiness..... What, one wonders, would really great happiness be like?

Rob.

To A GRADUATE STUDENT WORKING IN UGANDA

Massey College
University of Toronto
May 10, 1966.

[Dear _____:]

Matters respecting your thesis now stand thus: Your examiners, Professor Endicott* and I, have read it and approved it and have recommended you for the M.A. degree which can be conferred upon you in the autumn if you take steps to present your thesis in proper form. The form in which you gave it to us – carelessly typed and with some passages in red, and with frequent interlining – will not do for the Graduate School. They demand that two cleanly-typed copies, appropriately bound, be presented before they will grant the degree.

The cost of binding is $8.00, and you will not get the thesis typed for much under $60.00. My suggestion is that you send this money by International Money Order as quickly as possible to me and I will undertake to get this work done in time to ensure your degree in the autumn. I exhort you – for I know your temperament to be a somewhat dreamy one – to send this money as rapidly as you can in order that we may clear up your affairs and ensure your degree.

Yours sincerely,

[Robertson Davies]

To MICHAEL LANGHAM

Massey College
University of Toronto
May 12, 1966

Michael Langham had written and asked, "Why does Henry V refer to God more frequently than any other character in Shakespeare? It must surely be due to guilt."

[Dear Michael:]

Henry the Fifth's* keen sense of the nearness of God is only partly owing to guilt, and that guilt is not his but his father's. It is hard for us to understand the great importance laid on the Divine Right of Kings; we have to bear in mind that to our ancestors an election by God was every bit as important as election by a majority is to us. Henry IV had directly contradicted God's will by his murder of Richard II.* It was not superstition but psychological common sense for his son to assume that this might bring misfortune on everything that stemmed from such an act.

Henry, both in the play and in the Chronicles, appears as a profoundly religious man. When the Bishop of Ely calls him "a true lover of the Holy Church,"* he is not speaking ironically. Henry's rejection of Falstaff is evidence of his determination to cleanse himself for the holy vocation of kingship. The reason that Agincourt means so much to Henry is not only because it is a great and decisive victory, but because it is evidence that God has not visited his father's sin upon him. It is worth noting that Henry the Fifth's son, Henry VI,* was a man of uncommonly devout life and was adored as a saint in England for a century after his death.

The character of the devout warrior occurs repeatedly in history. During the last war Wavell and Montgomery and Patton* were examples of the type. We must not underestimate the power of their devotion; Patton once publicly prayed for the cessation of rain which interrupted one of his campaigns, and against all meteorological likelihood the rain stopped. These men have the secret of Joshua;* they know how to get God on their side. Any production of Henry V which fails to show Henry's complete belief in God and his sense that

God is the only superior he acknowledges, loses something which is vital to a full realization of the play.

Sorry to have lectured you.

Yours sincerely,

[Rob]

To CLAUDE T. BISSELL

Massey College
University of Toronto
May 25, 1966

Claude Bissell (1916–2000), Canadian, was president of the University of Toronto 1958–71. He was also a friend.

[Dear Claude:]

Enclosed is the piece about Michael Langham. It looks as though I had been so impertinent as to write a citation for you, but that was not my intention. When you told me that you wanted the comment as the basis for a citation, I could not think of it in any other form, but I think that what I have said about Michael is what is really important about him and more interesting than merely biographical detail. The fact is that he has adapted and refined Guthrie's style as no other protégé of Guthrie's has done, and although the Old Master is still unbeatable for sheer excitement, Langham is a much more scholarly director. The difference I suppose is that Guthrie is a genius, and like all geniuses he sometimes makes appalling mistakes: Langham is a very fine artist – not a genius – and he very rarely puts a foot wrong.

One of my difficulties in writing this piece for you was that I had already been asked by Michael to prepare a portion of the speech which he will give on accepting the degree, and it was very hard to keep these two things separate in my mind – indeed I didn't try.

With good wishes, I am

Yours sincerely,

[Rob]

To EARLE BIRNEY

Massey College
University of Toronto
October 31, 1966

*While Earle Birney was writer in
residence at the University of Toronto in
1966–67, he lived at Massey. He did read
a poem composed for the occasion at
Gaudy Night, the evening shortly before
Christmas when Massey College
entertains its friends.*

Dear Earle:

As you will see from your College calendar, we celebrate a Gaudy
Night at Christmas and this year it is going to be on Saturday, the
17th of December. We have music, and a ghost story, and a very lively
time. During the first three years we have always managed to have a
Christmas poem; the first year it was two charming translations from
the French by Robert Finch;* the second year it was a poem on a
Christmas theme by Douglas Lochhead; last year we had a novelty –
a dialogue between the three kings and the shepherds with the kings'
portion written by Finch and the shepherds' portion written by
Lochhead; it was an interesting experiment in collaboration and was
received with enthusiasm.

Would you consent to write a Christmas poem for us this year and
read it at the Gaudy? If you prefer not to do so you need not feel that
there will be any resentment, but I assure you that if you consented
the College would accept it as a great compliment. Whatever your
decision, I hope that you and your wife will be present on this occasion, which has always been one of the best affairs of the College year.

Yours sincerely,

Rob.

To SCOTT SYMONS

Massey College
University of Toronto
February 8, 1967

Scott Symons (1933–   ) is a controversial, combative, avowedly bisexual Canadian novelist and journalist. Place d'Armes was his first novel.

[Dear Mr. Symons:]

I read *Place d'Armes* last Sunday and have been thinking a good deal about it since. I gathered from our conversation on Saturday night that you felt some apprehension about its reception and I can understand why. You have stripped yourself naked and stood in the market place, and if you get the treatment of St. Sebastian* it will not be entirely surprising, particularly as you have rather outdone St. Sebastian and have thrown rotten eggs at all your enemies who are also in the market place. I must say that I feel your book would have been stronger if you could have denied yourself this gratification, because the tone of real protest and concern about Canada is very much diminished by these trivial personal enmities.

However, it was not to lecture you that I began this letter, but rather to congratulate you on the strong plea that you have made for deep emotional involvement with this country on the part of the people who live in it. It is the only thing that can possibly save us in the long run, and I wish I could be certain that it would make its appearance.

Yours sincerely,

[Robertson Davies]

To DOUGLAS LEPAN

Massey College
University of Toronto
April 6. [1967]

Dear Douglas:

I have left your letter to the last, in replying to the many kind notes
I have had about my father's death; I reserved some old friends until
after I had written more formal thankyous. So this is late.

Hamlet's uncle said* all that common sense suggests about the death
of fathers, and without much effect. Common sense has nothing to
do with it. One's concept of justice, one's concept of God, one's sense
of oneself – these are the things fathers shape before one is aware that
one is being shaped. Do you remember what Freud's father said* to a
friend? "My boy Siggy has more brains in his little finger than I have
in my whole body, but he would never think of contradicting me."
That is what a real father is.

My father had some strange qualities. Caprice, romantic egotism
(he lived a romance of his own composition), a gift for high-coloured
rhetoric (especially of the condemnatory kind) and mockery. But these
were the shadows of greater things – impatience with dull and trodden
ways, of a low idea of life, of dowdy talk and thought, and pompos-
ity. He always wanted things to be big and in Technicolor; he delighted
in vivid speech; he was a great *enjoyer*. Because he projected his image
(in the awful modern cant) so successfully, and acted so powerfully
onstage and off, I shall always feel rather second-rate and unworthy in
respect to him, though reason tells me I can do things he could never
have done. But one always wants to bend the bow of Achilles.*

So there it is. I have spoken to you frankly because you are one of
the very small group of people I know who really understands what
human relationships are about, and where the heart aches.

Rob.

To MAVOR MOORE

Massey College
University of Toronto
August 24, 1967

*James Mavor Moore (1919–   ) is a
Canadian actor, playwright, director,
radio and television producer, and arts
administrator.*

[Dear Mavor:]

Thanks for your interesting note about James Reaney's play.* I did not want to express myself too forcibly without having seen the whole of the play, particularly as I found myself unable to separate the contribution of the author from the very substantial contribution of the director. I am also somewhat hesitant about expressing opinions on matters relating to childhood, because my views are very much my own and perhaps a little too acid for general consumption. My own childhood was not a very happy one, although it had flashes of extraordinary happiness at rather widely spaced intervals. It is altogether too easy to blame other people for childhood unhappiness. I now think that it boils down to the fact that some people are temperamentally well suited to being children, and others are not. I have met many people who had very happy childhoods and never seemed to have had any happiness since, and I count myself fortunate not to be one of their number. Therefore, Reaney's portrait of childhood as a time of somewhat simple-minded ecstasy woke very little recognition in me, for if I were to write a play about childhood it would be like a 12-year Hallowe'en – a mediaeval Hallowe'en, not an Ontario one. I am, as a matter of fact, working on a novel [*Fifth Business*] in which some material of this kind will make an appearance, and I suppose that the critics who have always thought me rather harsh in my attitude toward life will be even further encouraged.

With good wishes, I am

[Rob]

To TYRONE GUTHRIE

[Massey College
University of Toronto]
September 19, 1967

[Dear Tony:]

. . . Brenda and I are both very well after an extremely busy summer, much of which I spent in work on my father's estate. Really it almost makes one afraid to die. Although my father left his affairs in very good order, getting everything sorted out and arranging for money to pay the succession duties is a long complicated business and I find that the assumption of the tax people is that everybody is dishonest and, therefore, everything must be proven several times over. It is a fact also that men very rarely provide their children with the kind of information that tax officials seem to want; it would never have occurred to me that I would require a birth certificate in Canada for a man who had been very well known here for at least fifty years, and had been a Senator. Nor would I have suspected that the birth dates of his grandparents would be required, and although I am fortunately able to dig these up, it all takes time. He took great pains to leave us with the least possible trouble relating to his property in Great Britain, but the least possible trouble is much more than one could have foreseen, and is complicated by the fact that English and Canadian lawyers attach different meanings to technical terms. Then, of course, there is the problem of personal possessions; he left some things to me which are to go to my children after I die; simple though this seems, it rouses the suspicions of the tax people that I might wickedly sell a few engraved trays and other things which he was given in recognition of various services, and thereby cheat my girls of part of their inheritance.

One of the stickers is that Rosamond must present a list of every gift that she received from her grandfather during the twenty years of her life, and the tax people cannot be perfectly certain whether this ought to include dolls and boxes of sweets or not. The only solution for this kind of thing that I can see is to contrive to die stark naked, in some foreign land, without any mark of identification. Part of the annoyance is that if I chose to be a crook about some of these things it would be quite impossible for them to prove it. Now that I come to consider the matter, I do believe that I have forgotten to list a 10¢ bag of humbugs which Rosamond got when she was seven.

Sorry about your ailing hand. I have one too and at times I can produce nothing but miser-like scratches.

Yours sincerely,

[Rob]

To ESCOTT REID

Massey College
University of Toronto
September 20, 1967

[Dear Escott Reid:]

Escott Reid (1905–99) was a distinguished Canadian diplomat, author of several important books on politics and diplomacy, and the first principal of Glendon College, York University, in Toronto.

As you no doubt know, some portions of your address to the students of Glendon College were reprinted in the *Varsity*,* and I am writing to tell you how interesting I found them, and how strongly I agree with what you have said. It is a very good thing that, at the present time, someone in authority in a university should say clearly that he holds his office by some right of appointment which is more secure than the favour of his students, and that his responsibility goes beyond what it may be in the power of students to comprehend at the present time. Such an attitude as you have clearly shown does not imply a lack of sympathy with students and their legitimate ambitions, but it is certainly very different from the terrified retreat which has been seen in some parts of the academic world, or the rigid position which has been seen elsewhere.

What no one seems yet to have had the courage to tell a group of students is that youth is not all glorious, and that ignorance and egotism are inevitably mixed up in the business of being young. Everybody has met with amusing evidences of this. The *Varsity* this morning carries an embittered complaint from a young man, appropriately named Duinker, that he was not given his degree for the trivial reason that he had failed one of his courses. Last year some of us here had to deal with a young man who wailed, "Is there no place in this university where I can write my own ticket?" If the universities are in difficulties at present it is, to some extent, their own fault; they have not held their heads high. But it is possible to recover the lost ground and I compliment you on what you personally have done about it.

With good wishes, I am

Yours sincerely,

[Robertson Davies]

To DOUGLAS LEPAN

Massey College
University of Toronto
Thursday. [September 28, 1967]

Dear Douglas:

Your gift of *Responsibility and Revolt** came yesterday and I sat down at once to read it, and have now read it for a second time. It is first-class, and I agree with it all, though I think I take a somewhat less pessimistic view of things than you. I sometimes feel that we are living in that sunless, moonless, starlit world that Apuleius gives us in *The Golden Ass** – full of the vicious, the avaricious, the false prophets, the disingenuous magicians, and a sneaking pack of priests who don't know what they are priesting about. And we, the bemused men of goodwill, are the asses, looking for a metamorphosis that will enlighten us. BUT – I think the metamorphosis and the illumination will come, if not in our time, in its own good time, and mankind will have taken another lurch forward, as it did when the Christian world got under steam. The world that is coming is bound to look frightening to most of us, but that is the usual thing. I'm sure Christianity scared the daylights out of everybody in the Roman world who was not too broken to care. But I fully agree that those of us who bear some responsibility in the world as it is must acquit ourselves like men; we are the boys on the burning deck,* and so far as I'm concerned I'm not budging an inch.

I enclose a little piece of mine* that is a kind of footnote to your fine essay. As you see, it was written as part of *a festschrift* for Vincent's birthday – an offering from the College, organized by the Junior Fellows. But – ah, high-hearted, generous youth! – they became involved in their own jealousies and incompetence and buggered it up, so that there is no book. My essay is not to be spoken of with yours, but it says something I think, and I offer it as a tribute to your essay, which I admire so much.

Rob.

To LOUIS DUDEK

Massey College
University of Toronto
November 16 [1967]

Dear Mʳ Dudek:

Louis Dudek (1918–2001) was a Canadian poet, critic, literary activist, and professor at McGill University 1951–82. In 1965–69, he wrote a column on books, film, and the arts for the Montreal Gazette.

Thank you very much for the generous notice of the *Almanack* in *The Gazette*;* one always considers criticism in terms of its source, and I value praise from you very highly, for I have admired your work for years, and know that you put high importance on matters of literary craftsmanship – as do I. It is rewarding and refreshing to read the comment of someone who understands that seemingly trivial and light-hearted things are not just thrown off in idle moments.

Of course you are right in your comment that slapstick and irrelevance are my besetting sins; I have never been able to control a relish for low comedy, and my entry into the academic world a few years ago has only served to add fuel to this flame. When so many people are engaged in discovering the Christ-symbol in *Peter Rabbit* or the Archetype of the Great Night Journey in "Hippety-hop to the barber's shop" it is an irresistible temptation to let go with some cheap jocosity. I don't suppose I shall ever get over it, though I am truly aware that it is poor stuff, and when I read it a few months later – too late to cut it out – I really do blush.

It was very kind of you to suggest that my work does not get the attention it deserves. Of course all writers feel this, and I try to avoid paranoia. But I think it is because my work is really rather old-fashioned – intentionally so, for I am absolutely no good at keeping up with literary modes. I cannot write a really modern prose, and at the same time say what I mean. Particularly I am no good at using dirty words: the really hair-raising obscenities are so often those wrapped in silk. So I must pay the price. Quite a lot of people like my things – some of them people like yourself, whose good opinion fills me with pride – but I shall never be fashionable. At least I shall avoid the sense of desolation that apparently comes with the discovery that one is – all of a sudden – *un*fashionable.

With thanks & good wishes.

Robertson Davies

What a dirty-looking letter! But I wanted to do it myself so that I could address you quite personally.

To SCOTT YOUNG

Massey College
University of Toronto
December 18, 1967

*Scott Young (1918–   ), Canadian, is a
sports journalist and author who had
become a friend when the Davies family
lived in Peterborough and he lived in
nearby Omemee. Davies used the
incident described in this letter in
What's Bred in the Bone 150–55.*

[Dear Scott:]

I was interested to read a review of your book about Senator O'Brien* [of Renfrew, Ontario] and I look forward to reading it.

There was one incident in the O'Brien story that you may not have heard about, but which I thought entertaining. The old Senator's son-in-law, Joe Murray, always held his head very high and on one occasion, when my father was publisher of the Renfrew *Mercury*, he called at the newspaper to say that in future, in any reference to him, he was to be spoken of as "Sir Joseph Murray" as the Pope had just appointed him a Knight of the Order of St. Gregory the Great. My father treated this announcement with coarse Protestant hilarity and Joe was deeply annoyed. It was not very long, however, before some busybody made it known to the Papal legate that Joe was more than ordinarily interested in his secretary, a girl named Blondie Dolan, who wore rolled stockings and smoked. As a result the Holy Father retracted the Knighthood and Joe was right back among the common people. This caused a lot of ill-natured giggling in Protestant circles among people who never had any real appreciation of tragedy. I think perhaps Joe's worst experience in connection with this was the bawling out he was given by the old Senator, who greatly disliked scandal touching his family.

With every good wish to you and Astrid and the children for Christmas and the New Year, I am

Yours sincerely,

[Rob]

To J. M. S. CARELESS

Massey College
University of Toronto
December 18, 1967

James Maurice Stockford Careless
(1919–) is an eminent Canadian
historian. He was a member of the history
department at the University of Toronto
1945–84, and a senior Fellow at Massey
College 1965–85.

[Dear Maurice:]

These are the notes that I promised you about Vincent Massey.

The thing which impressed me above everything else during the time that Massey College was being planned was his extraordinary personal concern with every detail of design and furnishing. This did not arise from any amateur enthusiasm for architecture or decoration but from an obvious keen conviction that quality in atmosphere goes far to create quality in living; the Massey Foundation was creating a college for some of the ablest minds in the graduate school and he was determined that the intellectual quality of those minds should be equalled by the artistic quality of the surroundings in which they lived.

This is a sort of idealism with which I have keen sympathy, though I think I am rather more aware than Mr. Massey of the many things that can go astray when you try to put it into action. It has been obvious in the five years of the College's life that the atmosphere in which the men live has an influence on them, though it is not always a predictable one. I think the point that has most impressed me is that the whole atmosphere of the College is not luxurious but good; everything is of excellent quality, excellent design, and is meant to last. It is a visible reminder that what is good is also likely to be enduring.

As I told you, Mr. Massey took a personal hand in some of the designing,* certainly he had many conversations with the silversmith, Eric Clements, who designed the tableware for the College, and on one famous occasion that I mentioned to you (February 22, 1963), he stood over a designer and directed him how to re-shape a chair by sawing a lot of needless wood from the model. He was also keenly interested in all the calligraphy in the College and worked directly with Allan Fleming in choosing how it should be done, so that even the signs on the doors of the washrooms are in a distinguished lettering and are in proper proportion to the total size of the door.

I want to emphasize that this is not mere aestheticism in the sense of imposing ornament where it would not, perhaps, normally be found, but an insistence that the most commonplace things should be of the best quality. This is a very rare spirit in Canada, or indeed anywhere else, and I think that it was Mr. Massey's principal contribution to this College. It is a contribution which will persist and influence the people who work here an unpredictable length of time beyond the span of his own life.

I hope that you were not embarrassed by my references to you* in the ghost story last night; the Gaudy is supposed to be a family affair and as all those present were friends I did not think that you would mind.

Yours sincerely,

[Rob]

To ROBERT FINCH

[Massey College
University of Toronto]
December 20. [1967]

Robert Finch (1900–95) was a poet, painter, harpsichordist, respected scholar of 17th- and 18th-century French poetry, and a senior fellow at Massey College 1961–95. Davies wrote this note in the copy of Samuel Marchbanks' Almanack *he gave to Finch.*

Dear Robert:

Since Sunday night snatches of your poems keep recurring to me, & always with a renewal of pleasure. I hope you will include the *Christmas Cards* in yᴸ next collection. Poetry is very dear to me – the bardic & rhapsodic especially; but you have given me a new appreciation of that cool, clearly perceived verse in which extraordinary sensibility reveals the quality of seemingly ordinary things, and I thank you.

This book brings Christmas greetings. Among the buffooneries there are a few things that may please you — perhaps the correspondence with Noseigh — pp. 94, 135, 198, & 201 — & of course the Christmas cards on p. 169.

Rob.

To RICHARD REOCH

Massey College
University of Toronto
December 20, 1967

Davies had read and commented on Richard Reoch's play Under the Sea to the Sunrise. *It had just opened at the Poor Alex Theatre in Toronto.*

[Dear Mr. Reoch]:

The notice of your play* which appeared in the *Globe* this morning was very harsh, and I hope that you will not mind if I offer you some advice at what I think may be a very important point in your career. It is painful to be criticized in such terms, and I expect that you feel deep resentment toward Kareda,* and my advice to you is this: do not stifle the resentment but allow it to burn, and in time it will burn itself out. If you choke back your feelings you will do harm to yourself.

Having said this I would like to point out to you that Kareda is as inexperienced as a critic as you are as a playwright. Because of his inexperience he hits too hard and takes pleasure in saying amusingly cruel things. It is sad to think that his harsh judgement of your play will reach more people than you are likely to attract into your theatre in a week, but you must remember that Kareda will always be a critic, and however good he may be, a critic is always a second-rate thing: it is not impossible that you may be a good playwright, and a good playwright is undeniably a first-rate thing. Kareda is already a failed actor: you are a playwright who has barely begun to make his way and there are great hopes for you. A writer, if he is any good, is an artist, and if you read Kareda's notice again, not as its subject but as a literary critic, you will see how badly he writes.

Having said this I remind you that when I returned your play I said that I thought it somewhat wordy, and this is one of the points that Kareda has emphasized. I did not say that I felt that the structure was weak because there are so many changes going on at present in the realm of playwriting that to talk of structure sometimes marks one as no more than old-fashioned. Nevertheless I do put this to you: a play is never a work of art unless it is first a piece of craftsmanship; the libraries are full of plays by people whose ideas were good but whose craftsmanship was weak.

I beg you not to be discouraged but to be strong and endure. It is vastly better to be stoned as an artist than to be snug as a nonentity. What you must do is to start thinking at once about your next play, and for heaven's sake do not allow your actors to begin tinkering with the play which is in performance now, simply because they think they can improve it. I expect you already know that the world is full of magnificent playwrights who have never written a play but are great hands at helping those who have done so. If you expect to do anything in this very difficult form you must first of all be true to yourself.

With sympathy and firm encouragement, I am

Yours sincerely,

[Robertson Davies]

To RALPH HANCOX

Massey College
University of Toronto
January 8, 1968

Dear Ralph:

At last I get a minute to thank you for your Christmas gift; it was most kind of you to think of us, and we thought of you with great affection. As you will have guessed, Vincent Massey's death caused a great deal of uproar here over the holiday time; the College seemed to be a source of information, and a focus for plans, and the 'phone rang literally *night* and day – people wanting 9-foot Canadian flags, potted biographies, and an extensive range of undertaking services. And, of course, protocol. *If* the Governor General came to the funeral at Port Hope* could I *personally guarantee* that the Bishop would usher him into the procession leaving the church, and that no unhallowed form would intrude itself between His Excellency and the Chief Mourners? My brief and spasmodic encounters with courtiers convince me that the eighteenth century must have been sheer hell.

But we got through it all, and the service at Port Hope was well done. Eight Junior Fellows of this College were the pallbearers, and it does wonders for a funeral when the pallbearers are young men and not doddering ancients, all of them obviously wondering which of them will be next to get the ride instead of the lift. When Lionel Massey was buried I was – believe it or not – the youngest pallbearer, and there were one or two who had carried nothing heavier than a briefcase since the Depression; I thought one man was going to fall into the grave; the result was that we got poor Lionel in sideways, and after some impotent jerkings of the straps had to leave him for the undertaker to get him level when we had gone. This is because of the Masseys' passion for real pallbearers, instead of undertakers' men, and it is a realm where amateurism is fraught with farcical possibilities.

Your letter to the *Globe** about Morley Callaghan was excellent. Of course it was idiotic to offer Morley a bunch of vegetables when roses had been heaped upon his great rival, MacLennan. But they should have given him a chance to refuse gracefully, instead of making a public thing of it; Irishmen should never be offered a chance to be disagreeable in public. Morley admits this himself. I think I would have done what he did, if offered the Booby Prize. We artists are all nerves, and sometimes we don't know what we are saying.

Yours sincerely,

Rob.

PS. Those things in the mouths of the dogs on the Robertson arms are not their tongues, they are purses. Those dogs are trained to pick the pockets of the English, at the word of command, which is "Hoot mon, a bawbee!"

To THE PRESIDENT, GREENSPOON BROS. LIMITED

Massey College
University of Toronto
April 25, 1968

Dear Sir:

I was aware that sooner or later Greenspoon knocked down everything in Toronto, but I had not thought that my turn would come quite as soon as it did. This afternoon, April 25th, at 4 P.M., I was walking up University Avenue past the site where your firm is demolishing the former Abitibi building; with me were Mr. W. H. Broughall of the National Trust, and Professors W. A. C. H. Dobson and W. E. Swinton* of this college. Suddenly the wind blew down two sections of the protective fence along the sidewalk and knocked me very forcibly to the ground, knocked Professor Swinton to the ground, and knocked Mr. Broughall out into the street. Professor Dobson, who was slightly behind us, escaped with having his umbrella broken. We asked to see the foreman on the job, and when he appeared he repeated, several times, variations on this sentence: "If you're hurt go to the doctor; I can't do anything about it; we've got insurance to cover this."

If your firm is really interested in creating a public image as Good Old Reliable Greenspoon That Everybody Trusts, may I suggest that you instruct your foremen that under such circumstances a word or two of ordinary human, decent regret and apology would not be amiss.

I do not know what the extent of my injuries may be, as I still feel somewhat dazed, but I assure you that if they are more than shock I shall consider you liable.

Yours truly,

[Robertson Davies]

To HORACE W. DAVENPORT

[Massey College
University of Toronto]
May 10. 1968

Shortly before this, Davenport's wife, Virginia, had died, leaving him to raise their two sons on his own. In his letter of sympathy on May 4, Davies had written, "I can only hope that your work is absorbing enough to give you some release from your situation." Davenport's reply has not survived, but its tenor can be surmised from Davies' letter.

Dear Horace:

Thanks for your long letter, which I value greatly and shall keep, as indeed I keep most of your letters. Not, I hasten to say, with a view to including them in my autobiography in eight volumes, but simply because I cannot bear to destroy really personal communications; they are written from the heart, and should be cherished.

I understand so well what you say about your quick dissatisfaction with your own work, however successful it may be. I have something of the same character. And I am oppressed by a sense of failure, as I get into the middle fifties. I hoped to do so much, and I have done what I could, and it doesn't amount to a very great deal. The joke is that externally I appear to many people to be very successful, because I have an assured air, and talk readily, and look more like a professor than most real professors. (In actual fact, I look like a Stage Professor, although I make no particular effort to do so.) But my desire was to be a writer of some consequence, especially for the stage, and time has shown that I have not the temperament for it; I do not work easily with other people, and that is essential for a dramatist. The tour with *Love and Libel* was hellish, and it seemed to me before the end that the text of the play was the least important element in the total. Also, such talent as I had for writing for the stage is now hopelessly old-fashioned, and not only am I unable to take to the new techniques – I don't want to, because they are totally unsuited to saying the kind of thing I want to say. The novel is a different matter; I can say what I want to say there, and technique is quite a different consideration. My three novels have had a flattering degree of success, without setting the Thames on fire. But now they are in paperback, and a lot of young people read them and respond very kindly to them, and this pleases me greatly. My most receptive audience has been in the States; England not so good, and Canada bitchy and small-spirited, as small nations so often are. Oddly enough I have had some success in Germany and Holland, which is gratifying.

It is here that I repose my hopes. I feel strongly that my best writing is still to come. I am just finishing up a volume for a new history of drama;* mine is the 1750–1880 volume. Then next autumn I shall get down to work on a novel [*Fifth Business*] I have been planning for years. It is autobiographical, but not as young men do it; it will be rather as Dickens wrote *David Copperfield* – a fictional reworking of some things experienced and much re-arranged – a spiritual autobiography in fact, and not a sweating account of the first time I backed a girl into a corner. I choose the word "spiritual" with intent, for during the past ten years the things of the spirit have become increasingly important to me. Not in a churchy sense – though as Master of this college I have to attend chapel and look serious – but in what I must call a Jungian sense. That may make you laugh, or spit, but through Carl Gustav Jung's ever-thickening veils of thought and fantasy

I discern something that gives great richness to my life, and helps me to behave rather more decently toward other people than my unaided inspiration can achieve. And that is important to me: the world is so full of self-seekers, crooks and sons of bitches that I am very keen to be a decent man – not a Holy Joe, or a do-gooder, but a man who does not gag every time he looks into a mirror.

This seems to be all about me, but it is your own self-revelatory letter that has brought it forth. You are one of a tiny group of people with whom I can be frank, even though we meet so rarely. For I cherish the memory of our earlier association, and get much sustenance from the realization that we both want to keep it alive. You speak of my "own troubles"; they are pretty trivial, and virtually all inward. But I have lots of duties, and I grow restive under duty; without a very happy marriage I couldn't stand it and would "Run Amok and Slay Four" like the people one reads about in the papers.

I think of you and the boys, and am very glad they are working out so well. Having no sons I don't know much about that side of things. My eldest daughter is just off to Vienna to work at the Conservatorium there; she has faced the fact that though a very good singer she is not of the top flight, and is putting her energies into opera with a hope of some day being a coach, or even a director, for which she has some flair, and has done well here. My second daughter is married. . . . [And] I think they are pretty happy. The youngest is still in university and is an unknown quantity, but a dear child. But girls become somebody else's, if they are lucky. I don't know about sons.

I shall write again. Write when you feel like it.

Rob.

To CLIFFORD LEECH

Massey College
University of Toronto
September 30, 1968

Clifford Leech (1909–77), English, was a professor of English and drama at the University of Toronto, a critic, and editor of The Revels History of Drama in English. *Davies had written a long section on "Playwrights and Plays" for the volume covering the period 1750–1880.*

[Dear Clifford:]

I now realize how you have gained your enviable reputation as an editor of scholarly works: it is by means that would have brought a blush to the cheek of Simon Legree.* You sent me five pages of single-spaced alterations, which you describe as "trifles that should not take up much of my time." You know jolly well that they would take a full week of the most drudging work, if I had a full week to devote to it. As it is, I am up to my neck in all the hubbub of the beginning of term, with its demands that theses be read and examination boards assembled and joined, in addition to the work that I have to do for this College. However, I have groaned beneath the lash of editors for the past thirty years and have never yet failed to lick the hand that was raised to strike me, so I shall do what I can to get all this stuff ready for you as soon as possible. I must say, however, that I dread the thought of adding more footnotes and scraps of information, because my own complaint about such books as the one upon which we are now engaged is that they are customarily so dense in their writing as to be virtually unreadable. In many instances in my text I have worked on information which I have acquired over thirty years, and which I know to be reliable. It can certainly be checked, and a footnote appended, but I have tried to avoid footnotes which refer to actors' memoirs of an almost illiterate kind that are of interest only to enthusiasts like myself, and the bibliographical information about which is extremely complicated. Something of this applies also to the editions of many of the plays to which I have referred; one reads them where one can find them, and I fear it is beyond my powers to guarantee that every edition of every melodrama to which

I have referred is the very first one. The publishers of plays, Lacy, Dicks and French,* knew nothing of such niceties and more often than not failed to date their editions.

It is good to hear that you will be back in Toronto at the end of the month and I hope that you will be able to spare time to visit your slave in his cell and discuss some of these matters directly. Meanwhile I shall get as much done as I can.

Yours sincerely,

[Rob]

To THE EDITOR OF *THE GLOBE AND MAIL**

Massey College
University of Toronto
November 1, 1968

[Dear Sir:]

May I comment on a front-page story in your issue of November 1 about Hallowe'en? Some people, it appears, have been putting razor blades, pins, needles and explosive or caustic substances in the candies and apples they give to children who call at their doors. Several children have been robbed of their UNICEF collection boxes.

Hateful, of course, but why is anyone surprised? A society more truly aware of itself, and less intent on pretending that the majority of people are good-hearted, dutiful, fun-loving extroverts, would have more sense than to send children out on the Eve of All Hallows; a mature society would keep its children indoors and provide treats for them at home.

Of course I do not believe that goblins and witches and bugaboos rage through the streets on Hallowe'en; at least, I do not believe it in quite that simple-minded way. But millions of our ancestors did believe it, and with good reason. Hallowe'en is the Celtic festival of the Death of the Year; it marks the change from autumn to winter (or does so in Europe) and the time when the souls of the dead revisit their old homes; but it was also the time when evil spirits had special license.

This was a psychologically sound idea; violence, hatred, malice and simple crankiness must have their outlet. Earlier religions than ours, and our own religion before it forsook the cure of souls for "social work," knew that people cannot be good all the time; sometimes the beast must be let off the chain. The time for that was Hallowe'en. The following day – All Saints' – the chain was back in place.

What have we done, in our wisdom? We have tried to clean it up, as part of the great campaign to make the world safe for cosy-minded, psychologically-stunted people. We have even tried to turn it into UNICEF Eve, and sanctify it as another charity-grab, like Christmas and Easter. But the old festival of evil is still vigorous, and apples with razor-blades in them are one sign of it. Evil has to be met and reckoned with – even compromised with – for it will not disappear. Our ancestors were wise to give evil its own special night.

The tax-burdened, law-burdened, regulation-burdened citizen of today gets a raw deal from society. It has turned his religion into a juiceless social service, it offers him forms of art that bamboozle and rebuff him and it provides him with governments, called "responsible," in which no one is finally and unmistakably responsible for anything. Whither shall he turn for succor and replenishment of the spirit? On the whole I am optimistic about the future, but I am certain it will not be made great or beautiful by the kind of psychological shallowness and immaturity that turns Hallowe'en into another Home and School Happening, and attempts to ignore the evil that is a secure and demanding inhabitant of the human heart.

Yours faithfully,

Robertson Davies

To KENNETH H. J. CLARKE

Massey College
University of Toronto
July 7, 1969

*Kenneth H. J. Clarke, Canadian, assistant
vice-president of the International Nickel
Company of Canada, was President of the
Stratford Shakespearean Festival
Foundation in 1968 and 1969.*

[Dear Ken:]

I have assumed for some years that my continued election to the Board of Governors of the Stratford Festival was owing to my special knowledge as a professor of drama and of the history of the theatre, which I have always been very happy to put at the Festival's service. Therefore I think I would be failing in my duty if I did not write to you about *Satyricon;** whatever its success may be with the public immediately, I fear that its long-term effect may be unfavourable to the Festival. My own opinion is that it is a piece of work that has no place in a classical theatre, as it is neither an old work of proven value or a new work of a kind which can be described as an innovation or an experiment. It is simply a piece of commercial theatre and not in the front rank in that category.

It is not the frankness of the dialogue that troubles me, for great freedom of dialogue is characteristic of much experimental play-writing in our day and we would be foolish to set our faces against it. Rather I resent the literary barrenness of the dialogue which is frank without distinction or wit, which is to say that a great part of the time it is merely dirty. There will always be people who are transported to hear an actor, or preferably an actress, say "kiss my ass" on the stage because they mistake this kind of gutter talk for a daring blow against conventional taste. More sophisticated play-goers weary of this kind of thing very quickly and its shock value is trivial.

Stratford may appropriately be as experimental as it can, but the presentation of scripts that are utterly without literary merit is against our best interests and contrary to our original principles.

I mentioned in my first paragraph that I felt that it was as a professor of the history of the theatre that I was of some value to the Festival. One of the things that the history of theatre makes amply clear is that when performances become common in which women are degraded and a homosexual appeal becomes prominent, great artistic dangers are clearly in sight. I do not wish to be misunderstood on this matter; homosexuality, treated as a serious theme by serious artists, is an entirely legitimate theme for theatre consideration. This, however, is a very different thing from the frankly faggoty bias of *Satyricon* and its cynical exploitation of cruelty and degradation to provide sensation.

May I propose two things that I think might help us? First, can we work out any plan whereby the governors are not obliged to give blanket approval to works of which they know nothing? I can see that this presents great difficulties. Second, when Sir Tyrone Guthrie is in this country this autumn could we get him to Stratford to talk to us about the first principles of the Festival, and perhaps get us back on the rails again? *The Three Musketeers,* which was admirable in its way, contained the seeds of a danger which has shown itself very clearly in *Satyricon* – that is the danger of the play written on the spot and subject to all the temptations of trivial and essentially unliterary invention. One more stride in this direction and we could put the Festival on the rocks.

With every good wish, I am

Yours sincerely,

[Rob]

MASSEY COLLEGE

in the University of Toronto

Dear Horace:

Your letter of July 20 luckily caught me
between two journeys;I was delighted to get
it because I have been hoping to hear from
you for some time--your last letter suggested great despair.But I am very happy to ∧
hear of your forthcoming marriage,and I
hope it will bring great happiness to all
of you.The news about the boys is very
good.Is Tom learning German for some
special pursuit,or simply to know it?
I am so out of touch with science that
I still suppose scientists must know German
to do their work,but common sense tells me
this must be wrong.Anyway,when you write to
him,give him my best regards.The news about
Rob is fascinating;he must be a very able
young man;one of my sons-in-law does a
good deal of work with computers (he does
research for the Department of Reform
Institutions here) but the only contact
I have with it is that he makes montages
of computer-punched paper and puts them up
in his kitchen;but at least he explains to
me in the simplest terms what a computer
does,which only gives richness to my ig-
norance.Give Rob my good wishes;he sounds
much too able to bother with boarding-
schools which,like schools in general,are
not for exceptional people.

SECTION

VI

July 1969–May 1972 – *Fifth Business* completed and published; *The Manticore* planned and written

avies, now 55, had made detailed outlines and notes for his "long-pondered" novel *Fifth Business* in 1968, and he had written the first two sections that fall. He completed it in the summer of 1969, and the book appeared in both Canada and the United States in fall 1970. The Canadian reviews were appreciative, but it was the American raves which made the book a bestseller on both sides of the border. Davies was particularly delighted by the letters he received from readers.

By June 1970, just months before *Fifth Business* appeared in print, Davies was already in the grip of his next novel. By the following May, he had it planned and had begun writing. When his Canadian publishers learned that the new novel was linked with *Fifth Business*, they urged him to complete it quickly to capitalize on the earlier novel's success. He managed to do so; the final typescript of *The Manticore* went to his publishers in late February 1972 for publication that fall.

Throughout this period, Davies continued with his responsibilities as Master of Massey College and professor in the Graduate School at the University of Toronto. Such travel as he managed had to be shoehorned into Christmas breaks. Immediately after submitting the manuscript of *Fifth Business* to his publishers in December 1969, he and Brenda spent a couple of weeks in London, visiting their daughter Miranda and soaking up theatre. They also flew to Paris to see their old friends the McInneses (Graham was seriously ill). The following December, they combined a research trip to Switzerland (to visit the Jung Institute and St. Gallen as background for *The Manticore*) with a period in London and Cornwall.

During the academic year 1969–70 Davies and Brenda worked with an architect on plans for a country house to serve as a weekend and summer retreat. "Windhover" was begun in 1970 and completed in May 1971, just in time for Davies to settle into the writing of *The Manticore*.

In 1971, Davies' eighteen years of service on the Board of Governors of the Stratford Festival came to an end.

To HORACE W. DAVENPORT

Massey College
University of Toronto
July 22. [1969]

Dear Horace:

Your letter of July 20 luckily caught me between two journeys; I was delighted to get it because I have been hoping to hear from you for some time – your last letter suggested great despair. But I am very happy to hear of your forthcoming marriage, and I hope it will bring great happiness to all of you. The news about the boys is very good. Is Tom* learning German for some special pursuit, or simply to know it? I am so out of touch with science that I still suppose scientists must know German to do their work, but common sense tells me this must be wrong. Anyway, when you write to him, give him my best regards. The news about Rob is fascinating; he must be a very able young man; one of my sons-in-law [Thomas Surridge] does a good deal of work with computers (he does research for the Department of Reform Institutions* here) but the only contact I have with it is that he makes montages of computer-punched paper and puts them up in his kitchen; but at least he explains to me in the simplest terms what a computer does, which only gives richness to my ignorance. Give Rob my good wishes; he sounds much too able to bother with boarding-schools which, like schools in general, are not for exceptional people.

My life is somewhat gummed up with student problems; not very bad, but time-consuming and so trivial that I get mad and wonder if this is what I have been shaping my life to do. My worst problems, though, are caused by senior men over whom I have almost no control (except for the final sanction of throwing them out, which would cause one of those long, whining academic wrangles) but whom I am expected to shepherd. The principle of academic tenure, in my view, is a preposterous Bill of Rights for bloody-minded, ego-drunk ruffians who have parlayed some sort of monkey-cleverness into a fat living. They think of me as a Daddy, and of course in modern terms the thing to do with Daddy is fry him. But I refuse to knuckle under to such nonsense, and a good deal of tension results.

Consequently I have been enjoying the last few weeks immoderately, for I have got myself out of the College – we go on for 12 months a year – & settled to the writing of a novel which has long been on my mind. It is a curious work, not like anything I have done before, and I doubt if anybody will like it much. But it has been on my mind for years, and demands to be written, so I am writing it and experiencing great catharsis therefrom.

In May I finished a study of Stephen Leacock* that I was asked to do. His centennial falls this year. I hope it is satisfactory; I have taken a view of S.L. much against the popular idea of the funny professor. Will send you a copy when it comes out.

And my contribution to the new many-volumed History of Drama is completed, and here again I have taken rather a new line on the 1750–1880 period I am covering; you may remember that at Oxford I was very much taken up with melodrama, and since then I have been plugging away at it, and now have a chance to say my say –

which is generally to the effect that its literary triviality has obscured its loud clear call to the hearts of audiences who saw in it a discussion of some of their own innermost concerns. The only trouble is that like all academic publishing it takes forever to get into print.*

Let me know how things are with you. Brenda and I are building a house in the country* – to escape to from here at weekends and holidays; it has a fine view. And we have another daughter married; husband a young biologist,* apparently promising, who is now going for an M.D. and then, I understand, back to biology. But he is very fond of people, and may practice instead, or teach and practice. We both like him very much. A child impends, so I shall be Old Gaffer Davies, carving ships out of pieces of kindling and telling fairy-tales in the chimney-corner. What life does to us! And so damned *fast*!

All the best

Rob.

To THE EDITOR OF *THE GLOBE AND MAIL**

Massey College
University of Toronto
[shortly before July 24, 1969]

[Sir:]

In the many comments you have printed on the dispute between Professors John T. Saywell and H. R. S. Ryan* I do not think anyone has mentioned a difference in attitude that underlies the definition of words in dictionaries. One group of lexicographers records what they believe to be the current use of the word – "prestigious" meaning "possessed of or conferring prestige," for example – whereas the other group defines words according to root, history, and usage by scholars and writers of repute. Let us call one attitude "popular" and the other "scholarly."

The trouble with the popular attitude is that it is so eager to keep up with changes in language that it encourages illiteracies that have become widespread. Such illiteracies are by no means confined to people whose schooling has been modest; indeed, people who are experts in fields other than language are among the worst offenders in this way. They like fancy words, but they cannot be bothered to find out what they mean. To give an example, the word "jejune" is a good, if somewhat unfamiliar, word for "hungry, meagre or barren" especially as applied to ideas or attitudes. But because it looks like the French word "jeune" – especially to speed-readers or smatterers – I have heard it used by people who seemed proud of their verbal jewel to mean "youthful, hopeful, charming." To admit this sort of usage is to create anarchy of language, and spread despair among those who value words and handle them like the edged tools they are.

I do not want to be stuffy and suggest that the *New English Dictionary* is the one true, apostolic dictionary delivered by the University of Oxford to the redeemed saints, but I must point out that dictionaries that are simple commercial products are apt to flatter careless and pretentious speakers and writers by recording and supporting their irresponsible mauling of our language. Many such dictionaries come from the United States, and I support N. Roy Clifton's comment* that their writ does not run here. A dictionary with a scholarly and historical bias is to be preferred. Most people regard a dictionary as an authority, not a key to fashionable foolishness.

[Yours sincerely,]

Robertson Davies

To GERALD LE DAIN

Massey College
University of Toronto
September 8, 1969

Gerald Le Dain (1924–   ), Canadian,
was professor of law at Osgoode Hall
Law School, York University, 1967–75,
and chairman of the Commission of
Inquiry into the Non-Medical Use of
Drugs, 1969–73.

[Dear Professor Le Dain:]

Thank you for your letter of September 5th. The subject of your Commission of Inquiry interests me very much indeed, for I am in touch with many students and hear quite a lot of conversation about the use of drugs. I do not feel, however, that I am qualified to present a formal brief to your Commission because I have no large body of fact upon which to build – only comments which have been made in conversation and in circumstances where they are not necessarily supported with indisputable evidence.

There is one aspect of this situation, however, about which I have an opinion which is supported by my own observation in this College and it is this: Many members of the medical profession seem to hand out what they call "tranquillizers" with remarkable freedom to students who are under stress and who sometimes exhibit symptoms of extreme disorder. In my conversations with these physicians, when I have talked to them on behalf of students known to me, they talk of "controlling" the neurosis. It appears to me from personal observation of students who are thus "controlled" that they have been partly stupefied, and although they are no longer a nuisance to the community they are unable to do their best work, and sometimes unable to do any work at all. It appears to me that we must be very cautious in condemning young people for their use of drugs when their elders and supposed intellectual superiors are extremely free with them. Indeed the drug problem seems not to be one of youth but of our age in general.

I am aware that the probable alternative to this wholesale distribution of tranquillizers is psychiatric treatment, which might be prolonged if the drug problem is as great as some people represent it to be, however, we might be wise to increase our training of competent psychiatrists and possibly turn our attention to that group whom Sigmund Freud called "lay analysts."

Yours sincerely,

[Robertson Davies]

To THE MASTER* OF BALLIOL COLLEGE

Massey College
University of Toronto
December 1, 1969

[Dear Master:]

On two occasions during the Mastership of Sir David Lindsay Keir,* I wrote to him on behalf of this College to ask if it would be possible for us to obtain one or two pieces of ornamental stone work from the facade of Balliol which was, at that time, being demolished. My reason for doing so was that this College, which I know you have visited briefly, was founded by the Massey family, four members of which had been Balliol men, and as I myself am a Balliol man, and so also are a number of our Fellows, we had hoped that we might incorporate one or two fragments of that College in our own building as ornaments. Sir David assured me that this could be done but I heard nothing further about it.

I am repeating this request to you, therefore, with assurance that we are happy to assume the cost of transportation and any charges that may arise. I hope that it is not too late for something to be done and would be happy to hear from you one way or the other.

This may appear to you to be sentimentality, but I am sure that you are also aware that sentimentality is one of the many kinds of glue that holds Colleges together.

With every good wish,

Yours sincerely,

[Robertson Davies]

To GRAHAM and JOAN
MCINNES

Massey College
University of Toronto
Jan. 5, 1970

The Davieses had spent the latter half of December abroad, primarily in London, but also in Paris, as they wanted to see their old friends the McInneses. Graham, who had become Canada's ambassador at UNESCO, was suffering from cancer.

Dear Graham & Joan:

We arrived home late on Saturday, and yesterday I spent all day going through accumulated correspondence; I always wonder what may jump out at me on such occasions, but this time all was calm. Today I am devoting to writing some personal letters, and yours must be the first. We both hope that the report from your physicians was encouraging, though I remember we agreed that they would be unlikely to commit themselves too strongly. Still, if they give you some modest encouragement you may hope for very much better results.

I need not stress how much it meant to us to see you both, and to be taken into your confidence at a bad time. Your courage and resolution were all that we would have expected of you – all that one could hope for in oneself in such a situation – but we pray (have indeed truly prayed) that things are not so irrevocable as you thought, and that many good years lie before you. Still, it is like you to assume nothing, and to be firm and strong; the only thing is, perhaps, that one should not be *too* strong, *too* resigned, *too* stoical in accepting the worst. I think I quoted you Hardy's fine lines –

If way to the Better there be
　　it exacts a full look at the worst –

but that was from a poem called *In tenebris*, and one can never be quite sure one has come to the darkness. Hope is not a delusion and a salve for weak spirits; it is a tremendous reality. So I hope, dear old friend, that you will not hurry to embrace the darkness when hope is still possible. I could do a lot of quoting; indeed the lines keep running through my head –

> Christ leads us through no darker rooms
>   Than He went through before –*

but I don't want to come the Holy Joe on you, for I know your outlook is different, and the only religion I respect is that in which a man is true to himself, and realizes himself most fully. You have been a Stoic for as long as I have known you, and Stoicism has its splendid resources as well as gentler – and perhaps in truth I should say – more romantic philosophies of life.

Now, I think that is quite enough from me about that. We had a tremendous bout of theatre-going in London, and saw much that was new as well as old, and quite the best thing we saw was *The Way of the World** at the Old Vic, done with a fine Swiftian edge that was delightfully different from the lace-hanky and snuff-taking style of Congreve production. Saw a panto, too – *Give a Dog a Bone* – and did not realize till we were seated that it was a Moral Re-Armament show! No wonder so many people despise religion! This dripped with glucose. But as a man who delights in words I relished the Congreve; modern attempts to regard the author as a nuisance and an odd-job man in the theatre are totally rebuked by such a feast of wit, elegance and the strength of mind without which elegance is as piffle before the wind,* to quote that notable stylist Daisy Ashford.

No more now. Write when you can.

Love from us both

Rob.

To MARGARET LAURENCE

Massey College
University of Toronto
Feb. 18 [1970]

*Margaret Laurence (1926–87) is one of
Canada's most important novelists. As
writer in residence at the University of
Toronto in 1969–70, Laurence had an
office in Massey College.*

Dear Margaret:

Because I had some work to do that could not wait, Brenda was
first to read *A Bird in the House* and was delighted with it; I finished
it myself last night and hasten to tell you how much pleasure it gave
me of a truly literary kind – I mean the deep pleasure that comes
from a really deep book, and has nothing to do with simple pastime.
I see what you mean about having waited until now to write auto-
biographically; the kind of thing you have in this book is distilled
feeling – not agreeable recollection of the externals of childhood.

The book struck a strongly responsive note in me as I am sure it
will with many Canadians; most of us have something of the atmosphere of Manawaka in our background. With me it was Renfrew,
in the upper Ottawa Valley, which, when I was a child there, was
certainly the Land that God Gave Cain.* Rural Ontario or rural
Manitoba, the spiritual deprivation is the same, and for the sort of
perceptive child who later becomes a writer, the sense of being
strange and alone is all-pervasive. I now know that what I suffered
from most painfully was unrequited vivacity: I wanted to be merry
and lively, and the leaden spirit of those sour-spirited Scotch kids,
whose vivacity expressed itself in torturing animals and jeering at the
crippled (the town boasted a notable dwarf who hanged himself
eventually, so jolly had life been made for him) that I was terribly
oppressed. Was life really like this, I wondered. Thank God, no.

Grandfather Connor and Grandmother MacLeod are very finely
realized. Oh, those granitic elders, sitting like images of Pharaoh in
their damned parlours! My grandmother – Dutch by descent – was
poison-pious. "I'll get to the market tomorra – *if I'm spared!*" she
would say, casting a gooseberry eye at me to see if I was appropriately impressed by the vanity of human wishes and the Conqueror

Worm. She was spared to a great old age, and as generals have horses shot under them in battle, she outwore two old maid daughters. My mother was the only one who had the "sand" (a much-admired quality) to marry, having to run away from home and have a row with her parents to do so. Ooooh, how Canada marks us, and mars us and maims us. But you have done the great thing: you have transformed these miseries into art, to which we can respond with the special blend of pain-in-recollection and joy-in-recollection that art of this sort provides. It cannot be utterly bad, we feel, if an artist can do this sort of thing with it. The wretchedness *did* have a form, and a validity; it was not merely gratuitous Hell.

So thank you more than I can say, and especially for your most generous gift of an early copy, with such a warming inscription.

And thank you, too, for your remarks about *At My Heart's Core*; if I were re-writing it now I would not make it so gabby; it has been acted a good deal in Canada. As for *Overlaid* it has been acted, I understand, more than any other Canadian play; it seems to get to the rural districts in the way I intended – not realism, God knows, but as a kind of *vaudeville* that allows a lot to be said in a small compass. Ethel comes right out of my mother's family – life-denying, bitter and (in the phrase they loved to use of other people) "kinda narra."

I hope you are surviving February: I reel under the blows of Fate.

Every good wish

Rob.

To TYRONE and JUDITH GUTHRIE

Massey College
University of Toronto
Feb. 27, '70

Dear Tony & Judy:

To reply to RSVPs first: Miranda is at 29 Cheyne Court, Flood Street, SW 3: second, I should be complimented if I were permitted to look over your text for the book on *ACTING** and would certainly make any comments that I thought might be useful..... & would of course send it back as soon as possible.

Now..... we are very sorry indeed to hear that you have to rest, for you don't like rest, and I think you are one of those people who gets admirable ideas when in full activity. But people who think best when on the hop are very likely to push themselves too far, so I suppose you must now cultivate the difficult art of thinking while inactive. Hard cheese! But 70 is as piffle before the wind, and if you rest you will not know yourself by the end of summer.

Sorry to hear bad news of Minneapolis.* Of course I knew that Douglas Campbell had left – and left Ann, as well, which saddens me, for I liked her greatly, though as you know I was never very keen about him. He too has taken a young mistress. These fellows like Michael [Langham] and Douglas are no wiser than Renaissance Popes; they have a superstitious belief in the revivifying effect of young flesh; they regard a Juicy Piece as the equivalent of a Voronoff transplant of goat's balls, or whatever the muck was. Ah, vain, delusive joys!

Last night the St. Lawrence Centre for the [Performing] Arts opened here; Mavor Moore's shop. Great hoo-ha, & scores of trendy folk in quaint garb lallygagging over a mixed media piece by Languirand called *Mankind Inc.** It is Wilder's *The Skin of Our Teeth* boiled and strained through a coarse and dirty colander, and served with a sauce of film, back-projection and lights that hurt your eyes. So what happens today? Mavor phones me, with mighty adjurations to secrecy,

to ask me to write him a letter of recommendation for a professorship at York Univ., where he will teach about the theatre! I groan in
the spirit. Here we have built this multi-million $ show-shop to
Mavor's personal specifications, and immediately it opens he is off
with the raggle-taggle academics, O!* Not that I blame him personally; the show-biz world of Canada would drive anybody into a university or a madhouse. Incidentally his director, Leon Major,* is
seriously considering my Casanova play for production next season;
would have done it this season except that they are doing *Faust* in a
splendid new translation by Barker Fairley.* If one has to be put to
one side it is nice to have it done by Goethe, whom I worship. And
Barker Fairley is a wonderful old chap, well over eighty, and I do not
a bit object to his getting his whack first. I don't think you know my
play, which is called *General Confession*, and is not in the least a dirty
play about seduction, but a sort of psychological fantasia. Michael
Langham said it has "lots of the old theatre magic" & would have
done it for the Davises if they had not decided to do J. B. Priestley's
The Glass Cage* instead – a flop, as it turned out.

Brenda is immensely cock-a-hoop because we have at last a grand-
son, Christopher David William Cunnington, and a fine sturdy child
he is, though at present he just stares about and takes his wittles reglar.*
So the human race is saved for at least one more generation. This,
and the prospect of building a house, are great diversions in our long
and treacherous winter.

I do not know whether I am about to burst into flower, with three
books in a row, or perhaps be blasted on the vine. If you are interested in Leacock I'll send one as soon as it appears; it is a very short
book, intended for students, mostly, but not therefore unreadable by
the intelligent adult. I send you also a copy of a poem* I wrote as a
jeu d'esprit for our College Poetry Evening, and which has had an
unforeseen success; I distribute copies like those pretentious abbés in
the 18th century who were above mere print but liked to be read by
their chums. As you will judge from it, I thought *Hair* stank – noisy,
dowdily dirty and amateurish. One girl of 17 told her mother that
my poem was the most horridly obscene thing she had ever read (she

obviously thought my quote from W. B. Yeats was original, and I
devoutly wish it were) but she gobbled up *Hair* without a blink. How
innocent the young tend to be.....

Strong, healing love from us both –

Rob.

To JOAN MCINNES

Massey College
University of Toronto
March 20, 1970

Dearest Joan:

When the news of Graham's death came I determined to wait a
little before writing to you, for I knew you would have a flood of
notes and letters, and I hoped that something from me might be
helpful later. But I fell into the clutch of the 'flu and was in bed for
a fortnight and have been at grips ever since with the wretched
depression and melancholy it leaves behind it, so this is much later
than I had meant.

Yet – I do not know what to say, because there is nothing to be said
that can make any difference to the brutal fact. However, as I lay in
bed I thought a lot about Graham and you, and thought how many
battles he had fought and won. He never spared himself, never gave
less than his uttermost, was indeed self-destructive in his attitude to
virtually any job he undertook. Yet as he gave greatly he received
greatly; he is one of the very small number of men I have known who
really took the trouble to look deeply and clearly into personal relationships, and if it was sometimes disillusioning and costly to him, it
gave him insights very few people achieve. He worked unsparingly at
all his jobs, and he won great prizes; after all, he died an ambassador,
and I think he brought to that work a degree of perception and a

quality of understanding and appreciation that must be very rare. He realized another part of himself in his literary work, and he had the immense satisfaction of returning to Australia and reaping some of the sweet harvest of success on his home ground. So it cannot be said that he died unfulfilled, though he missed the years of reconsideration and distillation which would have meant much to him, and of which he would certainly have made other and admirable books. A good life – a very good life. Unhappily, a life robbed of its Third Act.

I don't know if Brenda told you, but we got the news on Feb. 28. Next morning – Sunday – we had a celebration of Holy Communion in the chapel here, & we asked the chaplain to name Graham at the appropriate point, so that for us it was a memorial service for him. I well recall that he was with us when my Father died and went to Chapel with us the following morning, to what was also a memorial service; I shall not forget his kindness at that time, and at this service, which was for him, we thought of him with great love, and seemed to feel him very near, as he was then. I hope you do not regard this as aggressive religiosity; we find we need a form to contain our religious feeling, and we find it in Anglicanism, but I assure you it is by no means narrow or sectarian or even rigidly Christian. It is just our way of expressing a special kind of very deep feeling, which seems to require ritual and formal usage to body it forth.

You are the one who matters now, and you remember that I urged you not to let yourself be destroyed by Graham's death. Of course you have taken a dreadful knock, and nothing under a year will begin to ease that; you must grieve – it is natural and right, and healing, too. Grief repressed is a poison; legitimately indulged it is one of the few solaces we have in times of great trial and it brings its own healing. You have a long time to go, a life to re-direct, and much energy, experience, and beauty and charm of spirit to give to all kinds of people. No woman of your quality is ever wholly and solely somebody's wife; you are still you.

With all our love –

Rob.

To ANNA SZIGETHY

Massey College
University of Toronto
April 2, 1970

Anna Szigethy (1947–   ), was then
executive editor at the Canadian
publishing firm of McClelland and
Stewart. Since 1982, as Anna Porter, she
has been publisher of Key Porter Books.
(Davies turned to M&S again only in the
1990s for his last two novels, after
Douglas Gibson, his long-standing editor
at Macmillan, had joined the firm.)

[Dear Miss Szigethy:]

I am sending you with this a marked copy of *Stephen Leacock*. As you will see, the proof-reading has been very much neglected and the general preparation of the book has been so careless that in two places substantial portions of the text have been dropped. Even the material on the back of the cover contains errors. It seems also that the proof-reading has been entrusted to somebody who does not recognize such words as 'acuity' and 'spoliation' and who, on page 43, does not distinguish between £ and $. When the proofs of the book were sent here they were very carefully proof-read and returned with a list of at least 33 typographical errors; my secretary was assured, over the telephone by a Mr. _____ that the errors we were returning had already been corrected, but clearly this was not so.

I am sending you also some examples of alterations which have been made in the text and I judge that these have been the work of an editor who thinks I do not know how to write. I find this astonishing as I have been a writer for many years and this book is the twentieth that I have had published, and during that time I have had no complaints about my style – on the contrary have sometimes been praised for it. If I were so incompetent a writer as to need the attention you have given me, it would surely have been better not to ask me to write the book in the first place. At present a novel of mine [*Fifth Business*] is in process of publication by Macmillans, and when they are doubtful about anything I have written they ask me about it and we clear it up between us; this is the procedure that has been adopted by all the publishers that I have worked with, including Knopf, Chatto and Windus, Scribner's, Secker and Warburg – the sole exception being McClelland and Stewart, who do not seem to value my opinion in these matters.

The Leacock book is such a mess that I am ashamed to speak of it to my friends and could not dream of recommending it to students. It is humiliating to be associated with it. I feel compelled, therefore, to say that I will not sign a contract for *Feast of Stephen* [a Leacock anthology to be edited by Davies], or do any further work on its preparation, until I have a letter from McClelland and Stewart* guaranteeing that the whole of the material contained in *Stephen Leacock* will be printed as an introduction, that the text will be what I have written and not what your anonymous editor prefers (even to the matter of punctuation, in which I may be idiosyncratic but certainly not downright silly), and that corrections which I make in the proof will be heeded. I took a great deal of trouble in writing the small book, which you have treated so carelessly, and I should like it to appear in print in a form which does not humiliate me and confuse the reader. When I was approached about writing this book I was assured that the fee was to be small because it was, in a sense, a contribution on my part to Canadian literary studies. I receive the impression from what you have done, however, that you regard these simply as cheap books. I assure you that I am not a cheap author and deeply resent the way in which you have dealt with my work.

Yours faithfully,

[Robertson Davies]

To TYRONE GUTHRIE

Massey College
University of Toronto
April 7, 1970

*Tyrone Guthrie was descended on his
mother's side from Tyrone Power, whom
Davies once described* as "the early
nineteenth-century Irish actor whose gifts
and charm won him a high place before
his untimely death." On his father's side,
Guthrie was descended from Dr. Thomas
Guthrie, whom Davies characterized as
"the Scottish preacher and philanthropist,
a thundering orator, fighter for total
abstinence, and organizer of the Ragged
School movement to give elementary
instruction to the children of the poor.
This great-grand-father was as much a
charmer as the great actor."*

Dear Tony:

Herewith the MS and comment [some three and a half pages]. . . .

The book starts rather unimpressively and gets into high gear about
Chapter three, and is then full of meat, and really good counsel for the
serious beginner. Perhaps you might fatten the first two chapters. I
think you underestimate the weight of your reputation; you are a
power, and can thunder. But I sense Tyrone Power, rattling star of
Timmy the Tiler, at war with Guid Dr. Guthrie, Father of the Ragged
Schools, having an awful punch-up in your book. T.P. is all for the
Instinct; Dr. G. for Industry and Virtue. But both are Feelers; neither
is a Thinker, and so you are rather cranky about academics, whom you
suppose to Think a lot. They don't, you know; the best of them are
Feelers, too. If you will moderate your book not so as to geld it, but
so as to admit a decent debt from the stage to the universities – the
debt in reverse is generously acknowledged, even if the results are artis-
tically meagre, you will strengthen it. But at present it has an air of
grievance, whenever universities are mentioned, which is weakening.

By the way, the famous emendation about "he babbled of green
fields" is NOT Malone; it is Theobald.* I am sure you would not wish

to be in error on this point, as it might provoke sniggers in the Senior Common Rooms.

But these cavils aside, I think the book is fine – so good, indeed, that I think some expansion at the points I have indicated, on the philosophical and ethical side, would be welcomed by readers. After all, the artistic world is still ruthlessly undemocratic: those who have talent are set off from those who lack it by a gulf that no amount of Arts Council grants or other First Aid to the Hopeless can possibly bridge; and those who think of going on the stage ought to know it. I find that on this continent they find it very hard to swallow. And here is where your really strong anti-university argument lies: universities can do nothing for talent – they serve intelligent industry, and they damned well know it. They know they have no means of creating artists though – in music, for instance – they can teach them the customs of their trade. But in the Theatre, the world of dreams, the notion still lingers that Wishing Will Make It So. Here in Toronto, when we told the students that they could no more act their own plays than they could make their own clothes, and hired a professional co. to do it, the shrieks of injured vanity rent the skies for months, and still echo.

Our love to you & Judy,

Rob.

To the editor of *THE GLOBE AND MAIL**

Massey College
University of Toronto
[On or soon after July 3, 1970]

Sir:

This is an apology, directed to your theatre critic, Mr. Herbert Whittaker, to Mr. Patrick Crean,* whose fine revivifying of the works of Rudyard Kipling in his performance called "The Sun Never Sets" I so much enjoyed on Thursday July 2, and to anybody else whom I disturbed on that occasion. In his criticism (in your issue of July 3) Mr. Whittaker twice refers to my loud laughter,* which seems to have got his goat; he has spoken to me about it before, but never in print. Now I understand the sensations felt by my mother when, many years ago, she was rebuked from the pulpit for dancing.

These many years I have valued Mr. Whittaker as a personal friend, and admired – nay, reverenced – him as a critic. I am covered with shame at the thought that I have grieved that great and good man by laughing in the theatre.

There is an explanation, though it is a poor one. I simply can't help it. A loud laugh, like webbed feet or a vestigial tail, is a regressive trait that descends to a few people from our primitive ancestors. I am one thus afflicted, with the laugh only. When I am amused (or delighted by a notable show of skill, like Mr. Crean's in making fresh Kipling's art) I laugh, loudly. I used to think the noise had something to do with the shape of the roof of my mouth, but now I know it is because I am a throw-back to some noisy Welsh hillbilly whose brays of delight echoed down his native valleys, irritating the Normans on the other side of Offa's Dyke.

I cannot do much about it, but I suppose it would be decent of me to keep away from first-nights, when I may disturb the critics at their holy task. In future I promise to go only to Wednesday matinees, where no critic has been known to set foot.

Your humbled, apologetic reader,

Robertson Davies

To THE EDITOR OF *THE NEW YORKER*

Massey College
University of Toronto
November 30, 1970

[Sir:]

The large object pictured on page 147 of your edition of November 28th, illustrating your "On and Off the Avenue" department, was last seen in that form in 1951, a century after it made its appearance at the Great Exhibition.* My father caused it to be dismantled, and I have some portions of its magnificent carving in my possession.

The sideboard was of Austrian workmanship, and it was purchased for £1,400 at the Exhibition by John Naylor,* a Liverpool ship-builder, for his newly built house near Welshpool, Montgomeryshire. This was Leighton Hall, erected on the site of a Jacobean manor, which he destroyed for that purpose; Leighton was designed by Sir Charles Barry,* architect of the Houses of Parliament, in the Gothic Revival taste and it required massive furniture. The Naylors provided this in quantity, including a remarkable Swiss clock which occupied a tower to itself, and played national airs and favourite hymns on demand and on the hour; there were also marble likenesses of Mrs. Naylor, with her children kneeling in prayer before her, of Eve, and of Highland Mary, not to speak of suits of armour, Gothic writing-tables, a Turkey carpet 35' by 21', a piano with a special case incorporating the initials of the Naylors in *marqueterie*, and the arms of all the ancient princes of Wales in stained glass in a clerestory.

When my father bought Leighton in 1951 much of this grandeur remained because it was very hard to remove. The new owner, who was only 73 and Welsh, and therefore expected to live in the house for a good long time (he did so until he was 87) could put up with the marble and greatly liked the arms of Howel Dda and the other Welshmen, but decided that the Austrian sideboard was not to be borne.

It was the dogs that did it. My father's attitude toward dogs was reserved: the six three-foot wooden hunting-dogs, each with a carved chain around its neck, that may be seen in your illustration, were more than he could stand. They all wore that expression of moral superiority which the nineteenth century believed was proper to dogs, but otherwise they were dismayingly lifelike. The figures of the seasons, and of Ceres and Pomona* and other givers of good things he quite liked; the cupids with scythes and sickles were charming; the dead boar and the pheasants could have been endured; but the dogs – it might not be. So he had the great Austrian sideboard carefully dismantled by a cabinet-maker and stored the pieces in the stables.

It was like taking down a church. The workmanship was superb, the carving fine, and the joinery exemplary, so it all came apart in coherent sections. Some of the smaller pieces my father gave to his family; I have two magnificent cornucopia, and the cupid with a hat, who makes an excellent centrepiece for a Thanksgiving buffet. The wood of the carvings was fruitwood of every variety, worked as Austrian carvers knew how to do it.

So far as I know, the pieces that remain are where he put them, wrapped in straw and canvas.

I thought you might like to know.

Yours sincerely,

[Robertson Davies]

To HUGH MACLENNAN

Massey College
University of Toronto
January 13 [1971]

Dear Hugh:

Your letter of December 15 was waiting for me when I arrived home from a brief jaunt abroad, last weekend, and of a number of pleasing things that have been said about *Fifth Business* it is immeasurably the most delightful to me. You will know why; approval from readers and reviewers is what one seeks, but the understanding good word of another writer whom one greatly admires is what one hardly dares to expect, and is immensely flattered and humbled to receive. You really *know* what writing a novel means, and of how many people in Canada can this be said?

I particularly appreciated what you said about "that curious, ambiguous sphere which is the province of the older artist," because I am strongly conscious of the folly and self-destructiveness of trying to write in one's youthful vein when youth is past. At my age one ought to know more, and know it better, than was possible at thirty or forty. In middle life an artist – and surely we may both describe ourselves as artists, though many people shy at the word as applied to writers – has to change gears or perish; the impulses of youth should have given way to some achievement of insight, and without positively sounding like Grandfather Frog* he ought to write from a different ground of knowledge. But how many writers are wrecked in trying to round that point – or in fearing to do so. This is particularly the fate of humorists; they won't face middle age, and try to go on being youthful cutups when their antics have grown pitiful.

It is quite untrue that I wrote the book in two months; that is the sort of thing journalists like to believe. The writing took me about eight months, but the book was in my mind and in many notebooks for about twelve years, during which time I had to undertake and complete several writing tasks of very different nature. I am a slow writer and an even slower reviser, and furthermore I am a short-winded writer – two hours in a day is absolutely all I can manage. I am also secretive – hate talking about a book while it is in progress, because I find that while the broad outline of plot remains pretty firm, the means by which it is achieved keeps shifting, and usually does not declare itself until I am actually at work.

However, I would appreciate your advice about something relating to *Fifth Business* which is naggingly on my mind at present: I feel impelled to write another novel [*The Manticore*] about the same characters, but from a quite different point of view – that of Edward [David] Staunton, the son of Boy Staunton, who is said to have become a lawyer and a drunk. But I see this man as one of his father's principal victims, but a victim who in the end escapes his father's toils. He adored his father, and wanted to be like him, but for the obvious reason – that sons, in one way or another are impelled to live out the unlived portion of their father's lives, and because Edward is a man of greater sensitivity than Boy – he could not do it. The book would not be a sequel – no hint of *The Bobbsey Twins* at Long Island* being followed by *The Bobbsey Twins at Yellowstone Park* – but another aspect of a complex theme. How does a son face the reality of a dominant and successful father? I know something of this, for though my own father was no Boy Staunton (indeed, he detested such people) he was quite sufficiently dominant to have given my life a number of curious twists. So, although the book would be no more autobiographical than was *Fifth Business*, it would have a good lively imaginative springboard. Could you, some time, give me your opinion as a deeply experienced craftsman, and critic, and artist most of all, about such undertakings.

I do not remember the First World War except for burning the Kaiser and the kind of Victory Parade* I described, but it was very real in my family's history. My cousin, St. John Robertson* went down on the *Aboukir* as a midshipman, in the very early days of that awful business..... As for Eisengrim & his madness, I should like to take another look at him – and at the obsessed dottiness of the great public performer – in the book I speak of. Because it was Staunton's son who shouted the question "Who killed Boy Staunton,"* at the Brazen Head; he did so while he was drunk and miserable, and then of course he had to find out the answer to his question.

Again, heartfelt thanks for your letter,

Rob.

To AN ASPIRING PLAYWRIGHT

Massey College
University of Toronto
March 16, 1971

[Dear Mr. _____:]

I know that you will not mind if I reply to your letter briefly, for a full reply would run to the length of a book and neither of us has time for that.

The first point is that you must spell the word "playwright" and this spelling should tell you a great deal about how plays are put together. A "wright" is a man who wreaks something – that is to say who imposes a form upon raw material. The raw material is the idea that you have for your play and it may come to you either as a single dramatic incident, for which you must provide both the preparation and the resolution, or it may come as a complete dramatic narrative. Certainly before writing the play you should prepare a scenario which will enable you to put the scenes in the right order and to achieve the climax at the right place and you should stick to this scenario carefully. You should also prepare very elaborate notes on all your characters, and indeed there are many playwrights, of whom Henrik Ibsen was one, who wrote complete biographies for the principal characters in all their plays. Apart from this, the only advice that I can offer you is Stephen Leacock's: "Writing is simply a matter of jotting down things as they occur to you; the jotting presents no difficulty, but the occurring may be more difficult."*

There are playwrights who write novels and there are others who never write anything but plays. Whether an imaginative project is best suited to the novel form or to being a play is something that you will know by instinct.

A TV script is different from a play only in the limitations that the medium puts upon it; the dramatic form is essentially the same.

With good wishes,

Yours sincerely,

[Robertson Davies]

To MRS. A. E. McCULLOCH

Massey College
University of Toronto
April 21, 1971

Dorothy McCulloch (1929–2001),
Canadian, from Manitou, Manitoba,
wrote to Davies and many other notables,
asking for recipes, probably with the
intention of publishing them as a
collection.

[Dear Mrs. McCulloch:]

Thank you for your letter asking for a recipe. I am happy to send you my recipe for Old English Trifle, which I tested on countless occasions, and which I can guarantee to be the one true and proper way to make this dish.

OLD ENGLISH TRIFLE

Line the bottom of a pudding bowl with broken and crumbled stale sponge cake. The pieces should not be too small, but, upon the other hand, they should not be more than 1½" square. The sponge cake should half fill the bowl. It should then be soaked in a good quality of medium sweet Sherry. Canadian Sherry, I am sorry to say, is not satisfactory as it lacks the overtones which are vital to this delicious dish. Now cover the Sherry-soaked sponge cake with a generous coating of raspberry jam, and add a layer of sliced peaches. Cover this in its turn with a generous coating of liquid custard to which sufficient Jamaica rum has been added to give it a satisfactory flavour. The whole dish should now be chilled in the refrigerator, but only enough to make it cold, not enough to cool the flavour of the wine and the rum. Before serving put plenty of whipped cream on top and decorate it, if you wish, with chopped cherries, walnuts and almonds.

This dish is guaranteed to make a success of any party and should not be served in less than truly generous quantities.

Yours sincerely,

[Robertson Davies]

To PAULINE MCGIBBON

Massey College
University of Toronto
April 27, 1971

Pauline M. McGibbon (1910–2001), Canadian, served in many volunteer positions before becoming chancellor of the University of Toronto 1971–74, lieutenant-governor of the Province of Ontario 1974–80, and chair of the National Arts Centre 1980–84.

[Dear Pauline:]

I was struck by your remark at the concert on Sunday night last that you looked forward with dread to wearing the Chancellor's exceedingly heavy gown. I conjured up a vision of you doing so and felt that your misgivings were well-founded, and proceeded to give the matter some further thought. So far as I can discover, there is nothing at all that compels you to wear the gown as it exists. After all, you are the first woman to be Chancellor of the University and there is no earthly power that can stop you from having any gown you please, though obviously you will not want to fly in the face of tradition. However, the heavy gown of black silk decorated with gold bullion is the one that the University supplies and if you seriously want another you will probably have to provide it yourself.

Why not do so? New universities all over the world are devising new robes and some of them are extraordinarily beautiful. Cecil Beaton* has done some magnificent robes for the new English university at Brighton. They have a dash and dramatic sweep quite unknown to the ordinary academic robemakers. The Oriental universities also have gorgeous robes. Why not get a first-class Canadian designer to design a version of the Chancellor's robe especially for you in very light black silk and take account of the traditional gold ornamentation only by having a single beautiful gold ornament carefully placed – a tassel from the left shoulder or something of that sort, and, as I urged you on Sunday night, do not let them make you wear that black square cap; there was never a woman born who looked well in a mortar-board. You could get a beautiful cap made in silk which would be extremely becoming. If you are looking for any pictures from which to evolve a suitable design, may I recommend *A History of Academical Dress in Europe* by W. N. Hargreaves-Mawdsley.

One of the things which is a problem for women wearing academical dress is that they never seem to have the right things around their necks, and a naked neck and a considerable extent of exposed bosom coming out of an academic gown has a very bad theatrical effect and is, furthermore, unseemly, as these robes are essentially ecclesiastical in nature. Your designer could certainly prepare you a splendid blouse with either a fine white bow or a lace jabot to present the right effect.

All of this would cost you some money, but how better could you spend money than to show that a woman Chancellor can bring a fine new look of elegance to the Convocation ceremonies, which are so often dreadfully dowdy in their appearance? One of the things which I know for a certainty that you have learned in your public life is how to do things with style and this is certainly an opportunity for style, and God knows the University needs it.

With every good wish,

Yours sincerely,

[Rob.]

To P. B. JACKSON

Massey College
University of Toronto
May 27, 1971

*Philip B. Jackson (1917–   ), Canadian,
was president of the Jackson Lewis
Company, a construction firm, and, in
1971, president of the University Club of
Toronto. Davies was a member 1949–77.*

[Dear Mr. Jackson]

I am returning herewith the questionnaire about long range planning for the Club, which I have completed. I have examined also the memorandum about long range planning and I am certainly in agreement with anything that is done to make the Club a pleasanter place.

I was particularly interested in Section B, headed Aesthetic, and relating mostly to the washrooms. I think it is widely recognized that the water closets at the Club are such as no one can use with pleasure and, indeed, no one capable of exercising a choice in the matter would use them at all. For the main washroom, however, I have a certain affection and I think it stands with the corresponding accommodation at the York Club as one of the great unchanging monuments of civilization as we know it in Toronto. I hope, therefore, that any revisions would be undertaken with a gentle hand and that it would continue to have a clublike atmosphere and not that of a barber shop for ambiguous patrons which so many very modern washrooms resemble.

In conclusion may I say that I feel that there has been a decided improvement in the food and service at the Club during the past few months.

With good wishes,

Yours sincerely,

[Robertson Davies]

To J. BURGON BICKERSTETH

Massey College
University of Toronto
July 4: 1971

Dear Burgon:

Many thanks for your letter of June 22, which arrived the day after I had had excellent news of you from Jenny and Tom; they described you as being in wonderful spirits, and giving no sign of the wretched spell of ill-health we all knew you had suffered during the Winter and Spring. It was wonderfully kind of you to be so good to them; their visit to Canterbury was the high-light of their time in Britain.

I am so glad you liked the book [*Fifth Business*]. It has done much better than I had dared to hope. When you have a chance to read it, you will find that it is, in its way, a religious book, and as such it has been given a great welcome in the U.S., where a lot of readers seem to be sick of books about self-indulgent, nasty-living people. I am at present here in the country, working away at another book [*The Manticore*] about many of the same characters, and of kindred theme, though it is not precisely a sequel. Our house in the country is a great success. We need it, because when we retire from Massey we shall have to live somewhere, and we wanted a country retreat. So it is a full-scale house, not a cottage – unless one of those eighteenth century affairs called a *cottage orné*. It stands in 100 acres of hill country with a view toward Toronto, and we are delighted with it. Its name is Windhover (kestrel), because there are a lot of hawks about, and because it is the name of a favourite poem of ours by Gerard Manley Hopkins.* We were lucky enough to get a chunk of stone from Balliol (which is being re-done) to use as a corner-stone, with the date of building carved on it, and in my study I have a piece of oak beam from the house in which my father was born in Welshpool [Wales]: the date of building – 1738 – is carved in it. So you see it is a house of reminiscences, as Brenda also has lots of things in it from her family home. Did you know her family originally went to Australia from the

Shetlands? We have been back to see the family place of origin – a tiny parsonage right on the sea, from which young Petersons* went out to Australia, and India, and one to Canada; this one became President of McGill – Sir William Peterson. Another became a distinguished Sanskrit scholar; Brenda's great-grandfather just became rich, but his descendants have had cause to be glad of that.

But this is too much that is merely gossipy. What you say about your letters goes directly home with me. We should greatly like to have them,* and would value them extremely. Nor would this be wholly because of their own great interest. They would enormously extend the range and interest of our collection of Vincent's papers* – give it another dimension. As you know, I have kept a detailed diary of the history of Massey College since the day Vincent asked me to head it. It is diffuse and gossipy, as well as containing all the facts I could muster, and it contains much about College personalities, both among the junior and senior men. And of course a lot about the Massey Family and how things were when they were deciding the details of College building and character. I shall leave this to the College,* and I am vain enough to think that with Vincent's papers, and yours, it will form a body of university and Canadian history of substantial interest. It is not every day that three notably articulate men offer comment on a linked group of experiences.

As to putting an embargo on the use of your letters, that must be your decision. I can assure you, however, that we have been extremely discreet in the use of Vincent's papers. People write every week wanting to search them for something, but so far we have allowed nothing of the kind. The National Archive coolly suggested that we give them copies of everything! Not a chance! Lochhead and I take the conditions of the trust *au pied de la lettre* and allow no snoopers. It would be the same with yours.

No historian wants to write about Vincent, though the College would be glad if it were so, because we do not think his memory is best served by a 25 year postponement of *that*. Twenty-five years is too long, and not long enough, and when it is past, his career will be cold potatoes. But I tried Creighton* and Careless: the former is too old (he says – he is 71) and the latter too deeply committed. There was some talk that Claude Bissell might do it, but . . . he was not really sympathetic to Vincent's often curious ideas. So we must wait. But a biographer working on his papers would not be the same as somebody who was simply looting them for a book on some other subject. And the biography would have to please the College, for I expect we should be paying the shot – the family want a biography, but don't understand that such things do not fall from Heaven.

Once again, great thanks for your letter. I hope to get to England before too long, and will come to see you if you will have me.

Brenda joins me in affectionate good wishes

<u>Rob.</u>

To C. S. LENNOX

Massey College
University of Toronto
September 16, 1971.

C. S. Lennox was dean of Devonshire House, then a residence for engineering students at the University of Toronto. Devonshire House is located directly across the street from Massey College.

[Dear Dean Lennox:]

I am sorry to have to report to you so early in the term that difficulties have arisen between the men of Devonshire House and Massey College, but I feel that it is necessary to keep this record straight because I am apprehensive that on some such occasion damage will be done which will be truly serious and if that happens I do not think that it should be regarded as a single incident.

Last night, September 15th, I had a meeting at my house of a group of 16 people about some business unrelated to the University. This was the night when the Devonshire House students chose to douse passing cars with garbage pails full of water. They extended this game to throwing water over my garden wall, so that it was necessary for the guests to retire inside the house. When it was time to leave some students charged my front door and flooded my hall with water and drenched two of my guests to the skin. This is not irreparable damage, but the drying and re-waxing in the hall will take some time and I do not think that at least two of my guests will forget this aspect of university life. My impression was certainly that the disorder this year was greater than it had been in the past.

I am sure that you realize that there is nothing personal in these complaints but I feel that you should be informed of them as this sort of incident is making the occupancy of my own quarters in Massey College decidedly unpleasant and I should not like to find myself in a position where I cannot ask people to come to my house for fear that they will be assaulted or subjected to indignities.

Yours sincerely,

[Robertson Davies]

To FATHER PATRICK M. PLUNKETT S.J.

Massey College
University of Toronto
Nov. 4, 1971

Father Patrick Mary Plunkett (1911–75) was a Canadian Jesuit, a Catholic priest, and, for the last 20 years of his life, a professor of English at St. Paul's College, University of Manitoba.

Dear Father Plunkett:

. . . But to come to the serious part of your criticism [of *Fifth Business*]; I truly think I am a gnostic, if that means somebody who thinks that completion, or integration, or salvation of the spirit may be achieved by study and hard intellectual work. After all, as I have written in another novel,* Christ's birth was made known to three types of mankind in three appropriate ways: to the shepherds by portents and wonders, because they would not have known or heeded anything less; to the Magi by their studies and subtleties; to Simeon in the Temple by virtue of the vision given him by his great goodness. If I am going to achieve salvation, it will have to be as a Magus, because I am not simple, nor would I ever have the presumption to think I was particularly good – though I do my best. So, if that is a gnostic, I must bear the label.

There are other problems, too. I am much troubled by the problem of evil, and particularly the ambiguity of evil. Courses of life which seem to me to be evil nevertheless appear to bear good fruit; what is presented to me as virtue seems all too often in my eyes to be merely the avoidance of involvements which might imperil the "good" man (and you must understand that I do not mean by that the religious life, which I well know to be beset by perils of which the average sensual man knows nothing). My only honest conclusion is that, except in very gross matters, I cannot distinguish evil from good, and I marvel at the boldness of those Calvinist educators who brought me up, who seemed to be certain what was and was not God's will. Only Erich Neumann's discussion of what he calls the New Ethic* affords me any light in this dilemma. You comment that my chief character hedges his bets by balancing every bow to the Virgin with a salute to Venus; I hope I shall not dismay you by saying that only an appropriate regard for both can meet the obvious needs of life, and that the Virgin and Venus, wherever they have their being, must probably find one another excellent company.

It is impertinent of me to give you my amateur opinion on theological matters, for I have no training in that realm; I am, however, a student of many years' experience in the Analytical Psychology of C. G. Jung, who seems to be the only depth-psychologist who understands and gives weight to the necessity in man for religious belief. I cannot understand how people live without religion, for all the realm it deals with seems to me to be the greatest reality of life. But to make it manifest in one's life – that's the problem. To do so without avoiding anything, and without condemning courses of action which one cannot understand but which seem satisfactory and fruitful in other people; that's the puzzle.

Especially do I find this hard in the life I live now, as an educator and the head of a college for unusually intelligent young men. Most of them want nothing of religion; it seems to have no relevance to their lives, though I think that it will become so later, in many cases.

How they slough off the problems to which only religious feeling offers an approach is a continual puzzle to me. We have, of course, a chapel in this College, but it is impossible to persuade many of the men that it is a necessity in a place which tries to give the means of living a full and true life. Nor can I persuade myself that any good purpose would be served by holding fashionable services there – folk-masses and trendy delights of that kind, which seem to me to look backward toward paganism, or at best to be tricks to turn the chapel into an amusement place. All one can do is trust God and persist, but sometimes I wonder if God cares about formal worship. I do; but I am by temperament disposed to like formalities and rituals, as I suppose my book makes clear.

But I must not bore you. I am writing another novel now [*The Manticore*] which is not a sequel to *Fifth Business* but which uses many of the same characters, and in which I am again trying to come to grips with the question of evil. You will not like it all, because Venus does pop in now and then; I can't write about the life I know without giving her fair play; but I hope when it appears you will let me know what you think..... As I work on the book it becomes very plain to me that I really do believe in damnation, and think a lot of people achieve it in this world, even when they think they are going in the opposite direction.

With renewed thanks for your refreshing comments, and gratitude for the seriousness with which you have read my book –

I am yours,

Robertson Davies

To LORI _____

Massey College
University of Toronto
November 17, 1971

Dear Sister in Christ Lori:

As thou hast, without any previous acquaintance between us, addressed me by my Christian name, I judge thee to be one of the Society of Friends, vulgarly called Quakers, and shall try to reply fittingly. I know that thou wouldst not otherwise have the bloody gall to write as thou has done.

No, dear sister, I have never noticed any bias that might be attributed to sex in reviews of my work. As Christ died for us all, so is the redeeming work of the critic done without regard to sex or rank.

Because of the frankness that must exist between us, as Friends, dear sister, I am impelled to say that I think thy question a foolish one. Circumcise thy spirit, and forego such vain bibble-babble, or thou wilt end up a sociologist.

Thine in the love and charity of Christ,

[Robertson Davies]

To DR. CHRISTOPHER HILL

Massey College
University of Toronto
November 18, 1971

John Edward Christopher Hill (1912–   ), English, was master of Balliol College, Oxford, 1965–78. He is an eminent historian of 16th and 17th century English history.

Dear Master:

In the 1971 issue of the College Record you ask in your Letter for the opinions of former college men on the matter of admitting women to Balliol. Although it is many years since I was up (1935–38) and no longer know anyone at the college, I am still on its books and keep a warm place for it in my affections. Your enquiry, therefore, stirs me to say my say on a subject that concerns colleges everywhere, and which seems to me to be discussed, very often, in terms that do not fully come to grips with the real problem.

That problem, in the present instance, is this: can Balliol offer women the kind of education they need and deserve, or does it propose simply to make accessible to some women a kind of education it has brought to a high degree of excellence for the training of a particular kind of man? If Balliol is prepared to take a lead in educating women as women, I whole-heartedly support the move. If it proposes simply to educate women exactly as it has educated their brothers, I fear that the result will be to spoil a good college for men, without doing anything for women beyond a fashionable gesture toward a mistaken notion of equality.

I am not talking theoretically, for I am myself a teacher in a university where men and women are educated together, in the sense that they attend the same classes, write the same examinations, and are graded on the same principles. Only rarely do women excel, and when they do it is at a cost that anyone who really likes women must regret – the cost of learning to think like men, and argue like men of the First Class Honours kind; it is a good and useful kind, but it is not the highest kind of man. The woman who achieves this sort of distinction does it by subduing qualities, especially in the realm of feeling, that might have made her the highest kind of woman.

You will understand that I am not dealing here in the shallow nonsense that expresses itself in doubts about the intelligence of women or their fitness for careers of any kind they choose. But I feel that if society is to benefit in the fullest sense from the qualities that women can bring to the professions and to public life, they must be educated in a fashion that trusts and draws on their strength as women.

The strength of Balliol, over the past 150 years, has been its understanding of the Logos principle, and the typical Balliol man is a creature of Logos; this is admirable for many purposes, but it is a lucky thing for Balliol that some of its most famous sons have had other sources of inspiration. A first-class woman takes her psychological stand on Eros,* and the better she learns the Logos-attitude (which in her case will be merely Logos-tricks) the less she is her best self. When a thousand North American universities have demonstrated this basic psychological mistake to the satisfaction of any careful observer, does Balliol now want to climb on the band-wagon?

Perhaps this will seem to you to be a lot of Jungian gas; my recollection of Balliol is that it had small patience for what was not clearly demonstrable on strict Logos lines. But all that I hear of you, Master, suggests that you have more good sense than the usual Balliol man, and certainly more than the Master of my day, the late A. D. Lindsay* – a Logos man of the most intransigent kind. So I put it to you: why doesn't Balliol *really* do something radical for women by educating them *as* women? Not the subjects studied, but the approach and the conclusions would be different, and this would be revolution as education has rarely known it.

But as for admitting women merely to say, "Look we too have our women," that would be far too much like getting a cheap reputation for progressive thought by lugging in a few blacks, and trying to make them into third-rate whites.

With all good wishes,

Yours sincerely,

Robertson Davies

To A WOMAN IN OTTAWA

Massey College
University of Toronto
December 16, 1971

This correspondent drew attention to a miracle in Fifth Business *– Mary Dempster breastfeeding little Paul when her baby had been premature, she had been ill, and the baby bottle-fed for months.*

[Dear Miss _____:]

Your letter fills me with astonishment and dismay. I had always understood that after the age of 14 all women had milk all the time, and that if they had no infants it was reabsorbed into their system, producing the charm which is such a delightful characteristic of their sex. I had always thought that this was what was meant by the milk of human kindness. If this is not true, could you recommend some good book to me which would give me more accurate information?

Yours sincerely,

[Robertson Davies]

To GORDON SINCLAIR

Massey College
University of Toronto
March 23, 1972

[Dear Gordon Sinclair:]

Gordon Allan Sinclair (1900–84), Canadian journalist, author, radio commentator, and television panelist, had written to inquire: "What in Hell is enantiodromia? I know I never got to high school; but migod..... enantiodromia yet!"

Enantiodromia is a difficult word to express an even more difficult idea; it is Greek and it means literally "running together." It is used by psychologists to express the tendency of strongly felt emotions to run over into their opposites. I am sure you have observed how often people at funerals have difficulty in keeping straight faces and how people who break into hysterical tears very often turn to laughter. In other realms of human conduct we often observe that people who are strong supporters of a strict morality in public lead lives which contradict their teachings, that the good are often also the cruel, and that people of disorderly life are sometimes sensitive and kind. I suppose the most astonishing example of this tendency was the quick decline of the Nazi movement which began as an unbearably high-minded desire to drag the German people up out of a demoralized condition, into a dreadful tyranny which brought death to literally millions of people on grounds of racial purity.

One area in which this tendency seems to work almost with the regularity of a law is in the world of revolution. The French Revolution threw over one tyranny and in a few years headed straight into another. The story of the Russian Revolution is the same. Sometimes I think that the present so-called revolution of youth is leading us inevitably into a new age of repression, strict morality and extreme conventionality. It has happened so often before – the licence of the early nineteenth century rushing into extreme Victorianism – that there seems every reason for it to happen again.

I hope this clears up the problem, for as you can see, the word gives a name to something which can only be rendered clumsily into English by "the compensating and balancing principle of opposites" which is even worse than enantiodromia.

With good wishes,

Yours sincerely,

[Robertson Davies]

To JOSEPHINE ROGERS   *Josephine Rogers was with Davies' agents,*
                                    Collins-Knowlton-Wing, in New York.

Massey College
University of Toronto
May 8, 1972

[Dear Miss Rogers:]

Thanks for your letter of May 5th with the contract.

I am interested that you were able to flummox Cork Smith* by telling him about my dream of the maiden and the manticore. It tempts me to tell you that all the dreams in the book [*The Manticore*] are mine and although I have not interpreted them for David Staunton exactly as I would do for myself, I felt that the use of real dreams would help me to get the atmosphere of a dream convincingly, and I think that this is indeed what has happened. It is terribly difficult to make a dream in a book seem like a dream and not a poetic construction by the author, and I have winced at the dreams of dozens of fictional characters. Most of them are far too logical in an obvious way so that the clever reader can say, "Oh yes, it means *this*," whereas the logic of a dream is concealed and has to be ferreted out. I should be very reluctant, however, to have this known widely because I do not want press people haunting me about dreams and personal interpretations, which I most certainly would not give them. It is interesting that it was not until after Freud was dead that it became known that an extraordinary number of dreams in his book on dream interpretation were his own. I am not aspiring to the Freudian or the Jungian crown, but I feel that it is wise not to tell too much of one's personal life to people who cannot have any real concern with it. However, I thought that you might like to know.

Did I tell you that Macmillans in England now want to call the book *The Dream Prompter*? Do you think that there is any point in writing to Michael Horniman* and asking him to use his influence to press for *The Manticore*?

With good wishes,

Yours sincerely,

[Robertson Davies]

Dear Gordon:

We returned on Monday night,and
I got your letter--the one of June
10--on Tuesday morning first
thing,and it was a smack in the
eye,I can tell you!My instinct
was to write at once,but on
second thoughts 'which are the
best',I decided to defer writing
until I knew what I was going to
say,and to refrain from spray-
ing you with emotion and sympathy
which might be stupid and obtrusive.
So I have been dithering for some
days,during which I have had good
news of you through Moira.But after
all, we are old friends,and you
are I think the most truly good
and unselfish man I know,and if
one doesn't speak frankly when you
are seriously ill,when?

          This is your second
very serious encounter with that
great Balancer and Revenger,the
Belly.Only you know just what goes
on in there,but to an outsider--
a very concerned and truly affectionate outsider none the less--me--
it seems that this is the place
where you harbour all the frus-
trations and bitternesses which
in another kind of man would
find vent in complaint and
railimg against the gods,and
a few men.And of course it eats

SECTION
VII

JULY 1972–OCTOBER 1972 – *THE MANTICORE* AND *HUNTING STUART AND OTHER PLAYS* PUBLISHED, FIRST IDEAS FOR *WORLD OF WONDERS* CONCEIVED

 n August 28, 1972, Davies turned 59. He was still Master of Massey College and professor of English and drama in the Graduate School at the University of Toronto and still, with Brenda, an ardent play-goer.

What is fascinating about the outburst of letters in this section is the deliberate unfolding of Davies' preoccupations and thoughts from day to day through the summer of 1972. This sudden exposure of his inner self was precipitated by the grave illness of his old friend Gordon Roper, who was about to write the first serious scholarly book about Davies and his work. Davies had liked Roper's approach in the one article he had written about him, and very much wanted Roper to write the proposed book. He believed that Roper needed something to pique his critical interest. As an individual and as a writer *he* was the focus of Roper's current project, so what greater incentive could his old friend have to recover than a series of revelations that would be grist to his critical mill? So he opened his mind to his old friend.

To GORDON ROPER

Massey College
University of Toronto
July 1 [1972]
Dominion Day!

*Gordon Roper, now a professor of English
at Trent University in Peterborough, had
been preparing to write a book on Davies
for Twayne's World Authors Series. He
had had stomach ulcers earlier and,
recently, cancer of the bowel, which
necessitated a colostomy. Davies'
secretary, Moira Whalon, kept in touch
with the Ropers who were friends of hers
on visits home to Peterborough.*

Dear Gordon:

We returned on Monday night, and I got your letter – the one of
June 10 – on Tuesday morning first thing, and it was a smack in the
eye, I can tell you! My instinct was to write at once, but on second
thoughts "which are the best," I decided to defer writing until I knew
what I was going to say, and to refrain from spraying you with
emotion and sympathy which might be stupid and obtrusive. So I
have been dithering for some days, during which I have had good
news of you through Moira. But after all, we *are* old friends, and you
are I think the most truly good and unselfish man I know, and if one
doesn't speak frankly when you are seriously ill, when?

This is your second very serious encounter with that great Balancer
and Revenger, the Belly. Only you know just what goes on in there,
but to an outsider – a very concerned and truly affectionate outsider
none the less – me – it seems that this is the place where you harbour
all the frustrations and bitternesses which in another kind of man
would find vent in complaint and railing against the gods, and a few
men. And of course it eats into you.

It is not for me to poke my nose into the intimate problems of
your life, but I can offer some counsel, which is not a bit new, but
which is usually unheeded by people like you. The first thing is that
you must begin right away to pay some serious and realistic attention
to that person you gravely undervalue, and whom you treat as a beast
of burden: Roper. You are a man of remarkable qualities; I have heard

it said by many former students of yours, and I heard it from Miranda about ten days ago: you are the best teacher they encountered at the university. I was interested that Miranda, once a keen Brückmannite, and inclined to think Falle* a Man of Distinction, has decided after ten years that you were much the best. So that's one thing; a great teacher, and they are rare. The second thing is that you are a fine critic; I cannot comment on this without being personal and thus not objective, but as you are the only Canadian critic who was interested in taking the trouble to see what my work is *really* about, and to go beneath the surface, I think I know what I am talking about. You are a *real* critic, not a performer of variations on somebody else's theme. And these things accounted for on the professional and *persona* level, I tell you what you will be reluctant to believe – you are a very remarkable man spiritually, for you have fought a special kind of fight with circumstance, and you have won. You know very well that I don't just mean becoming a full professor (why are professors always "full" one wonders) after a shaky academic start; I mean becoming a wise and enlightened man, starting in the Ontario trash-heap of old ideas, and petty concerns.

When are you going to begin treating yourself as what you are, instead of shouldering everybody else's burdens and being, in fact, the Lamb of God who takes upon him the Sins of the whole World?

Of course you know that I am not suggesting that you kick your parents downstairs, and live entirely on champagne and oysters. But couldn't you close Roper's Free Lunch for Vampires for perhaps three days a week?

I am not going to write a long letter, because I don't want to weary you, and having begun, I shall write often – unless you send a message to choke me off. I shall send you gossip, funny jokes I hear in the street, and occasional dollops of the wisdom of the great Dr. Jung.

One more word for now. We must have you back on your feet, and don't be in too much of a hurry to say you won't write things. When you are in the convalescent stage you don't know what you may do. You live by the Spirit and the Word, and don't let any illiterate saw-bones cut you off from those things simply because they did not get into his medical training. The doctors can help you, but what will heal you is what you have fed upon for 58 years. So no more for the present except great love from Brenda to you and Helen, and as in our pernickety world I am not allowed to send great love to other men's wives or especially to men, I send an unidentified emotion indistinguishable therefrom.

Rob.

To GORDON ROPER

[Windhover
Caledon East]
Mon. July 3 [1972]

Dear Gordon:

I hope you don't mind being written to on what is obviously paper from a loose-leaf book; the only other paper I have here in the country is small, and not good for typing..... We have moved out to the country, and will stay here, with frequent expeditions to Toronto, until autumn. More & more I find that I *must* get away in summer, or the nagging detail of the College wears me down. This week I must go on Wednesday to take the new President, John Evans,* to lunch and explain Massey College to him; I am more hopeful than ever of turning it into a research college for senior men – not getting rid of the Junior Fellows, but changing the emphasis from them to the elders, and from youth to maturity. It will take money, and I continue in my search for it, immensely helped by Friesen and Lochhead; this will be our tenth year since foundation, and just the year in which to get the place on its feet financially..... But Oh, how this money-preoccupation grates! I left the world of business, where you could get money, quite easily, really, by working for it, to enter the academic world, where there never seems to be quite enough, and where neither quantity or quality of work bears any reference to reward.

But out here I want to get on with one or two tasks. I have under-taken to prepare an evening's entertainment for the Ben Jonson Society when it meets in Toronto in October; we shall have six people reading passages from the plays and poems, interestingly juxtaposed, and with some appropriate music. Remarkable what a lot of planning a modest venture like this entails.

My main concern, however, is to make notes and establish some plans for a new novel [*World of Wonders*]. I have talked to you of this one, I am sure. Briefly, it is about a young Englishman who in 1923–24 tours Canada as a member of an English theatrical company; the leader of the company, an English actor-knight whose repertoire is still heavily weighted toward the 19th century and the Irving tra-dition, is the other principal. The young man is very Post-War, very new, very much taken up with Freud and Aldous Huxley and the Bloomsbury Group* – not as a member but as a panting aspirant – and he regards the old man as a comic survival. But in the atmosphere of a new country, and new dimensions, and a new sort of life and responsibility and duty, he finds out a few things.

Sounds old stuff, doesn't it? But I have a few wheezes of my own. First, the Train on which the actors chug across the country, and which is a marvellous evoker of feeling, and breaker-down of little ideas. Then the Melodrama, for the old actor has several plays in his repertoire – *The Lyons Mail, The Corsican Brothers** – which hang on a "dual role," which is in effect a study of Good and Evil as contained in a single character; the young man has come along not primarily as an actor, but to carpenter a new play for the old man with one of these dual roles in it, and their struggle of ideas confronts Raw Freud with Old Cunning; Melodrama is powerful because it is one of the mirrors in which man can see himself. And I want to do something about the appeal of these plays of chivalry and honour to a society where such things seem at the farthest extreme from daily reality.

This is a tough nut to crack, and I am alarmed about it as I always am when beginning a new piece. Can I pull it off? Strange that experience doesn't really give one confidence; it gets a little harder every time.

Anyhow, that is what I am doing. And I shall need all your advice and wise encouragement to manage it. So don't just lie there; the world – me in the front rank – needs you!

Rob.

To GORDON ROPER

Massey College
University of Toronto
July 10, 1972

Dear Gordon:

I have just been talking on the 'phone to Moira, who gives me very good news of you, which is the best possible news I could get at this time. Getting to manage the mechanical thing is very rough, I understand, from a relative of Brenda's who did it; he was a soldier and he said it was the worst thing he ever encountered. But he mastered it, and lived to be over ninety, and one never sensed that he had any special problem. So my strongest sympathy goes out to you during the initiatory period; managing one's ordinary tripes is difficult enough, and to have to do it twice is an uncalled for insult from one's body.

This weekend I have been correcting the galleys of *The Manticore* and an odd experience it was. For one thing, the editor at Viking had tidied up the grammar in a rather schoolmarmish way; I OK'd most of the corrections, but some of them I could not permit; people talking under stress do not make such classy use of the subjunctive as this editor required. But I was puzzled; is the US the last stronghold of Rigorous Grammar? I have spent thirty years trying to learn *not* to write like a pedant, and this editor wants to reverse it all.

But what most puzzled me was that the book seemed strange, as though it had been written by somebody else. It was not only that a lot of my familiar mannerisms were gone, but the mode of expression, and so much of what it said, seemed unfamiliar to me. You are a critic;

how does this happen? I find it unnerving. Still, though I had the usual comings and goings about it, I thought the book satisfactory on the whole. What cheers me is that the publishers are enthusiastic about it. When I was in England I visited my agent [Michael Horniman] over there and also the Macmillan people, and their enthusiasm was very reassuring; they kept saying I was a "major" writer, and though I find this very hard to believe it is comforting to hear somebody say so – especially somebody who is risking money on what I write. Because, as I have told you many times, I have never been able to persuade myself that I am really a good writer, but only that a number of tricks of verbal facility and some humour have enabled me to kid the public to a slight degree. But the Viking Press people are also enthusiastic, and use very flattering words. This is why the somewhat unfamiliar face of *The Manticore* troubles me. Is this hardly-familiar writer really me? If so, I have been living under a cloud of illusion for nearly sixty years.

Moira says she spoke to you about your own book. Of course you must take your time, but I hope you won't set it aside, because on the strength of your article on *Fifth Business** I am sure it would be a first-class book, and not only a marvellous boost for me, but for all Canadian writers, who God knows need to be taken seriously. Sometimes the wisecracks around the University about Can. Lit. push me toward suicide. And such books as Elspeth Buitenhuis's thin little job* about me are hard to bear.

You must not imagine that I think of your book simply as an adjunct to what I have written; it is terribly difficult to write about it to you without sounding egotistical, and of course a measure of egotism and pride have to take their proper place. But I truly think that a *good* book about a Canadian writer would do the whole Can. Lit. world immeasurable good; our criticism has too often been condescending, or else stuff that sounds all too much like a half-drunken address at the Arts and Letters Club. The bitter fact is that there are so many people who, for reasons hard to fathom, *don't want* a Canadian literature that has any weight. Somehow it seems to offend their sense of propriety.

Moira says that when you can move a bit more freely you are making for the lake, and what could be more healing and restorative than that atmosphere? When you are up to it, perhaps we could drive over to Peterborough and see you? But we won't do it while you are in the first stages of convalescence, for even the best-intentioned visitors are exhausting. But can you think of anything you would like that we could send you? Any books? Cigars, cigarettes, chocolate bars? Do you pay much attention to gramophone records? Anything that would beguile the heavy-paced hours is yours, if you will name it.

Meanwhile, our thoughts are with you both, and our enthusiastic cheers for your victory sound for you both.

Rob.

To GORDON ROPER

[Windhover
Caledon East]
July 15 [1972]

Dear Gordon:

I hope you are obeying the counsel of the great physicians of the School of Salerno; my favourite nugget from their wisdom is –

Use three physicians still:
First, Doctor Quiet,
Next, Doctor Merryman
Then Doctor Diet.

May I appoint myself Doctor Merryman?

I am out in the country, and I had hoped to get some time to vegetate and form a few ideas for the next novel [*World of Wonders*] – the one of which I spoke to you – but no such luck. I have been up to my ears in proofs of *The Manticore*, which the publishers want at lightning speed, though they are not bringing it out until November 25 I find – just a month before Christmas! They assured me they would be

earlier, but at publishers' promises, they say, Jove laughs (Shakespeare).*
Anyhow, that is done now, and I have plunged into the proofs for the
book of three plays [*Hunting Stuart and Other Plays*] that New Press
is doing. I don't understand New Press; are they naive or crafty? My
agent doesn't understand them, either, for they keep sending me con-
tracts which look as if a child had composed them – but it proves to
be a child of uncommon shrewdness, who would have your pants off
if you weren't cautious. David Godfrey,* I know, is able to control his
enthusiasm for my writing; in his eyes I am one of the Dinosaurs of
Canadian Writing, and not among the New, Fresh Talents who are so
gloriously, orgasmically With It. But I deal with a chap called Mark
Czarnecki,* who seems to be a very nice fellow. But he is a schizo-
phrenic; he dresses like a proper New Press man, but his hair and his
bare feet are always clean, so obviously the Establishment is poised to
grab him.

In addition to these distractions, Brenda's mother is staying with
us, and though she is a prize as mothers-in-law go, all mothers-in-
law are great givers of advice, and tend to apply the brakes to the
wheels of life. She is now 80, and drives Brenda mad by remembering her (Brenda's) childhood all wrong, in such a way as to make B.
appear as a Comic Natural, while her Mother was always Wonderful
– a finer species of Mary Worth.* Master Roper, shall we be such
Sweet Pests at the distant time when Old Age claims us? I haven't a
doubt of it.

Last Tuesday we went to Stratford to see *The Threepenny Opera*.* It
was very well done; brilliant direction, and a treat to the eye. Everything, in fact, to make a fine evening in the theatre, and justify a 140-
mile round trip to see it. EXCEPT – I really do not like the work itself.
I greatly admire *The Beggar's Opera* because it is an embodiment of a
principle of literature very dear to me – the iron hand in the velvet
(or in this case, the chintz) glove; Gay invested his scoundrels with so
much charm, without thereby diminishing their roguery one jot. And
he did it by two strokes of genius: he gave them exquisitely phrased,
memorable things to say, and he embellished the piece with some of
the loveliest folk-tunes that ever were. So he produced exactly what
he intended: a Newgate pastoral. But what have Brecht and Kurt

Weill done? They have made the scoundrels stagey and unbelievable; they have written music which sounds worn-down and beat-up and *airless* (they are very fine, but they are German music of the great period of disillusionment) and they have loaded the play with a Message that would sink a battleship – the real old Brecht message: (1) there are no individuals, only classes; (2) all classes are made up of shits, but the poor shits are best because they are poor; (3) the only hope for mankind is to embrace a special kind of Sorehead Communism.

In fact, Brecht has done here what he did every time he stole a play; he has hammered away at disillusionment without any recognition that the originals from which he worked were disillusioned on a level far above his own, and therefore didn't have to sweat and grunt about it. I detest Brecht. A genius, in some sense, but a genius of low mind and vulgar spirit; a genius with a very bad breath.

Moira tells me the weather in Peterborough is no better than it is here; we have had the ultimate in Toronto summer – 90F, combined with great humidity. I hope this is not giving you a bad time as an invalid.

Of course I am very sorry you aren't up to doing the introduction to the three plays; New Press hoped very much that it might be possible, but I thoroughly understand that it isn't. When one is ill, mental work is just as much out of the question as chopping wood, which it so much resembles. They have asked Herbert Whittaker to do it. I tremble, for . . . [he] has some very eccentric views. But we shall see. All is best, though we oft doubt..... (Milton).*

And speaking of that, I have been having some rather delicate trouble with *Maclean's*.* They have done a piece about me as an author, which is excellent. But it has a short introduction which presents me as a farcical Oxonian, sipping claret, snorting up snuff, uttering Latin jokes, and in general an Over-ripe Fruit. This might be fair enough if they did not place this squarely in the context of Massey College, in a way which will make the young men furious, and the Seniors equally furious, and all with strong justification. This is just the kind of publicity the College does not need, and gets too often. I have written to the editor, begging him to mitigate this caricature insofar as the coll. is concerned, but I don't know what will come of it. The trouble is, when a journalist gets an idea into his head, nothing can convince him he is wrong; I was a journalist for 22 years, and I know the breed. They are sure they are clear-eyed critics of human-kind, and in 9 cases out of 10 they are bewildered, ill-informed, romantic ignoramuses. It has been said that there is no such thing as Bad Publicity (Matthew Arnold).* Believe me, it is not true.

And now I must fling myself into some more proofs. I do hope all goes well with you, and that the climb up the mountainside to health is progressing without too many crevasses and gravel slopes. I shall write again when I have something to say, and will try to be Doctor Merryman more successfully than this time.

Rob.

To GORDON ROPER

[Windhover
Caledon East]
July 21 [1972]

Dear Gordon:

One of the perils of living in the country is that one constantly encounters people who shout "Hot enough fer yuh?" in a jocose, yet punitive tone, as though the temperatures rising toward 90F were specially arranged to chasten your proud spirit. I hope the heat has not been making trouble for you; lying in bed is a very limited pleasure, even under the best circumstances.

Yesterday we adventured to Stratford in the burning heat to see *As You Like It*; it was worth every bit of the effort. This is a favourite comedy with me, and has been ever since 1932,* when I had the good luck to see a first-rate production, and rid myself forever of the bad impression the play made on me in school. Believe it or not, an old pedant named Willie Mowbray managed to teach it in great detail without ever letting us in on the secret that it was about love! I fell under the spell of the play at eighteen, and now, forty years later, I am even more delighted with it. I get so angry with people who twaddle about the improbabilities of the plot, and how silly it is for Oliver to reform suddenly and marry Celia, and how there aren't any lionesses in the forest of Arden (or as they hasten to explain, Ardennes, in North-east France.). It is like asking for probability from *Swiss Family Robinson*.* I realized last night, as never before, that what makes the Shakespearean comedies superlatively great is the immense spirit that lies behind them, a vital, optimistic spirit that believes in man. This hit me hard because when we were in London we saw a few of the most admired plays of the season, and they had behind them a little wizened spirit that didn't believe in anything except the possibility of making a success in the West End, by telling people that humanity was a fraud, love a horny joke, and the whole of life a lingering pseudo-philosophical fart. *ASYL* was like being put in touch with reality again, after a nasty dream.

This was all the more surprising to me because the production was by William Hutt, whose work until now I have not greatly admired. But it was very clean, if you know what I mean; no gimmicks, no extraneous "business," no attempt to prove anything on behalf of Kott* or some other trendy fraud, and a heart-warming dependence on the text itself, and a determination to get across what it said. And of course it worked like a charm; the great play bore them all aloft superbly, and the audience – full house, but not a literary or fashionable or informed house – responded heartily. Next to me was a young Chinese American I imagine, and a couple of girls, none of them over twenty; I got the impression they had not read the play; all the cracks were new to them, and they thought Touchstone was a hoot; their pleasure was extraordinary. So what did I care if they fidgetted and ate things all the time; I would have forgiven them anything, and somewhat envied them the freshness of their pleasure.

Somewhat – but not very much. After forty years of loving *ASYL* I think I get a squeeze of the fruit that the newcomer misses.

They had decided to do the play in 18th century costume and milieu, and it worked very well. Meant Rosalind in the forest wore a coat with enough tails to cover her bottom, which is what lies at the base of so many failures in this part. Extraordinary how, in the actor's art, some physical fact will undo the acquired art of a lifetime. I saw the famous *ASYL* in which Edith Evans played Rosalind with the young Michael Redgrave as Orlando. She *spoke* the part and understood it magnificently, but one could not rid oneself for an instant of the spectacle of a middle-aged woman with a monumental can exerting herself to charm a very handsome young man; there was a frowsy indecency about it. Rosalind and Orlando* have got to look fresh and fit for each other, which they did in this production. One of its merits was that Orlando was a merry fellow; so many Orlandos are solemn, or even sore-headed. Years ago at Stratford they did *AYLI** (I'll get it right sooner or later) and Irene Worth played Ros., and was just getting away with it – great art and too many years again; but the Orlando was Jason Robards, and if a bigger, stupider, more hairy-arsed and wooden-headed Orlando ever treads the stage, may it not be my misfortune to see him. But the young man they have this year is a cheerful, jolly chap, and worthy of Rosalind.

Touchstone is always a sticker. I am one of those who maintains that the Shakespearean clowns really *are* funny; but they simply must be *clowns*. That is to say, they must have the clown's ability to be funny in and of themselves; they must look funny, and be able to do immensely skillful and amusing things; they must also have some link with that world – almost lost, but you and I remember it from childhood – where word-catches, and riddles, and verbal absurdities were really funny, and the nervous wisecracking of the immobile TV comedians had not set a wholly new standard. In this production they had one of the really great clowns of our day, Edward Atienza,* to play Touchstone, and he gave a splendid rendition of a man whose livelihood was to make people laugh, and who delivered the goods, without sacrificing his human decency; he fell about, and squawked, and threw himself into strange postures, but he never ceased to be a man, to be *somebody*, to steer clear of mere abjection of the spirit. Great stuff..... A pretty good Jacques, too. Roly Hewgill,* a Kingston chap; but though he gave a very good impression of a philosopher – a real one, not the kind you usually meet onstage or in university departments – he was strangely ineffective in the Seven Ages speech. If I were directing the play, I should get Jacques to say that speech as if every word hurt him, and the end was so inacceptable that he could hardly bring it out. But thinking how I would produce plays is one of my great amusements. Nobody ever asks me to do it.

I have now completed correcting the proofs of the three plays [*Hunting Stuart and Other Plays*]. Reading them thus, after so many years of not looking at them, I am surprised to find them better than I remembered them; this is always my way with my work. I greatly wish somebody would do *General Confession*. But I wrote plays at a bad time. Only amateurs produced new Canadian plays, and they did them, very often, condescendingly and badly. I recall going into the London Little Theatre for the first night* of a production they did of *At My Heart's Core*, and one of the committee said, "Well, here we go for another of these rotten Canadian plays we do out of duty," to which he added Ha ha to show that it was a joke. But it had not been said quite as a joke, and the production which followed was sentimental, perfunctory and thoroughly bad. They had no real faith in the play because it had not come to them from London or New York..... But now a young playwright, with luck, can get quite a decent professional production, and if he is James Reaney the Stratford Festival will pour tens of thousands of dollars into showing him off. How I wish I had had that kind of chance! But I fear now my plays are both too old-fashioned, and too expensive, to interest anybody.

Hope all goes well: love from us both.

Rob.

To ARNOLD EDINBOROUGH

[Windhover
Caledon East]
August 2. [1972]

Dear Arnold:

I was not in town until yesterday, Tuesday, when I found your piece about *The Manticore*, and read it with blushes and rustic cries of "Zure, this never do be Oi!" Thank you enormously. I know the Bk-of-Mo does not expect you to pick holes in their books, but your generosity goes far beyond what they would require. And, frankly, I delight in it, because as you point out I have written 22 books and that not without sweat and heat, and it is nice to think one is not yet on the downhill grade.

We have talked often of the lot of the author in Canada. He practises a queer trade, for essentially nobody can do anything for him until he has finished his work. Canada Council grants will not change the quality of his work; indeed, unless he lives in real poverty, the presence or absence of money makes no great difference. He may decide to be an author and nothing else, like Morley Callaghan, or he may plug away in a bank and write very sparingly, like Sinclair Ross,* or he may be a teacher like MacLennan or me. But really it makes no difference to the final outcome..... He can be harmed, of course, and I often wonder whether the comparatively recent phenomenon of the Writer-in-Residence does not debauch some of the brethren. To be a licensed pundit; to hold the powers of life and death over young writers who are just getting their feet wet – is not this a heady draught for a man whose own soul is probably tortured by uncertainties, intimations of mortality, and fear of what the tonic ads call "waning powers"? Margaret Laurence performed this function admirably and with great honesty, but I have seen some of the brethren* grow dangerously gassy while holding such an office. The name of **rl* B*rn*y springs to mind, and also of J*ck L*dw*g; next year M*rg*r*t *tw**d takes a whirl at it, and we shall see what we shall see. But on the whole I am glad I have been a writer while doing other jobs, and quite honestly I still hate it when I am invited to posture as a Writer. Unfortunately some of this must be done; publishers think it good for sales (rum, ain't it, that the one thing they are dead certain would not affect sales is a good, generous advertising campaign?) and publishers have to be obliged because, as they are the first to say, where would literature be without them? Where would the poor cows go, with their engorged udders, if the kindly farmer were not at hand to relieve them?

But a truce to this puling, as somebody says in an eighteenth century play whose name I mercifully forget. A thousand thanks for your kindness; let's get together as soon as we can, which will probably be Sept., as I am up to my neck in laying plans for another book [*World of Wonders*], and must work against that grim day when the schoolbell rings and I have to give my mind to other things.

Love to Letty –

Rob. . . .

To GORDON ROPER

[Windhover
Caledon East]
August 4. [1972]

Dear Gordon:

It has been some time since I wrote to you, because I have been busy getting my mother-in-law safely away to Australia. I know that doesn't sound like a task that would present me with overwhelming difficulties, but surprisingly it took quite a lot of time, for we had to have some farewell parties for her so that she might say good-bye to the girls, and some other people wanted to entertain her, and I was busy completing her Book. These Books are a thing that has grown up over the years; whenever she visits us, I prepare a book for her to take home, which contains all sorts of collages, and drawings and water-colour pictures that present a cheerful record of what she has done while in Canada, and she likes to have them very much. You did not know I was a cheerful caricaturist, did you? Mrs. Newbold's Books are done very much in the vein of the pictures I did to illustrate the *Almanack*, and they take quite a bit of time.

Anyhow, we popped her on the 'plane, and Brenda and I sank into a coma for a day, then began to recover our true shape; the presence in the house of a strong personality, whose ideas and prejudices must not be flouted, makes decided demands, and sometimes results in covert warfare on a midget level. For instance, we have a cork board in the kitchen for bills, reminders and the like, and on it hangs a calendar which Rosamond gave us, of Russian Ikons, one for each month. Now, my Ma-in-law is fiercely atheist – she calls it agnostic but an agnostic is a seeker, and she don't seek – who professes a great regard for something she calls Nature. So she was nettled subcutaneously by the ikons, which B. and I both love. And on the cork board there are a lot of thumb-tacks, which, out of meanness and mischief, I arranged in the form of a small but clear cross. Every day I would find that my Ma-in-law had – for the best of reasons – found it necessary to disarrange this cross. So I would make a thumb-tack cross again. Not that I cannot live without crosses or want them in the kitchen, but out of sheer Old Nick. The matter of the little cross was never mentioned, but it was a hard-fought battle, I can tell you. I think Mrs. N. felt I was dragging her daughter toward Rome.

Psychiatry, too, was a bone of contention. Mrs. N. hates it, because someone she knows fell into the hands of a nut psychiatrist or witch-doctor in Tasmania. This person, mad already, killed herself. But also, like many of her generation, she has closed the manhole to the Unconscious, and sealed it with lead, and dreads any disturbance of the seal. I made the mistake of saying, "Well, would you expect to find a gifted practitioner of an extremely difficult art in such a knuckle-end of nowhere as Tasmania?" and this was not well-received. My Jungian bias kept pushing me to dispute this matter with Mrs. N., fruitless though I knew it to be; she was Animus-possessed and I was Anima-possessed,* and of course nothing could come of that. But we all got through the visit – which, as she stayed with us for ten days before going to England, was pretty much with us for a month there, and stayed nearly a month here, was a long one – with credit, and she liked her Book, which I had embellished with, among other things, a fine portrait of John Barrymore as Svengali,* labelled "The Hideous and Ever-Present Threat of Psychiatry."

We have made our second journey to Stratford, and saw *Lorenzaccio** and *King Lear*.

Have you read *Lorenzaccio*? Of course you have, and in French, too. So have I. Everybody has, in this great bi-lingual country. But it had somewhat slipped my mind, and the translation was a blow to me. It was, in the classic phrase, as flat as piss on a plate. Its history is of a kind not uncommon in the theatre; somebody was employed to do it; his version proved unsatisfactory, so "several hands" have been employed to tinker it, and the result is a botch. One chap told me, with a perfectly straight face, that the original translation had been in "flat American," and so attempts had been made to "Victorianize" it – by which he seemed to mean, to add some grace to the prose, and to find some 19th century English equivalents for the 19th century complexities of the French, which is very fancy. As you know –

Alfred de Musset
    Called his cat "Pusset";
His accent was affected,
    As was only to be expected.*

But the result is a welter of juiceless verbiage.

After about half-an-hour of *Lorenzaccio* I came to the conclusion that it was a prime example of the early 19th century tragedy which I set before my students; it might have been written by Sheridan Knowles or Bulwer,* for although the translation was far below their strength, the sentiments were unquestionably theirs. When an old Florentine noble declared, "I am a FATHER, and therefore, a REBEL," I knew right where I was – back at Covent Garden with Macready.* This was the staple of 19th century melodrama, with all the points in proper order: 1. – that though a weak priest may occasionally be a good fellow, all strong priests and especially cardinals are crooks; 2. that people in power are invariably evil and have to be put down, which means assassinated in as messy a style as can be contrived; 3. that mistresses abound, and do nothing between bouts of mistressing except bewail their fallen lot and abuse the cardinals; 4. that the best way to bring about the fall of an evil ruler is to make everybody think you are crazy and corrupt, and thus become the personal friend of the hateful ruler, who is too dumb to notice your dissembling, though every pinhead in the back row of the theatre can spot it immediately because you slink and leer so much; 5. that Liberty is a very fine thing, and easily defined, and if once The Peepul got some of it, all their troubles would end; 6. that the truly fine soul desires Liberty for others, but greatly prefers Death for himself; 7. that people who have been poisoned do not puke or void their bowels, but harangue the crowd while pressing the left hand to the side, as if suffering from gas. This is what the 19th century called "Poesy and Buzzem"* and *Lorenzaccio* is full of it. It looked good, and some good actors worked like cart-horses to drag it through, but it carried no conviction to my cynical heart. But as my friend Horace Davenport, who visited me last week, said, we have to see these things in order to remind ourselves how good Shakespeare really is.

Shakespeare had his innings with *Lear*. This is my favourite among the tragedies, and if it is even half-way well done it ravishes me. This was a good deal more than half-way well done; it was admirable so far as it went, but it fell short on Stratford's old weak point: the poetry was not allowed to do its full work. Stratford, over twenty years of my experience, always breaks down on the poetry of Shakespeare. Of course, it may be that my ideal performance would not please as many people as Stratford['s]; I would almost like it to be sung. But in this performance Bill Hutt, as Lear, had majesty, awesomeness and power, but he shouted the first part, and whined the rest, and if the leader does that, the other actors must also shout, or they will not be in key. Also, regrettably, Stratford has installed a new sound-system, which is the eighth wonder of the world, and can do anything except be poetic. So it produced a storm which would strike dread into the entire staff of Ontario Hydro, but which drowned Shakespeare's poetic storm, and allowed us to hear only an occasional shrieked word.

Still, it shook me, for there was a fine cast, and so many lesser things were made splendid because really good actors were doing them. The Fool was the best I have ever seen. Funny that until the 19th century the Fool was always left out, as a crude and incongruous blot on the tragedy; even the 19th cent. tended to put a girl in the part, for pathos. But this Fool was a sick man, given to spastic jerks and uncontrollable babblings – but so finely controlled that I was convinced that it would be just such a wounded man who would gain acceptance in a savage world by making himself a butt. The pathos of this performance was terrible, and I do not expect to see it bettered. But I have seen better Lears. Also, there were fashionable things which bothered me; when Cornwall and Regan put out Gloucester's eyes it is pretty well indicated in the text that Cornwall simply put his boot to the man's face, probably with a spur on it. But in this production Cornwall and Regan travelled with a Little Jiffy Home Torture Kit, on a rack, with gougers and diggers all complete; it was sadistic, rather than brutal, and a bit sick. Ah well, I am getting to be a real professor, with an Ideal Performance in my head, which I use to deride the work of theatre people. It was a good *Lear*, not great, but how often in a century is there a great *Lear*?

I have chattered rather at length, and I hope I have not wearied you. I hope you get better every day, and I promise that it will not be so long before I write again.

Rob.

To GORDON ROPER

[Windhover
Caledon East]
August 6. [1972]

Dear Gordon:

When last I wrote to you, I forgot to mention that I saw John Pettigrew* in Stratford, and he asked after you most kindly. It was at a party given after *Lorenzaccio* by Berners Jackson* of McMaster, on behalf of the seminar which McMaster runs at Stfd. for two weeks every year. Also present was a Professor Meisel,* to whom I was introduced and, as it was a theatre occasion I assumed he must be Martin Meisel, the Big Shaw Man, so I bespake him fair, and said how greatly his fine book had helped me in my own teaching; he looked rather confused, and I found later that he was Professor John Meisel, of Queen's, an economist! This is what Fate gives you for trying to be nice to people.

Indeed, that was not the only unfortunate academic encounter I had at Stratford. After *Lear* Brenda and I were standing by the refreshment counter, having a cup of coffee before setting out on our homeward journey. I was still very much *in* the play, and felt shredded, and so when a bearded, intense youth approached I was not giving him my full attention. He was reviewing the plays for _____ and he was, he explained, on the faculty of [an American university] (though he looked a hairy eighteen). He wanted to talk about a student of his called _____ who was at Toronto last year. Now _____ is a handsome young Jew with plenty of charm and high spirits, but no more brains than would butter a small biscuit. He took my Shaw course, and came out bottom because he could not form any idea of an age earlier than this, or a kind of life that was un-American, so his ideas about social progress were jejune, and he had no notion what Shaw was campaigning about. He had also, it must be noted, no idea of the English language, its grammar, vocabulary or use as a means of conveying thought as opposed to emotion. A Yankee dink, in fact.

But to this pixie _____ was "one of the best minds I have encountered in my career as a teacher" and he wanted to know how _____ measured up at Toronto. He buggered it up and dropped out, said I, only in academic lingo. What was the trouble, asked the pixie, astonished. He was pitifully ill-prepared for graduate work, said I; he had no idea of history, or the history of ideas, or social development in the 19th or any other century. Then I realized that the pixie had been one of the gang . . . who had formed, or scrambled, _____'s mind. But the pixie was equal to the occasion:

"At _____ we respect the student's RIGHT NOT TO KNOW!" he said, and withdrew, leaving me gaping. Brenda and I spent much of the homeward drive discussing this wholly new right (new, that is, to us). Are you aware of it? Is it in the Bill of Rights? In my stick-in-the-mud way I cannot distinguish it from ignorance, which I suppose is also a right, and one heavily insisted on by crowds of people – but not usually in Universities. But I was sorry to stab the pixie, who was a decent little fellow, though I fear of dangerously trendy beliefs. . . .

I sent off some books to you a while ago, including a Penguin of Thackeray's *Pendennis*, as I thought you might not have read it. I hadn't, and have just finished it. I take great delight in those long Victorian novels, and read and re-read Dickens with the greatest satisfaction. But Oh, what a pitfall that Monthly Number form* was! What padding! What amateur philosophizing! What downright bungling and muddling! Tremendous in their inventive powers, they were rotten planners and fumbling plotters. Wilkie Collins,* who plotted superbly, writes in a wearisome melodramatic style, and has a tin ear. Dickens just leaps from rock to rock, whelping plot and character as he bounds. Thackeray cannot keep from preaching, and won't stand still; one moment he is the Cynic, the next the Sentimentalist. *Pendennis* is full of good stuff, but if it had been half the length it would have been twice as good. The scene that really threw me back on my haunches is the one where Pendennis's Sainted Mum finds that her boy (who is all of twenty-five at the time) is still a virgin and was not, as she darkly feared, screwing his laundress; he kneels at her feet and recites the Lord's Prayer (brokenly, of course, for this bit of prose seems always to have had the Broken Treatment in the 19th cent.) and the old girl dies of a heart attack from sheer joy! In my dark heart I wished that Pendennis's Mum might be the victim of a particularly rough gang rape; she hated sex as only a Victorian Mother could, and her will was done when Pen finally married his cousin, whom he had grown up with and called his sister. There are splendidly incestuous abysses beneath *Pendennis* and yet I suppose that Thackeray, who was as level-headed and perceptive as they come, was not aware of what he was doing.

Do you suppose that the yearning of a few million Mothers in the 19th cent. really kept their sons virgins until they married some virgin girl? My guess is that it did so in multitudinous cases. But what a light this throws on the Rationalism, the Scientific Revolt, the High Church Movement and a dozen other great nineteenth century movements. It was Backed-Up Semen that created a lot of that enthusiasm, zeal, and idealism. The comparatively slack-twisted quality of so much modern thought among the young may be owing to the fact that they seem now to fornicate mindlessly at about ten, and can barely drag themselves out of the sack to get to High School.

Unhappiness and frustration are what make the wheels of progress turn, Master Roper. Last weekend I had a visit from an old friend of mine, from Oxford days – Dr. Horace Davenport of Ann Arbor, and one of the world's greatest authorities on the gastro-intestinal tract; he is a man notably uneasy in the world, gnawed by a thousand obligations, and tormented by the sense of a hundred thousand obligations which he cannot fulfill. Davenport, out of his frustrations and unhappinesses – and some very real distresses and griefs during his lifetime – has made a man of himself of remarkable quality, and has served mankind brilliantly, for the literature of his subject bristles with papers which begin "As Davenport has shown....." He makes me feel that a lot of rubbish is talked about *fulfillment* by people who interpret that word as a guaranteed full belly and an uncovenanted cheap lay. Yet Davenport is very merry company, and out of his great sorrows he makes first-rate jokes.

I embrace you in the bowels of Christ –

Rob.

To GORDON ROPER

[Windhover
Caledon East]
August 16, 1972

Dear Gordon:

All last week I was working like a Trojan, and a nailer, and a dog,
and a black, and all those other traditional toilers, to complete the
script of the Ben Jonson program I am preparing for the conference
next October 25. I think I mentioned it. Blissett* is getting it up, and
the arrangements are the usual academic confusion, but they want a
banquet and an entertainment, and I am providing the latter. I think
it might be quite a good show if we can pull it off effectively. But
what tough stuff Jonson is! I admire him, but not with my whole heart.
Whenever I have to do any work on him I am put off by the dirty
brutality of so much of his stuff, and by his coarse attitude toward
women. There are no women's parts in his plays that are not grotesques
that are worth a damn. If Shakespeare could write great parts for boy
actors, so could BJ if he had had it in him. But as well as the brawl-
ing, contentious Scot, plagued with piles and constipation (as Edmund
Wilson so pungently argues)* there is a man with great tenderness
toward children, and the wistfulness of the bully who wonders why
nobody likes him. I am including some of the unfavourable comments
on him in the program, to pepper it up. It will be a theatrically effective
thing, not too much sicklied o'er with scholarship.*

At the weekend we paid our annual visit to the Shaw Festival at
Niagara-on-the-Lake. One of the pleasures of modern Canada is that
one can do some very good playgoing – the best of the year, often –
in the summer. We saw *Misalliance* and *Getting Married*, both done
admirably. Indeed, I don't think I have seen either play done better,
or as well, and I have seen them both a few times. Can it be that
Niagara has got the range on GBS better than anyone else?

What made these productions so good was that they were played
all out for *theatricality*, which I am sure is what Shaw wanted. He said

it, over and over again. His plays are intellectual harlequinades, and he provides picturesque settings and fancy clothes – Bishops, generals, Lady Mayoresses, Aldermen and the like in full fig – and calls for lots of highly theatrical action. Shaw is *not* stupidly *talky*, except for people who have lost the ability to listen. If one can listen, the bewildering varieties of rhetorical device, the jokes and the variations of mood and tone are splendidly uplifting; we came away immensely refreshed and renewed. Fern Rahmel* met us in the foyer and shouted: "I think he's right! He *is* better than Shakespeare!"

Can't agree. He lacks the Shakespearean scope. Years ago – it was 1951 – Laurence Olivier and Vivien Leigh* presented Shakespeare's *Antony and Cleopatra* and Shaw's *Caesar and Cleopatra* on alternate nights in London, and Brenda and I saw them both. There was not a sliver of doubt as to who was the greater playwright. The Shaw play, which we saw first, delighted and refreshed as the greatest comedy does: but the Shakespeare gave one of those awesome peeps through the fog of everyday into the heavens where one became aware of the greatness and pathos of man's lot, and did it with poetry that could not be withstood. It went into regions where *thought* is secondary, and even trivial, as compared with *feeling*. No wonder Jung said that Shaw was not a sage but a wonderful adolescent, endlessly marvelling at the complexity of life. But Shakespeare – boozer, meat-eater and huckster as he probably was – knew what it was to reach a true maturity, and could tell us about it.

I have just got – with great difficulty – the second volume of Dan Laurence's edition of Shaw's *Letters*,* and I must gobble it before term starts, because my students, very properly, refer to them a great deal. It is far more interesting than the first vol. (1874–97) which contained a weary amount of business correspondence, and a lot of Shaw that explains why St. John Ervine* called him "a Dublin smartie." How admirable he was, but how little lovable! Not that I want to be rapt in adoration before great writers, but a few cracks in the armour become a man. But I am lecturing.

The two plays we saw had special interest for us because we have received word that Miranda is to be married next spring. Did I mention that? A charming young man, Michel Palaketis, a barrister and I gather a very good one. But they have made up their minds and next May we shall go to London for the doings. He is a religious oddity, for his father is Greek Orthodox, and his mother a Roman Catholic, and at present it looks as if they would be married by the RC rite. Miranda says she will not become a Catholic herself, and it is being done chiefly to please Michel's mother. Odd that two of our daughters should marry Catholics, for though I have a high regard for the upper levels of Catholic thought, nobody can live in Canada – especially in Peterborough – and not have reservations about Catholicism on the lower slopes. Still, I have strong intuitions that the Reformed Church is on the slippery slide, and in a century Catholicism may be the last stronghold of Christian belief. And what that will lead to, I shan't be here to see, but history teaches us not to be sure that any intellectual or spiritual movement is ever at an end! Christianity has survived rougher seas than those that now beat upon it. Not that I hold any strong brief for Christianity. The figure of Christ himself has always repelled me. Do you recall John Buchanan, once chaplain at Massey? I startled him once by saying that although I was on the best of terms with God, I couldn't make head or tail of His notionate, show-off boy. . . .

Poor Arnold Wilkinson* has died. He had a rough time as Warden for he was a sweet-natured man & the cantankerousness of student feeling during recent years gnawed at him. And in his own mind he lived in the shadow of Burgon Bickersteth, whom he adored with his whole soul. One pays a price for one's heroes. I have paid dear for several, & I dare say you have too.

Love to you both from both of us.

Rob.

To GORDON ROPER

[Windhover
Caledon East]
August 23 [1972]

Dear Gordon:

Got your letter of August 10 yesterday when I was in town. What a splendid letter! Do you know the story of Sam Goldwyn's amazement when he beheld a volume of the works of Shakespeare. "And to think he wrote it all wit' a feather!" he cried. I think of you driving your pen industriously and beautifully and legibly and am astonished even as was Sam. I can no longer write by hand. Writer's Cramp, my dear Numbbum, caused by thoroughly bad muscular habits. I can sign my name and make a few marks, but to write more than a paragraph with a pen is beyond me. And of course twenty years of daily journalism habituated me to the typewriter, and I believe I write more easily and better thereupon. Did you know Henry James* wrote on a typewriter, and not wit' a feather, as would have been more appropriate to his stately persona?

Brenda sends a message to Helen: *The Way of All Women* is not a young woman's book; she tried to interest our daughters in it, but it held nothing for them, because it was all theory in their eyes, and did not tie into anything they had been through – or knew they had been through. Says Brenda, freely adapting that mighty bard Edgar A. Guest,* "It takes a heap o' livin' to make a reader for Dr. Harding."

Did you know I once met Dr. Harding?* It was fifteen or so years ago, and I thought a Jungian analysis would be just the thing for me, if I could go to New York for a long weekend once a month and do it that way. So I consulted Dr. Harding, who said it would not work, and as I had not, in her words, "any gross symptoms" I gave up the idea. But I had an hour with her, and received an indelible impression of someone splendidly at home in her life; frank, charming, wise and without being in any way beautiful or young, certainly one of the most fascinating women I have ever encountered. If that is what a life under Jung's thumb does to you, let us have more of it. Brenda recurs to *The Way* about once a year and always finds something new. I know a man in Toronto – Jim Shaw,* the *éminence grise* of the Analytical Psychology Society [of Ontario],* who was analysed by Dr. H. He is not an intellectual person; indeed, he is the president of the Noxema company, and a manufacturer, and his training was as a chemist; when he returned from the war he was in a tangle, and involved in a bad marriage, and like a sensible chap he got himself analysed, got a divorce, and conceived a lifelong enthusiasm for Jung, which he now puts into practice by fostering the Analytical Psych. Soc. We meet in the Quakers' place in Toronto.* The president is a Dr. Paul Seligman,* a learned Jungian who is on the faculty at Waterloo; but alas the poor Doctor is a very dull pedant, and it is Shaw who makes the wheels go round, and incidentally makes the Noxema co. foot many a bill for mailing, correspondence, and the fees of speakers. I would urge you to join if it were not such a long jaunt to Toronto, but if you wanted to come up for an occasional specially worthwhile lecture – we meet once a month – we could put you and Helen up at the coll. with us. Unfortunately our membership contains the usual number of dotty people, and parsons who are trying to Reach Out, and young noodles who wish to devote the discussion periods to getting their dreams explained free of charge, but there are some serious and sensible types. I have rashly promised to give tongue on "Melodrama as a Drama of Archetypes" next season. It is a theme on which I harry my class in nineteenth century theatre.

You are very interesting on Trollope, and I want time to think about what you have said. I have always thought he had great psychological insight, of a kind quite different from that of Dickens. Dickens knew a lot of things because he was a genius, and didn't need to be told: Trollope knew a lot of things because he had seen them through those peepy little gold specs of his, and had seen them truly, and not under the delusions of the Time Spirit.

. . . I am anxious that you should become the Received Authority about me, for there are getting to be a few theses, and that awful, coarsely contrived mess by Frau Buitenhuis, which students must turn to if they turn to anything, and they are dreadful. This is delicate to say, but you know very well I do not regard you as my trumpeter or apologist, but as a scholar who by native wit, training and personal knowledge and sympathy with me knows what I am struggling to do, and I want your voice to be heard. It will be impossible then for anybody to ignore it, and criticism of my stuff will have to develop or depart from it; but at least the kind of nonsensical rubbish that depicts me as a sort of queeny, snuff-taking intellectual clown will have to go. Canada is such a bloody *belittling* place, and the brass-bowelled lack of intellectual curiosity and humility displayed by Frau Buitenhuis is very common.

Especially as I grow every year more opposed to the whole notion of autobiography. For me, that's to say. Macmillans have hinted at it, but I won't be drawn. For one thing, I am but a child, and my life has but begun. For another, I find the autobiogs of most other people revealing but in the wrong way. Everybody in them becomes a bit-player in the writer's personal drama, and this is grossly unfair even when it makes good reading. If I tried to give any true impression of what my life was up to the age of twelve it would take many volumes, and even then would not do the job. My family, in my eyes, appear in gaudy colours and strange characters. My father: composed of the Lord God Almighty, all the bards of Wales, the Devil, Mr. Micawber, Charlie Chaplin, a jeering, tormenting, hateful fellow-boy; a man who was soundly hated by the parents of many of the boys I played with; an innocent who thought that all the e-sounds in French were pronounced "ay" wherever they occurred; a great comedian; a hypochondriac, and an incorrigible meddler with other people's lives – to name but a few of his celebrated impersonations. My mother: less complex in form but extremely complex in depth, a sentimentalist, a Josh Billings,* a person frightened of almost everything in the external world, and unquestionably the most terrifying Primal Mother since Grendel's Dam* in *Beowulf.* How does one get that into an autobiography? Brenda has suggested that I write about various things that have interested me – the theatre, education, journalism and what not, leaving myself out of the foreground; but that sort of book doesn't really interest me.

I really hate delving into my past, though I do a certain amount of it. I face a task of that sort before I can get to work on my next novel [*World of Wonders*]. I have, during the past couple of years, recovered a large number of letters I wrote to a girl I was in love with* at the time, while I was at Oxford. I need much of what they contain for the book. But can I get at it? No, I shrink from re-greeting the young man I was. Do you know Heine's poem* in which he walks at night along a street where once lived a girl he loved; under her window he sees a figure, and realizes that it is himself! Schubert has set it, as one of the most blood-chilling songs in the world. (Another, by the way, is W. S. Blunt's *The Fox*,* set to marvellous music by Peter Warlock; it would take the skin off a bear to listen to it.) No, no; my youth and childhood are still too raw and painful in recollection; no candy-floss falsification palmed off as autobiography for me.

Don't think it *necessary* to write, though I delight in your letters. Your energy is for more important things, such as the unfreezing and metamorphosis of that numb bum, Numbbum. If its use is gone, you must develop its ornamental side.

Rob.

To GORDON ROPER

[Windhover
Caledon East]
August 31 [1972]

Dear Gordon:

I feel devilish queer. The modifier is carefully chosen, for there is something decidedly of the Dark Powers about it. Physically I am in my usual hog-like health, but my soul is exceedingly sorrowful. And I know why. It is the season of my birthday, and for many years it has brought with it this strangeness, a sense of boding, and very bad dreams. I don't pretend to know why. But fifty-nine years ago last

Monday, to a poor woodcutter's cottage in Thamesville, Ont., the fairies brought a little bundle of joy, which I suspect the poor wood-cutter & his wife would gladly have sent back again. Why? Because their second child [Arthur] had been born with *spina bifida* and was a source of anxiety; because their third child had been a still-born girl, and because when this fourth little bundle hove in sight, the poor woodcutter's wife was almost 45,* and had never been a great whooper-up for motherhood even in her youth. And what was the immediate upshot? The little bundle pined; it weighed less at six months than at birth; in the phrase of the time, it was Despaired Of. (Imagine that! I was Despaired Of!) and was a good deal of a nui-sance to raise. (Almost a little Paul Dempster.)

MEDICAL NOTE WHICH MAY INTEREST HELEN: there has been in the London *Times* of late weeks a correspondence about whether doctors should allow infants with *spina bifida* to live; their prognosis, it is asserted, is that they will not attain adulthood, that they will be obese cabbages of deficient intellect, unable to control their functions, and completely impotent. Well, the only *spina bifida* child I know is my brother Arthur, who was 69 on August 18, is hale and happy, has made a lot of dough and brought up two excellent sons, and has limped a little all his life, and now finds he likes to have a cane with a rubber tip, just to swat at things with. When he was born the doctor – Dr. G. K. Fraser, the local GP, and a good man but no Osler* – told my parents he would have to operate at once, and did so – on the kitchen table – within two hours of birth. Arthur was a frail child, but nobody ever thought he would be a vegetable, or impotent, or indeed any-thing but slightly lame. Behold, Numbbum, the positive side of Ignorance; nobody in the situation knew enough to Despair.

But to return to my mulligrubs. My birthday now is always a mile-stone, bringing with it decided psychic misery, bodeful dreams, and intimations of death. If I were a Psychological Strong-Man I would understand it, and pass it off with a laugh, but I'm not, and I don't. Sixty is going to be a brute.

There: I've never told anybody that before, except Brenda. You arouse the confessional spirit in me, Hezekiah.* You constellate the archetype of the Old Wise Man.

Brenda & I celebrated by going to Stratford to see *She Stoops to Conquer,** a play for which we both have a great affection, for we worked on it when we were at the Old Vic, know the text very well, and have seen every production we could manage since then, including some dismal ones. But this production was excellent. The tone was right; I mean that the director had placed the people accurately in the social scene – country gentry, but not as far from the rustics as they were from the city gentlemen. The mainstay was Tony van Bridge* – a very fine actor – as Squire Hardcastle; a real country squire, proud of his house and his ancestors and his people, a monument of good sense and real good breeding, but a whimsical old fellow all the same. So one could see why Tony Lumpkin got on his nerves, being both a boob and a profligate, though not a bad fellow. And the Squire's love for his daughter was touching and warming, and one knew in the first five minutes that she was the child of his first marriage, which is sometimes forgotten. Mary Savidge* was an excellent Mrs. Hardcastle, absurd in her ignorant yearning for fashion and her doting partiality for Tony, but not a fool. And Tony was very good indeed – a fat Tony, but boy's fat, and with a face like an apple; an ass but not vicious. Kate was played splendidly by Pat Galloway,* for she was so plainly her father's daughter; her rustic accent was good, but her speech when she was not pretending to be the barmaid was a little rustic too; and she had lots of spirit, without being a pushy girl. So this was a fine start; get the Hardcastles right, and you can't go far astray. Lots of other good performances, especially a young Englishman, Nicholas Pennell,* as Marlow. (Perhaps you saw him as Michael Mont in the *Forsyte Saga*?) He got very well over that primary hurdle of being bashful with ladies but a lady-killer with barmaids; that can be nasty unless Marlow has a likeable personality, which Pennell very notably has.

An American School group, predominantly black, sat near us & found the play weary work. The Right Not To Know, do you suppose, or am I right in thinking that cultural boundaries are often Grand Canyons?

So it was a first-rate evening, and we felt that we had once again refreshed ourselves at the clear crystal spring of a very great play. I rate it very high, and have warm admiration for Goldsmith; Sheridan is wonderful for his wisecracks; whole scenes of his bring a laugh on every line. But Goldsmith never makes a wisecrack; he has a truer humour, for his people are richly funny, and what they say is uproarious because of them, and not because of some fire-cracker joke. My one reservation was that the director, Michael Bawtree,* had "clarified" some passages by putting familiar words in place of unfamiliar ones and cutting things he thought nobody would understand. Example:* the bear-leader in the Inn Scene says: "May this be my poison if my bear ever dances but to the very genteelest of tunes; Water Parted or the Minuet in Ariadne." The second part of the line was cut. When I taxed Bawtree with it, he said, "Yes, but who knows or cares?" Well, I know and care, and everybody in the audience would know that two tunes so named were funny choices for a bear to dance to, and would laugh – as they laughed at many other lines they did not understand but which they knew in their bones to be funny. And another thing: Goldsmith writes prose that is every bit as *musical* in character as GBS; muddle them, or hack them, and a musical phrase is lost, and some of the great music of the play is missed. The effect is like those editions of Bach, on which some nineteenth century editor, trained in a conservatory in logical harmony, corrects the old man's daring and illogical progressions; the result is by so much the less the work of the great master, and something of the colour of his mind has been blotted. But I am lecturing. I wrote Bawtree a long letter about it, but who has ever been able to tell an Englishman anything?

I have been thinking a lot about Max Beerbohm. August 24 was the centennial of his birth. A bibliography and a book of his caricatures were published to mark the occasion, and I was interested that the critic in the *Times** said what I have always felt but feared to say about the caricatures: they are rotten drawings, and the colour is weak and weeshy; they are interesting because they show us what Rossetti and Wilde and George Moore and Wells* and Shaw and all the rest looked like to a very shrewd and irreverent mind and an eye that had seen them on the hoof, so to speak. I am an admirer of Beerbohm but I could never screw myself up into the abject, queeny admiration that possesses Norman Endicott, for instance. On August 24 I piously re-read a lot of Beerbohm's letters; astonishing in the light of Shaw's letters, which I had also been reading. Max writes so simply, even bone-lessly, to his friends, whereas GBS put a full battery of guns behind every laundry list. But the real give-away is that GBS writes a letter just as he wrote his plays and prefaces; the style is the same. Whereas Beerbohm obviously sweated and slaved over *his* famous style, and that is why his stuff always reads to me like the work of an architect who builds a house and then *applies* the architectural character afterward; thought and style are not one. Should they be? I don't really know, but the intimate Beerbohm is rather a dull little chap, and GBS couldn't have been dull if he had taken lessons..... Did you know I once met Beerbohm? And I knew his wife* rather better; a wonderful woman, the mark of which was that she always talked to everyone in precisely the same way – with intensity and truly thinking about what she was saying, because it was all feeling rather than intellectualizing. This made her an oddity to some young men, but I thought her a great darling.

I seem to have gobbled all my letter in literary opinions. Have I any *hard* news, as the papers consider it? Well, Jenny and Tom are going to Jamaica, to set up a manufacturing business; they go on Sat. They are excited and rather apprehensive, but I think it is a good thing, for otherwise they would wear away their lives in good, safe jobs here, and never stretch their abilities. They are going to make things from fibreglass, as a subsidiary of a Canadian firm which does this very successfully. But they are risking some money, and I expect they will be very thoughtful about every move. Moira W. goes on holiday next week: she has been poorly – headaches – & I have been worried about her. The young man who exercised his Right Not To Know in my GBS Seminar has *dropped out* of Grad. Schl. & gone to Hollywood as the kept man of an aging film star. Dare I say he has found his *niche*? A rather well-worn niche, I gather.

Don't answer. Husband your strength. Do you want any more books? Don't by the way, return the Stratford pamphlet; that one is for you.

Rob.

If my Mother were alive she would be 103 today.

To GORDON ROPER

[Windhover
Caledon East
Shortly after September 7, 1972]

Dear Gordon:

I am late in writing to you this week, for a variety of reasons, the first of which is that the far, clear call of the university is beginning to sound in my ears, and I have to go to town more frequently to cope with college affairs. And what affairs! They would depress the spirits of an archangel. I had one of my regular talks with [Colin] Friesen [the Bursar] on Wednesday, and in addition to his usual gloomy cry that the college cannot last without more money, he tells me that we now lose an average of $25 weekly in meals eaten by guests of the Junior Fellows, for which no chit is signed; that in the past six months eight dozen of cutlery has been stolen from the dining-room, and that this happens twice a year; that one of our departing Junior Fellows has made off with a chair belonging to the college; that another was apprehended when about to get away with eighteen dinner-plates and the cutlery to go with them. And that the House Committee was waiting to see him to complain that the standard of food was not what they thought it should be..... However, the House Committee has demanded that the college books be made open to them; they feel that *their* fees are not being spent to the greatest advantage. I wait gleefully for this encounter, because I hope to skin the hide off them. Pompous, ungrateful brutes! Most of them never ate so well in their lives, in the sod huts they inhabited out in Saskatoon or the fishy coves of Newfoundland. God, how I loathe the young! Do you suppose *we* were such grasping, crooked, self-important cabbageheads as these? I went to Queen's during the Depression, and as I remember it the student body was pretty scared, orderly and glad to be at a university, without getting any ideas that they ought to run it, and treat the officials of colleges as if they were defaulting cashiers.

Indeed, I think increasingly of resigning from the college. I have worked at several jobs, but never one in which I was treated as an incompetent lodging-house keeper by a rabble of pompous crystallographers, bioenterologists, medievalists, watch-menders, toaster-designers, and cannibals living off the scraps of Henry James. I often think that the whole concept of the college is a wrong one, unsuited to our times and our country, attempting to treat young men according to ideals of honour and decency which have no place in a fat-cat pseudo-democracy, where a "community of scholars" means a monkey-clever rabble of self-serving fatheads, with size 11 brains and size 2¼ souls.

As you may discern (if this reaches you on one of your intuitive days) I am a little out of temper, and it is for the second reason that makes me late in writing. I have the 'flu. Indeed, I am beginning to wonder if I do not have the 'flu for more days in the year than I enjoy freedom from it. This is the coughing, weeping, snuffling, gagging kind, complicated by sudden violent sweats and fits of weakness. This kind, medical friends tell me, takes two bites at you. I certainly had something like it three weeks ago, and thought I had banished it, but here it is again, refreshed by lurking unseen.

It came most inopportunely last Tuesday. I woke with no voice – not a croak – which was bad, because on Wednesday I was scheduled to read in the In Person series at the Museum; they get authors to read from their own stuff. So I had to go in for heroic courses of inhalation, hot baths and selective pummelling by Brenda (who has a gift for massage) and was able to read on Wednesday. Indeed, it went very well, and I had an overflow audience, and without immodesty I may claim to have wowed 'em. But the 'flu was not defeated; on Wednesday it was in full possession, and has been gnawing at me ever since. I can't do much, but I have done one most unaccustomed thing; I have watched the Canadian-Russian hockey match in Vancouver, and liked it better than might have been expected. I have also watched the telecasts from the Olympics, and enjoyed them hugely. There was a time when I took quite an interest in boxing, and there have been some nifty bouts at Munich; also the running and pole-vaulting were very fine. Canada seems to be doing better than usual, but as a nation we do not blaze in the sports firmament. I was very sorry for Esposito* of the Canadian hockey team when he spoke on the TV after the Vancouver game. He was a bit whiney, but he was right when he said that Canadians booed their own team cruelly for every error, and treated them as bums if they didn't win. This, of course, is very Canadian. We are an ignorant people, and by that I mean inexperienced, shallow and imperceptive; we only know the difference between winning and losing – nothing of the awful struggles to get into the competition at all, and the hundred variables that may make a good team today an ill-integrated mess tomorrow. We are without compassion, as children are – because we cannot understand what we have never felt.

I have also been whiling away the heavy, rheumy hours reading Dickens' *Our Mutual Friend*. I never read a Dickens novel without finding some new freshness on almost every page. I am continually astonished that the U of T English Dept. offers no single course in Dickens, but paws James, Lawrence* and Joyce almost to death. I firmly hold to the judgement that Dickens is second only to Shakespeare in the world of writing in our language. But of course he is long, and he makes extraordinary demands on the patience of inexperienced readers because of his gush and his sentimentality, and his splendours cannot be opened by any pinhead with a critical theory and nothing else.

What especially astonishes me this time around is his extraordinary understanding of Ignorance. I mean simple illiteracy, and not the school-trained, pus-gutted Canadian ignorance of which I was writing a moment ago. But Dickens penetrates with absolute certainty into the minds of people to whom the whole world of print, and all that books mean, is as little known as the moon is now – that is to say, the analphabets have heard tell of it, but they have no notion of its reality or how to reach it. Yet these unlettered people are not stupid; far from it. They have wonderful memories, and they have crude but effective ways of doing reckonings; what is amazing about them is the *cleanness* of their perceptions; they see what they see for themselves, and insofar as they can interpret it, they are individual. Very different this from the world in which we live where a vast body of commonly accepted, but dubious information is squarely between us all and anything we encounter. How we go whoring after whatever seems to be the latest and most miraculous explanation for anything. We can both remember when the germ theory of disease was newish, and seemed to be the explanation for all illness. Wipe everything with carbolic, and all will be well. But we have seen the rise of the virus, and the germ is beginning to look pretty cheap; indeed, my doctor son-in-law [John Cunnington] tells me the virus is in for some nasty surprises before long. But when the Germ was new, the Germ was King. Are we so much better off than savages who fall ill because they have swallowed a Spirit Snake while asleep?

This is a gloomy, spleeny letter, and I had better conclude it. I shall write again next week, before the jaws of the education-mill close upon me.

Rob. . . .

To GORDON ROPER

[Massey College
University of Toronto]
October 5, '72

Dear Gordon:

I have at last sequestered a few minutes in which to write to you. You know all the reasons and excuses – the manic urge of faculty and students at the beginning of term to do everything at once, and to appoint committees until halted by sheer dizziness. In addition, I have jobs to do about both the book of plays [*Hunting Stuart and Other Plays*] and the novel [*The Manticore*]. I call them jobs, because that is the light in which they appear to me; the publishers hold them out as delicious treats. To be at the CBC at five to nine in the morning to talk to somebody called Gzowski* (and to be overheard by millions, positively millions); to chew the rag with Elwood Glover* from 12 to 1.30 (and then rush back here to be at a graduate examination at which I am an appraiser at two); to hold myself in readiness to address people in Vancouver, Montreal, Philadelphia and points south (and on no account to take on anything which might conflict with possible but as yet undetermined dates). Well, there it is. I once yearned to be a successful author, and now I am something mildly in that order, and I must not whine. But when I yearned, I was young and had the energy of youth; now I get tired when I am thrust into the company of strangers, who regard me as a "property"; and when I am tired I entertain uncharitable thoughts.

Which brings me to your last letter, which I have read and re-read, and which Brenda has read, and about which we have talked a great deal. Your experience with the group with whom you went to school is very like my own. I had a group of special friends: one is dead of TB; one made a disastrous marriage and became somebody else; one became a boozer and drugger,* and blew his brains out (and he had more brains than any of us, but not enough character to put on a dime); one now a High School principal, married to a girl once a flaming Communist, but now anxious about knives and forks, and if she seats her guests correctly – and a Commie gone square is an awesome sight. But hardly a day passes that I do not see somebody with whom I was at Upper Canada College, and even if we were never on any sort of terms in those days, we wave genially at one another because we are greeting each other as survivors – which is what you said. But it was not only at UCC I was at school, as you know; I went to school with a lot of kids from what are now called "disadvantaged homes" but in those days were simply called The Pore. From time to time somebody sidles up to me, and extends a horny hand, and says "I bet you don't remember me" – and wins his bet. As we talk, it becomes plain that he is the boy he was, grown older, but essentially no different – a clod untroubled by a spark. I hate myself because I have nothing to say to him, but then reflect that Our Blessed Lord promised him the Kingdom of Heaven. These humbler people look so *old*: not poverty, but unused wits. The academic life preserves the appearance, if not of youth, of sanity – longer.

As for surviving, that is what I should like, but one must be careful about saying such things, because you can never tell Who may be listening, and it is always assumed that Who must be hostile or at least minatory. What a fine thing to live as long as Mann,* and write as well as he at the end! But it happens. The other day I saw a letter in the London *Times* from Sir Harry Brittain,* who was a friend of my father's; Sir Harry is pickled in alcohol and he is just about to be 99, and he writes with a clarity and concision I wish my students could achieve. . . .

So you are back in town? I hear good reports of you from my spies. But be careful. Coddle yourself. Spit in the eye of all demanders. SURVIVE! We need you. You know all the long list of people who need you, and I hope you have put my name good and high, because friends of your quality are damned few. So take a big swig of the medicine you have prescribed for me and SURVIVE!

Our best to you & Helen –

Rob.

To WILLIAM FRENCH

Massey College
University of Toronto
October 19, 1972

William French (1926–   ), Canadian, was literary editor for The Globe and Mail *1960–90.*

Dear Mr. French:

Thank you for your very kind review of *The Manticore** in this morning's *Globe.* I particularly liked being described as baroque; I am not certain that I can fully live up to this description but sometimes undeserved compliments are the sweetest.

With thanks and good wishes,

Yours sincerely,

Robertson Davies

To ROBERT FINCH

[Massey College
University of Toronto
soon after Friday October 27, 1972]

Dear Robert:

Very sorry that you are laid up, yet, in the blackness of my heart I reflect that if you are immobile you will be more disposed to hear my plea than if you were up and about: for once again the Gaudy impends, and I write to ask if you will favour us with yet another piece for that occasion. I am sorry to ask you so early, but Lochhead is asking *me* for the copy already for the invitation, which I understand is to be printed this year on paper made in our own paper-room. We who hope to delight our friends at Christmas have to set about the work while there are yet leaves on the trees.

Well, will you?

What about, sez you. Well, sez I, the choir are making a great feature of the fact that Vaughan Williams* was born a century ago, and they are going to do some fine things of his, and also a brand-new setting of Eliot's *The Journey of the Magi* by Benjamin Britten;* as Gordon Wry* is a friend of B.B. he has been favoured with an advance copy, and Massey College will be the first to offer this work on the North American continent! But if these circumstances suggest nothing that tickles your fancy, I remind you once again that John Donne* was born in 1572, and that might serve as a *donné* – have I got it right? (Perilous to pun in other than one's cradle tongue.) Or if that doesn't suit, you always have ideas up your sleeve, and what the Jacobeans called a pregnant wit.

If you could give me an answer soonish – just yea or nay, not a title or subject – I can satisfy the maw of the College Press. For you are our one poet who is bardic and will perform in public. LePan shrinks from it; Lochhead gets the bends at the mere thought. Not that I have asked them already; you are first choice; but they volunteered the information.

I am glad you did not come to the Jonson program on Friday last. The Jonsonians did not arrive until 9:55, and were many of them disguised in liquor. They were a poor audience. I am driven to the sad conclusion that many professors of Eng. Lit. do not care the bounce of a cracker for poetry. It is their "field" which they laboriously till; not a delight or a Muse they serve. How disillusioning the academic world is to us poor innocents who stray into it from the romantic, teeming world of business.

Rob.

Dear Mr. Pennell:

In your performance as Pericles
you have succeeded admirably in
one of the most difficult tasks
that can be set for an actor today: you have made a true hero
credible and likable and have won
the sympathy of the audience for
virtue and the heroic struggle.
My wife and I were delighted and
felt ourselves enriched by your
performance, for we are both very
keen on myth and legend and the
riches they contain for those who
can uncover such things. That is
what <u>Pericles</u> does, even in the
rather battered text we have--
show in mythical fashion man's
search for his inmost self, and
his terrible blindness to what lies
most immediately under his eyes.
A very great Jungian play, and you
have done wonders with it. Many
thanks from us both, and may you
have a great success in this
unlikely role--not a bad springboard
for Hamlet.

all good wishes,

Robertson Davies

Thurs.
July 26

SECTION

VIII

NOVEMBER 1972–DECEMBER 1975 – *WORLD OF WONDERS* PLANNED AND WRITTEN, *QUESTION TIME* PLANNED, WRITTEN, PERFORMED, AND PUBLISHED

avies had a sudden burst of new ideas for the story of *World of Wonders* early in November 1972, and gathered his resources through the following winter and spring. On July 2, 1973, he began to write, finishing the first draft on June 24, 1974. Then in July and August, he turned his attention to the writing of *Question Time*, an allegorical play about Canada's "identity crisis," commissioned by the St. Lawrence Centre for the Performing Arts in Toronto. The typescript of *World of Wonders* went to his publishers the following January and in the same month he completed his revisions to *Question Time*, which opened on February 25, 1975, to negative reviews but good houses. The play was published in September, and *World of Wonders* appeared in print in Canada that fall as well (in the United States it came out the following March). The most influential North American reviewers judged, albeit with some dissenting voices, that the Deptford trilogy, now complete, was indeed the *tour de force* that *Fifth Business* had promised.

Davies, inwardly insecure about his work, always appreciated formal recognition. In this period, two of Canada's greatest honours came his way: he was made a Companion of the Order of Canada in 1972, and he won the Governor General's Award for Fiction for *The Manticore* in 1973. The flow of letters from readers of the Deptford trilogy, especially *Fifth Business*, continued too, giving him great pleasure.

Davies continued as Master of Massey College and professor of English and drama in the Graduate School of the University of Toronto in this period. The student unrest of the late 1960s reached Massey late, and was most effective on the issue of the admission of women. Initially Davies resisted the students' demands, since he believed that women ought to be educated differently than men and knew that the founders of Massey (and Vincent in particular) had conceived of it as a College for men only. But once he had recognized that change was inevitable, he reversed his position and worked to ensure that the College corporation would support the admission of women.

So preoccupied was Davies with writing in these years that he and Brenda took only one trip, a jaunt to England and Wales in April of 1975. Like a similar trip in June of 1972, it returned them to old haunts and pleasures.

To GORDON ROPER

[Massey College
University of Toronto]
Nov. 6, 1972

Dear Gordon:

I thought you would like to know that I have decided to write a third book [*World of Wonders*] to complete the story that runs through *Fifth Business* and *The Manticore*.

It was never my intention to write a trilogy, or even to write the second book. It just happened. The story ran on, and required to be told. I have answered all enquiries about a trilogy with an assured No up to this time. But I have changed my mind.

Some time ago* I wrote to you about the book I was working on (making notes) during the summer. The trouble was that although I had a large quantity of detail and several characters, I had no plot, and I am not one of those who thinks plot does not matter. To think in that way suggests that life itself has no plot, and that is not my view at all, as you well know. I had the young man who was in search of himself, and I had the theatrical company, headed by the actor-knight and his remarkable wife, but although the amount of detail I can muster to clothe them is almost embarrassingly copious, *they don't do anything*. I was waiting for something to occur to me that would set the whole thing in motion. Slowly it did so, and it was the repeated question of readers and reviewers of *The Manticore* about more of the same. And quite suddenly – not unprompted by my humble petitions to Whatever It Is for some solution to my problem – the idea came: why not the story of Eisengrim, with all you have for the novel you have been planning used as a large section of his personal history? And there it was. Everything seemed to fall into place at once.

Of course Eisengrim will not appear as the callow young Englishman of my earlier plot; that fellow will remain, but as a secondary character. I have spent the past weekend scheming out the novel as it now seems to assert itself, and the plan looks like this: [a page of the letter is missing here, but Davies' "Works in Progress Notebook" makes it clear that the main elements of the plot of *World of Wonders* were now clear to him]. . . .

There; how d'you like *them* apples? I think I can round out the story, give a new twist to the mystery, and fatten out the whole thing in such a book because it will give me a chance to develop a few ideas that are shown in other aspects in the two preceding novels. The themes: the hunger in people for illusion, the mythical element in life, and the notion, not so much of Fate as of synchronicity,* which occupies my mind so much. And lots of the kind of technical detail which people seem to like in my books – the stuff about saints, and about the law, and about stage magic.

One thing bothers me, and perhaps you can throw some light on it, because it lies so near to me that I cannot see it clearly. It is obvious that sex will appear in this book, as it has done in the two others, as something nearly akin to servitude. Ramsay flees from it; Edward [David] rejects it; Eisengrim is "used" nastily by Willard. But there is another element. Ramsay finds sex as a fulfilling element in Liesl; so does Edward; so will Eisengrim. But why with such an ugly woman? Because, so far as I can see, she offers understanding, sympathy and a kind of adult sex that is far from the romance of the usual novel. Is this any good? I am puzzled by it, but as it is what I am impelled to write, I write it. Do you think it comes through?

Of course I am eager to know what you think. You have somehow woven your way into my work in a manner that makes you a very special person to me; I do with you what I had never thought to do with any critic – I trust you to give me genuinely perceptive advice, arising from your own critical sympathy and perceptiveness and real affection for literature. So if you can manage it, I should greatly like to have your opinion, because I am in rather a dither, having changed my plans so radically and so fast.

Every good wish –

Rob.

To HORACE W. DAVENPORT

Massey College
University of Toronto
Nov. 28, 1972

Dear Horace:

I have brought out another book – another novel [*The Manticore*] – and in a day or so I shall send you a copy of it. It is a companion to *Fifth Business*, and it has been getting flattering notices here and in the U.S., which sets at rest the anxiety which possesses me whenever I write a book. Will it measure up to the one just past? Have I begun the long decline toward the tomb and the Conqueror Worm which shows so painfully in the work of public entertainers? Well, for the moment the answers seem to be (a) Yes, and (b) No.

Ah, but I am at work on a third in this series [*World of Wonders*] – the book which will wind up the plot and the affairs of the principal characters. And in order to do this I need some help of a highly professional character in your line, and I write to you asking for information, if you can find time to write. Once before – in the 50s – you gave me invaluable information about the death of a woman who refused an operation for gall-stones, and I used it in a passage that has been admired by connoisseurs of fictional deaths. I like my medical details to be *right*.

This time I want to know something about acromegaly* – a disease which I first encountered at Oxford when you used to look dubiously at your very fine hands and demand of the listening air if you could possibly be getting it. Do you recall a character named Liesl in *Fifth Business*? A woman of hideous face, with big hands and feet, but a lot of charm? Could acromegaly be the cause of such ugliness? Could a woman have it, and not be affected mentally? Can medical science do much about it? Would it be likely to come on at puberty?

Such questions, I know, you answer off the top of your head. But are there any little quirks about acromegaly that I should know about, so as not to say silly things in describing someone who has it?

The other question, however, may be rather more of a poser. What can you tell me about the effects of long-continued buggery,* or sodomy, or whatever it is when a young man – a boy – is repeatedly invaded *per anum* by somebody's penis? Does he just get used to it? Surely it has an effect on his normal rhythm of evacuation? Is it obligatory to cut a muscle – called, I believe, the *forfex* – as used to be done among the Turks (and may still be, for aught I know). I once knew a fellow* who went in for this sort of thing, and he used to go into displeasing raptures about the sensation it caused him. (Oddly enough, it was at the Princeton School of Advanced Studies that he made these advanced studies.) But he was a kook, and finally shot himself, having lost all zest for anything except booze and drugs. My reason for asking is that I want to write about whatever it was that the character called Paul Dempster in *Fifth Business* experienced when he ran away with a circus and became the virtual slave of a sideshow man whose special interest was boys. Any information gratefully received about the physical or psychological effects of this nastiness.

Am working like a dog and coping with a certain amount of Student Unrest. The undergraduates have pretty well finished with it here, but it is just having a final fling in the Graduate School, and it takes the characteristic graduate form – tortured, mean-spirited, and needlessly complex.

The very best to you and Inge from us both.

Rob.

To FATHER PATRICK M. PLUNKETT S.J.

Massey College
University of Toronto
Nov. 30, 1972

Dear Fͬ· Plunkett:

I owe you so many letters that I scarcely know where to begin, but perhaps I had better start with an apology for my long silence. I have been up to my ears in work of one kind and another since the beginning of term, and have had to neglect many things that would have given me pleasure – including writing to you to thank you for your kindly criticism and refreshing point of view about my work.

However, I don't really think you have changed my mind, although you have given me many reasons to think about my opinions. The easy thing would be to say that we are both getting at the same thing from different directions, but you are much too acute to be fobbed off with that old chestnut. We are *not* getting at the same thing. You are putting forward a coherent opinion about the meaning and purpose of life which is based on long study of one of the most important bodies of belief and accompanying philosophy that the world possesses. I am putting forward some opinions derived from observation and intuition which is personal, and which has no authority behind it. You can present volumes of closely reasoned argument to support your beliefs, whereas all I can do is to say "This is how it looks to me." But I think you are mistaken if you suppose I present my ideas with any feeling that I am going to persuade other people to share them. When they do so, or when they do so in part, all I can say is that I have shown them some aspect of life in a new guise, which they will doubtless abandon when it suits them to do so. I do not write thus as if my vocation as a novelist were something I considered trivial: some of the very greatest of my craft have done what I try to do in a way that has shown the world something new. Dostoevsky,* for instance, is far from trivial, but he is also far from orthodox, and he has shown his readers a new aspect of compassion which they have valued and incorporated into their ideas about life. Thomas Mann has anatomized the psychological link between artistic creation and sickness as no one had done before him and we are all his debtors. I do not rank myself with these great ones, but I too, so far as lies in me, have offered an individual way of looking at life to my readers, and many of them have responded in a way that shows me that I have not done so in vain. I am not trying to proselytize: only to reveal a personal vision.

Here, I think, is the unbridgeable gulf between us, and it is the gulf between the orthodox Catholic view of life, and the Protestant one, which relies so heavily on individual exploration and approach. I tried, for a time, to ally myself with orthodoxy, but it simply didn't work. To have kept up a pretence would have been false to orthodoxy and false to myself, and I don't think any good can come of such falseness. You may say that I should have bent my neck to the orthodox yoke, and I am sure you could give me many good reasons for doing so, but you see I wasn't raised that way, and the whole tenor of my background and education was against it. Only some very striking conversion could have changed me, by changing me utterly, and I never met with any such experience. It was not that I didn't try. In my university days it was my good fortune to have some encounters with a most redoubtable member of your order, Father Martin D'Arcy,* who, quite understandably, had little time for me and my doubts and scruples; Father D'Arcy was a great fisher of souls, but he liked them big and showy, and undergraduates were not for him. Nor was he the only priest I approached, but I never found one who had much interest in converting me. I can well understand this: one of the most wearisome tasks of the priest must be that of explaining what is obvious to him to people who are drawn his way but want explanations to meet their usually cantankerous objections. So instead of becoming a Catholic – I had been raised a Presbyterian, and was discontented with what seemed to me to be its cruelty and intellectual bleakness – I became an Anglican, and what that means I leave it to you to fill in. In effect, I was thrown back on myself, and have had to make do with what I found there. Nor, may I say, am I now very much drawn by what I find of Catholicism in writers* who profess it noisily, like Graham Greene and Evelyn Waugh. Greene seems to me to be cruel and harsh enough for a Presbyterian, and for Waugh so much of Catholicism emerges as spiritual snobbery. So here I am, at 59, not likely to change the path in which I have travelled so long, which is a sort of solitary Protestantism, dismayed by the Protestant churches in their extraordinary variety.

The Manticore has been very well received both in Canada and the US, which is gratifying. I am puzzled by some of the things that are written about it, but that is understandable enough; any book with vitality means many different things because it rouses individual responses in readers who have an axe to grind, or a sore place that may be bruised anew by something that is read. The people who puzzle me most are those who think that the book must be disguised autobiography. Not a word of it! It is really astonishing how many people are incapable of believing that there is such a thing as imagination. One of the glories – as also one of the burdens – of my life has been an extremely active and profuse imagination. I suppose the people I create are, in some sense, aspects of myself, but they are, as it were, the unborn shadows of people I shall never be (which sounds like nonsense but I can't at present phrase it better); we are all many people, and I suppose a novelist has these lesser personalities more easily at call than others.

Now I must get back to work. You will know, as few of my other friends do, how much work and what a tangle of personalities even so small a community as this college can afford, and what a lot of work they make. Sometimes I wonder if all the tact and manoeuvring are worth the result.

If I do not have a chance to write to you again before Christmas, please accept my warmest good wishes for that season, which has such a very special meaning for you and also – I do assure you – for me.

Sincerely,

Robertson Davies

To MARGARET LAURENCE

Massey College
University of Toronto
January 5, 1973

Dear Margaret:

It has taken me an unconscionable time to reply to your letter of December 4, and the chief reason is that it is so hard to reply to such a generous message of encouragement and approval from a fellow-artist whom one respects profoundly and admires deeply as a human being. This is not just Welsh rhetoric: last night Brenda and I went to hear Mia Anderson's* one-woman show of pieces from modern Canadian writing, by women and about women; it was all pretty good and much of it was very clever, but it was when she concluded it with a noble passage from *The Stone Angel* that we felt that somebody of real size and capacity was speaking. Afterward we both agreed that it had been the authentic voice of Margaret, and made all the rest look

– well, pretty good and often clever..... Nothing that has been said or written about *The Manticore* has stirred and assured me as your letter has done, because I know that you know what you are talking about, as a fine craftsman as well as a writer of great authority and insight.

The book is going very well, which surprises me somewhat, because I thought the Jungian bias and the somewhat disagreeable nature of the main character would work against it. But it is selling well above *Fifth Business*. It has had splendid notices, and again I was surprised, because it is certainly not a modish novel. But its publication has been rather an exhausting experience, because both Macmillans here and the Viking Press [in New York] have wanted me to fly hither and yon to talk about it, and this is a kind of work I find very tiring. I really hate travel – short hops and one-day stands, anyhow – and fitting it in with university work has run me ragged. I even had to go to New York for four days between Christmas & New Year, which could have been fun if I had had a moment of free time; but my toughest day began at 9.30, and banged away till eleven at night, talking all the time, eating unsuitable food and drinking those ferocious drinks they have in N. Y. which would eat through a copper pot. So there it is. Brenda says, "Don't quarrel with success; you had long years when nobody would look at you." So I try to be philosophical. . . .

The literary scene in Canada is hotting up astonishingly, chiefly owing to the work of your friend Margaret Atwood. She is writer-in-residence here this year, but I see little of her, as she is tremendously organized and very busy. However, she has discussed with me her plan to get together an organization of Canadian writers [the Writers' Union] who are serious people – not a mess, like the Canadian Authors Association. I see great merit in the plan, but I am rather leery of it because it has a political tinge, strongly anti-American in a way I think naive, and ungrateful and unjustified. To indulge in a little amateur psychologizing, I wonder if Miss A. is not working off some of her resentment against her American husband, about whom she writes and speaks very sharply. Number Two* is on the horizon, and looks like a very nice fellow. . . . I do not want to get into anything that shouts for an enclosed Canadianism, because the US has treated me well, and I don't believe in nationalism of that kind. Let us *manifest* Canadianism in the quality of what we write; leave knocking the States to those who are bitter. Because of my age, and my own success in the States I should cut an absurd and cranky figure in an anti-American movement..... A lot of the movement seems, also, to insist on a particular kind of Canadianism, which springs, I feel, from Northrop Frye's concept of the Bush Garden: we are a bunch of poor, limited boobs, but by cracky we aren't Yanks – that seems to be the cry. I don't believe this. Miss A. has sounded the trumpet in her book *Survival*, which is enormously influential, but which will certainly bring many counter-blasts. I cannot agree with a *program* for survival; I have survived long enough to know that it is done by grabbing whatever opportunities come along, and they cannot be compelled to appear on schedule. I also feel – and this may be wrong but I sniff it – that they only want me because I am in the limelight at present, and I know that many of the younger writers think I am an ass, a pseudo-Englishman, and a writer of "entertainments" – which is apparently a horrid thing that looks like a novel but isn't one. So, I shall do anything I can for them that makes sense, but I won't mount the barricades.

I was delighted to hear about *The Diviners* and I hope all is going well with it. I think I know something of your method of work, and I know you must be slaving, for you are a Slaver. I am an Agonizer, which is different, and painful in another way. One of my great faults is my desire to please people, and it gets me into some messes. A dear old Jesuit in Manitoba [Father Plunkett] keeps writing to me, exhorting me to stop writing about Sin. What I am doing, he says, is to suggest that Good may come out of Evil, and this is very wrong-minded of me and may mislead my readers. Well, this is manifestly wrong-headed, even if deeply felt, but instead of brushing him off, I keep writing to him, trying to explain what I am really doing, which he cannot comprehend, because he lives according to a system, and his idea of a novel would be a dreadful object. Sometimes, as I set out to explain myself to him I am reminded of that incident in the Upper Library here when you attempted (with a charity and sincerity that I shall never forget) to explain to a girl of fifteen that you were not an enemy of Sex, just because Hagar had not found it all it might have been. The girl couldn't understand because she was talking from her own limited experience, and the modern doctrine that Sex is All. But you tried.

I have not been able to place your quotation THE VOICE OUT OF THE DARKEST CAVE WHICH SAYS ONE WORD ONLY..... REJOICE, but it sounds like Nietszche* (wrong spelling, but never mind). But how right you are; we all have to make a journey into the cave, and we are lucky if that is the voice we hear..... And I was flattered and humbled at once by your saying that *The Manticore* gave some suggestion of Grace to you. That is what I try for, but Grace is terribly out of favour, and one has to be sneaky about introducing it. Our age, loaded with guilt and stifled with luxury, fights the whole idea of Grace tooth and nail. We are ripe for a new Puritanism. I only hope it does not make its arrival in the form of a new Fascism. There are plenty of terrible hints on this continent that it could be so.

Again, deep thanks & love from us both –

Rob.

To GORDON ROPER

Massey College
University of Toronto
Jan 11. 1973

Dear Gordon:

Many thanks for your kind letter of Jan. 3. I was delighted to get the Companion of the Order of Canada, because I am that kind of person – I mean someone who takes great pleasure in public recognition, and who gets genuine reassurance from it. I am never able to sustain for long a sense of the value of my own work unless I have some echo from the outside. The roots of this profound lack of self-confidence lie very deep, and I cannot pretend to have traced them.

It is easy to be glib about such things, but the older I grow the less I trust quick and obvious explanations of anything. Anyhow, there it is, and the pleasantest part of it is the kind letters I get from friends – and some strangers – who think I am a fit person for this sort of award. Of course I value your generous comments, and if I may be so immodest, I think it is true that I have worked pretty hard to do some things that need to be done in Canada and which seemed to be my work more than most people's. I responded with special Hurrahs to your comment about the spirit of the university, so much of which is negative, and directly contrary to what one would have supposed and wished. Some members of the English Faculty seem almost to hate the stuff that sustains and justifies them..... But enough about that.

I am busy at the moment reading proofs of the first volume of the *Letters of C. G. Jung*, which the N/Y Times has asked me to review.* I was amazed by their request, for they must certainly have much better qualified people to do the job, but I did not hesitate, & grabbed the book before they could think twice. It is utterly amazing, and as I read it I am drowned in humility and a sense of unworthiness. The range of his knowledge and sympathy, patience and restraint under provocation is staggering. He seemed ready to write at length, and with the full weight of his knowledge and seriousness, to almost anyone who sent him a letter – often a very silly letter. Sometimes he is severe, and then the sparks fly, but usually he does his level best for anybody at all. How I am to make any sense of this in 1200 words I cannot now see, but something will have to be done.

The College is standing on its ear because tomorrow night the Governor General* comes to dinner, and all the young republicans and scorners of the Establishment are determined not to miss it. Men who have not been here for years are clamouring for seats. Well, well: who said that monarchy had lost its magic? I shall be glad when it is done and the *aides* and RCMP men and other appurtenances of glory are safely off the premises. I don't suppose anybody will throw a bomb at him, but in these days and in what Arthur Woodhouse* used to call this fallen world one can never tell.

Also, we have got a Visitor! Before Christmas the Junior Fellows made an uproar, and suggested that enormities and injustices were

being got away with – presumably by me and Friesen – and that a
Visitor was the only way to restore the reign of Justice. So we got one
in jig time. He is the Hon. Dalton Wells,* Chief Justice of Ont. and
a jolly good Fellow, and since then not a peep has been heard from
the malcontents. It is as well. We have mourned Vincent long enough,
and a Visitor has his place in such a rat-hole as this. We have a lot of
unrest and cloak-and-dagger this year, and some of it is fomented by
the Insidious Dr. Fu Manchu (Bill Dobson* to you). But poor old Fu
had better make the most of it, for by midsummer virtually all of his
arse-lickers will have gone elsewhere. . . .

Was in New York between Christmas and New Year, doing publicity, and to my astonishment everybody was trying to get me to
blackmouth Marshall McLuhan.* I wouldn't but I was certainly being
invited to. I sense that the Night of the Long Knives may be drawing
near for Marshall, and I shall not rejoice, because I like him, though
I think his ideas are dotty.

Our best to you & Helen

Rob.

To DAVID TENNEY

Massey College
University of Toronto
March 22, 1973

*David Tenney, of Sidney Kramer Books in
Washington, had failed to find Tho.
Overskou (who is quoted in the epigraph
to* Fifth Business) *in* Webster's
Biographical Dictionary, *and wrote
Davies to say that "It has been suggested,
rather maliciously I thought, that you
fabricated him."*

[Dear David Tenney:]

It distresses me to think that a bookshop in the capital of a great
nation should be brought so low as to depend upon Webster's dis-
credited *Biographical Dictionary* for information. If you would look in

the *Encyclopedia Americana* you will find that Tho. Overskou was a celebrated Danish actor and playwright, 1798–1873, and that he is remembered now for his history of the Danish theatre called *Den Danske Skueplads*, 1854–62.

How could you accuse me of fabricating a quotation?* If you will thumb through the many volumes of Overskou's great work it will immediately spring to your eye.

Yours sincerely,

[Robertson Davies]

To ANDREW KING

Massey College
University of Toronto
March 27, 1973

Andrew King (1885–1981), Canadian journalist and printer, was editor of the Estevan Mercury in Saskatchewan and a specialist in the printing of huge billboard posters for travelling shows and circuses.

[Dear Mr. King:]

May I appeal to you for some information about the carnival and show business as it existed in Canada around 1919–20. I write to you because I am sure that you will know the answers to my questions, and because you have been very kind to this College, and to our Librarian, Douglas Lochhead, in giving us some of the originals of your posters printed when you were in business in Estevan.

The kind of carnival I want to know about is the sort that used to visit villages like the one in which I was born – Thamesville, Ontario – and which had populations between 500 and 1000. These were one-day or at most two-day fairs. I remember the Midway at our village fair as a very small collection of rides and shows, though it seemed glorious to me when I was a child. I cannot remember any ride other than a merry-go-round, or any shows except a tent with a Fire-Eater, a Fat Woman, a Snake Charmer, a Ventriloquist, and a man who had no arms and could write with his feet. There were also a few games, at which you could win a Kewpie Doll if you knocked over some ninepins with a baseball.

It would help me greatly if you could tell me:

(a) how did such shows travel? By train? if so, how many cars would a small carnival have? Did the workers in the carnival eat and sleep on the train?

(b) What kind of money changed hands in such small carnivals? Did the local Fair Board have to put up a guarantee? Were the carnivals booked for village fairs by the season, or did they take a chance? Was everybody paid by the carnival boss, or was there a sharing system? What kind of pay would, for instance, the Ventriloquist or the Fat Lady get by the week?

(c) Where did they go in cold weather? Did they travel in the Southern U.S.A., or did they disband for the winter? Was there any trouble about crossing the U.S. border?

(d) Were most of the carnival workers Americans or were some Europeans and Canadians?

The reason for these questions is that I am working on a novel which makes some references to the carnival business in 1920–30 and I want to be sure that my details are authentic.

Yours sincerely,

[Robertson Davies]

To DOROTHY LIVESAY

Massey College
University of Toronto
April 2, 1973

Dorothy Livesay (1909–96), Canadian,
was a poet capable of dealing with
political and social issues and with
intimate emotion and reflection. Her
Collected Poems: The Two Seasons *was*
published in 1972.

Dear M<u>rs.</u> Livesay:

Many thanks for your kind letter of March 19th. I particularly appreciated hearing from you because, although we have never met, I have long been an admirer of your work and I feel that you, too, stand somewhat outside the popular and perhaps rather over-eager group of Canadian writers who seem anxious to provide us with a literature with a strongly political bias. I was very glad that you liked *Fifth Business* and *The Manticore*. I am at work now on a third volume which will complete that story and I hope add some interesting material to it.

Regarding your comment about your *Collected Poems* which you suggest might be criticized by a Jungian analyst, may I say that I hope you are joking. I have had the experience, since the appearance of *The Manticore*, of having that book of mine fairly extensively commented on by Jungian analysts and although I have been grateful for their attention, and for occasional light which they throw on the book itself, I have been very forcibly struck by their lack of understanding of the creative process. They seem unwilling to recognize that writing does not proceed from orderly thinking, or even from careful analysis of material that enters consciousness from the unconscious realm. They cannot comprehend the tumultuous quality of creation nor its intractability, and this in spite of the fact that they are invariably extremely intelligent and highly literate people. Therefore I would indeed suggest to you that you do your own job of analysis, if you think it necessary, but I would consider it much more likely that your poems have already told you most of their secrets. If you are interested in this theme, however, may I recommend Dr. C. G. Jung's marvellous autobiography called *Memories, Dreams, Reflections*, which tells you how he tackled the job of understanding his own life and how triumphantly he carried it through.

Yours sincerely,

Robertson Davies

PS: It may amuse you to know that Douglas LePan & I are now known to the ultra-nationalists as "colonialist writers"!

To ARTHUR HAILEY

Massey College
University of Toronto
April 10, 1973

Arthur Hailey (1920–   ), English-born Canadian, is a writer of best-selling novels including Hotel *(1966),* Airport *(1968), and* Wheels *(1971), and of movie scripts and television plays.*

Dear Arthur Hailey:

It was indeed kind of you to write to me, and send me the copy of what you had written to your daughter about my books. I appreciate it greatly, for though it is gratifying to receive kind words from critics, there is a special quality about praise from people who also write, and who know what a queer and often psychologically demanding job it is.

But I was also very pleased to hear from you, because we have friends in common, and I have heard about you from them. Particularly is this so, because I have been interested – and dismayed – by what seems to me to be an unjustified attack on you made during the past two years or so by a number of Canadian reviewers both of books and films, who seem to resent your extraordinary success. They write as if somehow it were contrary to God's manifest will that you should sell immense number of copies of your books, and that these books should so quickly be made into very successful movies. And they have not hesitated to word their criticism in terms which are not far short of personal attacks. I do not understand it, except as evidence of jealousy. But why are they jealous of a man who can do something they cannot do and – if they are to be believed – would not wish to do? Speaking for myself, I wish I had your ability to engross huge numbers of readers in my books, but I also know that it lies outside my range. But as for grudging you one jot of your tremendous popularity – I leave that sort of nonsense to the critics.

What does interest me greatly about your books – and I think it is a quality we share – is your interest in narrative as such. I have always been convinced that a story is vital to a novel, and that it should not be told in such a complex way that the average intelligent reader is bamboozled and thwarted. I have had several discussions with Morley Callaghan on this question of narrative, and it is one of the few subjects on which we are in full agreement. But I find that Canadian – not U.S. – critics refer to me habitually as "old-fashioned," and when I ask what they mean by that term, it is my insistence on narrative that comes up.

Nevertheless, when I look at the great classics of literature – not merely novels but the great epics and plays – it is clear that they are all strong in narrative. They give the public a story first, and then they give character and psychological insight, and then they provide that link with mythic background which university critics love, but which they so plainly fail to understand in anything but an intellectual way. So – what is wrong with narrative? I think the popularity of *Fifth Business* and *The Manticore* rests on the stories first and foremost. I am working now on a third book about the same characters and the same basic situation, and I am slaving away to get the story clear before I embark on the fancy-work. Taken as a trilogy, I hope that the books will make up one good story, with plenty of dimension; but the story is basic.

Why do I seem to be lecturing you like this? Only because I want to express my admiration for your own narrative sense, which seems to me to be the backbone of your books, and a very fine backbone, too. And if it is not impertinent in a stranger to say so, I hope you will not allow the critics who scold you for your strengths to depress your spirits. After all, as Sibelius* said, who ever erected a statue to a critic?

When next you are in Canada might we meet? I should greatly value an opportunity to talk to you. . . .

With thanks & good wishes,

Robertson Davies

To JOHN GRAY

Massey College
University of Toronto
April 25, 1973

John Morgan Gray (1907–78), Canadian, was president of the Macmillan Company of Canada, Davies' chief Canadian publishers since 1958. The Manticore had just won the Governor General's Award for fiction.

Dear John:

Many thanks for your kind letter of April 17th. I have been far too long in replying but there has been a great muddle of examinations and holidays and other disruptions in the interval. Of course I was delighted to get the award, particularly as it began to look as though I should at last be lowered into the tomb as the only Canadian author who had never done so.

I look forward to seeing you at the dinner next week, and perhaps we can chat further about it then.

Yours sincerely,

Rob.

To THE EDITOR OF THE *TIMES LITERARY SUPPLEMENT**

Massey College
University of Toronto
[Shortly before April 27, 1973]

This letter is rooted in the ethos of Oxford. In the 1930s when Horace Davenport and Davies were both graduate students at Balliol, the university was full of little dining clubs. Theirs (which involved only two or three other students) was called The Long Christmas Dinner Society after a play by Thornton Wilder.

Sir, –

It was a matter of keen satisfaction to me to read in Ian Hamilton's Viewpoint (March 16) that the Walter Pater Society of Brasenose* has made an award to Professor Horace W. Davenport of Ann Arbor, Michigan, for his apt and ingenious use of quotation from Pater when, in his *Physiology of the Digestive Tract* (Chicago, 1971), he described human flatus as burning "with a hard, gem-like flame."

May I, as permanent secretary of the Long Christmas Dinner Society (founded at Balliol on March 1, 1937, with H. W. Davenport as a founder member), call attention to the fact that the first edition of this notable work appeared in 1961; in that year Professor Davenport's old college honoured him for this same happy union of literature with science, when he was awarded the Society's Ben Jonson citation. It read, in full:

In the name of Ben Jonson
To Horace Willard Davenport
"The same that writ so subtly of the fart."
                    The Alchemist, II, 1*
From the Long Christmas Dinner Society.
                    March 1, 1961.

Robertson Davies

To NICHOLAS PENNELL

Massey College
University of Toronto
Thurs. July 26 [1973]

*Nicholas Pennell (1939–95) was a
talented English actor. He was to become
a stalwart of the Stratford Festival (which
presented Pericles in 1973), performing
there every season 1972–94.*

Dear Mr. Pennell:

In your performance as Pericles you have succeeded admirably in
one of the most difficult tasks that can be set for an actor today: you
have made a true hero credible and likable and have won the sympathy of the audience for virtue and the heroic struggle. My wife and I
were delighted and felt ourselves enriched by your performance, for
we are both very keen on myth and legend and the riches they contain
for those who can uncover such things. That is what *Pericles* does, even
in the rather battered text we have – show in mythical fashion man's
search for his inmost self, and his terrible blindness to what lies most
immediately under his eyes. A very great Jungian play, and you have
done wonders with it. Many thanks from us both, and may you have
a great success in this unlikely role – not a bad springboard for Hamlet.

All good wishes,

Robertson Davies

To LEIGH McC. GOSSAGE

Massey College
University of Toronto
July 31, 1973

*Leigh McCarthy Gossage (born c. 1902,
Canadian) was an intimate friend of
Vincent Massey's in the period when the
College was being planned and opened.
She was also a friend of the College and
a potential benefactor.*

[Dear Mrs. Gossage:]

I do not know whether the news has reached you that Massey
College is going to receive women as Junior Fellows after the autumn

of 1974, but I felt that it was owing to you to let you know how this came about and what we expect to come of it.

If you follow the University news in the papers you will know that there has been strong pressure to admit both sexes to all residences and to remove, as far as possible, any regulations which seem to discriminate against women. We have felt this pressure quite strongly in the College, and a year ago a petition from the Junior Fellows asked the Senior Fellows to consider it. We did so and replied that the College was founded as a trust and that we felt it was too early to re-interpret the intentions of the founders. Of course this reached Raymond, Hart and Geoffrey when the Minutes went to them and I received letters from them saying that, far from objecting to admitting women to the College, they were strongly in favour of it and wished this to be made known. Obviously when this information reached the Junior Fellows our situation would have been a very difficult one, so we discussed the question again at the Spring meeting of the College Corporation and decided, unanimously, to accept the wish of the living founders to admit women to the College, after our incorporating Act of Legislature had been appropriately altered.

We should have been compelled to do this eventually, though I had not foreseen that it would happen so quickly, and I am not pessimistic about its effect. The kind of girls who will want to live in a graduate residence are not likely to be any more rowdy in their way of life than are the young men and I am confident that we can deal with the situation and that it may lead to a stronger and more varied College. Of course, it is something that Vincent never anticipated, but he was extremely realistic and I think that if he were alive at present he would see that to continue solely as a College for men would greatly weaken our position in the modern university.

We are having some success in strengthening our position in the university and are at last moving towards what I have long wanted, which is a plan whereby we can provide some money to enable senior men to produce scholarly works of unusual quality. It appears at present as though the first of these would be a full-scale life of Vincent himself. The time is ripe for it, and if we delay too long it will be many years before interest in his life and career again reached a peak which would make a biography a practical undertaking. I am hopeful that we will be able to find enough money to support the research and work of a first-class biographer, but my efforts to raise money for the College during the past two or three years have not been encouraging. It is assumed, with some justice, that if the Masseys founded the College they should make it financially independent; certainly I am not prepared to enter into arguments with possible benefactors on this subject, though it becomes increasingly clear that what Vincent was able to provide for us is not sufficient to cover anything except barest necessities. However, I am hopeful that we shall find another benefactor if we are persistent. I am sure that I need hardly ask you if you should encounter any such person to let me know so that we can do whatever can be done to encourage him. It is not impossible, of course, if we are going to admit women, that a woman benefactor might appear.

With warmest good wishes,

Yours sincerely,

[Robertson Davies]

To MARGARET DAVIES

Massey College
University of Toronto
December 3, 1973

Margaret Ester Davies (1912–97), Canadian, was Rupert Davies' widow and RD's stepmother. She was then living in Wales.

[Dear Margaret:]

Have you any recent information about Mabel Jones [Rupert Davies' cousin] of Mold? I have had a rather confused letter from her which I cannot fully understand, but she seems to be extremely worried about her cats, five of whom she names, and then tacks etcetera on to the list, which suggests a considerable number. She wants me to make a contribution to the R.S.P.C.A. and this is in some way related to the fate of the cats. I understand that Eva is dead and I suppose Mabel is alone; she must be quite old and she was always a bit dull, and I wonder if she has gone off her head. I would gladly help out with the cat problem if it would make any real difference but I cannot tell from the letter what is really the matter, and I thought that you might know something about it.

I suppose you saw that Professor Roy* died at the age of 89 on November 29th. I am getting in touch with Michael [Davies]* to make sure that he has an appropriate send-off from the *Whig.* He had a marvellous obituary in the *Times** which I strongly suspect was written by somebody at Queen's, because it pumped up his career rather more than the facts will strictly support, but that is the Queen's way.

It was extraordinarily good of you to go to London for Miranda's concert and we were delighted to get your report. I hope that she and her friends are getting under way on something that will prove interesting and lively.

With love from us both,

[Rob.]

To ALISON BISHOP

Massey College
University of Toronto
December 14, 1973

Alison Mason Kingsbury was an artist and the widow of Morris Bishop. Bishop (1893–1973) wrote many volumes of light verse and a mystery story titled The Widening Stain. *He also wrote respected scholarly works and was professor of Romance languages at Cornell 1921–60.*

Dear Alison:

I did not write as soon as I received your letter about Morris's death, because I wanted time to think and I did not want to say anything to you that was not what I truly felt – as near as I could come to it. Morris meant something special to me, because from early years

I had so much admired his verses in the *New Yorker*. Of course they were widely admired, but they seemed to say something special to me, because they so plainly came from the kind of mind I admire most – the mind rich in scholarship but not confined by scholarship; it is a sort of mind I associate with the latter part of the eighteenth century and the early years of the nineteenth, when there seem to have been many men to whom scholarship was a delightful adjunct of life, rather than a reason for living. We see so many examples today of the solemn scholar who is lost in a dream of self-approbation because he knows a lot; but he does not live in a manner that suits his learning, and his learning seems to give him little pleasure; he is, indeed, burdened by his learning and not illuminated by it. Morris was illuminated by his scholarship and that quality of illumination showed in everything he wrote.

I began a correspondence with him rather shyly, because one always shrinks from disturbing writers and fears a rebuff. But it grew into something I valued enormously, and I have all his letters, and best of all, the extraordinary and bizarre postcards that he acquired, God knows how, and sent off as insouciantly as if they were views of Niagara Falls. You can imagine what a pleasure it was when I asked him to come here to speak to the Leacock Seminar [in October 1970], and he accepted. And that was when Brenda and I had the very great pleasure of meeting you as well as Morris, and knew that you were that sadly uncommon thing, a really well-matched and happy couple; it was enriching to be with you both, even for a short time, and we were sorry it was a one-time thing. Of course Morris was a wit far beyond Leacock's rather simple level, but he paid a fine tribute to Leacock, and was the making of the occasion.

Years ago we heard of you both from a couple who were close friends of ours, and who spoke of you with the greatest admiration. We, and they, had long been devotees of *The Widening Stain*. And of that book I often heard warm praises from that dear man Alfred Knopf. So when at last we met it was as though a net of association had at last been drawn close, and it made us very happy.

I shall not try to say anything consolatory, because I know how clumsy and intrusive such comment can be. But I am sure there must have been all sorts of people who loved Morris very much, and who have a better right to speak than we. But our warm goodwill and any comfort it may carry with it has gone out to you since first your letter came, and will long continue.

Morris was what Bernard Berenson* called a life-enhancing person; he was not only splendid in himself but he begot a kind of splendour in others. And his writing seems to me to be of the sort about which Joseph Campbell,* the mythology man, writes so finely; it was notable for more than what it said – it was great because of what it did. And what it did was to give one a sense of the rich quality of life, and the best aspects of mankind, without sentimentality (even with a splendid cynicism now and then) but with the warmth that is an aspect of a particular sort of greatness.

Thank you for sending us the news, which we would otherwise have missed. And please be sure of our love, and our gratefulness for everything that Morris was.

Rob. Davies

To H. J. HAMILTON

Massey College
University of Toronto
January 4, 1974

H. J. Hamilton was Director of Alumni Affairs at Queen's University in Kingston, Ontario.

[Dear Mr. Hamilton:]

Many thanks for your letter of December 21st, which has just reached me. Of course I would be delighted if you reproduced what I had to say about James Roy in the *Queen's Review*.

I was interested, too, in your information that Gerry Graham wrote the Obituary for the London *Times*.* I read it and told my wife that I would bet any money that it was written by a Queen's man because of its intensely Presbyterian reticences; there was no mention, for instance, of Roy's first marriage, which terminated at the church door, or of some of his more disreputable adventures while he was at Queen's, which were not really to his discredit but which caused terrible ructions at the time. If I had wanted to be mischievous I could have mentioned my own favourite story about him which concerned the Queen's Summer School; it had some drama instruction, under the direction of Herman Voaden,* and included some of that most dismal of dramatic effort, Choral Verse Speaking. The choir was to recite a new poem by James Roy, and at the right moment the group of solemn school teachers raised their arms heavenward and declaimed

"Would I were back in the Highlands
In the desolate lonely places....."

The choir was thrown off its stride when the audience burst into happy laughter because they knew at that very moment Jim Roy was in a Kingston jail under the care of Warden Hawkey, having been sent in for a few days after a case of drunken driving which could not be overlooked.

With good wishes,

Yours sincerely,

[Robertson Davies]

To MARIAN ENGEL

Massey College
University of Toronto
January 16, 1974

Marian Engel (1933–85), Canadian writer of fiction, was the first chairman of the Writers' Union of Canada 1973–74 and a member of its Public Lending Right committee. PLR legislation was eventually passed and in 1987 Canadian authors began to receive annual payments from the government for the use of their books in Canadian lending libraries.

[Dear Mrs. Engel:]

Thank you for your letter of January 14th. I have for some years made references in a variety of public speeches to the desirability of some form of public lending right, and very rarely have I done so without provoking angry response from librarians. Their indignation ranges between insistence that P.L.R. would burden them with extra work, and a waspish assertion that a writer should be pleased to have his work available to the largest possible public. Never do they come to grips with the essential point which, in my opinion, is that public lending of books is, in fact, an abridgement of property right, as a public body is taking something from an author which they then provide to their constituents, not always without fee, but without any recompense to the author beyond a single payment of royalty. If someone buys a book and lends it to 20 friends he is entirely within his right, but for a public body to do the same thing is to offer an advantage to some of its constituents at the expense of a single constituent and I do not see how this can be justified.

Argument on this subject on strictly legal grounds is difficult and it is by no means certain that a decision would go in favour of writers. Argument on moral grounds is a different thing. Why a community should offer free reading matter to its members when it would not, for an instant, think of offering them free theatre or free movies, is a curious question. I think that the custom is rooted in the nineteenth century idea that books are generally related to useful learning, although it is clear enough that a great many of them are strictly entertainment.

Whenever I discuss P.L.R. with writers the conversation is likely to break down into a series of angry anecdotes about rich people who borrow books but who find plenty of money for other kinds of entertainment. Undoubtedly it is a source of grievance to writers that people who will readily pay $10. or $15. for a dinner will not pay half that sum for a book. Whenever this point is made to librarians they immediately take the line that books are lent extensively to people of moderate means and to students. I still do not see that this is a justification for expecting authors to underwrite public generosity, as very few authors are well-to-do and, in any case, the matter of Right is not contingent on anyone's income.

I am afraid that these ideas will not be particularly helpful to you, but I thought that I should tell you the lines along which I have been arguing for a considerable time, and if I can be of assistance in clarifying anything further please let me know.

Yours sincerely,

[Robertson Davies]

To THE EDITOR OF THE *TIMES LITERARY SUPPLEMENT**

Massey College
University of Toronto
January 31, 1974

Sir:

Encouraged by James Redmond's article (*A Misattributed Speech in "Man and Superman"*) in your issue of January 18, may I call attention to a misprint in the Standard Edition of Shaw's works, which has been perpetuated in the Bodley Head Edition of 1971? This is also in "Man and Superman" but in the Epistle Dedicatory: on page viii (Standard) and 494 (Bodley) we read, "The question is, will you not be disappointed with a Don Juan play in which not one of that hero's *mille etre* adventures is brought upon the stage." The reference is to the "Catalogue Aria" in Mozart and Da Ponte's* *Don Giovanni* where Leporello tells Donna Elvira of his master's conquests, culminating in *mille e tre* (a thousand and three) in Spain.

    Ma in Ispagna son gia mille e tre

This silly mistake has enjoyed too long a life. It cannot be Shaw's, for he had an opera-lover's smattering of Italian, like

Yours faithfully,

[Robertson Davies]

To PAUL W. MILLER

Massey College
University of Toronto
February 4, 1974

Paul W. Miller was a professor in the department of English at Wittenberg University in Springfield, Ohio.

[Dear Professor Miller:]

I hope that you will forgive me for being so long in replying to your letter of December 14th. Part of my delay is owing to my doubts about what I should say in reply to your questions.

The town of Deptford is the village of Thamesville, Ontario, in which I was born, and although I lived there only until I was five years old I have very clear recollections of it, assisted by subsequent visits and by the memories that my parents had of it, stemming from their eleven years' residence there. However it is not of any particular value to identify localities or people in the village as it has changed substantially since then and because its character, as I drew it in the novel, is that of a number of small Ontario towns which are very much like small towns anywhere. One of the things that led me to write about the village as I did was that I have been distressed by the picture of village life that has become a commonplace in so much North American writing – the picture of which Peyton Place is a gross example. The notion that villages are hot-beds of vice is just as stupid as the idea, which village people used to cherish, that they were particularly virtuous in comparison with dwellers in cities. The special interest of village life to a child, of course, is that it is so much more fully comprehensible than life in a city. In a village of five hundred people it is possible for a child to be aware of almost everyone of distinctive character and to form an impression which lasts a lifetime.

With good wishes,

Yours sincerely,

[Robertson Davies]

To JOHN FANNING

Massey College
University of Toronto
February 4, 1974

John Fanning taught a grade 13 class at Keiller MacKay Collegiate Institute in Weston, Ontario. When discussing Fifth Business, *the class had been unable to decide "whether Boy Staunton commits suicide while he is fully aware of his actions or whether he does so under hypnosis."*

[Dear Mr. Fanning:]

I was pleased to receive your letter of January 30th because it presents such a pleasing picture of the interest that is taken in my work in your school. Understandably it is a matter of great satisfaction to me to know that Canadian students are being offered books of Canadian authorship and that mine are giving pleasure in these circumstances.

In reply to your question, however, I regret that I cannot give you a wholly satisfactory answer because the problem of why Boy Staunton died is one of the principal themes of the trilogy on which I am working, and of which *Fifth Business* and *The Manticore* are the first two volumes. In the third volume, which I am writing at the moment, I shall offer further information about all the principal characters and I hope that when it is concluded the question of Staunton's death will appear even more interesting than it is at present, but I question if many readers will find a completely satisfactory answer in it. The reason is that I am in rebellion against the idea that death comes arbitrarily and without some volition on the part of the person who dies. I do not regard death as simply the snuffing out of a personality but as the culmination of hundreds of thousands of circumstances which take place during a life, of which some are acts of conscious will and some the result of matters which are unconscious. There is also the effect of family circumstances, including those of the lives of the parents and possibly even of the grandparents of whoever it is that dies. You might think it strange if I told you that I know [knew] a man whose eventual suicide seems to me to be traceable in great part to the behaviour of his mother, who predeceased him by twenty years. There can be no wholly satisfactory argument about such matters, but it is impossible to escape very strong impressions that one receives which have almost the weight of evidence.

All the chief characters in the two novels which have been published undergo decided changes amounting to re-birth in their lifetime; Staunton might be said to have been re-born in terms of his association of himself with the Prince of Wales, or it would be more proper to say an ideal which he had built up and imposed upon the Prince of Wales. Was his death the result of some disappointment in that ideal? I do not think that there can be any total[ly] decisive answer to that but I am attempting to provide more evidence in [on] the matter in the book that I am writing now.

Perhaps you would like to read this letter to your class, and I hope that you will assure them of my keen pleasure in the message that you give me that they have enjoyed *Fifth Business*. If it has done anything to persuade them that life is a vastly more complex, enjoyable, fantastic and broad-ranging thing than it seems to be on the surface I shall feel that I have achieved my purpose.

With thanks and good wishes, I am

Yours sincerely,

[Robertson Davies]

To MRS. GORDON WALDRON

Massey College
University of Toronto
May 9, 1974

Mrs. Gordon Waldron wrote to Davies from Princeton, New Jersey. Liberata is one of the names of Wilgefortis, the bearded female saint who intrigued Dunstan Ramsay in Fifth Business.

[Dear Mrs. Waldron:]

Thank you for your letter and the picture of your painting of Saint Liberata. I was delighted to receive it and will keep the picture carefully because I have no other image of this rather uncommon saint. It is curious that although I have always been interested in saints, I never regarded myself as unusually interested in them until after the publication of *Fifth Business*, since when a number of people appear to think that I am an expert, which is by no means the case. I am rather frivolously interested in peculiar saints like Liberata, and I came upon a fine one the other day in the form of Saint Petronilla, who is supposed to have been the daughter of Saint Peter; she was so extremely beautiful that her father feared that she would turn men's thoughts from God, so he prayed that she would be struck with a fever which would rob her of her beauty, and in this apparently the beautiful Petronilla concurred entirely; later on someone who was undeterred by her illness wanted to marry her but she contrived to die the day beforehand, thereby escaping. The kind of thinking that lies behind such legends is wonderful to contemplate.

Again many thanks for the picture and your letter.

Yours sincerely,

[Robertson Davies]

To GORDON ROPER

Windhover
Caledon East
[June 24, 1974]

Dear Gordon:

I finished the novel [*World of Wonders*] this morning, and wish I knew what to make of it. It has been uncommonly tough chewing, because as you know I never intended a trilogy, and so had made no preparation for pulling three books into a unity; attempting to do this without violent warping, or recourse to such passages as..... "As my reader will recall, from our earlier volumes" (which was the method in the Tom Swift* books) nor yet chewing the old cabbage twice and even thrice, has been tedious in the extreme. But I think I have managed somehow, if not well, and have even managed a surprise or two. My temptation in this one has been to embark on long amateur-theological disquisitions; to try to set mankind straight on his relations to the Hidden World. This way madness lies, of course..... The book is not overtly Jungian, though of course that lies at the root of it. Jung and a helpful top-dressing of Kierkegaard.* I determined that this should be so, as foolish people have begun to type me as a Jungian, and they take aboard a little instant Jung, from a paperback, and set to work to explain me. Some girl read a paper on me as a Jungian novelist to one of the Learned Societies; she sure as hell knows nothing about Jung, if that is the way she behaves!..... It is the old trouble:

Canada has too few writers and too many critics. I was in Montreal recently to get a D. Litt. from McGill, for which I was truly thankful, as I have a high regard for McGill. But I was cornered by a variety of people all big with questions that I could not, or would not answer. People really should not ask the magician how he pulls the rabbit out of the hat; once he does that he is no magician, but a professor of rabbitology.

What comes next is the play [*Question Time*]. I have a basic idea but no more, and it will mean a busy summer. I want to write a fantastic comedy. Frankly, I want to write *Peer Gynt*,* but in such a way no Nosey Parker can catch me. But the NPs are getting so damned smart!

Rob.

Very sorry to hear about your Mother: news just came this morning. Our sympathy to you all.

To DONNA WINTERS

Massey College
University of Toronto
January 6, 1975

> *Donna Winters wrote to Davies from Windsor, Ontario, curious to know what Stoughton bottles were. They make an appearance in* A Mixture of Frailties *83 when Ma Gall says of the members of the Bridgetower Trust, "They just sat around that room like so many Stoughton bottles, and looked at us as if we was poison."*

[Dear Miss Winters:]

I am sorry to have been so long in replying to your letter of December 10th; I have been ill and am just back at work now.

A Stoughton bottle contained a popular nineteenth century tonic and bowel regulator, which originated in the U.S.A. and was the property of a man named Stoughton, who, I believe, called himself doctor, though whether he had any right to do so I cannot say. The characteristic of the bottle was that it was a chunky, flat-bottomed bottle which, when it appeared on the shelves of drug stores, had a squatting, somewhat stolid appearance, hence the application of the term Stoughton bottle to anybody who shared these characteristics. It was a very common term applied to children by their impatient elders, and when I was a child both my grandmother and my mother called me a Stoughton bottle many times, and such is the force of character that I am a Stoughton bottle still.

With good wishes,

Yours sincerely,

[Robertson Davies]

To SCOTT YOUNG

Massey College
University of Toronto
January 27, 1975

[Dear Scott:]

I hate to be contradictory, but whoever told you about Isaac Pedlow (in your column of January 27, about Lottie Whitton)* gave you an entirely wrong impression. He was no Honest ED, but one of the most literate men in Renfrew (not an Athens, but there were a few people who could read and write, and did). He had a large dry-goods store, and was locally notorious because he would not close it on Wednesday afternoons, as local ordinance demanded, but stayed open for trade, and paid his fine without complaint every week until the local authorities got tired of harassing him. His stand was that he would conduct his business as he pleased, and no bunch of cretinous Scotsmen were going to domineer over him. He was, you see, an Irishman (very combative) and a Quaker (very determined) and had more brains than the whole town council rolled into one.

In person he was small, extremely neat and very well dressed; he had a beautifully trimmed short white beard, and always cleared his throat before speaking, as if about to make a pronouncement. He went to Queen's after his retirement, and took his B.A. when he was over eighty, refusing to see anything extraordinary about it.

As for Lottie, she was a figure of fear in Renfrew, when she was secretary to the Hon. T. A. Low, who was our Liberal member, and Minister of Trade and Commerce. It was a local marvel that Tom Low employed a notoriously Tory secretary. Was she a Tory spy? I don't suppose so for a minute, for though a Tory she was honest. I well recall her in an extraordinary liberated outfit that included long gaiters up to her knees, struggling through the formidable snows of Renfrew on her way to work. I used to meet her on my way to school, and the rigour of her icy glance made the bitter Renfrew cold seem balmy by contrast..... Her brother Steve was the local comic, and part of the thrill of the High School Commencement Exercises was seeing what new comic role from Dickens or Thackeray would display the talents of Steve Whitton. I recall his Sam Weller* as the best I have seen in a lifetime of playgoing. Not all the Whitton wit and talent were confined in Lottie.

[Yours,

Rob]

To THOMAS COOPER

Massey College
University of Toronto
February 18, 1975

Thomas Cooper was a non-resident junior fellow at Massey College, 1973–77, studying drama.

[Dear Tom Cooper:]

Thank you for your letter of February 14th. I understand your difficulties about arranging the luncheon on February 27th. As you say, it is a difficult group to arrange properly* but there are one or two things that could be managed: you must bear in mind that you are the host and, although you are the most junior person present, the seating at the table must be related to yourself. If Schreiber is your guest of honour he should be on your right hand. You had better have the French Ambassador on your left (how is your French?). It would be courteous to have a few well-planned French observations up your sleeve. You had better have McLuhan next to Schreiber and Premier Davis next to the Ambassador, but be sure that you get the President of the University as close to the Premier as possible because they have to meet on so many business occasions it is useful for them to have some social meetings that are not arranged by themselves.

There: do you see how difficult it is to be a society hostess? As you are the host you must not be diffident; people sit down when you do and they will expect you to give the signal when to leave. If there is anything to drink you get it first; this is almost the only privilege a host enjoys. Certainly with such a group I think that you ought to arrange that they have drinks beforehand, if not actually at the table.

As you say, anything involving Marshall McLuhan is likely to be incalculable. Your best plan is to take the bull by the horns and encourage him to talk as this is what he likes and the others will be glad enough to listen without having to make much contribution.

If there is any other Emily Post advice that I can help you with do not hesitate to drop into my office.

I regret that I cannot be present on the 27th myself as I have another engagement, but I wish you well.

Yours sincerely,

[Robertson Davies]

To R. TOOKEY

R. Tookey was director of the British
magazine Punch.

Massey College
University of Toronto
March 13, 1975

[Dear Mr. Tookey:]

I am enclosing your re-ordering form for *Punch* but as I do so I feel that I should tell you why I allowed my subscription to lapse.

Like many others among your subscribers, I have been acquainted with *Punch* since childhood and indeed it is something like 55 years since I first became aware of it. I have seen it pass through many changes, and sometimes it seems to me that I have seen it change from a magazine of humour to an embittered and dirty magazine of political comment. I have reminded myself from time to time that *Punch* began its career as a radical paper and must be allowed to make its experiments in modern forms of radical thought. However, I cannot fight down a conviction that a magazine with such a splendid literary tradition betrays itself when it goes whoring after the modern cause of dirty words, dirty grammar and, most important of all, dirty attitudes. Certainly it was a very pompous and often silly magazine during the editorship of Sir Owen Seaman,* but I am almost compelled to long for his stuffed-shirt editorship when I look at *Punch* today, which seems to be edited by an ill-educated, disgruntled dwarf.* I feel, too, that in the worst of *Punch* in an earlier day there was pleasure to be gained from looking at the draughtsmanship and in so much of what you publish now I see only ugliness, unredeemed by talent.

Nevertheless, I find that I cannot do without my old friend Mr. Punch, though I wish that he were not so inclined at the moment to whine about modern affairs and embrace trashy and fleeting moral and political attitudes. I wish he would employ some critics of books and the theatre and not so many trivial people intent on exploiting their own tedious personalities, but I suppose I must bear with the cantankerous old gnome in the hopes that he may get over his present troubles.

Yours sincerely,

[Robertson Davies]

To R. A. WENDT

Massey College
University of Toronto
17 June 1975

R. A. Wendt was dean of the Faculty of Arts, Division II, Carleton University in Ottawa, Ontario.

[Dear Dean Wendt:]

Once again I am sorry that I must decline your invitation to give the Plaunt* Lectures in the spring of 1976. I am flattered by your invitation, and if it could be managed I should greatly like to do it, but I dare not add it to what I have already on my calendar.

You deserve a more detailed answer than a mere protestation of being engaged. Let me tell you, therefore, what I have on hand: there is the administration of this College, for a start, and as you know the smallness of an institution does not seem to diminish the amount of work it involves as much as one might suppose. I also teach regularly, and I am supervising sixteen Ph.D. theses. I am involved in several university committees, and I am up to my ears in a plan for the production of a series of studies in the history of the Canadian theatre. I have three books [*World of Wonders*, *Question Time*, and his contribution to *The Revels History of Drama in English*] coming out within the next twelve months or so, with all the attendant reading of proofs and at least a minimal amount of the brouhaha and tohubohu that publishers imagine to be necessary to such events. My doctor is becoming rather crusty with me, and threatens me with nameless horrors if I don't contrive to do less. I do not detail these things in the hope of impressing you, but rather to demonstrate what happens to someone who finds it difficult to refuse any interesting project that presents itself. I truly hope that one day I shall be able to do the Plaunt Lectures, but for the present I must beg to be let off. I do hope you will understand.

Sincerely yours,

[Robertson Davies]

To ROBIN PHILLIPS

Massey College
University of Toronto
August 6, 1975

Robin Phillips (1942–), English, was the artistic director of the Stratford Festival 1974–80.

[Dear Robin:]

I was in Stratford from July 27 until August 3, to take part in the Seminar, but I did not think it would be fair to attempt to speak to you then, as I knew you were extremely busy. Let me say how much impressed my wife and I were by what you have already been able to achieve at Stratford; we have now seen all the productions, including what was being done on the Third Stage, and everything confirmed the impression we received at the openings, that you have brought about a substantial and effective revolution.

May I now make a proposal that I have made to all the Stratford directors in turn – Guthrie, Langham and Gascon – which is that Stratford mount a production of Thomas Otway's tragedy *Venice Preserv'd*.* This is one of the few really great tragedies in English which is not by Shakespeare; it was a favourite on the stage from its first appearance in 1682 until the middle of the last century, and every first-rate actor or actress counted Jaffeir, Pierre or Belvidera among his most popular roles; in recent years it has had only one major production,* but it was a stunner, in which Paul Scofield and John

Gielgud gave magnificent performances, and the direction was by Peter Brook. But it has not been seen in Canada for about a century.

All the Stratford artistic directors thought the proposal a good one, but nothing happened, and indeed I could not persuade two of them – Guthrie and Gascon – even to read the play.

I think you could do it admirably, because you have not hesitated to give full weight to the homoerotic element in Shakespeare's plays, and *Venice Preserv'd* is unquestionably the greatest play of homoerotic love – and the only tragedy – in English. The struggle between Jaffeir and Belvidera for dominance in the affections of Pierre is the theme of the piece – a point which nineteenth century critics would not recognize – and it is brilliantly explored. I know from my experience in teaching this play to university students how powerful it is, and how it seizes the imagination of our time.

If you want to talk, or desire more information, I am

Yours sincerely,

[Rob. Davies]

To WILLIAM G. THOMPSON

Windhover
Caledon East
August 9, 1975

William G. Thompson was an editor at Doubleday, the New York publishers. Doubleday was bringing out a complete Saki in 1976 and Thompson had asked Davies for a quotation, probably for a book jacket or for publicity.

Dear Mr. Thompson:

Many thanks for the Saki* galleys; I have been going through them with pleasure in every spare moment since they arrived. As it is some time since I read him, he comes to me freshly.

A queer genius. I use the word genius advisedly, because nobody else is quite like him, he has had no successful imitators, and he imitated no one. Nevertheless Saki stands in the succession of English wit between the last enchantments of Oscar Wilde and the mature flowering of Wodehouse. Nor is he wholly English; he puts out a delicate root-system toward the wells from which Proust drew sustenance. His writing is the perfection of high-bred malice – a malice without ugliness. And of course these qualities do not arise from a trivial man; it takes a spirit of considerable depth to make the appearance of triviality so delightful, without ever dropping into the boredom of real triviality.

I do not know whether anything in the preceding paragraph is of any use to you. If not, let me try again. I am nothing if not obliging, and nobody wants to praise Saki in terms that would have drawn Saki's deadly fire.

With good wishes,

Robertson Davies

To ELISABETH SIFTON

Windhover
Caledon East
August 13 [1975]

Elisabeth Sifton (1939–) was senior editor at The Viking Press in New York. She became editor-in-chief 1978–84 and vice president of Viking Penguin and publisher of Elisabeth Sifton Books 1984–87. She was Davies' editor in New York 1972–87 and became a good friend.

Dear Elisabeth:

After I had written to you last, I remembered that I had forgotten to thank you for your kindness in sending me a pre-publication copy of *Humboldt's Gift*. I enjoyed it greatly. Every generation of writers makes its own interpretation of the evergreen theme of the intellectual in society, but Bellow* has done it with so much humour, and such splendidly wide range of perception and understanding that I expect his book to last as a record of what it was like to be an intellectual in North America, *now*. It is a delight to read a book by a writer with so much knowledge and so much ability to relate his own experience to it. So many new books are merely tedious adventures in the company of undernourished minds; in Shakespeare's phrase,* their writers have not fed of the dainties that are bred in a book, they have not, as it were, eat paper; they have not drunk ink; their intellect is not replenished. Nobody could say that of Bellow.

I have been going over the proofs of *World of Wonders* for the Canadian edition and have made a change in the text on page 135 of the typescript. Instead of talking about "a three or four-reel movie" I have changed it to "followed by a 'feature' film." The reason is, of course, that if I use the other, some know-it-all will write to me to say that movies were either two or five reels, or something of the sort. Would you please change it in your text.

Again, many thanks for *H's Gift* – a delightful addition to my summer.

Good wishes,

Rob. Davies

To CHARLES ANTHONY SHARMAN

[Massey College
University of Toronto
Fall 1975]

Davies was on the committee that was to examine Charles Anthony Sharman on his doctoral thesis in January 1976. The thesis was titled Bernard Shaw's Dramatic Theory and Practice: An Examination of Some Critical Approaches, with Emphasis upon Those of Shaw Himself.

Dear Mr. Sharman:

I think you have concluded your thesis admirably, and I congratulate you on the firm, but modest, tone of these final pages. Unquestionably some of my approval springs from the fact that what you say is what I myself feel – that Shaw was primarily a great literary artist, and only secondarily a reformer, or a theorist, or publicist, or whatever the label may be. As an artist, he encompasses many contradictions; like

Ibsen, he might have said that he found within himself both Right and Left. But I am convinced that if his ideas were the most important thing about him, five years of study would make us acquainted with those ideas: whereas an artist asks for a lifetime of contemplation, for at different periods of our own experience we encounter and respond to different aspects of his genius. So I wish you success with your thesis, and will do what I can, to ensure it.

As we have not met, perhaps I should at this point tell you what I usually say to students who are approaching the Ph.D. examination:

1. Bear in mind that when you enter the examination room you are pretty well assured of your degree; if your thesis were a failure, it would be halted by the departmental readers. Therefore, do not be thrown off your stride by a few minutes of what may appear to be unsatisfactory or even hostile questioning. The examiners, too, are expected to show off their brilliant plumage.

2. Do not be stung into giving aggressive or contumelious answers to what may seem to be foolish questions. Most examiners are gentle, compassionate and positive in their feelings toward you, but now and then some fur may be clawed off you, and you must not snarl, though you may wince.

3. Be respectful, but not servile. This is not such foolish advice as it may appear. The seniority of your examiners deserves your courtesy, but you need not defer in anything except matters of fact; you are expected to defend your opinions. I once was present at an examination where the candidate offered her examiners pieces of chocolate; she got the degree, but the chocolate worked against her.

4. Though your examiners may take an easy and informal attitude, you are best advised to maintain a certain formality. What are you doing? You are seeking the highest degree in your grasp, and the last one you will ever have to be examined to attain. You are, in effect, asking the examiners to admit you as an equal, in scholarly status, insofar as degrees can measure attainment. In respecting them, you respect yourself and the qualification you seek; in preserving a certain humility you are humble not before your examiners, but before the ideal of the learned life and the learned society you seek to join.

You are right in supposing that a bibliography is expected, but it is not expected that you will have all the details of all the books included in it at your fingertips, and you are quite within your rights in saying so, if the matter comes up.

I look forward to meeting you. Good luck.....

Robertson Davies

To PETER C. NEWMAN

Massey College
University of Toronto
December 8, 1975

Peter C. Newman (1929–　), Austrian-born Canadian journalist, author, newspaper and magazine editor, has written a series of immensely successful books about Canadian politicians, businessmen, and the financially powerful. His The Canadian Establishment *had just been published, and he wrote to say that he was "appalled" to see Davies declaring, in a taped television interview in Vancouver, that Newman "did not understand any members of the Canadian establishment."*

[Dear Peter Newman:]

I too am appalled by what you tell me you heard and saw in Vancouver. I can't explain it, because I have a rule I observe carefully *never* to offer comment on a book by another Canadian author, on radio or TV, if I cannot speak well of it. I do recall one of those terrible telephone-line TV interviews in Edmonton in which somebody asked me about your book, and I declined to answer because I had read only what had been excerpted in the *Globe and Mail*, and thus had no opinion worth hearing. I can only suppose that, driven to distraction by a great many interviews in a single day, I said something silly, and if that is what happened I apologize sincerely, because I admire your work and value my acquaintanceship with you, and would not do anything to harm it. I look forward to reading the book itself over Christmas.

Of course I have heard lots of talk about your book from other people – that Diefenbaker* is furious because you are outselling him (also an assurance from Macmillan that this is not true) – that you are mistaken in supposing that the very rich desire power, because all they want is all the money (this from a financial man) – that you have given 600 tapes to Massey College (by which I suppose they mean McMaster). You have created a great stir, and a vast amount of talk, and this is all to the good; I hope you sell enormously.

But as for any ill-will on my part – simply not so. On the contrary, I send you all good wishes,

[Robertson Davies]

Editorial Note

The early letters of Robertson Davies have a handsome appearance. In the period covered by this volume, 1938–1975, his handwriting gradually came to approximate the italic style whose beauty had captivated him when he was a schoolboy at Upper Canada College in Toronto. When he was at Queen's University in Kingston, Ontario, and at Oxford, he had given his letters an old-fashioned air by employing an elongated "s" and by sealing his envelopes with red sealing wax, but he had put such affectations aside by the time this collection begins.

Many of the letters in this volume were written entirely by hand. As the years passed, more and more were typed, either by Davies himself or by his secretary, but the typed letters have handwriting in them as well: the signature, corrections, postscripts, marginal notes, (often) the date, and from 1954 on, the salutation. Sometimes a whole letter is in green or purple, sometimes Davies used several colours in a single letter. When John Espey, an Oxford friend, decided to place his letters in a public collection, he commented, "I'll miss the colored inks!"

When Davies wrote or typed a letter, he put the date at the bottom left. His successive secretaries followed the more usual Canadian practice of typing the date at the top right until 1964 when his longest serving secretary, Moira Whalon, began to accommodate her practice to his, placing the date at the bottom left under the address of the person to whom the letter was written. In this volume, however, for the reader's convenience the date will be found at the top left following Davies' address.

From the beginning, Davies, the son of a printer who had taken pride in possessing fine personalized notepaper, chose to use letter paper of excellent quality and weight. Davies' correspondence was usually written on 20-pound bond, bearing his address at Oxford, at his father's house in Wales, at the *Peterborough Examiner*, at his Peterborough home, at Massey College in the University of Toronto, or at Windhover, his country home in Caledon East.

The originals of these letters are widely scattered, so it is not easy to consult them. Although this is not a scholarly edition, I have tried to maintain their integrity for the reader. Omissions have been kept to a minimum and are marked by conventionally spaced ellipsis points. Davies' enthusiasm for capital letters (which became even greater in the last twenty years of his life) has been preserved; his underlined passages appear here in italics except for the underlining of his signature. There the underline is preserved. I have retained the elevated (and, where appropriate, underlined) "r" in "Fr." and "rs" in "Mrs.", as these represent the beginning of a habit that later became his usual practice. Abbreviations are expanded where necessary for clarity. Punctuation remains as he wrote it, except for the addition of a few commas (usually the second of a pair). Occasionally he used strings of periods of variable length to indicate a minor break in thought or an ellipsis, and these are represented here by five unspaced periods. Paragraph breaks occur where he established them, with the addition in a few places of an extra paragraph division for clarity's sake.

Davies often said that he preferred the British usage in the matter of quotation marks. But in practice his own usage was inconsistent, often changing in mid-quotation and mid-letter, or following the British practice in one letter, the North American in another. When preparing a typescript for publication, his secretary always standardized to North American style, and I have adopted her policy. Davies' vocabulary and spelling, like most Canadians', contained elements of both British and American usage, though he leaned more heavily than most toward the British. If his spelling was supported by *The Oxford English Dictionary* or a standard American dictionary, it stands here as he wrote it. He often invented variants on words (or created new ones), and I have presented these, too, as he wrote them. While generally an accurate speller, he occasionally made mistakes, and he used a few idiosyncratic spellings like "accomodation." Such errors and typographical slips have been corrected.

I have used square brackets to denote my editorial additions (primarily names and dates, but also my guesses about the form Davies may have used in his salutation and signature when a secretarial carbon copy of a letter is the only available source).

I have supplied brief biographical headnotes on Davies' correspondents. Endnotes identifying people mentioned in the letters are likewise provided on the first occasion that they appear. Readers who need such information for subsequent references will find the index helpful.

Page references to Davies' books are to the Penguin editions. My biography, *Robertson Davies: Man of Myth*, is cited as *Man of Myth*.

Works by Robertson Davies mentioned in *Discoveries*

Shakespeare's Boy Actors (criticism, 1939)
Shakespeare for Young Players (school text, 1942)
Hope Deferred (play, first performed 1945)
Overlaid (play, first performed 1946)
The Diary of Samuel Marchbanks (belles lettres, 1947)
Eros at Breakfast (play, first performed 1947)
Fortune, My Foe (play, first performed 1948)
Eros at Breakfast and Other Plays (plays, 1949)
The Table Talk of Samuel Marchbanks (belles lettres, 1949)
King Phoenix (play, first performed 1950)
At My Heart's Core (play, first performed 1950)
Tempest-Tost (novel, 1951)
A Masque of Aesop (play, first performed 1952)
A Jig for the Gypsy (play, first performed 1952)
Renown at Stratford (criticism, 1953)
Twice Have the Trumpets Sounded (criticism, 1954)
Leaven of Malice (novel, 1954)
Thrice the Brinded Cat Hath Mew'd (criticism, 1955)
Hunting Stuart (play, first performed 1955)
A Mixture of Frailties (novel, 1958)
Love and Libel (play, first performed 1960)
A Voice from the Attic (essays, 1960)
Centennial Play (play, first performed 1966)
Samuel Marchbanks' Almanack (belles lettres, 1967)
Stephen Leacock (criticism, 1970)
Fifth Business (novel, 1970)
The Manticore (novel, 1972)
Hunting Stuart and Other Plays (plays, 1972)
World of Wonders (novel, 1975)
Question Time (play, first performed 1975)
What's Bred in the Bone (novel, 1985)
The Golden Ass (opera libretto, first performed 1999)

NOTES

p. 4: *The Rev. Mr Ridley*: Rev. M. Roy Ridley (1890–1967), English, was a fellow and tutor in English Literature at Balliol 1920–45, editor of the New Temple Shakespeare, and RD's chief tutor at Balliol 1935–38.

p. 4: *Sir Edmund Chambers and Dr. Percy Simpson*: Edmund K. Chambers (1866–1954), English, was a respected historian of the English stage and a civil servant; Percy Simpson (1865–1962), English, was a leading authority on the English playwright and poet Ben Jonson (1572–1637) and Elizabethan drama in general.

p. 5: *Fronfraith Hall*: RD's father, Rupert, who was born in Wales, purchased Fronfraith Hall in 1932. It is located on 179 pleasant acres, ten miles from Welshpool. Rupert spent his summers there, and RD spent periods of time there until his return to Canada in 1940.

p. 5: *Mr. Granville-Barker*: Harley Granville-Barker (1877–1946), English theatre scholar, actor, playwright, and director, had been asked by Dent's to give an opinion of RD's thesis.

p. 8: *Guild plays*: A series mounted by the Theater Guild of New York at the Royal Alexandra Theatre in Toronto.

p. 8: *W. H. Clarke*: (1902–55) Canadian, was manager of the Oxford University Press in Canada 1936–49 and president of the educational publishers Clarke, Irwin & Company Limited, which brought out RD's *Shakespeare for Young Players* in 1942.

p. 8: *call from Mrs. Ahrens*: Cora B. Ahrens (1891–1964) was a Canadian music teacher, lecturer, and pianist; her husband, Carl Henry Ahrens (1863–1936), was a Canadian artist. The conference was the first Conference of Canadian Artists, which was held in Kingston, Ontario, June 26–29, 1941. The "Cap and Bells" columns concerning Carl Ahrens appeared in the *Peterborough Examiner* and the Kingston *Whig-Standard* 26 and 28 June 1941: 4.

p. 8: *Guy Roberts*: (1896–1968) Canadian, director of the Roberts Gallery in Toronto 1934–48. The three-panel screen, which depicted theatrical figures, had been mounted within a single frame, roughly six feet by a foot and a half.

p. 8: *Mary [Keens]*: A helpful, kind single woman, considerably older than the Davieses. A Torontonian and lover of art and the theatre, she was a friend of Grant Macdonald's and became a friend of the Davieses. She visited them later in Peterborough from time to time.

p. 9: *I am Doin' Fine*: Line from the song "Doin' Fine."

p. 9: *the new Mr. Pinkerton . . . a v. good* poisoning *mystery, located at Richmond*: Probably a reissue of *Mr. Pinkerton Goes to Scotland Yard* by David Frome (pseudonym for Zenith Jones Brown), in which Mr. Pinkerton finds himself "head over heels in the famous Richmond poisoning case."

p. 10: *Ridpath*: Ridpath's is (and was then) a quality furniture store in Toronto.

p. 10: *Garner*: Harold L. Garner, general manager of the *Examiner* 1937–57.

p. 10: *St. David's day*: St. David is patron saint of Wales and his day is March 1. RD viewed himself as half Welsh because his father Rupert was born and grew up in Wales.

p. 10: *Craw*: G. Wilson Craw (c. 1904–67), Canadian, managing editor of the *Examiner* 1936–67.

p. 10: *I Breathed a Jolly but Grand Mood*: RD took lessons from the Irish voice teacher Bertie Scott (b. 1881) when he was at the Old Vic in 1938–39. Scott advised his students to "breathe the muhd" – i.e., to assume their characters so deeply that their very breathing would reflect the effects of emotion, age, and class.

p. 10: *Kennedy's*: Arthur R. Kennedy (1879–1941), Canadian, the *Examiner*'s previous editor.

p. 10: *station*: CHEX, the Peterborough radio station, began to broadcast in March 1942. Jointly owned by RD's father, Rupert Davies, and the future newspaper magnate Roy Thomson, it had its offices in the same building as the *Examiner*. Brenda Davies, experienced as a stage manager and in radio acting with the CBC in Toronto, might well have found a job with the station as traffic manager or radio actor.

p. 12: *fireplace good; not by the Brothers Adam*: Robert Adam (1728–92) was a Scottish architect and interior designer who often collaborated with his brother James Adam (1732–94) on the building of country and town houses in England and Scotland. Many of these have become national treasures.

p. 12: *both babies*: The Davieses' first child, Miranda, was born on December 24, 1940, and their second, Jennifer, would arrive on October 16, 1942.

p. 13: *Nemo . . . Tweeze*: Nemo, "no-one," was a nickname for Miranda both unborn and during her first year, and "Tweeze" refers to RD himself.

p. 14: *Kitty*: Wife of Richard Tattersall, music director at Upper Canada College when RD was there 1928–32. The Tattersalls were neighbours on Aylmer Avenue in Toronto.

p. 15: *filling in for Geo. McCracken*: On the editorial page of the Kingston *Whig-Standard* April–July 1940.

p. 16: *Roy's sale*: Roy S. Britnell, of the Albert Britnell Book Shop just north of Bloor on Yonge Street in Toronto, had an antiques and paintings shop a little further north on Yonge, which was managed by John Britnell.

p. 17: *Kawarthas*: Fourteen interconnected lakes stretching across Peterborough and Victoria counties in south central Ontario, a popular vacation area.

p. 17: Precious Bane: Country novel set in Shropshire by English writer Mary Webb (1881–1927).

p. 18: Cold Comfort Farm: Satirical novel by English poet and novelist Stella Gibbons (1902–89).

p. 19: *Stevenson's method – that of 'the sedulous ape'*: Robert Louis Stevenson (1850–94), a Scot, once observed, with regard to his own apprenticeship as a writer: "I have thus played the sedulous ape to Hazlitt, to Lamb, to Wordsworth, to Sir Thomas Browne, to Defoe, to Hawthorne, to Montaigne, to Baudelaire and to Obermann" (*Memories and Portraits*, chapter 4).

p. 20: *one play to a London producer [probably Tyrone Guthrie]*: The play was probably the one titled "The King Who Could Not Dream" or "King and Caliph," which concerns Ethelred the Unready and is set in the year 1000. Tyrone Guthrie (1900–71), English, was the director at the Old Vic in London when RD was a junior member of the company in 1938–39.

p. 20: *one-act piece on a Canadian theme*: Titled *Hope Deferred*, the little comedy concerns Count Frontenac (governor of New France, now Quebec) and the saintly Bishop Laval, and is set in 1793.

p. 20: *Molière's* Tartuffe: Jean-Baptiste Poquelin Molière (1622–73), French drama-tist and actor, was the author of some of the world's great comedies. The attack on religious hypocrisy in his play *Tartuffe* resulted in opposition and suppres-sion in France for many years; RD imagined a similar reaction in New France, years later.

p. 20: *Emily Carr's new book*: Emily Carr (1871–1945), Canadian artist whose canvases depict West Coast Indian villages and British Columbia forests. *The House of All Sorts* describes her period as a landlady and raiser of bobtail sheepdogs.

p. 22: To JAMES AGATE: Published in James Agate, *Ego 8: Continuing the Autobiography of James Agate* (London: Harrap, 1946) 115.

p. 22: *Hays Office*: With reference to William H. Hays (American, 1879-1954), president of the Motion Picture Producers and Distributors of America 1922–45. He administered the strait-laced motion-picture moral code prom-ulgated in 1934.

p. 22: Fanny by Gaslight: A melodramatic British film made in 1944. It is centred on the bastard daughter of a Member of Parliament who loves her father's socially prominent secretary. The latter saves her from a lustful lord.

p. 25: *reviews . . . Marchbanks*: See "The House That Mencken Built," *Peterborough Examiner* and Kingston *Whig-Standard* 2 January 1946: 4.

p. 26: Prejudices . . . American Language: Mencken's *Prejudices* (1919–27) gath-ered his critical essays in six volumes; his autobiographical volumes were

Happy Days, 1880–1892 (1940), *Newspaper Days, 1899–1906* (1941), and *Heathen Days, 1890–1936* (1943); his *A New Dictionary of Quotations on Historical Principles from Ancient and Modern Sources* appeared in 1942; and the first edition of *The American Language* was published in 1919.

p. 28: *The adjudicator's*: Charles B. Rittenhouse (1909–82), Canadian teacher, who directed, acted, and produced for the Montreal Little Theatre movement in the 1930s, '40s, and '50s.

p. 28: *French's*: Samuel French, publishers of plays.

p. 29: The New York Visit: Bettina Cerf Fetzke was with the Theater Guild. Brenda had met her and her husband earlier while visiting the Guthries in March or April 1946 and seeing Guthrie's production of Andreyev's *He Who Gets Slapped* at the Booth Theatre. The Old Vic productions opened May 6, 1946, for a six-week run in the Century Theatre. The friends in Ottawa were Graham and Joan McInnes.

p. 31: *bowel-shakers*: the Victorian *A Midsummer Night's Dream* (at the Old Vic in December 1937 and again in December 1938), the modern-dress *Hamlet* (at the Old Vic, October–November 1938), the Coronation *Henry V* (at the Old Vic in April–May 1937 with Olivier as Henry), and *The Country Wife* (at the Old Vic in October–November 1936). *The Country Wife* was written by the English dramatist William Wycherley (1640–1716).

p. 31: The Critic . . . The Good Natur'd Man: *The Critic* is a dramatic burlesque by Richard Brinsley Sheridan (1751–1816), Irish playwright. *The Good-Natur'd Man* is a lively, witty, humane comedy by Oliver Goldsmith (1730?–74), Anglo-Irish author.

p. 31: *Ralph Richardson*: (1902–83) English stage and film actor.

p. 31: *Beau Hannen*: Nicholas James Hannen (1881–1972), actor well-known on the London stage.

p. 31: *Joyce Redman . . . Diana Boddington*: Joyce Redman (1918–   ), well-known Irish stage and (later) film actress; Diana Boddington, stage manager with the Old Vic and (later) the National Theatre. RD met her first when he was a student at Oxford, probably in connection with the Oxford University Dramatic Society's production of *As You Like It* in May–June 1937.

p. 31: *José Ferrer do* Cyrano: José Ferrer (1912–92), Puerto Rican-born American actor, producer, and director. *Cyrano de Bergerac* is a play by French dramatist Edmond Eugène Alexis Rostand (1868–1918).

p. 31: *the Duke of Saxe-Meiningen's company*: The Meiningen Players tour of Europe 1874–90 transformed the way performances were handled. George II, Duke of Saxe-Meiningen, was the first to demonstrate the value of a director to a production, by imposing his vision on all aspects of presentation – acting, historically accurate sets and costumes, stage business.

p. 31: *Diaghilev's* Ballet Russe: Sergei Pavlovich Diaghilev (1872–1929), Russian ballet impresario and art critic, founder of the influential Ballet Russe in 1909. In his productions, music and scene design are integral to the dance.

p. 32: *new home . . . High Sheriff*: Rupert Davies had purchased Brookland Hall in order to have a home suitable for the entertaining done by the High Sheriff. His wife's ill health and death delayed his assuming the post until 1951, and by then he had purchased an even larger Welsh home – Leighton Hall.

p. 32: *My brother Arthur . . . & I am vice*: In 1946 Rupert Davies sold the *Examiner* to his three sons: Arthur L. Davies (1903–96) got 50%, RD 30%, and Frederic R. M. Davies (1902–54), 20%.

p. 32: *Dame Sybil*: Dame Sybil Thorndike (1882–1976) was a distinguished English actress. She was married to Sir Lewis Casson (1875–1969), the English actor and director.

p. 32: *John Gielgud*: (1904–2000) a renowned English actor, director, and producer. RD got to know him in 1936 when Gielgud directed the Oxford University Dramatic Society in Shakespeare's *Richard II* with RD as his stage manager.

p. 32: *Rabelais*: François Rabelais (1494?–1553), French humanist, satirist, and physician.

p. 32: *Van Druten's*: John Van Druten (1901–57), English-born American dramatist who wrote light comedies popular both in New York and in London.

p. 33: *Brenda's mother*: Muriel Newbold (1892–1976), Australian.

p. 33: *one of Bishop Bayle's moralities*: Namely *God's Promises* by John Bale (1495–1563), Bishop of Ossory in Ireland.

p. 33: *hard-handed men . . . this same play*: Lightly adapted from the description in *A Midsummer Night's Dream* 5.1 of the workmen who propose to present "A tedious brief scene of young Pyramus/And his love Thisby; very tragical mirth" for the amusement of the court.

p. 33: *Sir Osbert Sitwell's* The Scarlet Tree: Second part of a fine five-volume autobiography. Sitwell (1892–1969), English, wrote many books of poetry, fiction, biography, and autobiography.

p. 34: *Ottawa people . . . Overlaid*: RD's play *Overlaid* was performed on October 27 by the Ottawa Drama League Workshop under the direction of Amelia Hall (1916–84), English-born Canadian actress and director.

p. 35: *school stories in the* New Yorker: Espey had had stories published by the *New Yorker* since 1945. The one RD refers to is "Blasphemer" (23 February 1947: 72–77). The "school stories" were collected not as "Pine Tree Patrol" but as *Tales Out of School*.

p. 37: *LePan*: Douglas LePan (1914–98), Canadian, a friend from Oxford, was soon to become known as a poet and diplomat.

p. 37: *the letter . . . to the* New York Times: See "Democracy," *New York Times* 24 November 1946, Section 6: 27–28. The article that occasioned the letter was Helen Bryant's "Changing – Yet Unchanged – England," *New York Times* 3 November 1946, Section 6: 10, 67.

p. 40: *To THE EDITOR OF SATURDAY NIGHT*: Published in *Saturday Night* 26 April 1947: 4.

p. 40: *discussion of Mr. Donald Wolfit's performances (S.N. April 19)*: Donald Wolfit (1902–68) was a well-known English actor-manager. For the discussion, see Nat Benson, "Manhattan Playgoer: Minsky's Ghost Walks Again But Old Time Burlesque Was Better: Wolfit's Marks," *Saturday Night* 19 April 1947: 26. Sir H. is Sir Henry Irving (1838–1905), famous English actor-manager, first actor to be knighted.

p. 40: *Martin Harvey*: Sir John Martin-Harvey (1863–1944), English actor-manager.

p. 40: *opinion of Irving*: In *Ellen Terry and Bernard Shaw: A Correspondence* and in Shaw's reviews in *The Saturday Review* through the same period.

p. 40: *"Volpone"*: Play by Ben Jonson in which a rich, childless Venetian pretends that he is dying in order to elicit gifts from his would-be heirs.

p. 40: *Charles Cochran*: Charles Blake Cochran (1872–1951), English impresario.

p. 41: *Olivier's 'Lear'*: Olivier's 1946 performance of the role of King Lear was still fresh in mind.

p. 44: *Hardy, rather than Crabbe*: Thomas Hardy (1840–1928), the great English poet and novelist, rather than George Crabbe (1754–1832), English poet and cleric, a bleak, realistic observer of rural life and landscape.

p. 44: *D.P. girl*: The "Displaced Person" was Sylvia Pedak, a refugee from Estonia.

p. 44: *our Nativity Play*: In December 1946, '47, and '48, the Davieses directed the blue-collar parishioners of little St. George's Anglican Church in Peterborough in RD's own adaptation of the Coventry Nativity Play.

p. 45: *picture of me for* Mayfair: Line drawings of RD by Grant Macdonald accompanied RD's article "Advice to a Bride" in the May 1948 issue of *Mayfair*.

SECTION II

p. 50: The Abolition of Man . . . The Perennial Philosophy: RD had reviewed both books in the *Peterborough Examiner*, *The Abolition of Man* in "A Return to Greatness" 3 October 1945: 4 and *The Perennial Philosophy* in "Reviewer's Holiday" 4 September 1946: 4.

p. 52: *three papers here*: The Kingston *Whig-Standard*, the *Peterborough Examiner*, and the *Ottawa Citizen*. The first two carried the Marchbanks columns from the start in 1940; the *Ottawa Citizen* ran the Saturday Diary column from 1946 on.

p. 52: *as my grandmother*: RD's mother's mother, Lavina C. Langs McKay (1845–1924), Canadian.

p. 53: *Nothing human is alien to me*: RD chose to integrate Terence's *"Humani nihil a me alienum puto"* into the *Examiner*'s logo in 1950 when the paper's headings were redesigned.

p. 53: The Last Romantic: Maurice Willson Disher's book about Sir John Martin-Harvey.

p. 53: *dark backward and abysm of time*: See *The Tempest* 1.2.49.

p. 53: *agent*: From this point until 1952, Albert Stanley Knight, whose agency was

"Stephen Aske," Granville House, Arundel St., London, acted for RD in the U.K.

p. 53: *Harry the Horse*: A large walking stick whose handle was a carved horse's head. It was named after the small-time New York hustler in several stories by the American writer Damon Runyon (1880–1946). It vanished while Stead was away during World War II.

p. 54: *Vincent Rother*: Stead's Canadian brother-in-law, an architect who died prematurely in his 40s.

p. 54: *Piccini's Italian Punch*: Signor Piccini, a puppeteer, performed his Punch and Judy show in London, England, for John Payne Collier, who recorded the script, and George Cruikshank, who made illustrations, and the result was published in 1832. It has become an important source for the history of Punch and Judy shows.

p. 54: *Amy & Clair [Stewart]*: The Canadian designer Clair Stewart (1910–   ) and his wife Amy had been friends of the Davieses since the early 1940s.

p. 55: *Sutherland*: Arthur Sutherland (d. 1953 in his early 40s), Canadian actor and manager. He and Drew Thompson had just founded the International Players, which had successful summer seasons through 1953.

p. 58: *Hilda Kirkwood*: Regular reviewer for the *Examiner* in this period. She also reviewed books and wrote articles for the *Canadian Forum*, served as its book review editor 1959–69 and was on its editorial board 1970–83. She is also a published poet.

p. 59: *she threatened and bullied me*: See Jean Swanson, "A Diary with Sparkling Treatment of Ideas," *Saskatoon Star-Phoenix* 6 December 1947: 11.

p. 59: *Dr. Fitzpatrick*: Irish pediatrician, briefly in Peterborough.

p. 60: *Little Theatre plays*: *The Play of the Weather* is a short comic dialogue written by English dramatist John Heywood (1497?–1580?). *The Tinker's Wedding* is a play by Irish poet and dramatist John Millington Synge (1871–1909), which depicts the bleak and tragic lives of Irish peasants and fisherfolk. The third play on the program was RD's *The Voice of the People*.

p. 61: *Maxwell Wray*: (b. 1884) minor English director.

p. 61: *The Lady's Not for Burning*: Wry comedy, written in verse and set in the Middle Ages, in which love overcomes prejudice and hypocrisy, by English dramatist Christopher Fry (1907–   ).

p. 63: *Ma Moore & Mavor*: See RD's letter to Dora Mavor Moore, June 29, 1945. James Mavor Moore (1919–   ), Canadian actor, playwright, producer, and professor, helped launch the New Play Society in Toronto, the first indigenous professional theatre company after World War II. It produced many Canadian plays in the late 1940s and '50s.

p. 63: *Summer Theatre . . . at Ottawa . . . Robt Gill*: The Peterborough Summer Theatre performed *At My Heart's Core* August 28–September 2, 1950; the Ottawa Repertory Theatre did it January 9–13, 1951; Robert Gill (1911–74), American-born Canadian and influential director of the Hart House Theatre at the University of Toronto, did not do it.

p. 64: *to Calgary*: To the annual playoff of the Dominion Drama Festival. Michel Jacques Saint-Denis (1897–1971), French actor, teacher, and director, was adjudicator of that year's finals.

p. 64: *copy of* The Forum: RD refers here to W. S. Milne's "Drama Festival Afterthoughts" (*Canadian Forum* July 1950: 82–83).

p. 66: Harvey: Pulitzer-winning comedy written by American playwright Mary Coyle Chase (1907–81). RD had reviewed the Peterborough Summer Theatre's production of the play in the *Examiner* on June 27.

p. 69: *much notice*: RD was unduly pessimistic. The play was reviewed coast to coast and sold well.

p. 72: *its week in Ottawa*: The Ottawa Repertory Theatre presented *At My Heart's Core* to capacity houses January 9–13, 1951. Brenda Davies played Mrs. Frances Stewart.

p. 74: *Miss Robson*: Flora Robson (1902–84), English actress, active on the stage until 1969.

p. 74: *Athene Seyler*: (1889–1990) outstanding English comic actress, active on stage until 1966.

p. 75: Heart's Core *at Knowlton*: RD directed *At My Heart's Core* for the Brae Manor Theatre in Knowlton, Quebec, July 4–7, 1951, with Brenda in the role of Mrs. Frances Stewart.

p. 75: The Listener: See William Plomer's review of *The Table Talk of Samuel Marchbanks*: "A Canadian Man of Letters," *Listener* 21 June 1951: 1005.

p. 76: Chums: Weekly British magazine for boys, which was gathered into annual volumes.

p. 76: *Richmal Crompton*: Richmal Crompton Lamburn (1890–1969), English writer, was the creator of the popular *Just William* books for children.

p. 76 *Though his . . . tempest-tost*: Macbeth 1.3.

p. 76: *saw a horse electrocuted*: During the dress rehearsal of the Oxford University Dramatic Society's production of *As You Like It* in 1936. RD was stage manager.

p. 81: *Hugh Kenner*: (1923–   ) acclaimed literary critic, author of 30 books on modern American and British literature, including definitive studies of T. S. Eliot, Samuel Beckett, Ezra Pound, and James Joyce (1882–1941), the influential Irish writer whose novel *Ulysses* ranks among the great works of world literature. Kenner was born in Peterborough.

p. 84: *Herbert's nice piece*: Herbert Whittaker's "Show Business" column (*Globe and Mail* 3 March 1952: 8) concerned the Eastern Ontario Drama Festival, which took place, for the first time, in Peterborough. Whittaker spoke of Peterborough as having become a "theatre town" as the result of the sparkling efforts of the Davieses, he as playwright, director, and actor and she as actress.

p. 84: *Clayton Ridpath*: Vice president of sales at Ridpath's (a quality furniture store in Toronto), nephew of John I. Ridpath, a founder and the president of the store.

p. 85: *Galt*: George Michael Galt (1904–61), Canadian, was English master at the UCC Prep.

p. 85: *they are doing it the week we shall be in St. John*: The Prep was to perform *A Masque of Aesop* May 2–3, 1952, days which fell in the week the Davieses were to be in Saint John, New Brunswick, for the final competition of the Dominion Drama Festival.

p. 85: *Dr. Sowby*: Rev. C. W. Sowby (1902–75), English-born Canadian, Anglican cleric, and principal of Upper Canada College 1949–65.

p. 85: *Décor by Anna Pedak, Shoes by Gamba, Wigs by Clarkson*: Anna Pedak was the mother of Sylvia Pedak, the Displaced Person who became the Davieses' housekeeper in 1947. Anna succeeded her daughter in 1948, staying until she retired in the late 1960s. Gamba were makers of theatre shoes, and Clarkson, famous wig makers. Both would be acknowledged in phrases like this on theatre programs in London, England.

p. 85: *Mrs. Shields . . . Boo, Catherine and Cawoll*: The little girls were Rosamond Davies, Catherine Shields, and Carol Knox, all then roughly five years old. The Shields and Knox families were neighbours.

p. 85: *the Festival*: The Eastern Ontario Drama Festival, a preliminary heat of the Dominion Drama Festival, at which the Peterborough Little Theatre under RD's direction had a great success with *The Merry Wives of Windsor* with Brenda as Mistress Page.

p. 86: *Approbation from Sir Hubert Stanley is praise indeed*: Quotation from *A Cure for the Heartache* 5.2 by English dramatist Thomas Morton (1764–1838).

p. 86: *how superb you looked*: In his "Show Business" column (*Globe and Mail* 3 March 1952: 8), Herbert Whittaker described Brenda Davies, on stage on Saturday evening to receive the award for best actress, as "the glamorous Mrs. Davies."

p. 86: *Saint Mellangel*: Doubtless Saint Melangell of Wales (+ca. 590), in the folds of whose skirts a hare, hunted by the Prince of Powys, found protection. The church of Pennant Melangell, which claims to stand on the site of this happening, is in Montgomeryshire where Rupert Davies had his Welsh homes.

p. 86: *Ross Matthews*: Ross Munro Matthews (1909–82), Canadian, Peterborough pediatrician.

p. 87: *Marston*: John Marston (1576–1634), English satirist and dramatist.

p. 87: *The costume problem*: For the skating carnival. Mrs. Susi was a friend of Mrs. Pedak's. Gwenny is Gwen Brown (1921–), Canadian, a neighbour on Weller Street. Mrs. Mitchell was Mary Mitchell, wife of Dr. Addison Mitchell.

p. 88: *my Mother*: Florence (McKay) Davies (1870–1948), Canadian.

p. 88: *a Great Sawney*: A great fool, a simpleton (a usage current in Ireland and England).

p. 88: *your stepfather*: Claude Henry Newbold. See *Man of Myth* 224-25.

p. 88: *frampold*: Obsolete word meaning disagreeable.

p. 89: *Maisie*: Lady Maris Joyce Drysdale (1915–2001), Australian.

p. 89: *Richard Larking . . . velvet cloth*: Richard Larking (1850–1908), English-born Australian, was Brenda's grandfather. RD gave his photographic interests to Senator James McRory in *What's Bred in the Bone*.

p. 91: Quo Vadis . . . Lady Precious Stream: *Quo Vadis* is the 1951 MGM movie about a Roman officer (Robert Taylor) who falls in love with a forbidden Christian girl (Deborah Kerr) during the reign of the mad emperor Nero (Peter Ustinov). *Lady Precious Stream* is a conflation of several versions of an old famous Chinese dramatic theme by translator S. I. Hsiung. The play was first published and produced in London, England, in 1934.

SECTION III

p. 96: William IV: (1765-1837) King of England 1830-37.

p. 98: *Art Theayter conducted by Mrs. Goulding*: Dorothy Massey Goulding managed the Toronto Children Players 1934–59. Whittaker had devoted part of a column to its Easter performance in Eaton's Auditorium. See "Show Business," *Globe and Mail* 10 April 1953: 25. He noted that "The Lame Duck" (the second of three plays performed) was done in pantomime "behind a gauze."

p. 98: The Family Reunion *in Victoria*: Whittaker had won at the Central Ontario Drama Festival with his production of *The Family Reunion* by T. S. Eliot (1888–1965), the American-born English poet, playwright, and critic. He was to take *The Family Reunion* to Victoria for the final competition of the Dominion Drama Festival.

p. 99: *April 21 (birthday of You Know Who) 1954*: Queen Elizabeth was born on this day in 1926.

p. 99: *Yeats*: William Butler Yeats (1865–1939), Irish poet and playwright, a major figure in 20th century literature.

p. 99: *James Mason*: (1909–84) English stage and film actor, an international star from the 1950s on.

p. 99: *Guthrie . . . another book*: *Twice Have the Trumpets Sounded*, which commemorates the Festival's second year as *Renown at Stratford* commemorates the first.

p. 100: *shonnachie . . . father . . . Saturday Night*: Shonnachie (also shanachie, and senachie), a skilled teller of tales or legends, especially Gaelic ones; McInnes' father, Scottish baritone and teacher of elocution and singing, James Campbell McInnes (1873/4–1947), combined (in RD's view) "the qualities of an interpretative artist of the first rank with the ungovernable temperament of a Highland Celt" ("Introduction," *The Road to Gundagai*). RD reviewed *Lost Island* in "Books: For Hammock and Deck Chair," *Saturday Night* 24 July 1954: 13–14.

p. 100: *tetter*: See Leviticus 13:39 in the Revised Version of the Bible.

p. 101: *a Trollope novel*: A novel by the great English Victorian writer Anthony Trollope (1815–82).

p. 101: A Jig for the Gypsy: Play written in 1945. The BBC Welsh Region produced it in 1952.

p. 101: *Vincent Massey, Canada's Governor General*: Canadian politician, diplomat, governor general 1952–59.

p. 101: *Eddys*: Eddy Match Company, manufacturer of wooden matches, based in Hull, Quebec, across the River from Ottawa.

p. 101: *Ben Jonson-Inigo Jones to the James I*: Ben Jonson collaborated with the English architect and artist Inigo Jones (1573–1652) on a number of masques – spectacular entertainments combining music, poetry, scenery, and elaborate costumes – which were presented at the court of James I (1566–1625, Scottish King of England 1603–25).

p. 101: *Charlotte Whitton*: (1896–1975) Canadian social worker, politician, feminist. Pugnacious and energetic, she was Ottawa's mayor during the 1950s and 1960s.

p. 102: *Arnold Edinborough*: (1922–) English-born Canadian. He and his wife, Letitia, had been good friends of the Davieses since they met in Kingston in 1948.

p. 102: *R. M. Ballantyne*: (1825–94) Scottish writer of popular adventure stories for boys, which were set in distant places.

p. 102: *your kinsman Rudyard . . . Max Beerbohm*: McInnes' mother (novelist Angela Thirkell) was cousin to the English writer Rudyard Kipling (1865–1936), who is best known for his stories about India, the jungle and its beasts, and the army. Max Beerbohm (1872–1956), English essayist, caricaturist, and parodist, wrote about Kipling's "manlydom" in "Kipling's Entire," *Saturday Review* 14 February 1903, and reprinted in Beerbohm's *Around Theatres*.

p. 103: *a good American agent*: Willis Kingsley Wing (1899–1985), who was based in New York. Wing was the agent of Scott Young (1918–), Canadian sports journalist, author, and friend. Young introduced RD to Wing by letter.

p. 104: *Questors Theatre*: Questors Little Theatre in Ealing (a suburb of London), one of Britain's leading amateur groups.

p. 104: *Ella Wheeler Wilcox and Godfrey Winn*: Ella Wheeler Wilcox (1850–1919), American poetaster, was a prolific writer of romantic, unctuous verse. Godfrey Winn (1908–71), English actor, novelist, and journalist, wrote whimsical, sentimental columns for the *Daily Mirror* and the *Sunday Express* in the 1930s and early 1940s.

p. 104: *Mrs. M.:* Pamela Kellino (1915–), English actress and author, married to James Mason 1941–65. Her background was in film rather than the stage: her father Isidore Ostrer controlled half of the British film industry in the late 1930s and early '40s; her first husband, Ray Kellino, was a cameraman turned director; she herself was an actress in films.

p. 105: *Michael, Susan and Simon*: The McInneses' children, born respectively in 1941, 1944, and 1948.

p. 106: *Macaulay's* Essays: Thomas Babington Macaulay (1800–59), English politician and historian, wrote many essays on literary and historical topics.

pp. 106–07: *piece about the Tillotsons . . . Dr. Leavis*: See "Pertinent and
   Impertinent Critics," *Saturday Night* 29 January 1955: 11–12. In this article,
   RD reviewed several books, including Kathleen Tillotson's *Novels of the
   Eighteen-Forties* and Geoffrey Tillotson's *Thackeray the Novelist*. F. R. Leavis
   (1895–1978), English, was one of the most influential literary critics of the 20th
   century and a fellow at Downing College, Cambridge. William Makepeace
   Thackeray (1811–63) was one of the great English novelists of the 19th century.
   The Brontës – a family of English novelists that included Charlotte (1816–55),
   Emily (1818–48), and Anne (1820–49) – wrote two of the great English novels,
   Jane Eyre (by Charlotte) and *Wuthering Heights* (by Emily).

p. 107: The Road to Xanadu: John Livingston Lowes' brilliant study of Samuel Taylor
   Coleridge (1772–1834), English poet, critic, and philosopher of Romanticism.

p. 107: *a coming* SN *article*: See "Catching Your Great Man," *Saturday Night* 19
   February 1955: 14–15. This article considers several books, including Joan
   Evans' *John Ruskin*. Ruskin (1819–1900) was an English social theorist and a
   critic of art and architecture. RD appears not to have reviewed the book on
   Lord George Gordon Byron (1788–1824), English Romantic poet.

p. 107: *C. S. Lewis and Dr. Chapman . . . Edmund Chambers*: RD encountered
   these three at Oxford 1935–38: Clive Staples Lewis (1898–1963), well-known
   English author of the Narnia stories, was a fellow and tutor of English at
   Magdalen College, 1925–54; R. W. Chapman (1881–1960), eminent Scottish
   editor of the works of Jane Austen and Samuel Johnson, was a fellow of
   Magdalen College, 1921–47; and, of course, Edmund K. Chambers was one of
   the examiners of RD's B. Litt. thesis.

p. 107: *Paul Bacon*: The son of one of Gordon Roper's neighbours in Toronto.
   Bacon was, in Roper's recollection, in his final year at Trinity College, University
   of Toronto.

p. 108: *Stendhal's* Diaries: *The Private Diaries of Stendhal*, edited by Robert Sage.
   Davies reviewed this book in "Catching Your Great Man," *Saturday Night* 19
   February 1955: 14–15. Stendhal was the pseudonym of Marie Henri Beyle
   (1783–1842), one of the great French novelists.

p. 109: *Mrs. Roy*: Peterborough dress maker.

p. 110: *Saw* Hamlet: In CBC's "Scope" series. It aired April 24, 1955. Kate Reid
   (1930–93) was an English-born Canadian actress and Robert Christie
   (1914–96), a Canadian actor and director. For Herbert Whittaker's assessment,
   see "Showbusiness," *Globe and Mail* 26 April 1955: 13. The film from which
   "the production had been hooked" was Laurence Olivier's 1948 *Hamlet*.

p. 110: *Dr. Honey*: Ralph Honey, Peterborough dentist and neighbour.

p. 111: *Lloyd Hale . . . Marcella Buck*: Of these, Lloyd Hale and Glen Jagerman
   were not in the cast when the play was presented November 19, 1955, during
   the Peterborough and District Drama Festival.

p. 113: *directing a play*: Ten Nights in a Barroom (an old temperance play), for the
   Straw Hat Players in Port Carling and Gravenhurst, Ontario, August 15–27, 1955.

p. 113: *a new one of my own . . . Toronto*: RD's new play *Hunting Stuart* ran from November 22 to December 3 at the Crest Theatre in Toronto. It was not produced again for many years.

p. 113: *disturbing time*: Davenport was eager to leave Utah and had been interviewed for the chair of physiology at the University of Michigan in July, but then heard nothing. Meantime, he was offered a similar appointment at the newly founded University of Florida and had to make his decision (it was negative) without knowing Michigan's decision. That was not made until late November, when he was offered the post.

p. 113: *Old Testament, but menstruous rags*: Possibly a conflation of two verses: "Ye shall defile also the covering of thy graven images of silver, and the ornament of thy molten images of gold: thou shalt cast them away as a menstruous cloth; thou shalt say unto it, Get thee hence" (Isaiah 30:22) and "But we are all as an unclean thing, and all our righteousnesses are as filthy rags; and we all do fade as a leaf; and our iniquities, like the wind, have taken us away" (Isaiah 64:6).

p. 114: *Slough of Despond*: One of the trials encountered by Christian on his way to the Celestial City in *The Pilgrim's Progress*, an allegory written by English Non-Conformist preacher and author John Bunyan (1628–88).

p. 114: *Broadway producer*: Joseph M. Hyman (1901–77), American, who held an option on the dramatic rights for two years.

p. 114: *Eliot Emmanuel*: A contemporary at Balliol.

p. 116: *first a play*: *General Confession*, but in the event he did not write it until 1958.

p. 117: *Langham*: Michael Langham (1919–   ), English artistic director of the Stratford Festival 1955–67.

p. 119: In a Great Tradition . . . Stanbrook: The book's full title is: *In a Great Tradition: Tribute to Dame Laurentia McLachlan Abbess of Stanbrook by the Benedictines of Stanbrook*. It does indeed contain several letters written by G. B. Shaw to the Abbess.

p. 120: *important writers of the day*: Sylvia Townsend Warner (1893–1978), English novelist and poet; Christopher Fry (1907–   ), English dramatist; Aldous Huxley (1894–1963), English novelist and writer of short stories and essays; Robert Graves (1895–1985), English poet, novelist, and critic. Of these, only Christopher Fry appears in Karsh's *Portraits of Greatness* (1959).

p. 121: *To BROOKS ATKINSON*: Published in *The New York Times* 28 October 1956, Section 2: X3.

p. 121: *Miss Nancy Mitford's revelations about U and Non-U speech*: "U and Non-U speech" refers to Upper Class and non Upper Class usage and pronunciation. Nancy Mitford (1904–73), English novelist and biographer, had her say on the subject in *Encounter*. Her article was reprinted, along with others on the subject, in *Noblesse Oblige: An Enquiry into the Identifiable Characteristics of the English Aristocracy* by Alan S. C. Ross and others.

p. 123: *my attitude to the matter*: RD's attitude, in the end, was that he should be paid for the adaptation and in due course the Stratford Festival paid him $500. For a full account, see *Man of Myth* 377–79.

p. 127: *Lilian Baylis*: (1894–1937) important English theatre manager, famed for mounting the entire Shakespearean canon at the Old Vic. In 1936 Brenda Davies had auditioned successfully with Lilian Baylis for a place in the Old Vic's drama school in London.

p. 127: *already been chosen*: Irving had been spoken for already, so the Davieses then dedicated the third seat to Sir John Martin-Harvey (successor to Irving, also famous in Shakespearean roles, and an actor whose performances had enchanted RD when he was a boy). The seats, including Irving's, are located on either side of aisle six at B27–29 and B30.

p. 128: *evidence . . . local Judge*: See "Compromise Sought by Judge: Denies Trying to Influence *Examiner's* Editorial Policy, Absurd to Attempt to Do So," *Peterborough Examiner* 19 July 1957:1, 2, 26–27. The judge was John de Navarre Kennedy.

p. 129: *LePan . . . diplomatic service*: Douglas V. LePan was a member of the Department of External Affairs 1945–59. He developed an expertise in economics, served in Washington as minister-counsellor, and in 1958–59, became assistant undersecretary of state.

p. 130: Maria Stuart: Play by German poet and dramatist Friedrich Von Schiller (1759–1805), which brings together Elizabeth I and Mary Queen of Scots (who in real life never met). Translated as *Mary Stuart* and directed by Tyrone Guthrie, it opened at the Phoenix Theatre in New York on October 8 and ran for seven weeks.

p. 130: Macropoulos: *The Makropoulos Secret*, Tyrone Guthrie's new version of a play by Czech playwright Karel Capek (1890–1938), about a woman who learned the way to eternal life. It opened at the Phoenix Theatre in New York on December 3 and lasted a month.

p. 130: Faust *in Edinburgh*: Goethe's *Faust* performed by a group from Dusseldorf during the Edinburgh Festival, September 1949.

p. 130: Peg's Paper . . . The Happy Mag: *Peg's Paper* was published in London, England, 1919–40 and *The Happy Mag* was likewise published in London, England, 1922–40 and 1940–   .

p. 130: *fretting scall*: See Leviticus 13:29–51 in the King James Version of the Bible.

p. 131: *Oberammergau Passion Play*: Passion plays were medieval religious dramas which dealt with events from the Last Supper to the Crucifixion of Christ. The best known of the few still performed is the one done by the villagers of Oberammergau in Bavaria.

p. 131: *Ethel Barrymore in* The Corn Is Green: Ethel Barrymore (1879–1959), leading American actress, starred on Broadway in 1940 as Miss Moffat in *The Corn Is Green*, a play by Welsh dramatist Emlyn Williams (1905–87).

p. 131: *Goin' Home!*: This ballad has many verses; but its concluding stanzas give a feel for the whole:

> By and by, buddy, we'll all get a pardon,
> Get to go home, my Lawd, get to go home.

> Doncha hear yo', hear yo' mother callin'
> "Run, son, run, my Lawd, run, son, run"?

> I'm gonna break right, break right pas' dat shooter
> I'm goin' home, my Lawd, I'm goin' home.

p. 131: *skelping . . . in the* Ex: "Passion Play Acting Poor, Attendance too," *Peterborough Examiner* 18 October 1957: 17, 29.

p. 132: *Morley Callaghan*: (1903–90) Canadian novelist and writer of short stories.

p. 133: *Angry Young Men*: A group of English writers of the 1950s including playwrights John Osborne and Arnold Wesker and novelists Kingsley Amis, John Braine, John Wain, and Alan Sillitoe. They were critical of the English establishment and disillusioned with themselves and their accomplishments.

p. 133: *Dr. W. A. MacKintosh . . . Royal Society*: William A. MacKintosh (1895–1970) was professor of economics at Queen's University, Kingston, 1920–51, principal and vice chancellor 1951–61, and vice chancellor 1961–65. RD quotes from "These Seventy-Five Years," *Transactions of the Royal Society of Canada* 3rd Series 51 (1957): 53–62.

p. 135: *Huxley's . . . statement*: RD refers here to a statement in *Ends and Means* (London: Chatto & Windus, 1937) 326.

p. 137: *an imitator of Angela Thirkell*: Thirkell (1890–1961), prolific English novelist, chronicled the lives of the principal county families of rural Barsetshire with a trenchant acerbity. Her tone and her choice of character types – "exquisitely aristocratic but nitwitted old women," "demure and well-bred young women," "honourable, stupid young men" – are quite unlike RD's. (See his review of Thirkell's *Peace Breaks Out*, "Latest Report from Barsetshire," *Peterborough Examiner* 14 May 1947: 4.)

SECTION IV

p. 141: *Sir George Parkin*: (1846–1922) Canadian educator, principal of Upper Canada College 1895–1902, secretary of the Rhodes Scholarship Trust 1902–22.

p. 141: *William Mowbray*: (1874–1946), Canadian, English Master at Upper Canada College for much of the period 1902–34; House Master of Wedd's (one of the Houses for boarders) 1925–34. RD was resident in Wedd's 1928–32.

p. 141: *Pauline Johnson . . . Sir William Peterson*: Pauline Johnson (1861–1913), Canadian poet, daughter of a Mohawk father and English mother, a gifted performer of her own poems; Sir William Osler (1849–1919), eminent Canadian physician, writer, and educator; Sir John A. Macdonald (1815–91), Scottish-born Canadian lawyer, politician, and first prime minister of Canada; Goldwin Smith (1823–1910), English-born Canadian historian and journalist; Bliss Carman (1861–1929), Canadian poet, editor, and journalist; Sir William Peterson (1856–1921), classical scholar and educationist, principal of McGill University in Montreal 1895–1919.

p. 143: *Mayor Fournier*: Sarto Fournier (1908–80), Canadian, member of parliament, judge, senator, and mayor of Montreal 1957–60.

p. 144: *T's book*: His autobiography, *A Life in the Theatre*, published later in 1959 by McGraw-Hill.

p. 145: *horde of guests*: There were 19 while RD was there, a few just for a meal, most for a few days to a week.

p. 145: *Joe Hone*: Joseph Hone (1937–   ), Irish radio and television critic, reviewer, writer, editor.

p. 145: She *by a fella named Haggard*: *She* is a celebrated novel of adventure written by the English writer Sir Henry Rider Haggard (1856–1925).

p. 145: *wee Morris*: Guthrie was 6′5″ tall and RD himself a portly 6′.

p. 145: *Sandgate*: Lulie Westfeldt's farm in Vermont.

p. 147: *Reas & Peter Zeisler*: Oliver Rea was from Pittsburgh, and his wife was a Montreal woman whom the Davieses had met at Brae Manor; Peter Zeisler was a Broadway stage manager and theatre administrator. Together with Tyrone Guthrie, they wanted to found a theatre in the U.S.A. for producing classics. The theatre they founded was the Minneapolis (later the Guthrie) Theater of Minneapolis, which opened in 1963.

p. 147: *J. B.*: Verse dramatization of the Book of Job by the American poet and playwright Archibald MacLeish (1892-1982). Just before leaving for Ireland, RD had written a column about *J. B.* See "A Writer's Diary: Audiences Mad at God Not Play," *Toronto Daily Star* 11 July 1959: 28.

p. 147: *Lord Rossmore*: (1931–   ), Irish, 8th Baron Rossmore of Monaghan (Ireland) and 7th Lord Rossmore of Monaghan (United Kingdom). His name is William Warner Westenra.

p. 147: *Mrs. Stewart*: Frances Stewart (1794–1872), Irish-born Canadian. Her letters were published as *Our Forest Home*. She and her husband, Thomas, were among the early settlers of Peterborough, Ontario, and she figures as a character in RD's play *At My Heart's Core*.

p. 148: *Hugh McCraig's advice*: RD had visited astrologer Hugh McCraig in New York the previous December. McCraig said that the collaboration with Tyrone Guthrie "will be difficult but if I treat him with kid gloves his jealousy of me may be blunted" (RD, Diary, December 8, 1958).

p. 148: Hamlet . . . *Chris Plum*: Christopher Plummer (1927–   ), eminent, versatile

Canadian actor, active in Canada, the U.S., and Britain. In the event, Tyrone Guthrie did not produce *Hamlet* in London with Plummer playing the lead role.

p. 149: *Christopher Scaife*: Tyrone Guthrie's oldest friend, professor of English Literature at the University of Lebanon.

p. 149: *His pick*: Micheál MacLiammóir (1899–1978), Irish actor, designer and dramatist; Esmé Church (1893–1972), English actress and director whom RD knew at Oxford and at the Old Vic; William Shatner (1931–   ), Canadian actor who performed at the Stratford Festival 1954–56 and later became known internationally as Captain Kirk in the *Star Trek* television series and movies; Nancy Malone (1935–   ), American film and television actress, later director and producer for television and film; William Hutt (1920–   ), Canadian actor and director capable of performing a broad range of parts, stalwart of the Stratford Festival; Eric House (1923–   ), skilful Canadian comic stage and film actor; Douglas Campbell (1922–   ), Scottish-born Canadian actor and director, long associated with the Stratford Festival, an excellent character actor; Davy Gam, Esq. See *Henry V* 4.8 where King Henry learns that the French lost 10,000 men at Agincourt, including many of position and power, while his English army lost only "Edward the Duke of York, the Earl of Suffolk,/Sir Richard Ketly, Davy Gam, Esquire;/None else of name; and of all other men/But five and twenty"; Amelia Hall was the only one of Guthrie's "pick" to be part of the actual cast.

p. 150: *black babies*: The Davies family used "black babies" to mean illegitimate children.

p. 151: *Dr. Steele*: An English anaesthetist who, with his wife and young sons, had come two days earlier to visit the Guthries.

p. 151: *what the hell, Archie*: Phrase often used by Mehitabel (the alley cat who traces her lineage back to Cleopatra) when describing her experiences to Archy (the cockroach with the soul of a poet), in light verse by Don Marquis (1878–1937), American newspaper columnist, poet, and playwright.

p. 152: *Mermaid*: The play RD saw at the Mermaid Theatre was *Lock Up Your Daughters*, adapted by Bernard Miles from Henry Fielding's comedy *Rape upon Rape*, lyrics by Lionel Bart and Music by Laurie Johnson.

p. 152: *present for WRD*: Present for Rupert Davies' 80th birthday.

p. 153: *Miss W.*: Moira Whalon (1924–98), English-born Canadian, RD's secretary.

p. 153: *that article*: See RD's "A Writer's Diary: Man Could Be Girl, Hag or Harlot," *Toronto Daily Star* 22 August 1959: 30.

p. 154: *Mr. Strauss . . . misusing the word comprise*: Strauss edited the manuscript of *A Voice from the Attic*. Knopf quoted several of his comments in his otherwise warmly positive letter about the manuscript of *A Voice*, including this: "And I am startled at the constant misuse of the word 'comprise.' On page 56, people do not comprise a doctor's practice. On page 189, such texts do not comprise the real closet drama. On page 245, people do not comprise a theatre audience. In each case it is the other way around."

p. 155: *Miss Seaman*: Belinda Hartnet Seaman (1912–92), Canadian, was head of the English department at BSS, Dean of Women at the University of New Brunswick 1960–63 and Principal and Dean of Women at St. Hilda's College, Trinity College, University of Toronto 1963–78.

p. 156: *Greenhill*: Ralph Greenhill (1924–96), English-born Canadian photographer, historian of photography, and collector.

p. 157: *same posture as . . . Bernard Shaw*: In Karsh's *Portraits of Greatness*, Shaw is seated in a chair set at an angle to the camera. The back of the chair is toward the right of the photo, Shaw's left arm rests on the arm of the chair, his right hand holds his spectacles, his head is tilted a little toward his left shoulder, his eyes alert, his expression genial.

p. 158: *David Hays*: (1930–) American lighting and set designer, and, recently, best-selling author. He did the sets and lighting for more than 50 broadway plays and musicals; he also founded and led the National Theatre of the Deaf.

p. 158: *Dennis King*: (1897–1971) English-born, aging American matinée idol, who played the eccentric organist Humphrey Cobbler. King appears not to have been in *The Desert Song*; RD was probably thinking of *The Vagabond King* (1930).

p. 158: *The Tenth Man*: Play by Paddy Chayefsky (1923–81), American writer of television and stage plays. Tyrone Guthrie produced it at the Booth Theatre in New York in 1959, where it ran for 623 performances.

p. 158: *Jacques Barzun*: (1907–) American scholar (born in France), teacher, editor, critic.

p. 161: *Davies had declared*: See "Stratford 1961: A Comedy of Noble Lunacy," *Peterborough Examiner* 24 June 1961: 4.

p. 162: *Nathan Cohen . . . Lou Applebaum*: Nathan Cohen (1923–71), Canadian, was a theatre critic and radio and television broadcaster. See "Nathan Cohen at Stratford: 'Love's Labour's Lost' Is Tribute to Langham," *Toronto Daily Star* 22 June 1961: 20. Louis Applebaum (1918–2000), Canadian, was a prolific composer, conductor, and administrator. He wrote and conducted music for over 75 of the Stratford Festival's productions.

p. 162: *Fragonard*: Jean-Honoré Fragonard (1732–1806), French painter of polished and delicately erotic scenes of love and gallantry for the court, including one called "The Swing."

p. 162: *a Watteau As You Like It*: RD saw this at the Old Vic in London some time between November 10 and December 5, 1936. Edith Evans (1888–1976), the celebrated English actress who made her theatrical debut in 1912, played Rosalind, and Michael Redgrave (1908–85), English actor just setting out on a long, busy career, played Orlando. For another discussion of this same production, see RD's letter of July 21, 1972.

p. 162: *Arne's*: Thomas Augustine Arne (1710–78), English composer of operas, oratorios, instrumental music, and incidental music for plays.

p. 163: *Jack Cooke*: Jack Kent Cooke (1912–97), Canadian-born American, self-made magnate who built empires in newspapers, radio, cable television, and owned several sports teams. He owned *Saturday Night* 1952–61.

p. 163: *canning my* Star *column*: Actually RD continued with his *Star* column until June 1962.

pp. 163–64: *Corvo and Logan Pearsall Smith* . . . *Babbitt*: Corvo and Logan Pearsall Smith represent byways of English literature. Baron Corvo, whose real name was Frederick William Rolfe (1860–1913), was an English novelist whose style was replete with learned allusions and arcane vocabulary; Logan Pearsall Smith (1865–1946) was an American-born English writer of exquisite essays. (For RD's "A Writer's Diary" columns about Smith and Rolfe, see the *Toronto Daily Star* 5 August 1961: 24 and 7 October 1961: 33.) *Babbitt* was a satiric novel by American journalist, editor, and novelist Sinclair Lewis (1885–1951).

p. 164: *May you be to this unawakened earth the trumpet of a prophecy*: RD refers to "Be through my lips to unawakened earth/The trumpet of a prophecy!" from "Ode to the West Wind" by Percy Bysshe Shelley (1792–1822), English Romantic poet.

p. 165: *Sir James Barrie*: James Matthew Barrie (1860–1937), Scottish novelist and dramatist, best known for *Peter Pan*.

p. 165: *my collection*: At a later point RD was given to understand that the collection didn't mesh well with the library's holdings so it will not end up at Massey.

p. 166: *Massey association with Balliol*: Vincent Massey, the dominant member of the Massey Foundation, took his B.A. at Balliol; Massey was Canada's High Commissioner to London when RD was at Balliol, and he entertained Balliol's Canadian students from time to time; there were Massey scholarships to Balliol; Vincent Massey's sons Lionel (1916–65) and Hart (1918–97) were both undergraduates at Balliol when RD was there.

p. 167: *Dr. Claude Bissell*: (1916–2000), Canadian, professor of English, president of the University of Toronto 1958–71, reviewer of RD's early work, friend.

p. 167: *Jowett*: Benjamen Jowett (1817–93), English educator and Greek scholar, was master of Balliol College 1870–93.

p. 167: *not remember . . . affection*: This is not quite accurate. Davenport barely knew Lionel and Hart, though with the latter there was tension. Davenport, a tall man, was aware that Hart, who was tiny, was extremely conscious of the disparity.

p. 168: *The others*: Hart Massey was an architect; Raymond Massey (1896–1983), Canadian-born American actor associated with the role of Abraham Lincoln on stage and in film; Raymond's son was Geoffrey Massey (1916–), Canadian architect practising in Vancouver; their financial advisor was Wilmot H. Broughall of National Trust.

p. 173: *In 1942*: September 27, 1940.

SECTION V

p. 180: *Colin Friesen*: (1922–) Canadian, bursar of Massey College 1962–88.

p. 181: *our librarian [Douglas Lochhead]*: (1922–) Canadian poet, librarian, bibliographer, professor, and printer. He was the College's librarian 1963–75.

p. 182: *B. K. Sandwell*: Bernard Keble Sandwell (1876–1954), English-born Canadian, editor of *Saturday Night* 1932–51.

p. 182: *Mackail . . . Burne-Jones*: Graham McInnes' mother, Angela Thirkell, was the daughter of the eminent John Mackail (1859–1945), English, distinguished administrator at the Ministry of Education and classical scholar, literary critic, poet, and biographer. Angela Thirkell's brother was Denis George Mackail (1892–1971), the prolific and successful English novelist, and her grandfather was the English pre-Raphaelite painter Sir Edward Burne-Jones (1833–98).

p. 183: *his brother*: Colin MacInnes (1914–76), English (but brought up partly in Australia).

p. 184: English Court Hand: *English Court Hand, A.D. 1066 to 1500: Illustrated Chiefly from the Public Records*, 2 vols., by Charles Johnson and Hilary Jenkinson.

p. 185: *John Barker*: (1934–) Canadian, non-resident junior fellow at Massey College 1963–67.

p. 185: *Joe McCulley*: Joseph McCulley (d. 1977), Scottish-born Canadian educationist, warden of Hart House 1952–65. He was 74 when he died.

p. 185: *How odd . . . the Jews*: Anti-Semitic doggerel minted by the English journalist and humorist William Norman Ewer (1885–1976).

p. 185: The Cenci: Verse tragedy exploring moral deformity by Shelley.

p. 186: *run by three men*: Clifford Leech (1909–77), English, professor of English and drama at the University of Toronto; John Howe Sword (1915–2001), Canadian educator, at this point executive assistant to the President of the University of Toronto.

p. 190: *Thomas Surridge*: (1930–2002) Jamaican-born Canadian psychologist.

p. 190: The Beggar's Opera: Popular ballad opera combining political satire and burlesque of Italian opera, by John Gay (1685–1732), English poet and satirist.

p. 191: *Professor Endicott*: Norman Jamieson Endicott (1902–79), Canadian (born in China), professor of English at University College, University of Toronto, expert in Sir Thomas Browne and the modern British novel.

p. 192: *Henry the Fifth*: (1387–1422) King of England 1413–22. He was the eldest son of Henry IV (1366–1413), who was King 1399–1413. He resumed the Hundred Years War, winning the battle of Agincourt in 1415.

p. 192: *Richard II*: (1367–1400) King of England 1377–99. Henry Bolingbroke seized the throne in 1399 as Henry IV. Richard died the following year in mysterious circumstances.

p. 192: *a true lover of the Holy Church*: See *Henry V* 1.1.22.

p. 192: *Henry VI*: (1421–71) King of England 1422–61, 1470–71.

p. 192: *Wavell and Montgomery and Patton*: Archibald Percival Wavell (1883–1950), British field marshal; Bernard Law Montgomery (1887–1976), British field marshal; George Smith Patton Jr. (1885–1945), American general.

p. 192: *the secret of Joshua*: See Joshua 1:1–9.

p. 194: *Robert Finch*: (1900–95) poet, painter, harpsichordist, respected scholar of 17th and 18th century French poetry, and a senior fellow at Massey College 1961–95.

p. 195: *St. Sebastian*: Martyr who was shot with arrows.

p. 196: *Hamlet's uncle said*: RD refers here to the speech given by King Claudius, *Hamlet* I.2.87 ff., which begins:

> 'Tis sweet and commendable in your nature, Hamlet,
> To give these mourning duties to your father;
> But you must know your father lost a father;
> That father lost lost his; and the survivor bound,
> In filial obligation, for some term
> To do obsequious sorrow. But to persever
> In obstinate condolement is a course
> Of impious stubbornness; 'tis unmanly grief. . . .

p. 196: *what Freud's father said*: See Ernest Jones, *Sigmund Freud: Life and Work, Vol. 1, The Young Freud 1856–1900* (London: Hogarth, 1953) 21.

p. 196: *to bend the bow of Achilles*: RD probably refers to the bow of Odysseus. During Odysseus' 20-year absence at and after the war in Troy, his wife Penelope is besieged by suitors. Finally she agrees to marry the one who can bend the bow of Odysseus and shoot an arrow from it through the holes in the backs of 12 axes; all fail – except Odysseus himself, home at last, disguised as a beggar.

p. 197: *James Reaney's play*: *Colours in the Dark*. James Reaney (1926–   ) is a Canadian poet and experimental playwright. In 1967, the Stratford Festival gave *Colours in the Dark* a professional production of the sort RD yearned for when he was an aspiring playwright.

p. 199: *reprinted in the* Varsity: See "Does an Opening Address Have to Be Dull?" *Varsity* 20 September 1967: 5.

p. 200: Responsibility and Revolt: See *Queen's Quarterly* 74.2 (Summer 1967): 201–21. Escott Reid's address (see the previous letter) made use of ideas in this article.

p. 200: *Apuleius gives us in* The Golden Ass: Lucius Apuleius (c. 124-c. 170) was a North African writer, satirist, and rhetorician. *The Golden Ass* concerns a vain man who is turned into an ass and who has a series of adventures. He gains wisdom and in the end becomes a priest of Isis. RD's interest in *The Golden Ass* began at Oxford in the 1930s. In his novel *A Mixture of Frailties* (1958) he had his characters write and perform an opera based on *The Golden*

Ass, and in 1994–95, in the last year of his life, he himself wrote the libretto for such an opera. It was performed by the Canadian Opera Company in 1999.

p. 201: *the boys on the burning deck*: With reference to the once popular poem "Casabianca" by English-born Welsh poet Felicia Dorothea Hemans (1793–1835), which begins, "The boy stood on the burning deck,/Whence all but he had fled." It concerns a lad who remained at his post during the battle of the Nile after the ship had caught fire and all guns had been abandoned. He died when the vessel exploded.

p. 201: *a little piece of mine*: "What Do You See in the Mirror? A Footnote to the Psychedelic Revolution," *University of Toronto Graduate* 1.2 (March 1968): 60–4. This is an article about LSD and drugs that release and enlarge consciousness. It considers witches, saints, ecstatics, and Aldous Huxley.

p. 201: *notice of the* Almanack *in* The Gazette: See "Almanacks Galore – Who Could Ask for More?" Montreal *Gazette* 11 November 1967: 44.

p. 203: *your book about Senator O'Brien*: The book is titled *O'Brien* and was written by Scott Young and Astrid Young.

p. 204: *personal hand in some of the designing*: Eric Clements (1925–   ) is an English award-winning designer, much admired for his understanding of function, respect for detail, and love of form and shape. Ronald James Thom (1923–86), Canadian architect who planned Massey College and Trent University, was the person Vincent Massey compelled to remove excess wood from a piece of furniture. A later version of this story appears in *Man of Myth* 409. Allan Fleming (1929–77) was a Canadian graphic designer. He created the calligraphy and oversaw the application of lettering in quotations, signs, and the corner stone. He also devised the clock face and the first version of the College coat of arms.

p. 205: *my references to you*: See "The Charlottetown Banquet" in *High Spirits*.

p. 206: *The notice of your play*: See Urjo Kareda, "Theatre: An Author at Odds with His Fantasy," *Globe and Mail* 20 December 1967: 15.

p. 206: *Kareda*: Urjo Kareda (1944–2001), Estonian-born Canadian critic, later artistic director of the Tarragon Theatre in Toronto 1982–2001.

p. 208: *Port Hope*: Vincent Massey's home, Batterwood, was near Port Hope, east of Toronto.

p. 208: *Your letter to the* Globe: See "Letters to the Editor: Order of Canada" 6 January 1968: 6. In 1967, the year Canada established the Order of Canada, there were two ranks, Companion and Medal of Service. Hugh MacLennan was given the first and Morley Callaghan the second. Callaghan refused the Medal.

p. 209: *Professors W. A. C. H. Dobson and W. E. Swinton*: W. A. C. H. Dobson (1913–82), Scottish, was head of the department of East Asiatic Studies 1952–65, professor of Chinese, productive scholar, and senior fellow at Massey College 1962–72; W. E. Swinton (1900–94), also Scottish, was a specialist in dinosaurs, a member of the scientific staff of the British Museum

(Natural History) 1924–61, a professor of zoology at the University of Toronto 1962–66, a senior fellow of Massey College 1966–81.

p. 211: *a volume for a new history of drama*: RD contributed "Playwrights and Plays" to *The Revels History of Drama in English. Vol. 6: 1750–1880*: 147–286.

p. 213: *Simon Legree*: Brutal slave-owner in *Uncle Tom's Cabin* by American novelist Harriet Beecher Stowe (1811–96), who has Tom whipped to death for refusing to divulge the whereabouts of some runaway slaves.

p. 214: *Lacy, Dicks and French*: T. H. Lacy, John Dicks, and Samuel French.

p. 214: *To* THE EDITOR OF THE GLOBE AND MAIL: Published 5 November 1968: 6.

p. 216: Satyricon: Burlesque based on material from Petronius, Juvenal, Tacitus, and Minsky. The book and lyrics were by Thomas Best Hendry (1929–   ), Canadian playwright and administrator, and the music by Stanley Silverman. It was performed at the Stratford Festival in 1969.

p. 217: The Three Musketeers: Adapted from the novel by French dramatist and novelist Alexandre Dumas père (1802–70) by Peter Raby (1939–   ), British writer. It was produced at Stratford in 1968.

SECTION VI

p. 220: *Tom*: Thomas Landis Davenport (1952–89), American, the older of Horace's two sons. He became a computer programmer.

p. 221: *Department of Reform Institutions*: At the time, this was called the Ministry of Correctional Institutions, Government of Ontario.

p. 221: *Stephen Leacock*: (1869–1944) English-born Canadian humorist, writer, teacher, political economist. RD's little book was titled *Stephen Leacock*.

p. 222: *forever to get into print*: The volume to which RD contributed was not published until 1975.

p. 222: *a house in the country*: Called "Windhover," the house is set on a hundred-acre parcel of land near Caledon East and overlooks a long sweep of unspoiled countryside. The actual building commenced in 1970 and was completed in May 1971.

p. 222: *another daughter married; husband a young biologist*: Rosamond was married to John Cunnington 1969–83.

p. 222: *To* THE EDITOR OF THE GLOBE AND MAIL: Published 24 July 1969: 6.

p. 222: *Professors John T. Saywell and H. R. S. Ryan*: John T. Saywell (1929–   ), Canadian, was then professor of history and environmental studies at York University, and H. R. S. Ryan was a professor in the Faculty of Law, Queen's University, Kingston. The dispute was headed "English Usage" by *The Globe and Mail* whenever a fresh letter on the subject appeared.

p. 223: *N. Roy Clifton's comment*: See "Letters to the Editor: English Usage," *Globe and Mail* 21 July 1967: 6.

p. 225: *THE MASTER*: John Edward Christopher Hill (1912–   ), English, was master of Balliol College 1965–78. He is an eminent historian of 16th and 17th century English history.

p. 225: *Sir David Lindsay Keir*: (1895–1973) Scottish, Master of Balliol College 1949–65. His field was English constitutional history.

p. 227: *Christ leads us . . . through before*: From the hymn by Richard Baxter (1615–1691), English Puritan divine and writer, which runs

Lord, it belongs not to my care
Whether I die or live;
To love and serve Thee is my share,
And this Thy grace must give.

If life be long, I will be glad,
That I may long obey;
If short, yet why should I be sad
To welcome endless day?

Christ leads me through no darker rooms
Than He went through before;
He that unto God's Kingdom comes,
Must enter by this door. . . .

p. 227: The Way of the World: Comedy by William Congreve (1670–1727), one of the great English dramatists. The play is a witty, penetrating study of love and marriage in a mercenary world. The Irish writer Jonathan Swift (1667–1745) is one of the greatest satirists in the English language.

p. 227: *piffle before the wind*: Phrase from chapter 5 of *The Young Visiters*, a novel by Daisy Ashford (1881–1972), English, written at the age of nine.

p. 228: *the Land that God Gave Cain*: Cain's punishment for murdering his brother Abel was to be exiled from Eden to the land of Nod (Genesis 4); RD may also be recalling the title of the novel *The Land that God Gave to Cain* by Hammond Innes (1913–94), English writer of adventure novels.

p. 230: *text for the book on* ACTING: See *Tyrone Guthrie on Acting*.

p. 230: *Minneapolis*: The Minneapolis Theatre in Minneapolis, Minnesota, planned by Tyrone Guthrie as a professional classical repertory theatre, opened, under his direction, in 1963. Douglas Campbell acted in many of Guthrie's productions there, and was artistic director, briefly. Campbell's first wife was Ann Casson, daughter of Dame Sybil Thorndike and Sir Lewis Casson. Serge Voronoff (1866–1951), Russian transplant pioneer, grafted chimpanzee and baboon testicles onto forty men during the 1920s and '30s, seeking to prevent aging and achieve rejuvenation.

p. 230: *Mavor Moore's shop . . . mixed media piece by Languirand called* Mankind

Inc.: Mavor Moore was director of the St. Lawrence Centre at the time. Jacques Languirand (1931–) is a Canadian playwright, actor, and critic. *Mankind Inc.*, a vehicle to show off the resources of the new theatre, involved film, dance, song, and live actors and was loosely based on *Everyman*. RD compares *Mankind Inc.* to *The Skin of Our Teeth*, a drama surveying man's narrow escape from disaster through the ages, by Thornton Wilder (1897–1975), American dramatist and novelist.

p. 231: *the raggle-taggle academics, O*: With reference to the ballad called "The Wraggle-Taggle Gypsies" concerning a lady who left her new Lord and her fine possessions to go with "the wraggle-taggle gypsies, O."

p. 231: *Leon Major*: (1933–) Canadian, director of plays and opera in Canada, the United States, and Europe. He did not do RD's Casanova play, *General Confession*.

p. 231: *Barker Fairley*: (1887–1986) English-born Canadian poet, artist, professor of German at the University of Toronto 1915–32 and at University College, University of Toronto 1936–57, expert on Goethe, Heinrich Heine, Nietzsche, and others.

p. 231: *Davises . . . J. B. Priestley's* The Glass Cage: Priestley wrote *The Glass Cage* specially for the Canadian acting family of Murray and Donald Davis and their sister Barbara Chilcott for production at the Crest Theatre in Toronto in 1957. RD was also asked to write a play for the Davis family, namely *General Confession*. For the full story see *Man of Myth* 384–89.

p. 231: *takes his wittles reglar*: As Sam Weller in Dickens' *Pickwick Papers* might say.

p. 231: *a poem*: Titled "Lines Written in Dejection after seeing a performance of HAIR on Epiphany, 1970." His "quote from W. B. Yeats" – "Love has pitched his mansion in/The place of excrement" – is from "Crazy Jane talks with the Bishop."

p. 235: *a letter from McClelland and Stewart*: Anna Szigethy wrote on April 9, 1970, to say that "the material printed in STEPHEN LEACOCK" would be "newly printed as an introduction to FEAST OF STEPHEN, incorporating the errors and corrections you have listed and marked in the copy of the book." In addition, *Stephen Leacock* was reissued and the proof-reader fired.

p. 236: *Davies once described*: For the quotations about Tyrone Power and Dr. Thomas Guthrie, see "Tyrone Power and Dr. Thomas Guthrie in Canada," *Drama Survey* 3.1 (May 1963): 91–6.

p. 236: *the famous emendation . . . NOT Malone; it is Theobald*: This emendation concerns Falstaff's dying words in *Henry V* 2.3, which, in the folios, read "His nose was as sharp as a pen, and a table of green fields." This was changed to "His nose was as sharp as a pen, and 'a babbled of green fields'" by Lewis Theobald (1688–1744), English Shakespearean scholar and author of poems, essays, and dramatic works. Edmund Malone (1741–1812), Irish, was a later Shakespearean scholar and critic.

p. 237: *To THE EDITOR OF* THE GLOBE AND MAIL: Published 9 July 1970, Metro Edition: 7.

p. 237: *Patrick Crean*: (1911–) British-born Canadian, fencing master and actor on stage and in film, who toured his one-man show "The Sun Never Set," based on the writings of Kipling, across North America.

p. 238: *twice refers to my loud laughter*. See Herbert Whittaker, "Laughter, Silence Greet One-Man Rediscovery of Kipling," *Globe and Mail* 3 July 1970: 13.

p. 239: *the Great Exhibition*: In London, England, in 1851.

p. 239: *John Naylor*: A liverpool banker.

p. 239: Sir Charles Barry: (1795–1860) English architect.

p. 240: *Ceres and Pomona*: Ceres was the Roman goddess of agriculture (grains, corn, bread) and Pomona, the Roman goddess of fruit trees and orchards.

p. 241: *Grandfather Frog*: In a series of once popular children's books, Thornton W. Burgess (American, 1873-1965) whimsically depicted nature and animal life. Grandfather Frog figured as a wise, aged being, whose utterances were widely respected.

p. 242: The Bobbsey Twins: Series of once popular children's books written by Edward Stratemeyer (1863-1930) and his daughter Harriet Stratemeyer Adams (1894-1982).

p. 242: *burning of the Kaiser . . . Victory Parade*: See *Fifth Business* 101–2 and 94–95.

p. 242: *St. John Robertson*: Rupert Davies' cousin Diarmid Robertson, son of Dr. Robert Robertson of Ventnor in England, went down on the *Aboukir*. The confusion is with Dr. Robertson's stepson St. John Nicholson. The cruiser *Aboukir* was sunk on September 22, 1914, by the German submarine *U9*.

p. 242: *Who killed Boy Staunton*: See *Fifth Business* 266.

p. 243: *Writing is simply . . . difficult*: Usually quoted as "Writing is no trouble: you just jot down the ideas as they occur to you. The jotting is simplicity itself – it is the occurring which is difficult."

p. 245: *Cecil Beaton*: (1904–80) English designer of theatrical costumes and scenery, also a photographer.

p. 248: *Gerard Manley Hopkins*: (1844–89) English Jesuit poet, innovative with rhythm and language.

p. 249: *young Petersons*: The Peterson who went to Australia and became Brenda's great-grandfather was William (1823–98). The one who went to India and became a Sanskrit scholar was probably Peter, who published editions and translations of Sanskrit treatises and classical texts in Bombay in the 1880s. Sir William (1858–1921), principal of McGill University in Montreal 1895–1919, belonged to the next generation. He was a nephew of the Australian William.

p. 249: *your letters . . . have them*: For a time these were housed in the Massey College Library, but they are now in the University of Toronto Archives with other Hart House material.

p. 249: *Vincent's papers*: Now in the University of Toronto Archives.

p. 249: *I shall leave this to the College*: Now held by the National Archives of Canada (closed until 2016).

p. 249: *Creighton*: Donald Grant Creighton (1902–79), eminent English Canadian historian who taught in the history department at the University of Toronto 1927–71, and was a senior fellow at Massey College 1969–74.

p. 251: *as I have written in another novel*: See *A Mixture of Frailties* 375–79.

p. 252: *Erich Neumann's discussion . . . New Ethic*: See *Depth Psychology and a New Ethic* by Erich Neumann (1905–60), German-born Israeli psychologist, disciple of C. G. Jung.

pp. 255–56: *Logos principle . . . Eros*: In *Aion, The Collected Works of C. G. Jung* 9 ii, paragraph 29, Jung writes: "I use Eros and Logos merely as conceptual aids to describe the fact that woman's consciousness is characterized more by the connective quality of Eros than by the discrimination and cognition associated with Logos. In men, Eros, the function of relationship, is usually less developed than Logos. In women, on the other hand, Eros is an expression of their true nature, while their Logos is often only a regrettable accident."

p. 256: *A. D. Lindsay*: (1879–1952) Scottish educationist, socialist, Quaker, master of Balliol College 1924–49.

p. 258: *Cork Smith*: Corlies M. Smith (1929–) American, senior editor at The Viking Press in New York and RD's editor for *Fifth Business, The Manticore*, and the Compass paperback edition of *A Voice from the Attic*.

p. 259: *Michael Horniman*: Horniman was with Messrs. A. P. Watt, RD's London agents at this time.

SECTION VII

p. 263: *Brückmannite . . . Falle*: Patricia C. Brückmann and George Falle were both members of the English department of Trinity College, University of Toronto. Falle (1915–84) was Canadian and his research and teaching were focused on literature of the 17th and 18th centuries. Brückmann (1932–), an American-born Canadian, was at Trinity 1958–97; her teaching and research have been focused on Chaucer and 18th century literature.

p. 264: *John Evans*: John Robert Evans (1929–), Canadian, president of the University of Toronto 1972–78 and a doctor known for innovative reforms in medical education.

p. 265: *Bloomsbury Group*: A literary group centred on Bloomsbury Square in London from 1904 to World War II. It included Lytton Strachey, Virginia Woolf, Leonard Woolf, E. M. Forster, Vita Sackville-West, Roger Fry, Clive Bell, and John Maynard Keynes.

p. 265: The Lyons Mail, The Corsican Brothers: *The Lyons Mail* is the name under which Henry Irving produced *The Courier of Lyons* by English novelist and playwright Charles Reade (1814–84). *The Corsican Brothers* is a translation by Irish Playwright Dion Boucicault (1820–90) of a French dramatization of Alexandre Dumas père's *Les Frères Corses.*

p. 267: *your article on* Fifth Business: See Gordon Roper, "Robertson Davies' *Fifth Business* and 'That Old Fantastical Duke of Dark Corners, C. G. Jung,'" *Journal of Canadian Fiction* 1. 1 (1972): 33–39.

p. 267: *Elspeth Buitenhuis's thin little job*: *Robertson Davies* in the series *Canadian Writers and Their Works* (Toronto: Forum House, 1972) 80 pp.

p. 269: *at publishers' promises, they say, Jove laughs (Shakespeare)*: RD here plays with "at lovers' perjuries/They say Jove laughs" (*Romeo and Juliet* 2.2).

p. 269: *David Godfrey*: (1938–) Canadian writer, publisher, and academic, was cofounder of both the House of Anansi and New Press. His novel *The New Ancestors* won the Governor General's Award for fiction in 1970.

p. 269: *Mark Czarnecki*: (1945–) Canadian, editor at New Press, subsequently a theatre critic and audit advisor.

p. 269: *Mary Worth*: Key figure in a comic strip of that name in many North American papers from 1938 on. A kindly, wise, sophisticated older woman, Mary Worth gives advice to chance acquaintances who come and go in her life. As a result the strip considered a wide range of social problems.

p. 269: The Threepenny Opera: An adaptation of John Gay's *The Beggar's Opera* by Kurt Weill (1900–50), German-born American composer, in collaboration with Bertolt Brecht (1898–1956), German dramatist, poet, and Marxist.

p. 270: *All is best, though we oft doubt..... (Milton)*: See the beginning of the Chorus's last speech in *Samson Agonistes* by the great English poet John Milton (1608–74).

p. 270: Maclean's: See Peter C. Newman, "The Master's Voice: The Table Talk of Robertson Davies," *Maclean's* September 1972: 42–43. The introduction includes the following sentence concerning Massey College and its Master: "Inside its elegant walls he moves among his Junior Fellows in their gowns, looking quite magnificent in a necromancer's beard, living in the Master's Lodge, presiding once a month at High Table, sniffing snuff out of Aram's [a ram's] horn, sipping claret, responding with superb indifference to all charges that the college is snobbish, anachronistic, sexist and maybe even absurd."

p. 271: *no such thing as Bad Publicity (Matthew Arnold)*: The originator of this oft quoted phrase is unknown, and was certainly not, as RD knew, Matthew Arnold (1822–88), English poet and influential critic.

p. 271: *ever since 1932*: In the summer of 1932, RD saw *As You Like It* in the Memorial Theatre at Stratford-upon-Avon in England.

p. 272: Swiss Family Robinson: A classic for children about the adventures of a family wrecked on a desert island, by Johann David Wyss (1743–1818), Swiss.

p. 272: *Kott*: Jan Kott (1914–), Polish critic and literary historian, who published some unusual views about Shakespeare's plays in the 1960s.

p. 273: *Rosalind and Orlando*: Rosalind was played by Carole Shelley (1939–   ), English stage and film actress, active subsequently in Canada and the United States. Orlando was played by Nicholas Pennell (1939–95), fine English actor, a stalwart at the Stratford Festival 1972–94.

p. 273: *Years ago at Stratford they did* AYLI: In 1959. Irene Worth (1916–2002), American actress; also active in London, England, and in film and on radio; Jason Robards (1922–2000), American stage and film actor, known for his interpretations of Eugene O'Neill.

p. 273: *Edward Atienza*: (1924–   ) Canadian comic actor.

p. 273: *Roly Hewgill*: Roland Hewgill (1929–98), Canadian who acted in major theatres across Canada, in film, and on television.

p. 274: *London Little Theatre for the first night*: May 3, 1951.

p. 275: *Sinclair Ross*: (1908–96) Canadian writer whose *oeuvre* consists of four novels and 18 short stories.

p. 275: *some of the brethren*: Earle Birney; Jack Ludwig (1922–   ), Canadian novelist; Margaret Atwood (1939–   ), influential Canadian poet, critic, and best-selling novelist.

pp. 277–78: *Animus-possessed . . . Anima-possessed*: In Jung's theory, as explained by Anthony Storr in *The Essential Jung* (Princeton: Princeton UP, 1983) 414, the anima and animus are the "personification of the feminine nature of a man's unconscious and masculine nature of a woman's. . . . Anima and animus manifest themselves most typically in personified form as figures in dreams and fantasies ('dream-girl,' 'dream-lover'), or in the irrationalities of a man's *feeling* and a woman's *thinking*."

p. 278: *John Barrymore as Svengali*: John Barrymore (1882–1942), American actor who was memorable as the evil mesmerist Svengali on stage and in the 1931 movie called *Svengali*.

p. 278: Lorenzaccio: Historical drama by Alfred de Musset (1810–57), French poet and playwright, about the assassination of the unpopular Alexander de' Medici by his young cousin Lorenzo.

p. 278: *Alfred de Musset . . . expected*: A clerihew (a pseudo-biographical quatrain, rhymed as two couplets, with lines of uneven length, more or less in the rhythm of prose) by Maurice Evan Hare (1886–1967), English, who is remembered for this and a couple of other light verses.

p. 278: *Sheridan Knowles or Bulwer*: James Sheridan Knowles (1784–1862), Irish-born playwright; Edward George Bulwer-Lytton (1803–73), English novelist and dramatist.

p. 278: *Macready*: William Charles Macready (1793–1873), English actor and manager, an exceptional tragedian.

p. 279: *Poesy and Buzzem*: Quoted from "John and Freddy" in *The Bab Ballads* by W. S. Gilbert (of Gilbert and Sullivan). The context is as follows: "But *Freddy* tries another style,/He knows some graceful steps and does 'em – /A breathing Poem – Woman's smile – /A man all poesy and buzzem."

p. 281: *John Pettigrew*: John S. Pettigrew was an English-born Canadian. RD shared the teaching of a course with him at Trinity College, University of Toronto, 1960–62. He was the first Registrar at Trent University, Peterborough, Ontario, 1964–65, then taught in the English Department at Trent 1965–68.

p. 281: *Berners Jackson*: Berners A. W. Jackson (1916–   ), English-born Canadian, taught in the English department, McMaster University, Hamilton, Ontario, 1956–81. The Shakespeare Seminar was sponsored by a consortium of Canadian Universities and organized by the Department of Extension at McMaster under Jackson's directions.

p. 281: *Professor Meisel*: (1923–   ) Canadian (born in Vienna), respected political scientist, at Queen's University, Kingston, Ontario, since 1949, chair of the Canadian Radio-Television and Telecommunications Commission from 1980–83, past president of the Royal Society of Canada.

p. 282: *Monthly Number form*: Novels were published in monthly installments.

p. 282: *Wilkie Collins*: (1824–89) English novelist, best known for *The Woman in White* and *The Moonstone*, and for writing the first full-length detective novels in English.

p. 284: *Blissett*: William Blissett (1921–   ), Canadian, professor of English at University College, University of Toronto 1965–87, an expert on Shakespeare, Ben Jonson, Edmund Spenser.

p. 284: *Edmund Wilson so pungently argues*: Edmund Wilson (1895–1972) was an influential American literary and social critic. See his "Morose Ben Jonson" in *The Triple Thinkers: Twelve Essays on Literary Subjects*, 2nd edition (New York: Oxford UP, 1948) 213–32.

p. 284: *too much sicklied o'er with scholarship*: Here RD plays with a thought from Hamlet's "To be or not to be" soliloquy, in 3.1: "Thus conscience does make cowards of us all;/And thus the native hue of resolution/Is sicklied o'er with the pale cast of thought. . . ."

p. 285: *Fern Rahmel*: Fern Alma Rahmel (1914–   ), elementary and later secondary school English teacher in Peterborough, assistant to the editor of *Saturday Night* 1953–56, creator of educational radio plays for children, director with the Peterborough Little Theatre.

p. 285: *Vivien Leigh*: (1913–67) outstanding English stage and film actress, married to Laurence Olivier, and best known for her Scarlett O'Hara in the film *Gone With The Wind*.

p. 285: *second volume of Dan Laurence's edition of Shaw's* Letters: See *Bernard Shaw: Collected Letters 1898–1910* (1972).

p. 285: *St. John Ervine*: See St. John Greer Ervine, *Bernard Shaw: His Life, Work and Friends* (London: Constable, 1956) 295.

p. 286: *Arnold Wilkinson*: (born c. 1916–72) Canadian. Wilkinson's whole career was at Hart House, the centre for men students at the University of Toronto, beginning in 1938–43 as assistant secretary, then as assistant comptroller, assistant warden activities, acting warden, and finally warden 1966–72.

p. 287: *Henry James*: (1843–1916) American novelist and critic who lived much of his life in Europe and England, and often contrasted American and European character.

p. 287: *freely adapting that mighty bard Edgar A. Guest*: (1881–1959) English-born American newspaper poet. He wrote a daily poem for the *Detroit Free Press* which was widely syndicated. His poems had a homely, saccharine morality. The line RD adapts (from the poem that gave Guest's book *A Heap o' Livin'* its title) originally ran "It takes a heap o' livin' in a house t' make it home."

p. 287: *I once met Dr. Harding*: RD consulted her in New York on May 8, 1959. See *Man of Myth* 351–52.

p. 288: *Jim Shaw*: James M. Shaw (1920–2002), American-born Canadian.

p. 288: *the Analytical Psychology Society of Ontario*: RD helped to found this Jungian group in 1970, and he and Brenda were regulars at its meetings for many years.

p. 288: *the Quakers' place in Toronto*: The meeting house of The Religious Society of Friends, at 60 Lowther Avenue, not far from Massey College.

p. 288: *Paul Seligman*: (1902/3–85) German-born Canadian, professor of philosophy at the University of Waterloo 1963–75, a distinguished teacher whose areas of expertise were ancient philosophy, Jewish thought, and the philosophy of religion.

p. 289: *Josh Billings*: Pen name of Henry Wheeler Shaw (1818–85), American humorist and lecturer, known for his homespun philosophies and peculiar spelling.

p. 289: *Grendel's Dam*: In the 8th century English epic *Beowulf*, Grendel and his mother are terrifying water monsters.

p. 290: *a girl I was in love with*: Eleanor Anne Sweezey (1915–   ), Canadian medical illustrator. RD fell in love with her when they were both students at Queen's University in Kingston, Ontario.

p. 290: *Heine's poem*: "Der Doppelgänger" by Heinrich Heine (1797–1856), German lyric poet. The poem was given a musical setting by the Austrian composer Franz Schubert (1797–1828).

p. 290: *W. S. Blunt's The Fox*: This is one of RD's rare slips. "The Fox" was written not by English poet, diplomat, traveller, anti-imperialist, and Arabist Wilfrid Scawen Blunt (1840–1922) but by Bruce Blunt (1899–1957), the journalist and bon vivant. Peter Warlock (pseudonym for Philip Heseltine, 1894–1930), was an English composer of delicate songs and chamber music.

p. 291: *wife was almost 45*: Florence Davies was 43 at the time of RD's birth.

p. 291: *no Osler*: Sir William Osler (1849–1919), Canadian doctor, author of the authoritative *The Principles and Practice of Medicine*, first published in 1892.

p. 291: *Hezekiah*: Wise king of Jerusalem, a contemporary of Sennacherib, King of Assyria, and of the prophet Isaiah. He is described in 2 Kings 18:5 as one who "trusted in the Lord God of Israel; so that after him was none like him among all the kings of Judah, nor any that were before him."

p. 292: She Stoops to Conquer: Lively, witty comedy by playwright Oliver Goldsmith.

p. 292: *Tony van Bridge*: (1917–) English actor and director, active in Canada since 1954 with the Stratford and Shaw Festivals.

p. 292: *Mary Savidge*: (d. 1982) English-born Canadian actress, active in theatres across Canada (including the Stratford Festival) and on CBC radio and television from the mid-1950s until her death in her fifties.

p. 292: *Pat Galloway*: (1933–) English-born Canadian actress and director, leading performer at the Stratford and Shaw Festivals.

p. 292: *Nicholas Pennell*: (1939–95) English actor, stalwart at the Stratford Festival 1972–94. *The Forsyte Saga* was a celebrated British period drama series first televised in 1967, based on novels by the English author John Galsworthy (1867–1933).

p. 293: *Michael Bawtree*: (1937–) Australian director, co-founder of the Comus Music Theatre (Toronto), head of the theatre wing of the Banff Centre for the Arts for a time, founder of the Atlantic Theatre Festival, professor and director of drama at Acadia University, Wolfville, Nova Scotia.

p. 293: *Example*: The passage that was cut was a favourite. It is quoted in *A Mixture of Frailties* 305, and RD considered using part of it – "Water Parted" – as the title of the novel. He knew and loved Thomas Augustine Arne's song "Water Parted."

p. 293: *the critic in the* Times: See "Dear Max: A Birthday Puzzle" 24 August 1972: 7.

p. 293: *Rossetti and Wilde and George Moore and Wells*: Dante Gabriel Rossetti (1828–82), English poet and painter, a founder of the pre-Raphaelites. Oscar Wilde (1854–1900), Irish playwright, poet, story-writer, novelist, and wit. George Moore (1852–1933), Irish-born English novelist who introduced naturalism into the Victorian novel. H. G. Wells (1866–1946), English writer best remembered for his works of science fiction.

p. 294: *I once met Beerbohm? And I knew his wife*: Beerbohm's wife, the American actress Florence Kahn (1878–1951), played the Duchess of Gloucester in the Oxford University Dramatic Society's production of *Richard II* in February 1936. RD was stage manager. Beerbohm came to visit his wife in her dressing room and, at the supper after the final performance, he responded to the toast to "The Guests" with wit and ease.

p. 296: *Esposito*: Philip Anthony Esposito (1942–), Canadian hockey player, who with Bobby Orr led the Boston Bruins to Stanley Cup victories in 1970 and 1972. He gave inspired leadership during the Canada–Soviet Hockey series of 1972, which began with a loss, followed by a win, a tie, and then the 5–3 loss in Vancouver during which Canadian fans booed the home team.

p. 297: *Lawrence*: D. H. Lawrence (1885–1930), English writer who influenced the development of 20th century fiction.

p. 298: *Gzowski*: Peter Gzowski (1934–2002), Canadian broadcaster, journalist, writer, and editor. He was host of CBC radio's "This Country in the Morning" 1971–74, the show RD was on.

p. 298: *Elwood Glover*: (1915–90) Canadian radio and television broadcaster. The show RD was on – "Luncheon Date with Elwood Glover" – ran on CBC television 1963–75.

p. 299: *a boozer and drugger*: John Pearson (1915–58), Canadian, a friend from Upper Canada College 1928–32. For other discussions of Pearson's life, see RD's letter of November 28, 1972, and *Man of Myth* 527–28.

p. 300: *Mann*: Thomas Mann (1875–1955), influential German novelist and essayist. Mann lived to be 80 and, as RD once observed, concluded "his career as a writer with the first volume of a novel which is worthy of what had gone before," namely *Confessions of Felix Krull, Confidence Man*. See "The Last of Fortune's Favorite," *Saturday Night* 29 October 1955: 26–8.

p. 300: *a letter in the London* Times *from Sir Harry Brittain*: See "Squiggly Signatures," *The Times* 3 October 1972: 15. Brittain (1873–1974) was a politician, director of numerous daily and weekly papers and other businesses, author, and notable eccentric. Rupert Davies knew him through their newspaper interests.

p. 300: *your very kind review of* The Manticore: See "William French: Magical Davies," *Globe and Mail* 19 October 1972: 15. French concludes: "If approached on conventional terms, *The Manticore* and *Fifth Business* are baroque, and demand more than the normal suspension of disbelief."

p. 301: *Vaughan Williams*: Ralph Vaughan Williams (1872–1958), English composer influenced by medieval and Tudor music and by folk song.

p. 301: *Eliot's* The Journey of the Magi *by Benjamin Britten*: *The Journey of the Magi* is a poem by T. S. Eliot. Benjamin Britten (1913–76), the most important English composer since Purcell, wrote vocal music.

p. 301: *Gordon Wry*: (d. 1985) Canadian tenor, founding member of the Festival Singers, and long-time member of the Mendelssohn Chair. With Giles Bryant he founded the Massey College Singers, an exceptional group of 18 or 20 individuals who sang at College Chapel services, gave College concerts, and performed at Gaudy Night each year during RD's tenure as Master.

p. 301: *John Donne*: (1572–1631) English poet and divine, the greatest of the metaphysical poets.

SECTION VIII

p. 307: *Some time ago*: See RD's letter of July 3, 1972.

p. 307: *synchronicity*: RD once defined synchronicity as "encountering what is important and necessary at the right time . . . a kind of falling-together of circumstances. You cannot compel it, but you can be ready for it and worthy of it." See *For Your Eye Alone* 53.

p. 309: *acromegaly*: Rare disease characterized by abnormal enlargement of the skull, jaw, hands, and feet. Davenport forwarded two medical accounts for RD's use.

p. 309: *What can you tell me about the effects of long-continued buggery*: Davenport's answer in a letter written December 16, 1972, was: "First, I know nothing about it myself. I hadn't run into anything on the subject in my reading. I tried the head of our Psychiatry Department with no results. . . . Then I tried an English-trained gastroenterologist with the enclosed zero."

p. 309: *I once knew a fellow*: John Pearson. See RD's letter of October 5, 1972, for another account of Pearson's life.

p. 311: *Dostoevsky*: Feodor Mikhailovich Dostoevsky (1821–81), great Russian novelist, profound psychologist, and philosopher.

p. 312: *Father Martin D'Arcy*: (1888–1976) English Jesuit, philosopher, connoisseur, and major figure of the modern Roman Catholic Church in England. He was Master of Campion Hall, Oxford, 1932–45.

p. 312: *Catholicism in writers*: Graham Greene (1904–91), English, was a prolific Catholic novelist and playwright; Evelyn Waugh (1903–66), English, was a satiric, witty, sophisticated, Catholic writer. Waugh was baptized by Father Martin D'Arcy.

p. 313: *Mia Anderson*: Canadian poet and actress for stage, radio, and television. Her one-woman show was titled "10 Women, Two Men and a Moose."

p. 314: *her American husband . . . Number Two*: Atwood's American husband was James Polk, a writer. The marriage lasted less than five years 1967–72. Number Two is the Canadian novelist and cultural activist Graeme Gibson (1934–   ).

p. 316: *Nietszche*: Friedrich Wilhelm Nietzsche (1844–1900), German philosopher.

p. 317: Letters of C. G. Jung . . . *review*: See *New York Times Book Review* 25 February 1973: 31.

p. 317: *Governor General*: Resident representative of the Crown. Roland Michener (1900–91), Canadian lawyer and politician, was Governor General 1967–74.

p. 317: *Arthur Woodhouse*: Arthur Sutherland Piggott Woodhouse (1895–1964), Canadian teacher, scholar, humanist, and head of the department of English at University College, University of Toronto 1944–64.

p. 318: *a Visitor . . . Hon. Dalton Wells*: The position of Visitor had been instituted to give Vincent Massey a ceremonial role in the College, and had been quietly dropped in 1970 when the statutes were amended. The students had gotten hold of an outdated copy of the statutes, which said that there should be a formal visitation every five years, oftener if necessary. They argued that the role of the Visitor was to provide a final court of appeal beyond the College Corporation. The Hon. Dalton Courtwright Wells (1900–82), Canadian, was chief justice of the High Court of Ontario from 1967 to 1975.

p. 318: *Bill Dobson*: Professor W. A. C. H. Dobson, initially an asset to the College, had become a divisive force, causing unrest among the students and picking away at RD's authority. In May 1972 his fellowship had not been renewed, though his influence continued for a time.

p. 318: *Marshall McLuhan*: Herbert Marshall McLuhan (1911–80), Canadian communications theorist, famous for his studies of the effects of mass media on thought and behaviour, was a member of the department of English at St. Michael's College in the University of Toronto from 1946 on, and director of the Centre for Culture and Technology from 1963 on.

p. 319: *fabricating a quotation*: In fact, RD *did* fabricate this particular quotation. But see his explanation in *For Your Eye Alone* 43.

p. 323: *Sibelius*: Jean Julius Christian Sibelius (1865–1957), Finnish composer. The quotation is variously worded in English.

p. 325: *To THE EDITOR OF THE* TIMES LITERARY SUPPLEMENT: Published 27 April 1973: 473.

p. 325: *Walter Pater Society of Brasenose*: Brasenose is an Oxford college. Walter Pater (1839–94) was an English essayist and critic and a fellow of Brasenose. "To burn always with this hard, gemlike flame, to maintain this ecstasy, is success in life" is drawn from the "Conclusion" of Pater's *Studies in the History of the Renaissance.*

p. 325: *"The same that . . . The Alchemist, II, 1"*: Actually *The Alchemist* II.2.

p. 329: *Professor Roy*: Professor James Alexander Roy (1884–1973), Scottish, poet, writer of fiction and criticism, biographer, and professor of English at Queen's University in Kingston, Ontario. RD took his courses at Queen's 1932–35.

p. 329: *Michael [Davies]*: (1936–   ) the older of Arthur L. Davies' two sons, RD's nephew, general manager, then publisher, and eventually owner of the Kingston *Whig-Standard* 1962–90.

p. 329: *marvellous obituary in the* Times: See "Prof James Roy: Teacher and Biographer" 29 November 1973: 20.

p. 331: *Bernard Berenson*: (1865–1959) American (Lithuanian by birth) art historian, connoisseur of Italian art, and philosopher.

p. 331: *Joseph Campbell*: (1904–87) American professor and writer interested in culture and mythology.

p. 331: *Obituary for the London* Times: See RD's letter of December 3, 1973.

p. 332: *Herman Voaden*: (1903–91) Canadian playwright, director, educator, and editor. Voaden's unusual plays fused poetic choral speech, music, dance, and unrealistic lighting and settings.

p. 334: *To THE EDITOR OF THE* TIMES LITERARY SUPPLEMENT: Published 15 February 1974: 158.

p. 335: *Da Ponte*: Lorenzo Da Ponte (1749–1838), Italian poet who wrote librettos for all the leading Viennese composers of his day, including the one for Mozart's opera *Don Giovanni.*

p. 339: *Tom Swift*: Hero of a series of books for boys by American writer Edward Stratemeyer (1863–1930).

p. 339: *Kierkegaard*: Søren Kierkegaard (1813–55), Danish philosopher and religious thinker. RD probably meant to say Spengler rather than Kierkegaard: he makes some play with the "Magian World View" of Oswald Spengler (1880–1936), German historian and philosopher, in *World of Wonders* 287–88.

p. 340: [Question Time] . . . Peer Gynt: *Peer Gynt* is a verse drama by the Norwegian dramatist and poet Henrik Ibsen (1828–1906), which explores the Norwegian character through the mythic life story of one man. *Question Time* explores the Canadian character: its central character is the Prime Minister of Canada, Peter Macadam, whose plane crashes in Canada's frozen north, and whose survival is dependent upon his learning how to draw on the resources of his neglected inner man.

p. 341: *your column of January 27, about Lottie Whitton*: Lottie Whitton was Charlotte Whitton. See "Lottie Whitton," *Globe and Mail* 27 January 1975: 27. The relevant sentence runs: "She was a student at Queen's [in 1917] when Laurier's Liberals picked their candidate, Isaac Pedlow, a sort of Honest Ed of his time, running a cut-rate store in Renfrew."

p. 342: *Sam Weller*: Mr. Pickwick's facetious, resourceful, and devoted servant in Dickens' *The Pickwick Papers.*

p. 343: *a difficult group to arrange properly*: Jean-Louis Servan-Schreiber (1937–) is French. His *Le Pouvoir d'Informer* (1972) had been translated as *The Power to Inform, Media: The Information Business* (1974); William Grenville Davis (1929–), Canadian, was the Conservative Premier of Ontario 1971–85; the President of the University of Toronto was still John Robert Evans.

p. 344: *Sir Owen Seaman*: (1861–1936) English poet, satirist, parodist, and editor of *Punch* 1906–32.

p. 344: *disgruntled dwarf*: William Davis edited *Punch* 1969–77.

p. 345: *Plaunt*: Alan B. Plaunt (1904–41) devoted his life to national unity, public broadcasting, economic reform, and pacifism.

p. 346: *Gascon . . . Thomas Otway's tragedy* Venice Preserv'd: Jean Gascon (1921–88), French Canadian actor and director, was artistic director of the Stratford Festival 1967–74. *Venice Preserv'd* is written in blank verse. The English dramatist Thomas Otway lived 1652–85.

p. 346: *only one major production*: This was the revival of 1953 at the Lyric Theatre, Hammersmith, in London, England. Paul Scofield (1922–) is a well-known English stage actor whose range is extraordinarily broad, and Peter Brook (1925–) is one of the great English directors of the last half century, known for his innovative productions.

p. 347: *Saki*: Pseudonym of Hector Hugh Munro (1870–1916), English author and journalist (born in Burma) known chiefly for his short stories.

p. 348: *Bellow*: Saul Bellow (1915–), Canadian-born American novelist. *Humboldt's Gift* won the Pulitzer Prize.

p. 349: *Shakespeare's phrase*: See *Love's Labour's Lost* 4.2.

p. 352: *Diefenbaker*: John George Diefenbaker (1895–1979), lawyer, politician, Conservative Prime Minister of Canada 1957–63.

Acknowledgements

The copyright for Davies' letters is held by Brenda Davies, his widow. She and her daughter Jennifer Surridge, under the name of Pendragon Ink, manage Davies' literary estate. They have given invaluable assistance as this collection of letters took shape, smoothing the way with the owners of some of the letters, and supplying suggestions for passages that only those privy to details of Davies' private life could clarify. They read successive drafts in a timely way and with great care.

After them, my chief debts are to the many recipients of Davies' letters who searched their files, forwarded copies and supplied details of themselves, their letters, and their relationships with him. Their contributions are evident in the head- and endnotes. Several of Davies' frequent correspondents – Horace W. Davenport, Arnold Edinborough, John Espey, Ralph Hancox, Tanya Moiseiwitsch, Gordon Roper, and John Stead – were especially helpful. Also, many individuals mentioned in the letters kindly responded to my queries. The information they supplied enriches the endnotes.

I also want to acknowledge the contributions of those who searched for letters on my behalf or who suggested where they might be found: Nancy Bartlett and Anne Frantilla, reference archivists at the Bentley Historical Library, Ann Arbor, Michigan; Claude Bissell, Vincent Massey's biographer, now deceased, but then resident in Toronto, Ontario; Robert Blount of Peterborough, Ontario; Lisa Brant, Archivist, and Brigitte Lawson, of the Director's Office, at the Stratford Festival, Stratford, Ontario; Dr. Richard Davis of Guelph, Ontario; Dr. Bernadine Dodge, University Archivist at Trent University, Peterborough, Ontario; John Fraser, the current Master of Massey College in Toronto, Ontario; James Forsyth, Tyrone Guthrie's biographer, Haywards Heath, Sussex; Anne Goddard, Manuscript Division of the National Archives of Canada, Ottawa, Ontario; Michael Riese, Comptroller of St. Paul's College at the University of Manitoba, Winnipeg, Manitoba; Carl Spadoni, Research Collections Librarian, Mills Memorial Library, McMaster University, Hamilton, Ontario.

Several friends and colleagues solved conundrums – in particular, David Gardner, who supplied leads for a number of theatre people; Susan Howson, who lent assistance with pounds, shillings, and pence; David Klausner, who helped with the Welsh bits (in letters that were, in the end, not included); Ann Saddlemyer, who located a graduate student to sort through the Tyrone Guthrie materials in the vaults of the Ulster Bank Dublin Trust Company, Dublin; Carl Spadoni, who forwarded information about Berners Jackson; and Germaine Warkentin, who solved the problem of "wittles."

In addition, I would like to thank a few of the many other individuals who answered questions and looked up information: the archivists of the Anglican Diocese of Toronto, Toronto, Ontario; Margaret Angus of Kingston, Ontario; Father Patrick Boyle of Regis College in Toronto, Ontario; Jane Britton of the University of Waterloo Library in Waterloo, Ontario; Gwen Brown of Peterborough, Ontario; Eileen Bruce, secretary to Michael Davies, Kingston, Ontario; Robert Conner of Red Lake, Ontario; Gwen Craw of Peterborough, Ontario; Peter Dalgleish, Ross Mortimer, and John Ridpath (all connected with Ridpath's) of Toronto and Ottawa, Ontario; Bernadine Dodge, University Archivist at Trent University, Peterborough, Ontario; Jane Edmonds, archivist, and Ellen Charendoff, archives assistant, at the Stratford Festival Archives, Stratford, Ontario; Pat Kennedy, Marie Korey, and P. J. MacDougall, all of Massey College, Toronto; The Law Society of Upper Canada in Toronto, Ontario; Edith Leslie of the C. G. Jung Foundation of the Ontario Association of Jungian Analysts in Toronto, Ontario; Barbara Love of the Kingston Frontenac Public Library, Kingston, Ontario; Simon McInnes of Ottawa, Ontario; Celia Roberts of Toronto, Ontario; Marian Spence, archivist of Upper Canada College, Toronto, Ontario; Andrea Tufts of Bishop Strachan School, Toronto, Ontario. And finally, I'd like to express my gratitude to the many librarians at the Robarts Library, University of Toronto, and at the Toronto Reference Library who displayed great resourcefulness in suggesting possible approaches to finding answers to a wide range of queries.

A number of people (in addition to those I have mentioned in *For Your Eye Alone*) found letters that I have not been able to include, but I am grateful to have been able to consider them when making my selection: Birthe Jörgensen at the Joan Baillie Archives of the Canadian Opera Company, Toronto, Ontario; George Brandiak, Curator of Manuscripts, Special Collections and University Archives Division, University of British Columbia; Patricia Beharriell CM of Kingston, Ontario; Major John Conrad of the Canadian Armed Forces; Professor C. Abbott Conway, Department of English, McGill University, Montreal; Mary Lou Fallis of Toronto, Ontario; Mary Flagg, University Archivist, Harriet Irving Library, University of New Brunswick in Fredericton, New Brunswick; Birgitta Rydbeck Heyman of Lidingö, Sweden; John Hols of Spokane, Washington; Susan Howson, Department of Economics, University of Toronto, Toronto, Ontario; Kathleen Jacklin (Archivist) and Lorna Knight (Curator of Manuscripts), Cornell University Library, Ithaca, New York; James Neufeld, Department of English, Trent University, Peterborough, Ontario; Fern Rahmel of Bailieboro, Ontario; Donald Ryerson, now deceased, of Toronto, Ontario; Eleanor Anne Sweezey of Montreal, Quebec; and Ian E. Wilson, Archivist of Ontario, Toronto, Ontario.

The originals of many of the letters in this volume are still in private hands. Those to the following recipients are in public places –

J. Burgon Bickersteth's in the Warden's Office, Hart House, University of Toronto, Toronto, Ontario.

Earle Birney's, some of Robert Finch's, William French's, and Douglas LePan's in the Thomas Fisher Rare Books Library, University of Toronto, Toronto, Ontario.

W. H. Clarke's, Harold Raymond's (of Chatto & Windus), and R. W. W. Robertson's with the Clarke, Irwin papers in the Archives and Research Collections of McMaster University, Hamilton, Ontario.

Horace Davenport's in the Michigan Historical Collections, Bentley Historical Library, University of Michigan, Ann Arbor, Michigan.

Hugh Dent's and Mr. Bozman's with the J. M. Dent and Sons Papers in the Southern Historical Collection, University of North Carolina Library, Chapel Hill, North Carolina.

Louis Dudek's in the National Library of Canada, Ottawa, Ontario.

Some of Robert Finch's and Moira Whalon's in the collection of Dr. Richard Davis, Guelph, Ontario.

John Morgan Gray's, Amelia Hall's, Yousuf Karsh's, and Raleigh Parkin's in the National Archives of Canada, Ottawa, Ontario.

Tyrone and Judith Guthrie's, in the possession of Guthrie's biographer James Forsyth and also of the Ulster Bank Dublin Trust Company, Dublin.

Christopher Hill's in the Archives of Balliol College, Oxford.

Alfred A. Knopf's in the Knopf, Inc. archive, Harry Ransom Humanities Research Center, The University of Texas at Austin, Texas.

Margaret Laurence's and some of Herbert Whittaker's in the Archives and Special Collections, Scott Library, York University, Toronto, Ontario.

Dorothy Livesay's in Archives and Special Collections, Elizabeth Dafoe Library, University of Manitoba, Winnipeg, Manitoba.

Grant Macdonald's in the Queen's University Archives, Kingston, Ontario.

Hugh MacLennan's in the Department of Rare Books and Special Collections of the McLennan Library, McGill University, Montreal, and in the University of Calgary Libraries Special Collections, Calgary, Alberta.

Vincent Massey's in the University of Toronto Archives, Toronto, Ontario.

H. L. Mencken's in the Enoch Pratt Free Library, Baltimore, Maryland.

Vernon Mould's and Alan G. A. Stephen's in the Archives of Upper Canada College, Toronto, Ontario.

Nicholas Pennell's in the Stratford Festival Archives, Stratford, Ontario.

Father Plunkett's in the Jesuit Community Archives, Regis College, Toronto, Ontario.

Gordon Roper's in the Trent University Archives, Peterborough, Ontario, and in the National Archives in Ottawa, Ontario.

The copies of correspondence concerned with the management of Massey College are held by the College itself (notably the letter to a student dated January 14, 1965, and the ones to John N. Buchanan, J. M. S. Careless, Gerald Le Dain, the Master of Balliol College, and Thomas Cooper).

The copies of Davies' business correspondence are in the National Archives in Ottawa, Ontario.

INDEX

OTHER TITLES FROM
DOUGLAS GIBSON BOOKS

PUBLISHED BY MCCLELLAND & STEWART LTD.

FOR YOUR EYE ALONE: Letters 1976-1995 *by* Robertson Davies
These lively letters, selected and edited by Judith Skelton Grant, show us the private Davies at the height of his fame, writing family notes and slicing up erring reviewers. "An unmitigated delight." *London Free Press*
 Belles lettres, 6 × 9, 400 pages, facsimile letters, notes, index, trade paperback

HAPPY ALCHEMY: Writings on the Theatre and Other Lively Arts *by* Robertson Davies
"Far more personal than anything published under Davies's name, and all the more enjoyable for it" (*Edmonton Sun*), this collection shows the full range of his wit and wisdom.   *Non-fiction, 6 × 9, 400 pages, hardcover*

THE MERRY HEART: Selections 1980-1995 *by* Robertson Davies
"A marvellous array of Davies' speeches and reviews, interspersed with bits of his personal diaries." *Hamilton Spectator*   "It's a happy thing that the voice from the attic is still being heard." *Montreal Gazette*
                         Non-fiction, 6 × 9, 400 pages, hardcover

THE CUNNING MAN: A novel *by* Robertson Davies
This "sparkling history of the erudite and amusing Dr. Hullah who knows the souls of his patients as well as he knows their bodies" *London Free Press* is "wise, humane and constantly entertaining." *The New York Times*
                         Fiction, 6 × 9, 480 pages, hardcover

MURTHER AND WALKING SPIRITS: A novel *by* Robertson Davies
"Brilliant" was the *Ottawa Citizen*'s description of the sweeping tale of a Canadian family through the generations. "It will recruit huge numbers of new readers to the Davies fan club." *Observer* (London)
                         Fiction, 6¼ × 9½, 368 pages, hardcover

HATESHIP, FRIENDSHIP, COURTSHIP, LOVESHIP, MARRIAGE:
by Alice Munro
A new collection of nine stories by Alice Munro at her remarkable best. Simply unforgettable. Literature at its best by the writer Cynthia Ozick called "our Chekhov."   *Fiction, 6 × 9, 320 pages, hardcover*

LIVES OF MOTHERS AND DAUGHTERS: Growing Up With Alice Munro
by Sheila Munro
"The book will thrill anybody with a serious interest in Alice Munro." *Edmonton Journal* "What Sheila Munro says about her mother's writing

could be just as aptly applied to her own book; you trust her every word." *Montreal Gazette*

        Biography/Memoir, 6 × 9, 60 snapshots, 240 pages, trade paperback

THREE CHEERS FOR ME: The Journals of Bartholomew Bandy, Volume One *by* Donald Jack
The classic comic novel about the First World War where our bumbling hero graduates from the trenches and somehow becomes an air ace. "Funny? Very." *New York Times*

        Fiction/Humour, 5½ × 8½, 330 pages, trade paperback

THAT'S ME IN THE MIDDLE: The Journals of Bartholomew Bandy, Volume Two *by* Donald Jack
Canadian air ace Bandy fights at the front and behind the lines in the U.K., gallantly enduring the horrors of English plumbing. "A comical tour-de-force." *Montreal Gazette*

        Fiction/Humour, 5½ × 8½, 348 pages, trade paperback

IT'S ME AGAIN: The Journals of Bartholomew Bandy, Volume Three *by* Donald Jack
Bart Bandy's back, landing behind enemy lines in France, causing havoc in Halifax, and trying to roll back the red Russian Revolution in Archangel. "Outrageously funny!" *Hamilton Spectator*

        Fiction/Humour, 5½ × 8½, 420 pages, trade paperback

ME BANDY, YOU CISSIE: The Journals of Bartholomew Bandy, Volume Four *by* Donald Jack
It's 1920, and fresh from fighting Bolsheviks in Russia, Bartholomew Bandy is in New York trying to establish an airline, a movie career, and a romance with a tycoon's daughter. "The Bandy Papers deserve to be read in private, where insane giggling can go unnoticed." Jack Granatstein

        Fiction/Humour, 5½ × 8½, 304 pages, trade paperback

ME TOO: The Journals of Bartholomew Bandy, Volume Five *by* Donald Jack
"Vote for Bandy" proves to be an irresistable slogan when our hero comes slouching home again, hurrah, and is so desperate for work that he stumbles his way into Parliament. "Read this book at your own peril."

        Fiction/Humour, 5½ × 8½, 404 pages, trade paperback

THIS ONE'S ON ME: The Journals of Bartholomew Bandy, Volume Six *by* Donald Jack
It's 1924 and ex-MP Bandy is back in the Old Country, blundering into trouble everywhere, from boarding house bedrooms to No. 10 Downing Street. "One of Canada's finest comic creatures, bashful Bandy." *Toronto Star*

        Fiction/Humour, 5½ × 8½, 434 pages, trade paperback

REMEMBERING PETER GZOWSKI

This lively and varied volume of tributes includes pieces from well-known friends like Robert Fulford, Alice Munro and Shelagh Rogers, and from ordinary people touched by Peter Gzowski's life and work.

Anthology, 5½ × 8½, 248 pages, including photographs, hardcover

A PETER GZOWSKI READER

The famous writer-broadcaster's last book, a wide-ranging selection of the very best pieces from his writing life that comes close to being an auto-biography. *Anthology, 6 × 9, 274 pages, trade paperback*

RAVEN'S END: A novel of the Canadian Rockies *by* Ben Gadd

This astonishing book, snapped up by publishers around the world, is like a *Watership Down* set among a flock of ravens managing to survive in the Rockies. "A real classic." Andy Russell

Fiction, 6 × 9, map, 5 drawings, 336 pages, trade paperback

THE GRIM PIG *by* Charles Gordon

The world of news is laid bare in this "very wicked, subversive book . . . it reveals more than most readers should know about how newspapers – or at least some newspapers – are still created. This is exceedingly clever satire, with a real bite." *Ottawa Citizen*

Fiction, 6x9, 256 pages, trade paperback

THE CANADA TRIP *by* Charles Gordon

Charles Gordon and his wife drove from Ottawa to St. John's to Victoria and back. The result is "a very human, warm, funny book" (*Victoria Times Colonist*) that will set you planning your own trip.

Travel/Humour, 6 × 9, 364 pages, 22 maps, trade paperback

AT THE COTTAGE: A Fearless Look at Canada's Summer Obsession *by* Charles Gordon *illustrated by* Graham Pilsworth

This perennial best-selling book of gentle humour is "a delightful reminder of why none of us addicted to cottage life will ever give it up." *Hamilton Spectator* *Humour, 6 × 9, 224 pages, illustrations, trade paperback*

THE SELECTED STORIES OF MAVIS GALLANT *by* Mavis Gallant

"A volume to hold and to treasure" said the *Globe and Mail* of the 52 marvellous stories selected from Mavis Gallant's life's work. "It should be in every reader's library." *Fiction, 6⅛ × 9¼ , 900 pages, trade paperback*

CONFESSIONS OF AN IGLOO DWELLER *by* James Houston

The famous novelist and superb storyteller who brought Inuit art to the outside world recounts his Arctic adventures between 1948 and 1962. "Sheer entertainment, as fascinating as it is charming." *Kirkus Reviews*

Autobiography, 6 × 9, 320 pages, maps, drawings, trade paperback

Dear Madam:

I think I understood you to say, in your Wednesday night radio address, that the tempo of living in Australia is _markedly slower than that of this continent._ Madam, beware! You have trodden on the rattlesnake of local patriotism! Here in Peterborough I venture to say that we can show you a tempo of living slower than any in the world! Let the kangaroo tremble in his bed! The Beaver of the Kawarthas can out-drowse him any day of the week! Adieu, rash Antipodean—

One of the Seventy Times Seven
Sleepers of Peterborough

—

...nce as Pericles
...ded admirably in
...t difficult tasks
...set for an actor to-
...ve made a true hero
...and likable hero for
...athy of the audience for
...fe and the heroic struggle.
...ourselves enriched by your
...and I were delighted by your
...formance for we are both very
...riches they contain for those who
...een on myth and legend and the
...can uncover such things that is
...what Pericles does, even in the
...rather battered text we have—
...show in mythical fashion man's
...search for his blindness to what lies
...his terrible blindness to his eyes.
...most immediately under his eyes.
...A very great Jungian play, and you
...have done wonders with it. Many
...thanks from us both, and may you
...have a great success in this
...unlikely role—not a bad springboard
...for Hamlet.

All good wishes,
Robertson Davies

MASSEY COLLEGE

in the University of Toronto   MASTER

Dear Horace:

Your letter of July 20 luckily caught me between two journeys; I was delighted to get it because I have been hoping to hear from you for some time—your last letter suggest-ed great despair. But I am very happy to hear of your forthcoming marriage, and I hope it will bring great happiness to all

PETERBOROUGH EXAMINER
PETERBOROUGH, ONTARIO

September 11, 1954

EDITOR

Dear Alan:

Thanks for your letter of September 10th. It will give me the greatest pleasure to go to the performance of A Masque of Aesop in December and I would be very greatly obliged if you could extend your invitation to include my daught... who are extremely anxious to see the play.

I really haven't any idea wh... could be done with the $250; I am absolutely and unshakeably agains... ...ing it spent on a picture of ...e no desire to see my m... ...in oil paints and ... ...of the money ...Nor d...